Radio and the Politics of Sound in Interwar France, 1921–1939

In December 1921, France broadcast its first public radio program from a transmitter on the Eiffel Tower. In the decade that followed, radio evolved into a mass media capable of reaching millions. Crowds flocked to loudspeakers on city streets to listen to propaganda, children clustered around classroom radios, and families tuned in from their living rooms. *Radio and the Politics of Sound in Interwar France* examines the impact of this emerging auditory culture on French society and politics, revealing how broadcasting became a new platform for political engagement, transforming the act of listening into an important, if highly contested, practice of citizenship. Rejecting models of broadcasting as a weapon of totalitarian regimes or a tool for forging democracy from above, the book offers a more nuanced picture of the politics of radio by uncovering the competing interpretations of listening and diverse uses of broadcast sound that flourished between the world wars.

REBECCA P. SCALES is an assistant professor in the Department of History at the Rochester Institute of Technology.

Cambridge Social and Cultural Histories

Series editors:
Margot C. Finn, *University College London*
Colin Jones, *Queen Mary, University of London*
Robert G. Moeller, *University of California, Irvine*

Cambridge Social and Cultural Histories publishes works of original scholarship that lie at the interface between cultural and social history. Titles in the series both articulate a clear methodological and theoretical orientation and demonstrate clearly the significance of that orientation for interpreting relevant historical sources. The series seeks to address historical questions, issues or phenomena which – although they may be located in a specific nation, state or polity – are framed so as to be relevant and methodologically innovative to specialists of other fields of historical analysis.

A list of titles in the series can be found at:
www.cambridge.org/socialculturalhistories

Radio and the Politics of Sound in Interwar France, 1921–1939

Rebecca P. Scales

CAMBRIDGE
UNIVERSITY PRESS

CAMBRIDGE
UNIVERSITY PRESS

University Printing House, Cambridge CB2 8BS, United Kingdom

One Liberty Plaza, 20th Floor, New York, NY 10006, USA

477 Williamstown Road, Port Melbourne, VIC 3207, Australia

314-321, 3rd Floor, Plot 3, Splendor Forum, Jasola District Centre, New Delhi-110025, India

79 Anson Road, #06-04/06, Singapore 079906

Cambridge University Press is part of the University of Cambridge.

It furthers the University's mission by disseminating knowledge in the pursuit of
education, learning and research at the highest international levels of excellence.

www.cambridge.org
Information on this title: www.cambridge.org/9781107519619

© Rebecca P. Scales 2016

First published 2016
First paperback edition 2017

A catalogue record for this publication is available from the British Library

Library of Congress Cataloging in Publication data
Scales, Rebecca, 1976–
Radio and the politics of sound in interwar France, 1921–1939 /
Rebecca Scales.
Cambridge, United Kingdom : Cambridge University Press, 2016.
| Series: Cambridge social and cultural histories | Includes
bibliographical references and indes.
LCCN 2015039572 | ISBN 9781107108677 (hardback)
LCSH: Radio broadcasting – Political aspects – France – History – 20th
century. | Radio broadcasting – Social aspects – France – History – 20th
century. | Sound – Political aspects – France – History – 20th century. | Sound –
Social aspects – France – History – 20th century. | Mass media – Political
aspects – France – History – 20th century. | Mass media – Social
aspects – France – History – 20th century. | Politics and culture –
France – History – 20th century. | France – Politics and government –
1914–1940. | France – Social life and customs – 20th century.
| BISAC: HISTORY / Europe / General.
LCC HE8697.85.F8 S34 2016 | DDC 384.540944/09042–dc23
LC record available at http://lccn.loc.gov/2015039572

ISBN 978-1-107-10867-7 Hardback
ISBN 978-1-107-51961-9 Paperback

Contents

Illustrations

Acknowledgments

Although writing is very much a solitary endeavor, many institutions, organizations, and individuals contributed to the labor contained within the covers of this book. Grants and fellowships from the Social Science Research Council, the Embassy of France in the United States, the American Philosophical Society, and the Western Society for French History supported multiple years of archival research in France. A Paul and Francena Miller Fellowship from the College of Liberal Arts at the Rochester Institute of Technology provided me with critical teaching release time to complete a final draft of the manuscript. Archivists and staff at the Bibliothèque Nationale de France, the Centre des Archives Nationales, the Centre des Archives d'Outre-Mer in Aix-en-Provence, the Service Historique de la Défense, and the Paris Préfecture de Police provided invaluable assistance in tracking down sources and making reproductions. I would also like to thank the editors of the Cambridge Social and Cultural History Series, and particularly Colin Jones, for their support of this book, as well as Elizabeth Friend-Smith, Rebecca Taylor, and Amanda George at Cambridge University Press for shepherding the manuscript through each stage of the review and production process. Earlier versions of Chapters 2 and 5 appeared in *French Historical Studies*, 31, 4 (2008), *Comparative Studies in Society and History*, 52, 2 (2010), and *Media History* (2013). I thank the editors of these journals for allowing me to reprint these materials here.

During my academic career, I have had the privilege of working with many talented historians whose influence continues to shape my thinking. At the University of Georgia, where I began graduate school, Joshua Cole's inspired teaching and intellectual generosity first compelled me to think seriously about becoming an historian. I am reminded of his courses every time I sit down to prepare an assignment or draft a syllabus, and I hope to pass on to my students even a few of the lessons I learned from him about critical textual analysis. Many of the ideas in this book grew out of Michael Adas's comparative history seminars at Rutgers University, where our conversations about the global circulation of technologies, ideas, and people challenged many of my preconceptions about European history. In very different ways, Matt Matsuda and Joan Scott each taught me a great deal about writing, the performance of teaching, and the immense pleasure to be derived from intellectual labor. Bonnie Smith has championed this book from its inception, always encouraging me to think better and write faster. Her relentless cheerfulness, indefatigable work ethic, and consummate professionalism continue to inspire me. I am so fortunate to have been her student, and I cannot thank her and Don Kelley enough for their continued support of my career, as well as for many wonderful dinners on both sides of the Atlantic.

This book has also benefited from the transformative insights of a number of colleagues, including Caroline Campbell, Jeffrey Jackson, Catherine Kudlick, and Rosemary Wakeman, all of whom commented on earlier portions of the manuscript or the book proposal. Keith Wailoo and the members of his medical history research group at Rutgers – Greg Swedburg, Julie Livingston, Richard Mizelle, Marc Matera, Michal Shapira, and Melissa Stein – also provided invaluable suggestions for revisions to early chapter drafts. Conversations with colleagues at the annual meetings of the Society for French Historical Studies, the French Colonial Historical Society, and the Western Society for French History deepened my analysis and refined my arguments. Jennifer Sessions deserves special thanks for reading multiple versions of the entire manuscript, from its earliest iteration through the final revisions. I am grateful for her incisive questions and her willingness to engage in lengthy conversations about a research topic so different from her own. I never would have completed the research for this book without the support of Teresa Delcorso, whose guidance in writing grant proposals made every trip to France possible. Her friendship and professional guidance continue to sustain me. Finally, I thank my colleagues in the History Department at the Rochester Institute of Technology for providing a welcoming environment in which to begin my teaching career and finish this book.

In New York, Washington, DC, and Paris, many friends supplied delicious meals, good humor, and stimulating conversations that buoyed my spirits after long days in the library and the snow. Special thanks to Joshua Arthurs, Jonathyne Briggs, Tamar Carroll, Claire Eldridge, Sarah Ellerman and Brad Smith, Darcie Fontaine, Amy Freund, Carmen and Ed Gitre, Gillian Glaes, Jessica Anderson Hughes, Laura Kalba, Kate Keller, Jennifer Knight, Lisa Hermsen, Rob Lewis and Cathy Carlisle, Joel Revill, Louisa Rice, Danielle McGuire Rosh, Karen Routledge, Erin Slattery-Duda, Jennifer and Mark Tharp, Sarah Thompson, Corinna

Schlombs, and Nick and Elizabeth Wolf. As this project came to a close and a new one began, Zina Weygand welcomed me into her family and scholarly networks, making Paris feel like home.

Finally, I could not have written this book without the love and support of my family. My grandmother, Jeanette Scales, was the first person in her family to go to college. She worked hard to make sure her husband, children, and grandchildren all had the same opportunity, and her monthly checks kept me afloat for many years of graduate school. I am sad that she did not get to see me cross the finish line, but I hope she would have been proud of the work I have accomplished. My aunt Pat has played many roles in my life, from family feminist to political *provocateur*. Most importantly, she made sure that a kid growing up without a library or bookstore nearby always had something to read. Even though we each read different types of books these days, her influence can be seen throughout these pages. My parents, Larry and Sandra, have always believed that I could achieve anything I set out to do, even when I doubted it myself. They first inspired my love of history and my interest in different cultures, and I am immensely grateful for my adventurous childhood spent traveling through airports and down dirt roads. For giving me the world, and for loving me enough to always let me go, I dedicate this book to them.

Introduction

In December of 1921, three years after the Armistice that ended the First World War, a former army radio transmitter on the Eiffel Tower broadcast France's first public radio program, composed of weather and stock bulletins and a short musical concert. A decade later, twenty-five state-run and commercial stations were transmitting radio broadcasts across France. Radio had evolved from the pastime of a few tech-savvy wireless amateurs into a mass media capable of reaching millions of listeners. Urban crowds gathered on city streets and in stadia to listen to fiery propaganda speeches broadcast via loudspeakers, schoolchildren clustered around radio receivers in their classrooms, and families tuned into music and news from the comfort of their living rooms. By 1936, the composer and music critic Emile Vuillermoz could write in the illustrated weekly *Le Miroir du monde* that French audiences were "gorging themselves tirelessly in uninterrupted listening to radio, sound films, and the phonograph."

Invited by the magazine's editors to contribute to a special issue exploring the *mentalité* of the "youth of today," Vuillermoz highlighted the frenzied consumption of broadcast sound as the defining characteristic of the postwar generation. "Their radios are on from the moment they wake up," he reported. "They complete their *toilette* while listening to foxtrots ... read newspapers to the sounds of tangos ... and take their meals accompanied by rumbas." An adjacent photo spread captured the visible features of this new auditory culture in glossy black and white: a loudspeaker perched atop a café awning diffusing sounds onto the terrace below; adolescents spilling out of a listening salon in a record store; a couple enjoying a portable gramophone on a countryside holiday; young men dining in a nightclub; and a group of women smiling through the windows of a "radio-taxi" – this latter innovation a Parisian sensation of 1935. Over-exposed to syncopated rhythms and to the "shrill sounds, aggressive dissonances, and corrosive timbres" of amplifiers and loudspeakers, Vuillermoz lamented, French youth had become "victims of that collective deformation of our time – that special organic perversion

1

known as the love of noise. An entire generation has become adapted to the shrill voice of today's civilization."[1]

Vuillermoz's commentary reflected his personal distaste for popular music and *le jazz hot*, but he also heard the proliferation of radios and a host of other electro-acoustical technologies, from the gramophone to the public address system, as the origins of a "sound revolution" that was transforming French society and culture. Although the telephone and phonograph debuted during the fin de siècle, access to recorded sound remained limited to social elites and city dwellers until the eve of the First World War, making the postwar democratization of radios and gramophones across all social classes appear sudden and dramatic.[2] "Just as there are states of collective soul in the subjects of literature, painting, theater, and leisure," Vuillermoz argued, "there is equally a 'state of the ear' characteristic of certain periods in the history of people. Our senses develop through interdependence and mimicry. Over ten, twenty, or thirty years, one observes the same tendencies." The postwar generation might find nothing remarkable about the ubiquity of broadcast sound, but those born in the previous century could hear how modern sound technologies had dramatically altered their environments by dispensing sounds indiscriminately into public and private spaces, making everyday life louder and filled with sound. Even more important, radios and gramophones newly privileged listening as a means of engaging with the world.[3]

Vuillermoz was not alone in his conviction that the advent of radio, as the technological centerpiece of this broader "sound revolution," would usher in a distinctive sensory regime grounded in the ear – a possibility at once thrilling and disconcerting. "Wireless, or the communication of sounds by intermediary material, is in the process of disrupting the world," the physician and parapsychologist René Sudre told an audience at the Collège de France in 1929. "Of all the scientific discoveries of the century, none, not even the cinematograph, has had a greater influence on social life. It's a sort of 'miracle' analogous to printing." Just as the invention of the printing press centuries earlier provoked a shift from orality to literacy in Western Europe, Sudre proposed, the era of radio would elevate hearing to a new place of preeminence in the modern world.[4]

---

[1] Emile Vuillermoz, "La peur du silence," *Le Miroir du monde: hebdomadaire illustré*, April 6, 1935, 55–57.

[2] Sophie Maisonneuve, *L'invention du disque: genèse de l'usage des médias musicaux, 1877–1949* (Paris, 2009), 19–102; Annegret Fauser, *Musical Encounters at the 1889 Paris World's Fair* (Rochester NY, 2005), 279–312.

[3] Emile Vuillermoz, "La peur du silence," *Le Miroir du monde*, April 6, 1935, 55–57.

[4] René Sudre, *La psychologie de la radio. Conférence donné à l'Institut général de psychologie* (Paris, 1929), 1–16.

These enthusiastic predictions about radio's future, however, could not entirely counter contemporaries' fears about the potentially harmful effects of broadcast sound on its audiences. "Devices of mechanical music have acquired a hitherto unknown importance," the engineer Pierre Hemardinquer observed in 1934, but how would the impending "twentieth century of noise" affect France's citizens?[5] Emile Vuillermoz, for his part, feared that constant listening would only fuel mass distraction, and regarded his contemporaries' penchant for broadcast sound as an unfortunate byproduct of the political and economic anxieties of the age. "We live in an epoch of uncertainty and anguish," he worried, defined by a "vertiginous race for money . . . the universal apotheosis of violence and brutality, the Americanization of our values . . . and a generalized *gangsterisme* that invades all aspects of activity." Far from predisposing people to meditative silence, this tumultuous climate instead propelled them to seek refuge in that sort of "light opium that is uninterrupted rhythm." Would anyone, he wondered, be willing to seek a "detoxification cure?"[6]

This book investigates how France's incipient auditory culture sparked a series of virulent debates about the role of broadcast sound and listening in modern life, as people from across the social spectrum encountered a sound media that disrupted conventional modes of sensory perception and infiltrated nearly every arena of society and politics. What Emile Vuillermoz hailed as the distinctive postwar "state of the ear" – the democratization of radio and a host of related electro-acoustical technologies, the new listening practices they generated, and their subsequent transformations to the soundscape of everyday life – quickly became the source of myriad disputes between ordinary listeners and a range of public and political figures. How, when, and where should people listen to the radio? When did broadcast sound become "noise?" What effects did sound waves have on the human body? How did constant listening affect the acquisition or retention of knowledge? These questions also preoccupied a number of self-proclaimed sound professionals, who launched investigations into the physiology of hearing and the psychology of listening and experimented with practical applications for radio and other sound media. If their studies produced little consensus about the impact of broadcast sound on the French population, it was because their findings quickly became entangled in the turbulent politics of the interwar decades.

While exploring the simultaneous fascination and anxiety surrounding the emergence of a new auditory culture, this book also

---

[5] Pierre Hemardinquer, "Les recherches physiques récentes sur l'ouïe," *Annales de prothèse auriculaire. Revue d'acoustique physique appliquée à l'étude de l'ouïe*, June 1934, 5.
[6] Emile Vuillermoz, "La peur du silence," *Le Miroir du monde*, April 6, 1935, 56.

investigates how broadcasting transformed the dynamics of politics in France and its empire. Examining a series of debates about the political and social uses of radio that unfolded in the pages of the mass press, the halls of parliament, and in a range of bureaucratic and elite circles, I uncover how French people progressively came to conceive of the airwaves as a "radio nation": a new type of collective space in which they could come together to debate both the definition of the body politic and the terms by which citizens could participate in the life of the nation. In the process, radio listening came to be seen as an important, albeit highly contested, everyday practice of citizenship. For not everyone in France welcomed the incursions of a broadcast media into politics. Nor did audiences become the passive consumers of sound imagined by Vuillermoz. Instead they developed innovative ways of using their radios and the sounds that emerged to participate in national life. In doing so, they ensured that the role of broadcast sound in French society would remain the subject of fierce controversy into the Second World War and beyond.

Creating and contesting the "radio nation"

Radio's development as a mass broadcast media coincided with the final years of the Third Republic, two decades when domestic politics and international affairs became closely intertwined as France struggled to recover from the material and psychological destruction of the First World War. The onset of total war had temporarily halted the protracted nineteenth-century ideological battle between secular republicans and right-wing supporters of the Catholic Church that exploded into violence during the Dreyfus Affair of the 1890s. When the German Army invaded Belgium and northern France during the autumn of 1914, the parties of the left and right temporarily abandoned their differences to rally behind national defense in a *union sacrée*. Wartime propaganda, rationing, and military service all chipped away at persistent cultural and linguistic divides among citizens of different regions as the state expanded its control over previously sacrosanct areas of private life. But the war also destroyed a generation of young men, disrupted conventional family life and conventional gender roles, and exacerbated class and racial hostilities, leaving in its wake a fractured and disillusioned population divided over the war's legacies and its meaning in their lives.[7]

---

[7] Jean-Jacques Becker, *The Great War and the French People*, trans. Arnold Pomerans (New York, 1986); Mary Louise Roberts, *Civilization without Sexes: Reconstructing Gender in Postwar France, 1917–1927* (Chicago, 1994); Tyler Stovall, *Paris and the Spirit of 1919: Consumer Struggles, Transnationalism, and Revolution* (Cambridge, 2012).

The celebrations marking the Armistice and the frenzied hedonism of the immediate postwar years could not entirely mask lingering anxieties about the war's impact on France's future. How could hundreds of thousands of physically and mentally disabled veterans be reintegrated into society? Might national unity be restored in the face of growing economic divides between a wealthy bourgeoisie and an increasingly impoverished industrial class? Could France, threatened on its imperial peripheries by anti-colonial nationalism and challenged as a leading diplomatic player on the Continent, ever regain its prewar geopolitical prestige? Governments vacillated from right to left and collapsed in dizzying succession in the 1920s as legislators struggled to answer these questions while rebuilding the destroyed "red zones" of northern France and contending with rampant inflation.[8]

After 1930, the global economic depression, an influx of immigrants from Eastern Europe and the colonies, and the rise of authoritarian regimes in neighboring Italy and Germany further inflamed partisan tensions between left and right. In February of 1934, when far right extra-parliamentary leagues and veterans' associations took to the streets to protest government corruption and the inefficacies of parliamentary democracy, they nearly toppled the Republic. The ensuing conflicts between the left-wing Popular Front coalition that rallied in defense of democracy and its opponents on the far right only exacerbated citizens' anxieties about France's future as another European war loomed on the horizon.[9] For these reasons, historians have long regarded the 1930s as the "inexorable march to war of a society that was, and yet was not, helpless to affect its fate." Paralyzed by the material and psychological destruction wrought by the First World War, preoccupied with the nation's political and intellectual "decadence," and looking backward to make sense of the future, France's leaders could do little to forestall its impending defeat by Nazi Germany in the summer of 1940.[10]

However, broadcasting began to transform the dynamics of politics during the same tumultuous years, as contemporaries turned to a modern

---

[8] Benjamin Martin, *France and the Après-Guerre* (Baton Rouge, 1999); Chris Millington, *From Victory to Vichy: Veterans in Interwar France* (Manchester, 2012); Antoine Prost, *In the Wake of War: Les anciens combattants and French Society, 1914–1939* (Oxford, 1992); Sophie Delaporte, *Les gueules cassées. Les blessés de la face de la grande guerre* (Paris, 2001).

[9] Julian Jackson, *The Popular Front: Defending Democracy, 1934–1938* (Cambridge, 1998), 1–51; Jessica Wardhaugh, *In Pursuit of the People: Political Culture in France, 1934–1939* (London, 2009), 1–93.

[10] Eugen Weber, *The Hollow Years: France in the 1930s* (New York, 1994), 6–10. Omer Bartov, "Martyr's Vengeance: Memory, Trauma, and Fear of War in France, 1918–1940," in Joel Blatt, ed., *The French Defeat of 1940: Reassessments* (New York, 1998), 60–90. For the classic thesis on French decadence during the interwar decades, see Jean-Baptiste Duroselle, *La décadence: 1932–1939* (Paris, 1979).

media technology for solutions to the many challenges facing the postwar nation. Long before a radio receiver had entered every home, people began to imagine the airwaves as a "radio nation": a new type of space composed of sounds and radio signals where they might come together to negotiate the boundaries of the body politic and the means by which citizens could participate in national life. From its very origins, the media historian David Hendy suggests, radio exuded an "aura of democracy" by presenting itself in a "language stoked in demotic values."[11] Even more than the mass newspapers of the mid-nineteenth century that encouraged people to imagine themselves as members of a monolingual national community, radio waves' defiance of geographical distance and the perceived boundaries between public and private life promised audiences the opportunity to experience national politics more intimately and immediately than ever before.[12] "One of the things about radio that should make us love it is its power of unity," the journalist André Forèze wrote in the far-right Catholic newspaper *Choisir* in 1934, for "despite distance, thousands and even millions of listeners can come together by hearing the same words."[13] Radio's indiscriminate address and its ability to speak to listeners simultaneously as individuals and collectives, combined with the apparent universality of listening as a sensory experience, all suggested that radio could reach audiences of widely divergent social, economic, and educational backgrounds.[14] It was precisely this "radiophonic ubiquity," the left-leaning dramatist Carlos Larronde proposed the same year in the state's *Annuaire de la radiodiffusion nationale*, that allowed the airwaves to serve so many different political agendas, whether they carried "pacifist messages or militarist diatribes."[15]

Radio broadcasting began to mediate contestations over citizenship, relations between Paris and the provinces, and the interactions between colony and metropole, as a diverse range of political stakeholders sought to harness the interwar "sound revolution" for a variety of public and political ends. In the late 1920s, philanthropists and social reformers argued that radio listening could reintegrate disabled veterans into civil

[11] David Hendy, *Radio in the Global Age* (Oxford, 2000), 195–96.
[12] Benedict Anderson, *Imagined Communities: Reflections on the Origins and Spread of Nationalism* (London, 1983, 2006), 33–36.
[13] André Forèze, "La vie provinciale et la radio," reprinted from *Choisir* in *Le Petit radio*, December 7, 1934.
[14] Jason Loviglio, *Radio's Intimate Public: Network Broadcasting and Mass Mediated Democracy* (Minneapolis, 2005), xiii–xxviii; Kate Lacey, *Listening Publics: The Politics and Experience of Listening in the Media Age* (Oxford, 2013), 35.
[15] Carlos Larronde, "L'universalité de la radio," *Annuaire de la radiodiffusion nationale 1934* (Paris, 1934), 102–6.

society through the airwaves, with broadcast sound serving as a "prosthesis" to rehabilitate their damaged bodies and minds. At the same time, state bureaucrats, colonial lobbyists, and politicians labored to construct a network of state radio stations that could reach rural audiences in the remotest regions of metropolitan France and the empire, while simultaneously working to carve out a distinctive space for French voices on the European radio spectrum. By the mid-1930s, questions about precisely which sectors of the French population could access radio technology, as well as how, when, and where they tuned into broadcasts, became controversial and divisive. For the leaders of the Popular Front movement, democratizing access to the airwaves became a new political imperative. They hoped to mitigate class tensions and combat the rise of fascism by deploying radio to instill a common cultural capital in France's youth, drawing on a modern pedagogy of the ear to discipline the listening and speaking habits of schoolchildren through on-air radio lessons. In French North Africa, European settlers tried to exploit broadcasting to strengthen ties between Algiers and Paris and reinforce France's "civilizing mission" among the Muslim population.

Yet these varied efforts to deploy broadcasting in the service of the nation or for more specific political agendas frequently clashed with the desires of radio audiences, who rejected elite constructions of listening and developed unconventional uses for radio technology well outside the realm of information or entertainment. Disabled veterans converted their radios into hearing aids to portray themselves as able-bodied; amateur radio enthusiasts sought out foreign signals and radio programs, often in languages they could not even understand; and colonial populations used their radios to access Arab cultures outside the sphere of French control. Radio listening, as we shall see, turned out to be highly subjective and broadcast sound difficult to manipulate and control. Moreover, as radio audiences' everyday listening habits became embroiled in local, national, and even international affairs, fierce disputes erupted over the meaning of listening and the role of the state in regulating the emerging "radio nation" in the airwaves and in cultivating a distinctly French auditory culture.

The debates about radio listening featured in this book demonstrate the centrality of broadcast sound to twentieth-century French politics by highlighting the ways in which political subjectivity and sensory perception have historically been intertwined. Where a vast scholarly literature has examined the role of material and visual culture, from national monuments and paintings to the mass press, film, and even television, in shaping French political culture and national identity over the course of the nineteenth and twentieth centuries, the auditory dimensions of politics have rarely been studied outside the circumscribed domains of singing and music.[16] This lacuna results in part from a historiography that has privileged vision as critical to the development of rationality and modern governmentality and linked the rise of print media and reading publics to the emergence of individualism and nationalism.[17] Understanding the pivotal role that broadcasting came to play in interwar politics requires us to jettison longstanding assumptions about listeners as passive consumers of sound, and instead, as Kate Lacey recently proposed, to consider listening as an intersubjective activity bridging the "conventionally political realm of debate and deliberation and the realm of sensory, embodied experience."[18] That French people of the interwar decades began to conceive of listening as a form of political participation illustrates how broadcasting transformed the experiential dimensions of citizenship, or what the historian Geoff Eley has described as the "set of practices – juridical, political, economic, and cultural, which define a person and through which persons define themselves as members of society."[19] When elites began to try to mold citizens through broadcast sound, the very act of listening became the site of multiple power struggles, as audiences used their radios to negotiate the terms of their participation in the "radio nation" in the airwaves.

Revisiting interwar politics through the framework of auditory culture consequently revises conventional portrayals of the *entre-deux-guerres* as a period of political stagnation and entrenched ideological struggle between "Two Frances" – one deeply Catholic, conservative, and proto-fascist, and the other secular and republican – that culminated in the triumph of the far-right collaborationist Vichy regime of the

[16] Representative examples of this literature include Richard Thomson, *The Troubled Republic: Visual Culture and Social Debate in France, 1889–1900* (New Haven CT, 2004); June Hargrove and Neil McWilliam, *Nationalism and French Visual Culture, 1870–1914* (New Haven CT, 2005); Simon Dell, *The Image of the Popular Front: The Masses and the Media in Interwar France* (Basingstoke, 2006); Tamara Chaplin, *Turning on the Mind: French Philosophers on Television* (Chicago, 2007); and Joel Vessel, *Drawing France: French Comics and the Republic* (Oxford MS, 2010). Works exploring the relationship between music, auditory culture, and French politics include James Johnson, *Listening in Paris: A Cultural History* (Berkeley, 1996); Regina Sweeney, *Singing our Way to Victory: French Cultural Politics and Music During the Great War* (Middletown CT, 2001); Jane E. Fulcher, *French Cultural Politics and Music: From the Dreyfus Affair to the First World War* (Oxford, 1999); Jane E. Fulcher, *The Composer as Intellectual: Music and Ideology in France, 1914–1940* (Oxford, 2005); Barbara L. Kelly, ed., *French Music, Culture, and National Identity, 1870–1939* (Rochester NY, 2008).

[17] For examples, see Donald Lowe, *A History of Bourgeois Perception* (Chicago, 1982); Chris Otter, *The Victorian Eye: A Political History of Light and Vision in Britain, 1800–1910* (Chicago, 2008).

[18] Lacey, *Listening Publics*, 13–17, 35.

[19] Geoff Eley and Jan Palmoski, eds., *Citizenship and Nationality in Twentieth Century Germany* (Stanford, 2007), 1–14. Eley also cited by Lacey, *Listening Publics*, 7.

Second World War.[20] Without denying the existence of profound political and social divisions or the rhetorical and physical violence that contributed to a climate of undeclared civil war in the mid-1930s, the battles over radio listening highlight important areas of fluidity between left and right that have only recently drawn the attention of scholars. In the struggle between democracy and authoritarianism, Jessica Wardhaugh argues, there was a "constant evolution of rhetoric and practice within the dynamic opposition of left and right," as politicians battled to win the support of the masses.[21] Radio intensified this sensation of rapid change by carrying news of political coups and assassinations across the Continent and transporting the voices of striking industrial workers and street demonstrators into cafes, homes, and public squares across France.

More important, the "radio nation" in the airwaves constituted a unique type of auditory space whose borders remained in constant flux, subject to the temporality and short duration of radio broadcasts, as well as to listeners' access to radio technology, the quality of their reception, and their own desire to tune in. Audiences might one day participate in the "radio nation" only to be excluded from it the next, unable to hear French stations' signals through the stream of static and foreign voices surfacing from their radio loudspeakers.[22] Radio listeners, including some from marginalized social groups, found ways to participate in separate and overlapping radio publics both within and outside the borders of the "radio nation," thus undermining broadcasting's ability to produce social or political cohesion. At the same time, listeners demanded greater state involvement in developing the "radio nation," even while rejecting controls over broadcasting that they perceived to be an assault on their "right to listen" in the ways they chose. These demands for state intervention followed no clear left–right trajectory, fueling the tensions between securing individual rights and promoting collective national interests that lay at the very heart of the Third Republic's struggle for political legitimacy. The anxieties and aspirations that animated interwar politics – over France's vulnerable geopolitical status, the nation's deeply rooted class and religious differences, and the fate of its colonial

---

[20] Julian Jackson, *The Popular Front: Defending Democracy, 1934–1938* (Cambridge, 1988); Herman Lebovics, *True France: The Wars over Cultural Identity, 1900–1945* (Ithaca NY, 1992); Samuel Kalman, *The Extreme Right in Interwar France* (Aldershot, 2008); Sean Kennedy, *Reconciling France Against Democracy: The Croix de Feu and the Parti Social Français* (Montreal, 2007).

[21] Philip Nord, *France's New Deal: From the Thirties to the Postwar Era* (Princeton NJ, 2010); Jessica Wardhaugh, *In Pursuit of the People: Political Culture in France, 1934–1939* (London, 2009), 17–22.

[22] Lacey, *Listening Publics*, 115.

empire – cannot be understood without attending to the ways that broadcasting contributed to the multivalence of democracy. More important, the politics of auditory culture in interwar France invite us to rethink standard accounts of radio's role in the European crisis of liberal democracy and the centrality of listening to twentieth-century political life.

Rethinking interwar broadcasting

In surveys of twentieth-century European history, broadcasting typically makes a brief appearance in chapters devoted to the turbulent depression years, suggesting that radio's primary historical significance resided in its transformation of mass politics. Certainly, radio's expansion as a mass media coincided with the crisis of liberal democracy: decades when communist and fascist leaders challenged the legitimacy of parliamentary regimes and battled to win the hearts and minds of the European masses. Because many Western European governments regarded wireless as an extension of existing telecommunications such as the telephone and telegraph, they quickly claimed a legal monopoly over the airwaves, facilitating the emergence of national state-run broadcasting systems.[23] As a result, many European politicians, intellectuals, and cultural critics regarded broadcasting as the quintessential mass media of the modern era, and as such, either a "newly democratic forum" or a "pernicious threat to participatory democracy and an effective public sphere."[24] Perhaps unsurprisingly, historians have in turn been preoccupied with investigating whether radio bolstered democracy or hastened its demise, producing two dominant interpretations of interwar broadcasting.

In Mussolini's Italy and Hitler's Germany, fascist propagandists rapidly seized control of radio microphones to eliminate political dissent and manufacture consent for one-party dictatorships.[25] Both regimes sponsored schemes to cultivate radio listening across social classes

---

[23] Kate Lacey, "Radio in the Great Depression: Promotional Culture, Public Service, and Propaganda," in Michelle Hilmes, ed., *Radio Reader: Essays in the Cultural History of Radio* (London, 2002), 26–32; Suzanne Lommers, *Europe on Air: Interwar Projects for Radio Broadcasting* (Amsterdam, 2013), 45.

[24] Lacey, *Listening Publics*, 7.

[25] J.H.P. Bergmeier, *Hitler's Airwaves: The Inside Story of Nazi Radio Broadcasting and Propaganda Swing* (New Haven CT, 1997). Regionally produced radio programs that flourished during the Weimar Republic of the 1920s rapidly disappeared under centralized propaganda directives from Berlin following Hitler's seizure of power. We know considerably less about radio policy in Italy during the 1920s. See Giana Isolo, "Italian Radio: History and Historiography," *Historical Journal of Film, Television, and Radio*, 15, 3, 1995, 393–99; Enrico Menduni, "An Unheard Story? The Challenges for Radio Studies in Italy," *The Radio Journal: International Studies in Broadcast and Audio Media*, 2, 1, 2004.

through the state-subsidized production of inexpensive and deliberately weak radio receivers designed to prevent listeners from tuning into foreign signals. State propagandists promoted collective radio listening through rural village cooperatives, at party meetings, and during political rallies, with the goal of exposing the masses to the voices of their "all-powerful" leaders.[26] Influenced by the Frankfurt School's critique of mass culture and Habermasian anxieties about the decline of an autonomous public sphere, studies of German radio have portrayed broadcasting as an agent of cultural standardization and political manipulation.[27] Although recent scholarship has begun to complicate this narrative by uncovering how radio listening could function as a form of political resistance, historians continue to emphasize fascist propagandists' efforts to deploy broadcast sound to colonize the ears of citizens in public and private spaces.[28]

Studies of British broadcasting, in contrast, have focused on the efforts of English political and intellectuals to exploit radio as a counter-weight to the introduction of universal suffrage by molding the religious views, cultural tastes, and political perspectives of the working masses to more closely resemble their own. Purged of the taint of mass consumer culture and shielded from excessive government intervention, early British broadcasters argued, a public service broadcasting monopoly would forge a more egalitarian democracy by giving every citizen access to a common national culture.[29] Under the domineering hand of John Reith, the first director of the British Broadcasting Corporation (BBC), radio programs papered over racial and class divisions within British society, often to the chagrin of many listeners, who judged the highbrow

---

[26] Victoria de Grazia, *The Culture of Consent: The Organization of Mass Leisure in Fascist Italy* (Cambridge, 1981), 103–125; Shelley Baranowski, *Strength Through Joy: Consumerism and Mass Tourism in the Third Reich* (Cambridge, 2004).

[27] Karl Christian Führer and Corey Ross, eds., *Mass Media, Culture, and Society in Twentieth-Century Germany* (London, 2006), 1–13. Recent scholarship has highlighted the diversity of listening experiences during the Weimar period. See Kate Lacey, *Feminine Frequencies: Gender, German Radio, and the Public Sphere, 1923–1945* (Ann Arbor, 1996); Adelheid von Saldern, "Volk and Heimat Culture in Radio Broadcasting during the Period of Transition from Weimar to Nazi Germany," *The Journal of Modern History*, 76, 2, 2004, 312–46; Karl Christian Führer, "A Medium of Modernity? Broadcasting in Weimar Germany, 1923–1932," *The Journal of Modern History*, 69, 4, 1997, 722–53.

[28] Muriel Favre, "Quand le 'Führer parle': Le public des cérémonies radiophoniques du Nazisme," *Le Temps des médias*, 2, 3, 2004, 108–17; Carolyn Birdsall, *Nazi Soundscapes: Sound, Technology, and Urban Space in Germany 1933–1945* (Amsterdam, 2012). Andrew Stuart Bergerson, "Listening to the Radio in Hildesheim, 1925–1953," *German Studies Review*, 24, 1, 2001, 83–113.

[29] Asa Briggs, *The History of Broadcasting in the United Kingdom*, 5 vols. (Oxford, 1961); D.L. Le Mahieu, *A Culture for Democracy: Mass Communication and the Cultivated Mind in Britain Between the Wars* (Oxford, 1988); Paddy Scannell and David Cardiff, *A Social History of British Broadcasting. Vol. 1: Serving the Nation, 1922–1939* (Oxford, 1991), 13; Jennifer Doctor, *The BBC and Ultra-Modern Music, 1922–1936* (Cambridge, 2002).

cultural and religious programs to be boring and irrelevant to their daily lives. Despite these criticisms, most histories of the BBC concur with Paddy Scannell's conclusion that broadcasting reinvigorated civil society and contributed "unobtrusively to the democratization of everyday life."[30]

French radio does not fit easily into this binary historiography that casts broadcasting either as the powerful weapon of an authoritarian state or as a tool for forging democracy from above. In many social and cultural histories of the interwar period, radio appears as a popular domestic entertainment that launched the careers of the recording stars Maurice Chevalier and Edith Piaf, or alternatively, as an underdeveloped medium with only marginal influence on mainstream politics.[31] In Eugen Weber's blunt assessment, "technical equipment was poor, power weak, fading frequent, sound indifferent, blurring, scrambling, interference, [and] failure of broadcasting stations frequent," while the programming itself was "unsophisticated and uncoordinated."[32] Thanks to the work of Christian Brochand, Cécile Méadel, and Caroline Ulmann-Mauriat, among others, we know a great deal about the administrative and legal history of early French broadcasting that contributed to its dismal retrospective reputation.[33] In contrast to the strict state monopolies established elsewhere in Europe, in France a dual commercial-public broadcasting system took root haphazardly over the course of the 1920s and 1930s, revealing profound political disagreements about how the airwaves should be developed and regulated.

In the aftermath of the First World War, radio amateurs and enterprising businessmen who had learned about wireless during their military service claimed the right to construct radio transmitters and broadcast programs. The French Postal Administration (Postes, Télégraphes, et Téléphones, or PTT) held the legal monopoly over wireless communications, but a succession of postal ministers granted private stations concessions to broadcast, while choosing to ignore others that began

---

[30] Paddy Scannell, "Public Service Broadcasting and Modern Public Life," *Media, Culture, and Society*, 11, 1989, 135–66.

[31] Andrew Dudley and Steven Ungar, *Popular Front Paris and the Poetics of Culture* (Cambridge MA, 2005), 192–203; Charles Rearick, *The French in Love and War* (New Haven CT, 1997); Jacques Kergoat, *La France du Front Populaire* (Paris, 1986), 359.

[32] Weber, *The Hollow Years*, 64–65.

[33] Cécile Méadel, *Histoire de la radio des années trente: du sans-filiste à l'auditeur* (Paris, 1994); Caroline Ulmann-Mauriat, *Naissance d'un média: histoire politique de la radio en France, 1921–1931* (Paris, 1999); Christian Brochand, *Histoire générale de la radio et de la télévision en France*, 2 vols. (Paris, 1994); Jean-Jacques Cheval, *Les radios en France: histoire, état, et enjeux* (Rennes, 1997); René Duval, *Histoire de la radio en France* (Paris, 1980); Michel Amoundry, *Le Général Ferrié: naissance des transmissions et de la radiodiffusion* (Grenoble, 1993); Frank Tenot, *Radios privés, radios pirates* (Paris, 1977).

transmitting without official authorization. These early commercial broadcasters, who relied heavily on advertising revenues for their operations, found important backers among a coalition of radio boosters that included radio-electric manufacturers, amateur radio clubs, and professional scientific societies, who together campaigned to shield the entire industry from state regulation. State-affiliated PTT stations also began to appear in regional cities, managed by local radio clubs and listeners' associations composed of community leaders, artists, and intellectuals appointed to represent the "public interest."[34]

For much of the 1920s, defenders of the state broadcasting monopoly, who included radical and socialist politicians and unionized PTT workers, battled with proponents of commercial broadcasting over who had the right to transmit programs, each side's arguments complicated by economic instability, electoral turmoil, and frequent ministerial turnover. In 1928, under the conservative Poincaré government, legislators voted to ban the creation of any future commercial stations, a gesture that implicitly legalized those already in existence. By 1930, fourteen commercial stations were broadcasting alongside eleven in the state-run PTT network, and France's commercial broadcasters faced no subsequent challenges to their existence until the Second World War.[35]

However, bureaucrats in the state radio administration did begin to exert greater control over the airwaves by monitoring the content of news bulletins, delimiting stations' frequency attributions and transmitting power, regulating the use of radio in elections, and slowly purging commercial advertising from state stations. In the early 1930s, the state purchased the commercial station Radio-Paris to become France's flagship national station and launched the Ferrié Plan, a decade-long project to construct a state radio network that would cover all of France with broadcast sound. Yet public radio, funded through revenues to the annual radio license fee introduced in 1933 as well as appropriations from the national budgets for fine arts and education, faced growing competition from commercial stations, including the Poste Parisien and Radio-Toulouse, whose vast advertising revenues enabled them to hire the most talented radio dramatists and reporters.[36]

By 1936, audiences could hear significant differences in the programs and broadcasting style of the state and commercial stations. That year, the advertising entrepreneur Marcel Bleustein-Blanchet revolutionized commercial broadcasting when he created the Parisian station Radio-Cité, which pioneered game shows and soap operas based on the American

[34] Ulmann-Mauriat, *Naissance d'un média*, 5–47.   [35] Ibid., 51–218.
[36] Méadel, *Histoire de la radio*, 26–28.

model of corporate sponsorship. His own advertising firm Publicis supplied the bulk of contracts for Radio-Cité and other commercial stations, including the neighboring multilingual Radio-Luxembourg. Leaders of the left-wing Popular Front coalition government of 1936–1938, fearful of the growing corporatization of the media, responded by imposing a hefty tax on radio advertising.[37] However, the expansion of commercial broadcasting also fueled demands on the part of politicians, intellectual elites, and listeners of varied political convictions that the state should play a greater role in developing high-quality cultural programming for France's citizens, something that could only be achieved through greater centralization of the airwaves. Rising diplomatic tensions on the Continent and an increased number of foreign propaganda attacks by fascist and Nazi radio transmitters after 1936 fueled additional demands that the state develop a comprehensive counterpropaganda program to represent France's interests internationally, leading the radical premier Edouard Daladier to impose significant restrictions on the airwaves on the eve of the Second World War.

This complex institutional history takes center stage in previous studies of French broadcasting, with the result that the competition between public and commercial stations has emerged as the dominant narrative for understanding the "politics" of interwar radio. Media historians cite the state's relatively late intervention in broadcasting, a comparatively low number of registered radios (5.5. million in 1939 to Great Britain's nearly 8 million), and the uneven distribution of state radio transmitters across national territory as evidence of France's failure to measure up to the highly centralized and comparatively well-funded BBC and German Rundfunk. French broadcasting, they suggest, could do little to bolster the ailing democracy of the Third Republic. For Cécile Méadel, this failure reflected public radio's local roots as well as the absence of a strong conception of broadcasting as a "public service" among lawmakers and cultural power brokers.[38] Joelle Neulander's recent study of post-1936 commercial broadcasting, which examined the narrative structure and content of popular radio plays and song lyrics, likewise concluded that private radio captured a larger share of radio audiences through programs that reflected the conservative, Catholic, and bourgeois values that would go on to define the Vichy regime of the Second World War.[39] However,

[37] Joelle Neulander, *Programming National Identity: The Culture of Radio in 1930s France* (Baton Rouge, 2009), 23–44; Victoria de Grazia, *Irresistible Empire: America's Advance Through Twentieth-Century Europe* (Cambridge MA, 2005), 243.
[38] Ulmann-Mauriat, *Naissance d'un média*, 30–31; Méadel, *Histoire de la radio*, 375–77. Méadel argues that French broadcasting could not transform the practices of democracy because no strong conception of radio as a "public service" existed in France before the Second World War.
[39] Neulander, *Programming National Identity*, 185–91.

by elevating the BBC as the standard bearer for state radio in a democracy or American commercial broadcasting as the model for France's private stations, these studies obscure the novelty radio held for so many people and the multiplicity of uses they imagined for broadcast sound. Moreover, the very absence of firm state control over the airwaves into the mid-1930s permitted many different political stakeholders to participate in the creation of radio programs and the day-to-day management of state stations.

This book departs from the institutional history and analyses of radio programming that characterized much of the earlier scholarship on French broadcasting by investigating how broadcast sound resonated in multiple arenas of cultural, intellectual, and political life. Rather than asking whether radio reinforced or undermined democracy, I examine the progressive development of a "radio nation" in the airwaves whose ever-shifting borders contributed to the political confusion of the era. According to Lisa Gitelman and Rick Altman, all new media undergo an initial phase of "identity crisis," when their meanings and uses remain in flux, until they become "adapted to existing categories of public understanding about what the medium does for whom and why."[40] France's "radio nation" occupied a space at once physical and discursive – produced by the radio signals that carried sounds across vast distances as well as by the varied social and political tasks that contemporaries assigned to broadcasting and to wireless technology. This space did not emerge solely through the top-down initiatives of legislators and state bureaucrats, but in dialogue with radio audiences and other interested parties, all of whom imagined very different aesthetic and utilitarian futures for the airwaves amid the rapidly evolving domestic and international political climate of the 1930s. Nor would it be accurate to speak of the existence of a national radio audience in this period as a fixed body of listeners. Instead, multiple and overlapping radio publics interacted with the "radio nation" that they imagined and heard through their radio receivers. In fact, it was precisely this "interpretive flexibility" of early radio that contributed to such fierce disputes about the potential uses and abuses of broadcast sound.[41]

In this book, then, I am less interested in analyzing the content of radio programs than in examining the battles that surfaced over the meanings of radio listening as a public or political act.[42] This does not mean that

[40] Lisa Gitelman and Geoffrey Pingree, eds., *New Media, 1740–1915* (Cambridge MA, 2003), xi–xxi; Rick Altman, *Silent Film Sound* (New York, 2004), 15–21.
[41] Lisa Gitelman, *Always Already New: Media, History, and the Data of Culture* (Cambridge MA, 2008), 63.
[42] Lacey, *Listening Publics*, 6–7. Lacey's recent work examines these questions from a theoretical and historiographical perspective.

audiences did not care about the content or quality of the radio programs they heard. Listeners expressed firm opinions about their sonic preferences in memoirs, personal correspondence, and in the pages of a flourishing specialized radio press. Radio newspapers, whose circulation numbered in the hundreds of thousands by 1930, published weekly radio program schedules and reviews by professional critics as well as listeners' columns where readers wrote in to rank their favorite programs or complain about the poor quality of others.[43] Yet the absence of comprehensive archival collections of radio scripts or musical set lists makes it difficult to determine exactly which programs aired and when, for radio newspapers printed incomplete listings and stations frequently changed their schedules unannounced. Concrete efforts on the part of radio programmers to determine the age, sex, or social class of their audiences, or what we might today call market research, did not begin in France until after the Second World War.[44] Indeed, it was the very difficulty of determining how audiences interpreted the sounds they heard that made listening the subject of both fascination and anxiety among those seeking to exploit a broadcast media that they did not yet fully understand.[45] Throughout the book, I address the radio programs that people listened to, but only to the extent that they reflect particular conceptions of radio listening or illuminate audiences' perspectives about sound. Instead, by situating the history of broadcasting with broader debates about the potential impact of "sound revolution," I want to reassert the importance of listening to studies of twentieth-century history, mapping the ways that contemporary investigations into broadcast sound became intertwined with larger socio-political debates to produce a dynamic politics of auditory culture.

Listening, broadcast sound, and modern life

When Emile Vuillermoz described the emergence of a distinctive postwar "state of the ear" to *Le Miroir du monde* in 1935, he raised a provocative question that captivated many of his contemporaries and would continue to preoccupy generations of later scholars: were different historical eras dominated by particular sensory regimes? And if so, how did they shape the cultures and worldviews of the past? Alain Corbin has traced the first forays into the history of the senses to the 1930s, when the Annales School historians set out to uncover the structures of emotion and perception

---

[43] Brochand, *Histoire générale de la radio, Vol 1: 1921–1944*, 662–71.
[44] Susan J. Douglas, *Listening In: Radio and the American Imagination from Amos 'n' Andy and Edward R. Murrow to Wolfman Jack and Howard Stern* (New York, 1999), 147–60.
[45] Lacey, *Listening Publics*, 6.

undergirding early modern societies as part of their history of *mentalités*.[46] Yet despite living through a period that so many people experienced as louder and more filled with sound than ever before, the *Annalistes* provided the intellectual foundations of a narrative charting "decline of listening in the face of the ascendant power of vision" that would dominate the history of the senses for decades.[47]

As the Annales School cofounder Lucien Febvre set out to investigate the "mental equipment" of the past, he drew upon anthropological traditions dating to the late eighteenth century that employed measurements of sensory acuity to explain cultural differences, and which ranked "primitive" peoples lower on the scale of human civilization because of their supposed reliance on the "baser," animalistic senses of smell and touch.[48] This differential hierarchy of the senses infused Febvre's classic 1942 book *The Problem of Unbelief in the Sixteenth Century*, in which he proposed that hearing, smell, and touch were the more developed senses before the scientific revolution elevated seeing as the critical faculty for interpreting the material world.[49] Although Febvre offered little historical evidence for this claim, his provocative notion that a reordering of the Western sensory hierarchy occurred in the seventeenth century informed another influential framework within the history of the senses: the "great divide" model elaborated by communications theorists Marshall McLuhan and Walter Ong.[50]

Writing in the 1960s, McLuhan argued that stages of human development and social organization could be explained by transformations in the "ratio of the senses" produced by the advent of different communications and media technologies. The invention of the printing press, followed by an eye-centered Renaissance and Enlightenment, ushered in a world where "vision came to dominate Western thinking, serving as the authenticator of truth, courier of reason, and custodian of the

[46] Alain Corbin, *Time, Desire, and Horror: Towards a History of the Senses*, trans. Jean Birell (Cambridge, 1995), 181–82.
[47] Eric Leigh Schmidt, *Hearing Things: Religion, Illusion, and the American Enlightenment* (Cambridge MA, 2000), 17–20.
[48] David Howes, *Sensual Relations: Engaging the Senses in Culture and Social Theory* (Ann Arbor, 2003), 6–10. Early twentieth-century anthropologists, Howes suggests, turned to photographic equipment and phonographs to record their observations of different cultures, resulting in a tendency to classify them as either "eye" or "ear" cultures. See also Constance Classen, *Worlds of Sense: Exploring the Senses in History and Across Cultures* (New York, 1997).
[49] Lucien Febvre, *The Problem of Unbelief in the Sixteenth Century: The Religion of Rabelais*, trans. Beatrice Gottlieb (Cambridge MA, 1942, 1985), 424, 432–37.
[50] On the Annales School within the genealogy of the history of the senses, see Martin Jay, *Downcast Eyes: The Denigration of Vision in Twentieth-Century French Thought* (Berkeley, 1994); 33–35; Robert Jütte, *A History of the Senses: From Antiquity to Cyberspace* (Cambridge, 2005), 11–13.

intellect," in turn marginalizing the senses of taste, touch, and smell. Critical to McLuhan's thesis was the distinction between sound, which "penetrated and surrounded viewers," and vision, which "gave the viewer perspective, distance, coolness, detachment, and a growing sense of self." For McLuhan, this hegemony of vision distinguished rational Western societies from the ear-dominated "oral and intuitive cultures" of so-called tribal peoples.[51]

Although the binary nature of "great divide" theory and its reliance on a racialized other for its explanatory power has since sustained considerable criticism, the hegemony of vision in the post-Enlightenment world has remained an important theme of historical scholarship, as evidenced by a vast literature exploring the "scopic regimes of modernity" undergirding print and reading cultures, Western intellectual traditions and scientific practices, bureaucratic states and modes of surveillance, and of course, the spectacles and simulacra of modern consumer cultures.[52] An emerging interdisciplinary field of "sound studies" has recently begun to challenge this ocularcentrism by exploring how sound has shaped modern forms of social and political organization and the cultural life of modernity.[53] Yet our understanding of auditory cultures remains dominated by what the media historian Jonathan Sterne has termed the "audiovisual litany": a powerful set of tropes associating hearing with passivity, irrationality, and subjectivity, and linking seeing to activity, rationality, and objectivity. Rather than serving as the starting point for critical analysis, Sterne suggests, these distinctions are often taken as biological or physiological facts. Moreover, by explaining "history as something that happens *between* the senses" when a "culture moves from the dominance of one sense to another," the audiovisual litany ignores the simultaneous interplay of multiple senses while masking the

---

[51] Mark M. Smith, *Sensing the Past: Seeing, Hearing, Smelling, Tasting, and Touching in History* (Berkeley, 2007), 6–10; Marshall McLuhan, *The Gutenberg Galaxy: The Making of Typographic Man* (Toronto, 1962); *Understanding Media: The Extensions of Man* (Cambridge MA, 1994 [1964]); Walter Ong, *Orality and Literacy: The Technologizing the Word* (New York, 1982, 2012).

[52] Martin Jay, *Downcast Eyes*, and "Scopic Regimes of Modernity," in Hal Foster, ed., *Vision and Visuality* (Seattle, 1998), 2–23; Jonathan Crary, *Techniques of the Observer: On Vision and Modernity in the Nineteenth Century* (Cambridge, MA, 1990); David Michael Levin, *Modernity and the Hegemony of Vision* (Berkeley, 1993); James C. Scott, *Seeing Like A State: How Certain Schemes to Improve the Human Condition Have Failed* (New Haven CT, 1999).

[53] A number of recent sound studies anthologies provide samplings of this work. Jonathan Sterne, ed., *The Sound Studies Reader* (Abingdon, 2012), 2; Les Back and Michael Bull, eds., *The Auditory Culture Reader* (London, 2003); Trevor Pinch and Karin Bjisterveld, eds., *The Oxford Handbook of Sound Studies* (Oxford, 2012); Mark Michael Smith, *Hearing Histories: A Reader* (Athens GA, 2004); Veit Erlmann, *Sound Cultures: Essays on Sound, Listening, and Modernity* (Oxford, 2004).

ways in which seemingly biological or natural phenomena are constructed through language, culture, and technology.[54]

When interwar cultural commentators described the emergence of a new auditory culture, they predicted that radio and other new sound media would usher in, for better or worse, a sensory regime in which the ear would once again dominate the eye. For Emile Vuillermoz, the growing popularity of broadcast and recorded sound provided clear evidence of civilizational decline and of French society's regression to a more primitive state, while René Sudre celebrated the potential restoration of listening and oral language. Both claims, grounded in a rigid notion of a hierarchy of the senses, would be difficult to substantiate given the visual culture of cinema, photography, and glossy print magazines that flourished in the 1930s. Instead, by situating the history of broadcasting within contemporary debates about the potential impact of a "sound revolution," I seek to demonstrate why broadcast sound and the act of listening itself became so contested as a new auditory culture was coming into being. Doing so requires both an examination of how people listened to broadcast sound and an analysis of the cultural and intellectual premises that shaped contemporary interpretations of listening.

In the pages that follow, I explore the diverse range of new listening practices generated by radio and a host of related electro-acoustical technologies, from the phonograph to the public address system. I consider the ways in which these technologies and their component parts (such as headsets, loudspeakers, aerials, microphones, and dials) framed the act of listening and the reception of sound. Examining how audiences manipulated these devices demonstrates how the cultural meanings of technologies are historically contingent, dependent not only upon their evolving mechanical configurations but also upon the ways that users understood and exploited them.[55] Early radio audiences left abundant descriptions of their own listening habits, but I also analyze listening through a diverse range of print sources concerned with sound. At a moment when discoveries in acoustics were revolutionizing basic knowledge about human hearing and the physics of sound, a self-defined group of "sound professionals" – including pedagogical theorists, physicians and auditory rehabilitation specialists, engineers, and acousticians – all

---

[54] Jonathan Sterne, *The Audible Past: The Cultural Origins of Sound Reproduction* (Durham NC, 2003), 2–3, 14–16.
[55] Wiebe E. Bijker, Thomas P. Hughes, and Trevor Pinch, eds., *The Social Construction of Technological Systems: New Directions in the Sociology and History of Technology* (Cambridge MA, 1987); Weibe E. Bijker, *Of Bicycles, Bakelites, and Bulbs: Towards a Theory of Sociotechnical Change* (Cambridge MA, 1995); Nelly Oudshoorn and Trevor Pinch, eds., *How Users Matter: The Co-Construction of Users and Technologies* (Cambridge MA, 2003).

claimed expertise in new sound-related disciplines.[56] Their investigations into the physiology of hearing and the psychology of listening illustrate how radio's arrival resonated in domains as diverse as urban planning and public hygiene, medicine and welfare policy, education, colonial policy-making, and even international affairs. More important, their studies reveal why cultural constructions of listening cannot be divorced from the tumultuous political context of the interwar years.

Following the lead of the listeners who turned the dials of their radio receivers to navigate the radio spectrum, the five thematic and loosely chronological chapters of this book each tune into a moment of particularly vibrant debate about broadcast sound, charting the progressive politicization of radio listening and the emergence of the "radio nation" over the course of two decades. Chapter 1 explores how radio transformed the soundscape, spurring virulent arguments over the meaning of "noise" and "quiet," and producing a new everyday politics of listening preoccupied with questions of when, where, and how people listened to broadcast sound. In Chapter 2, I analyze discussions in parliament and the mass press about radio's ability to reintegrate veterans of the First World War into civil society, uncovering how people began to define listening as a practice of citizenship and conceive of the airwaves as a "radio nation." Chapter 3 examines the relationship between geography and sound as another framework through which contemporaries imagined the "radio nation," charting the efforts of politicians and state bureaucrats to create a distinctive space composed of French voices and radio signals in the airwaves over Europe, a project challenged by audiences' persistent desire to tune into foreign radio signals.

Chapters 4 and 5, both set in the mid-to-late 1930s, explore the efforts of different stakeholders to exploit the "radio nation" for a particular political end, from the Popular Front's efforts to discipline the listening habits of schoolchildren to colonial policymakers' attempts to control and manipulate Algerian radio audiences. Central to these debates were questions about the appropriate broadcasting policies of a democratic, republican nation and the work that should be accomplished by a "French" auditory culture at home and abroad. But to understand how broadcasting and listening first became the subjects of public and political debate, our story begins in the streets of Paris, where many people encountered radio broadcasting for the first time.

---

[56] Leora Auslander, *Taste and Power: Furnishing Modern France* (Berkeley, 1994), 195–96.

1   Radio broadcasting and the soundscape of interwar life

"Noise is the most striking characteristic of our modern world," a journalist for the popular health magazine *Guérir* announced in 1933. The streets of Paris and other cities resounded with the "noises of motors, auto horns, the jerky crackling of drilling machines demolishing the roadways, the beep-beeps of traffic horns, the whistles of policemen, [and] the rumbling of the autobus . . . making houses tremble from the basement to the attic." Nor could Parisians take refuge from the cacophonous streets in the privacy of their homes, where a "phonograph plays constantly, while on nearby floors you hear the deafening echoes of your neighbor's wireless. The factory resounds with the brouhaha of machines, the office with the tic-tac of typists and telephone rings . . . Noise, always noise!"[1] Similar assessments filled the pages of newspapers and magazines during the interwar decades, as journalists, physicians, engineers, and essayists penned hundreds of articles describing their cacophonous surroundings. Life in the capital had become a "monstrous charivari," thanks to the "rhythm of the traffic, the emergence of mass transit, the apotheosis of the noisiest instruments of the orchestra, and the inhumane sound systems of certain cinemas," the composer and music critic Emile Vuillermoz remarked in the illustrated weekly *Le Miroir du monde* a few years later. "Ours is the era of noise."[2]

Complaints about the noise of the capital did not suddenly begin in the 1930s. Although cultural historians have portrayed nineteenth-century Paris as a preeminently visual city, whose wide boulevards and overflowing café terraces inspired the quintessentially urban practice of *flânerie* and contributed to the birth of a modern consumer culture defined by the spectacular displays of the department store window and the world's fair, for many of its residents the City of Light had long been a city brimming with sounds.[3] Parisians had denounced the "noises" of their city – or sounds they perceived to be disruptive, intrusive, or excessive – since the

---

[1] "Le bruit," *Guérir. Revue mensuelle de vulgarisation médicale et scientifique*, May 1933, 9.
[2] Emile Vuillermoz, "La peur du silence," *Le Miroir du monde*, April 6, 1935, 56.
[3] For examples, see Vanessa R. Schwartz, *Spectacular Realities: Early Mass Culture in Fin-de-Siècle Paris* (Berkeley, 1999); Rosalind Williams, *Dream Worlds: Mass Consumption in Late*

late eighteenth century, even as they relied on them to order their social and political worlds.[4] Urban chroniclers of the 1780s such as Louis-Sébastien Mercier invoked the music of street performers and the clattering of vehicles on cobblestones to juxtapose the hustle and bustle of city life with the comparative calm of the provinces. Bourgeois residents retreated indoors during the 1830s and 1840s to distance themselves from the noises of the "dangerous classes" in the streets, whether the cries of street vendors or the angry shouts of political agitators. Church bells, which had served as quotidian reminders of religious and state power since the Middle Ages, gradually became sonic nuisances for city dwellers, only to be replaced in the 1870s by the machine and traffic sounds of an emerging secular and industrial age.[5] The seventeenth-century poet Boileau may have been the first Parisian to comment on the din of the capital, the psychologist Pierre Vachet claimed in his 1928 treatise *Remèdes à la vie moderne*, but urban noise had "only increased every day since, while noises have also multiplied in number. Tramways, metros, whistles, and sirens all create an infernal racket to which orchestras and jazz, each more numerous, add their dissonant notes." [6]

Despite the clamor of the fin-de-siècle industrial city, many Parisians experienced the deafening artillery bombardments of the First World War as a sonic threshold marking France's turbulent passage into the twentieth century, ushering in a world that not only seemed significantly louder, but also one that was filled with a range of new and distinctly modern sounds.[7] From the early 1920s onward, radios, gramophones, loudspeakers, and public address systems overtook city streets, public venues, and the intimate spaces of homes, ensuring that intermittent moments of repose competed with the near-constant presence of broadcast sound, according to one journalist. "To relax, you dine with music and then dash off for a Negro dance hall, where your ears are assaulted

---

Nineteenth-Century France (Berkeley, 1982); T.J. Clark, *The Painting of Modern Life: Paris in the Art of Manet and His Followers* (Princeton NJ, 1999); Aruna D'Souza and Tom McDonough, eds., *The Invisible Flâneuse? Gender, Public Space, and Visual Culture in Nineteenth-Century Paris* (Manchester, 2008), Hazel Hahn, *Scenes of Parisian Modernity: Culture and Consumption in the Nineteenth Century* (New York, 2009).

[4] David Garrioch, "Sounds of the City: The Soundscape of Early Modern European Towns," *Urban History*, 30, 1, 2003, 5–25.

[5] Peter Bailey, "Breaking the Sound Barrier: A Historian Listens to Noise," *Body and Society*, 2, 49, 1996, 49–66; Jean-Pierre Gutton, *Bruits et sons dans notre histoire: essai sur la reconstitution du paysage sonore* (Paris, 2000), 120, 130–34.

[6] Pierre Vachet, *Remèdes à la vie moderne* (Paris, 1928), 122.

[7] Jean-Pierre Rioux and Jean-François Sirinelli, *Histoire culturelle de la France, Vol. 4: Le temps des masses* (Paris, 1998), 160. The authors describe the "*sonorisation brusque*" of the 1920s. Hillel Schwartz, *Making Noise: From Babel to the Big Bang and Beyond* (New York, 2011), 571–76.

with syncopated dissonances, while ingenious portable phonographs and wireless devices allow fanatics . . . to broadcast sound wherever they go." [8] Even in the rural hamlet of the Val d'Oise where the physician-turned-essayist Georges Duhamel spent his summer holidays, the "voices of modern titans," from rattling railways to revving automobiles, drowned out the murmurs of the local stream, while the sounds of "mechanical pianos, orchestrions, phonographs of all sorts, and *téhessefs* [wirelesses] of every plumage" resounded through the windows of nearly every home in the village.[9] "It has become a common formula to say that wireless is the death of silence," the journalist Georges-Armand Masson quipped in 1935, but "for my part, I never knew the true meaning of silence before the age of radio."[10]

Broadcast sound, as much as the flickering cinema screens or neon lights that increasingly dotted city streets, came to symbolize for many people the rapid pace of modern life, the sensorial disruptions provoked by new communications and media technologies, and the social and political dislocations produced by the First World War. Avant-garde composers and Modernist artists, from the Futurists to the Surrealists, celebrated the disembodied voices emerging from their phonographs and the roars of loudspeakers as provocative inspirations for their compositions.[11] Yet for all those who reveled in broadcast sound's transgression of sensory norms, others heard it as a harbinger of France's moral and physical disintegration. "We are living in the century of noise," the physician Paul Vigne lamented in 1937, the "inevitable consequence of the hectic manner in which postwar society is organized."[12] Emile Vuillermoz, for his part, worried less about the "few delicates" tortured by broadcast sound than the growing insensitivity so many of his contemporaries displayed toward their cacophonous surroundings and their concomitant, if unconscious, "fear of silence." The postwar generation fled contemplative quiet to seek refuge in the screeching sounds of radios, phonographs, and loudspeakers, he lamented, a phenomenon that should "worry our educators, moralists, and hygienists."[13]

[8]   "Le bruit," *Guérir*, May 1933, 9.
[9]   Georges Duhamel, *Querelles de famille* (Paris, 1932), 12–13.
[10] Georges-Armand Masson, "Le mort du silence," *Le Haut-parleur: journal pratique, artistique, amusant des amis de la radio*, February 10, 1935, 76.
[11] Douglas Kahn, *Noise, Water, Meat: A History of Sound in the Arts* (Cambridge MA, 1999); Douglas Kahn and Gregory Whitehead, eds., *Wireless Imagination: Sound, Radio, and the Avant-Garde* (Cambridge MA, 1992), 1–29, 139–88; Karin Bijsterveld, *Mechanical Sound: Technology, Culture, and Public Problems of Noise in the Twentieth Century* (Cambridge MA, 2008), 137–58.
[12] Dr. Paul Vigne, "Le bruit. Danger social? Réflexions d'un résigné," *L'Avenir médical*, April 1937, 111–12.
[13] Emile Vuillermoz, "La peur du silence," *Le Miroir du monde*, April 6, 1935, 56.

This chapter examines the simultaneous fascination and anxiety surrounding what Emile Vuillermoz hailed as a distinctive postwar "state of the ear": the auditory culture created by the democratization of radio and a host of contemporary electro-acoustical technologies, the new listening practices they generated, and their subsequent transformations to the soundscape of everyday life. Following the historians Alain Corbin and Emily Thompson, I employ the concept of the soundscape to refer both to the physical environment produced by sounds and to cultural perceptions of that same environment.[14] I focus on Paris as the stage for broadcasting's debut, tracing radio's move from city streets into domestic spaces and from urban centers into the provinces, investigating the varied meanings that contemporaries assigned to wireless technology and to broadcast sound. In the early 1920s, radio boosters and sound entrepreneurs introduced radio to audiences as a modern media that defied barriers of space, time, and distance to create potentially vast national and international audiences. Yet as radios and loudspeakers became permanent fixtures in public spaces and private homes over the course of the next decade, complaints about broadcast sound as a disruptive form of noise led many people to conclude that the soundscape should be carefully monitored and controlled, in turn producing a new everyday politics of listening.

In the pages that follow, I develop three intertwined arguments about broadcasting's impact on interwar France. First, scholars have long portrayed radio as a predominantly domestic medium, drawing on nostalgic recollections of families gathered around their receivers on cold winter nights to conclude that radio's primary historical significance resided in a "public" media reaching into the "private" sphere of the home.[15] Radio found important domestic audiences, to be sure, but the entrepreneurs who introduced wireless to the public did not immediately envision families as their primary audiences. In fact, the uneven democratization of radio technology ensured that alternative public and semi-public spaces for radio listening flourished into the late 1930s. Radio might better be understood as a media that contributed to a "sustained crisis in definitions of public and private" – a phenomenon that owed as much

---

[14] Alain Corbin, *Village Bells: Sound and Meaning in the Nineteenth-Century French Countryside*, trans. Martin Thom (New York, 1988), xx. Corbin uses the phrase "auditory landscape." Emily Ann Thompson, *The Soundscape of Modernity: Architectural Acoustics and the Culture of Listening in America, 1900–1933* (Cambridge MA, 2002), 1–2. For the history of the concept of the soundscape, see Jonathan Sterne, "Soundscape, Landscape, Escape," in Karin Bijsterveld, ed., *Soundscapes of the Urban Past: Staged Sound as Mediated Cultural Heritage* (Bielefeld, 2013), 181–91.

[15] Interwar radio has primarily been studied as a source of domestic entertainment. See Neulander, *Programming National Identity*; Rearick, *The French in Love and War*, 212–25; Dudley and Ungar, *Popular Front Paris and the Poetics of Culture*, 182–94.

to radio waves' defiance of spatial boundaries as it did to the amplified sounds of loudspeakers resonating through buildings and parks.[16]

Second, factors such as gender, social class, and geographical region complicated access to radio technology and listeners' reception of broadcasts. Long after radio boosters and political stakeholders began to imagine forging a mass national radio audience, multiple radio publics continued to coexist and overlap with one another. Radio listeners sometimes chose where and with whom to tune into the radio, but at other moments became unwitting publics for broadcast sound they could not control. Consequently, while elite cultural critics such as Vuillermoz worried about the narcotizing effects of broadcasting on France's citizenry, his fears about radio fueling cultural standardization remained largely unfounded. Radio may have contributed to the homogenization of the interwar soundscape by exposing audiences across France to a common set of programs, but it also provoked widely divergent reactions to broadcast sound.[17]

Finally, radio's impact on French society and politics cannot be understood without considering it as the technological centerpiece of a much broader transformation to the soundscape, as evidenced by contemporaries' growing complaints about noise. After 1930, conflicts erupted between municipal authorities, businessmen, the police, and ordinary radio listeners over how, when, and where it was acceptable for people to listen to broadcast sound. While forcing people to acknowledge the inherent subjectivity of concepts such as "noisy" or "quiet," the diffusion of radios and electro-acoustical devices pitted those seeking to control the soundscape against others defending their "right to listen" in any way they chose. This everyday politics of listening would in turn shape debates about the potential political uses for radio broadcasting that feature in subsequent chapters of this book. To understand why the arrival of broadcast sound became so enthralling and so controversial, we turn first to the streets of Paris, where many people encountered radio for the first time.

Sound in the City of Light: encountering radio in the streets of Paris

In the cultural imagination of the 1920s, radio's emergence as a broadcast media was intimately linked to the physical spaces of the capital – the

---

[16] Lacey, *Listening Publics*, 117; Loviglio, *Radio's Intimate Public*, xvi.

[17] Matthew F. Jordan, "Discophile ou Discomanie? The Cultural Politics of Living-Room Listening," *French Cultural Studies*, 16, 2, 2005, 151–68; David Goodman, "Distracted Listening: On Not Making Sound Choices in the 1930s," in David Suisman and Susan Strasser, eds., *Sound in the Age of Mechanical Reproduction* (Philadelphia, 2010), 40–45.

stage for France's first radio broadcasts and for the numerous demonstrations that introduced wireless technology to the general public. Journalists acknowledged radio's international origins in the contemporaneous discoveries of Russian, Italian, and American scientists, but elaborated a distinctive history for French broadcasting that began with the physicist Edouard Branly's laboratory experiments at the Institut Catholique, where he produced the world's first radio coherer capable of receiving wireless signals in 1890. Seven years later, the industrialist Eugène Ducretet successfully transmitted signals between two of the city's tallest landmarks, the Panthéon and the Eiffel Tower. On the eve of the First World War, General Gustave Ferrié installed a radio transmitter on the Eiffel Tower, permitting the army to exploit the iconic landmark as a liaison center for the transmissions of field radio operators along the Western Front.[18] This wartime use of the Eiffel Tower permanently altered the monument's place in Parisian memory, the journalist Pierre Descaves later recalled, transforming it from a "precious and legendary ornament on the skyline of the capital" into a radio tower worthy of the "pride of the Nation."[19] In 1921, just a few years after the Armistice, the Eiffel Tower became France's first state-run radio station, joining the privately owned Radiola, the latter station exploited by the veteran Emile Girardeau and his Compagnie Française de T.S.F. (CSF), in broadcasting record concerts, meteorological reports, and news bulletins for a few hours every morning and evening.[20]

The mass daily L'Oeuvre captured the public's fascination with these early radio broadcasts in a whimsical 1923 account of the inanimate Eiffel Tower's "voice" stopping harried Parisians in their tracks outside the Gare de l'Est train station on a Monday afternoon. "Ladies and Gentlemen," a voice rang out across the Boulevard de Strasbourg, "you are going to hear a speech by Monsieur Poincaré at this very moment," the journalist Emmanuel Bourcier recounted. Startled by the sounds, the passers-by halted before the "double door of a boutique, where they saw a sort of ebonite funnel from which a voice emerged ... it was Monsieur Poincaré, invisible and present, speaking to the crowds through wireless telegraphy." This was not an isolated incident, however, for a few hours later on the Boulevard Poissonière, the "the same formidable voice raised itself, very clear and strident, despite the fracas of the traffic," and went

---

[18] Amoundry, Le Général Ferrié: naissance des transmissions de radiodiffusion, esp. Chapters 3 and 4. Ferrié presided over the army's telegraphy school at Mont Valérien and participated in Marconi's first wireless transmission in 1899. He created the army's radio-telegraphy service in 1900.
[19] Pierre Descaves, Quand la radio s'appelait Tour Eiffel (Paris, 1963), 69–70.
[20] Brochand, Histoire générale de la radio, 1: 44–46.

on to read the stock market report and the evening news bulletin to anyone who would stop to listen. Loudspeakers resonated "on the *bateaux-mouches*, in the studios, in front of the photograph stands and the knick-knack displays ... in the wireless shops, in the *grands magasins*, the dance-halls, and in the bistros." Although the Eiffel Tower's initial broadcasts could not have been heard by more than a few thousand people, Bourcier celebrated their potential to defy barriers of space and distance, uniting city residents before reaching into the provinces to create a mass national audience. In every *quartier* of Paris, Bourcier imagined, the "same formidable voice could be heard, just as it was in all of the towns, the *bourgs*, and the hamlets of France ... the Eiffel Tower has spoken."[21]

In the years that followed, an informal coalition of radio boosters that included radio clubs, radio-electric manufacturers, and professional scientific societies endeavored to turn Bourcier's fantasy of a mass national radio audience into a reality by transforming radio listening from the hobby of a tech-savvy few into a more widespread practice. Central to this community of radio boosters were *sans-filistes*, or wireless amateurs who took their name from the phrase "wireless telephony" (*téléphonie sans fil* or *T.S.F.*). They included many veterans of the First World War who had learned about radio during their military service and returned home eager to use their recently acquired skills in radio tuning and construction in civilian life.[22] The postwar vogue for wireless, the musicologist André Coeuroy later commented, "found its explanation in the possibility that exists for everyone to construct his own receiver."[23] *Sans-filistes* reveled in listening to distant radio stations from Europe and around the globe, and as participants in the numerous radio clubs that began to appear across France, competed with one another to build more powerful and sophisticated radio receivers, and in some cases, small radio transmitters that they used to send Morse code signals – all skills demonstrating their technical prowess and fascination with scientific modernity.[24] Radio clubs, whose combined membership numbered 60,000 by the end of the decade, frequently enjoyed informal relationships with radio-electric manufacturers and the first radio stations, and thus played a critical role in introducing

[21] Emmanuel Bourcier, "La voix qui parle aux foules," reprinted from *L'Oeuvre* in *L'Antenne. Journal français de vulgarisation de T.S.F.*, May 2, 1923, 8.
[22] Méadel, *Histoire de la radio*, 187–91. The air force distributed 18,000 wireless receivers during the First World War, creating a sizeable population of veterans skilled in radio-electric construction.
[23] André Coeuroy, "L'évolution de l'industrie radioélectricité," *Machines parlantes et radio. Publication officielle de l'Office Général de la Musique*, August 1930, 538–39.
[24] See Douglas, *Listening In*, 67–69; Sterne, *The Audible Past*, 154–62; and Kristen Haring, *Ham Radio's Technical Culture* (Cambridge MA, 2006), 39–48.

Figure 1.1 "The oldest radio station in France," *Je sais tout* (1923).
Image courtesy of the Bibliothèque Nationale de France.

broadcasting to wider audiences through the publication of technical manuals, specialized radio newspapers and programming guides, and above all, through demonstrations of wireless technology.[25]

The confluence of scientific and industrial interests in northern France and the emergence of several fledgling radio stations in the capital ensured that Paris became the site of many of the largest wireless

[25] Robert Prot, *Dictionnaire de la radio* (Grenoble, 1997), 271–72; Ulmann-Mauriat, *Naissance d'un média*, 24–25.

demonstrations. In 1923, the popular science magazine *Je sais tout* and the CSF-affiliate Société Française de Radioélectricité (SFR), the firm responsible for constructing both the Eiffel Tower and Radiola transmitters, staged a "Festival of the Airwaves" at the Trocadéro Palace to honor Branly as the "father of wireless" and introduce Parisians to broadcasting.[26] Under the shadow of the Eiffel Tower, the "oldest radio station in France," SFR engineers turned the Trocadéro's amphitheater into a giant "radio receiver and transmitter," permitting the estimated 4,000 spectators inside to listen to radio concerts broadcast by the Eiffel Tower and Radiola stations, the new Paris PTT transmitter managed by the Ecole Supérieure des PTT, and to experimental transmissions from two military radio-telegraphy stations in southern France [Figure 1.1]. Loudspeakers installed on the façade of the Trocadéro and on nearby boulevards invited strolling Parisians to stop and listen to the concerts, the dignitaries' speeches, and the engineers' technical explanations of the transmissions.[27] *Je sais tout* followed up the Trocadéro festival with a tour of wireless demonstrations, backed by the PTT, in forty cities across France. A team of Parisian technicians drove cars equipped with a small transmitter and loudspeakers into the Roman amphitheater in Nîmes, and reportedly drew a crowd of 7,000 in Rennes.[28] Later that autumn, the newspaper *Le Petit parisien* organized its own series of touring radio concerts featuring a car mounted with a giant Gaumont loudspeaker, which drew crowds numbering in the thousands to listen to the Eiffel Tower station. The newspaper used the publicity to launch its own radio station, the Poste Parisien, which went on to become one of the most popular commercial stations of the 1930s.[29]

Interwar wireless demonstrations built upon decades-old traditions of mass urban spectatorship that combined scientific pedagogy and entertainment to attract middle-class men interested in technological progress as well as wider audiences seeking curiosities and thrills. Electro-acoustical technologies, until quite recently overlooked in the historiography of Parisian cultures of display, had played a central role in the world's fairs of the fin de siècle. Crowds thronged to exhibition pavilions to marvel at Edison's phonograph and listen to the *théâtrophone*, which used telephone

---

[26] *Je sais tout. La revue de la découverte.* May 1923. Other public radio demonstrations preceded this event in 1921–1922. Ulmann-Mauriat discusses this event briefly in *Naissance d'un média*, 35.

[27] "La radiodiffusion d'une grande soirée," *Je sais tout*, May 16, 1923, and "Notre fête de la T.S.F. française," *Supplément de Je sais tout*, June 15, 1923, i–ii.

[28] "'Je sais tout' organise des galas de T.S.F. dans toute la France," *Je sais tout*, June 15, 1923, 380–81; "Le raid de nos autos-radios," *Je sais tout*, November 1923, 581.

[29] "Les radio-concerts du *Petit parisien* sont terminés," *Le Petit parisien*, October 17, 1923, 2.

wires to relay the sounds of Parisian stages to seats equipped with hearing tubes.[30] By the 1920s, many people had become accustomed to acoustic listening (in which the original source of sound remained invisible), but the physics of wireless transmission remained something of a mystery.[31] Radio boosters consequently staged the invisibility and immateriality of wireless transmissions and the "liveness" of broadcast sound as the new media's principal attractions, deploying a variety of technical tricks to astonish the public. In the summer of 1923, the commercial station Radiola broadcast a classical concert from its studios on the Boulevard Haussmann to an audience gathered in the suburban Parc Montmorency. At the close of the evening, the station used a wired connection to pick up the sounds of a jazz band playing in a brasserie adjacent to the park, before rebroadcasting the music to create an outdoor "radio dance-hall." Later that year, the station's staff locked its star announcer Marcel Laporte, popularly known as "Radiolo," in a sound-proofed glass box with a microphone wired to the studio. Observers looked on eagerly as Radiolo's voice, transported by invisible sound waves, surfaced from a loudspeaker on the sidewalk.[32]

Radio spectacles also tapped into a growing cultural fascination with amplification, and radio boosters touted loudspeakers' distinctly modern sound as a critical element of their entertainment factor.[33] Visitors to the 1929 International Wireless Salon at the Parisian amusement park Magic City, the journalist René Bruyez reported in the radio magazine T.S.F. Programme, were captivated by "The Voice of the Giant," a powerful loudspeaker whose "deafening, tyrannical voice monopolized the attention of the crowd."[34] As Emily Thompson has argued, by the 1920s decades of research by telephone engineers and phonograph manufacturers had eliminated the interference of outside "noise" in electrical sound signals. This engineered sound not only proved to be louder than natural sound, but it was direct, penetrating, and non-reverberating, in turn producing a bigger sensory impact on listeners.[35] For Bruyez, the enormous loudspeaker heard by thousands of exhibition attendees

[30] Carolyn Marvin, *When Old Technologies Were New: Thinking about Electric Communication in the Late Nineteenth Century* (New York, 1998), 208–12. Fauser, *Musical Encounters at the 1889 Paris World's Fair*, 280; M. Testavin, *L'Organisation actuelle du théâtrophone* (Paris, 1930), 2–26. The Compagnie du Théâtrophone attracted a bourgeois clientele through a permanent home service that operated into the 1920s.

[31] Stephen Kern, *The Culture of Time and Space, 1888–1914* (Cambridge MA, 1983), 184.

[32] R. de Laromiguière, "J'écoute: le radio-concert du 12 août à Montmorency," *L'Antenne*, August 22, 1923. A similar experiment took place in the Place des Vosges in June of 1923. See *L'Antenne*, June 20, 1923, 1.

[33] Schwartz, *Making Noise*, 629.

[34] René Bruyez, "Chronique de T.S.F.," *T.S.F. Programme*, October 10, 1929, 6–8.

[35] Thompson, *The Soundscape of Modernity*, 235–42.

provided a sonic manifestation of how "wireless dominates the world." As he observed, "while participating in collective life, radio alone can become an integral part of the private patrimony of every man, however distant he may be from his brothers."[36] Conflating the amplified sound emitted by public address systems with radio waves' defiance of distance, journalists for radio newspapers and the popular scientific press fetishized the size of loudspeakers and their ability to reach enormous crowds, insisting that broadcasting would reinvigorate abandoned auditory traditions such as church bell ringing. "Progress, far from killing old religions, gives them new weapons," *Fil et sans fil* opined, and "thanks to wireless, the sermons of great preachers [and] the most famous sacred choirs can be heard at once by thousands of distant listeners" – a prediction at least partially fulfilled in 1924 when loudspeakers appeared inside Notre Dame, the Gothic cathedral anointing the Ile de la Cité.[37] Manufacturers such as Amplion fueled audiences' desires for novel auditory experiences by promising visitors to a wireless demonstration at the 1925 Exposition des Arts Décoratifs the opportunity to hear the same devices used to "make the Pope's voice audible to 70,000 pilgrims at the Vatican" during the beatification ceremonies for Saint Teresa.[38]

Urban radio demonstrations – in which audiences participated as part of a socially heterogeneous crowd that might include adults and children, men and women, or bankers and street vendors – invited listeners to imagine how radio waves transcended the boundaries between street and home, the *quartiers* of the capital, or Paris and the provinces to unite individuals across vast distances through a simultaneous and collective listening experience. With this goal in mind, France's first radio stations, whether state-run or commercial, competed to design grandiose spectacles that showcased radio's potential to become more than a mere technological curiosity, but rather a medium of national or even international significance. In 1924, when the newly elected *cartel des gauches* government transferred the remains of the socialist Jean Jaurès to the Panthéon, the secular temple honoring France's "great men," the

[36] René Bruyez, "Chronique de T.S.F.," *T.S.F. Programme*, October 10, 1929, 6–8.
[37] *Fil et sans fil*, October 15, 1929; *La Nature. Revue des sciences et de leurs applications aux arts et à l'industrie*, April 4, 105; "Le beffroi haut-parleur," *La Nature*, March 1924, 14–43.
[38] Bibliothèque Historique de la Ville de Paris. Brochure for Amplion, "Le roi des haut-parleurs," ca. 1930. In the Amplion auditorium, fairgoers sat in risers overlooking a stage with a giant radio displayed before a backdrop painted to represent the mysterious "ether" through which sound waves traveled. Loudspeakers distributed sounds around the auditorium. See "Les appareils anglais de radiophonie," *L'Illustration*, October 31, 1926.

fledgling state station Paris PTT provided live coverage of the ceremonies, installing loudspeakers in front of the building and along the streets of the Latin Quarter to allow passers-by to listen.[39] In the decade that followed, the PTT regularly stationed loudspeakers across the capital to permit residents to hear the sounds of military bands, cathedral choirs, and dignitaries' speeches during state funerals, Armistice Day commemorations, and July 14 celebrations.[40] On these occasions, the crowds massed on the sidewalks became participants in live broadcasts staging radio's future as a medium of the masses. During the state funeral of Maréchal Joseph Joffre in 1931, the murmurs of the crowds gathered outside the Hôtel des Invalides and Notre Dame harmonized with the refrains of a military band and the funeral mass to create a perfect sound décor for the radio reporters, *Radio-Magazine* described, as the "miracle of radio gave objective reality to the collective emotion of an entire nation, crystallized before loudspeakers during the commemoration."[41]

The editors of the Parisian daily *L'Intransigeant* also devoted considerable efforts to developing technically innovative live broadcasts that demonstrated radio's potential to create a transatlantic, if not global, audience.[42] On September 3, 1930, the French aviators Dieudonné Costes and Maurice Bellonte hoped to break the world's record for the longest nonstop flight with a Paris-to-New York crossing. The American Charles Lindbergh had captivated Parisians a few years earlier when he landed at Le Bourget airfield after his solo transatlantic flight, turning the aviator into an emblem of "pacifistic heroism." The French aviators' crossing now promised to become a potent symbol of France's postwar renewal in a twentieth century defined by international travel, commerce, and communication.[43] To commemorate the event, *L'Intransigeant* collaborated with Radio-Paris to broadcast the aviators' New York landing through a complicated series of relay exchanges between stations in

---

[39] "Carnet de la T.S.F.," *Le Matin*, November 23, 1932, 7. The PTT placed loudspeakers outside the Palais-Bourbon (where Jaurès's body lay in state) and at several other locations around Paris.

[40] Avner Ben-Amos, *Funerals, Politics, and Memory in Modern France, 1798–1996* (Oxford, 2000), 283, 308–10, 330, 344–48; Evelyne Cohen, *Paris dans l'imaginaire national de l'entre-deux-guerres* (Paris, 1999), 36–44.

[41] "Les funérailles du Maréchal Joffre," *Radio-Magazine*, January 11, 1931, 7; Paul Roux, "La radiodiffusion des obsèques nationales du Maréchal Joffre," *Le Petit radio*, January 10, 1931, 1.

[42] Transatlantic short-wave broadcasting has recently attracted scholarly attention. See Derek Vaillant, "At the Speed of Sound: Techno-Aesthetic Paradigms in U.S.-French International Broadcasting, 1925–1942," *Technology and Culture*, 54, 4, 2013, 888–921.

[43] Modris Eksteins, *Rites of Spring: The Great War and the Birth of the Modern Age* (New York, 1989), 263–65.

Schenectady, Rugby, and Paris.[44] On the day of the historic flight, photos of Marie Costes listening at home with a headset for the sounds of her husband's arrival dotted the front pages of multiple mass dailies, but *L'Intransigeant* invited Parisians without personal radios to gather in the Place de la Concorde, where loudspeakers lined the terraces of the Automobile Club de France.[45]

By 9 p.m., the teeming crowd in the square forced traffic on the adjacent Champs-Elysées to a standstill, leaving vehicles trapped until the following morning. "With power and clarity thousands and thousands of listeners … *lived* the minutes of the landing," *L'Intransigeant* proclaimed the next day, as the loudspeakers broadcast the "ovation of the transported American crowd and a rendition of the *Marseillaise*" by a brass band.[46] According to *L'Antenne*, France's first weekly radio newspaper, radio had united the Old and New Worlds through the "charming intimacy of listening," for only "wireless allowed us to enjoy this minute that we must describe as an historic moment in both aviation and broadcasting."[47] Given the fragility of the relay connections and the size of the crowd, not everyone massed in the Place de la Concorde would have been able to hear the broadcasts. Yet journalists rhapsodized about the moment when the aviators' voices, "serious, energetic, and a little terse," surfaced above the cheers of New Yorkers.[48] Eager not to be outdone by corporate interests, the state station Paris PTT claimed the right to broadcast coverage of the aviators' triumphant return to France. The state installed loudspeakers along the Rue de Rivoli to permit residents to celebrate the "French Lindberghs" by gathering on sidewalks to listen to broadcasts of the dignitaries' speeches and the aviators' testimonies during a ceremony at the Hôtel de Ville.[49] Radio spectacles like these would become increasingly integrated into the capital's entertainment offerings in years to come. State-affiliated stations broadcast

[44] Fernand Divoire, "En écoutant … Le jour de gloire," *T.S.F. Programme*, September 10, 1930, 4. For the 1930 Bal des petits lits blancs, an annual fundraising gala for children with tuberculosis, *L'Intransigeant*'s staff tried unsuccessfully to broadcast a performance by the *chansonnier* Maurice Chevalier from Hollywood through radio and telephone relays. Jean Antoine, "Comment a été diffusée l'arrivée du '?' à New-York," *L'Intransigeant*, September 4, 1930, 6.

[45] Maurice Prax, "Le merveilleux exploit de Costes et Bellonte," *Le Petit parisien*, September 3, 1930, 1–2.

[46] Jean Antoine, "Comment a été diffusée l'arrivée du '?' à New-York," *L'Intransigeant*, September 4, 1930, 6.

[47] Le Navigateur, "Costes, Bellonte, et la T.S.F.," *L'Antenne*, September 7, 1930.

[48] Fernand Divoire, "En écoutant … le jour de gloire," *Lumière et radio*, September 10, 1930.

[49] Archives of the Paris Préfecture de Police DB532. Secrétariat des Conseils Municipal et Général. Service des Fêtes Municipales, October 23, 1930.

retransmissions of "national" celebrations into the streets and commercial stations organized live performances by their musicians and star reporters at expositions, street fairs, and the annual radio salons organized by manufacturers to sell their products, practices that linked radio to urban crowds and city life in the cultural imagination into the 1950s.[50]

* * *

Radio demonstrations created an urban soundscape that many people experienced as louder and more filled with sound than ever before, but they also illustrate how broadcasting's identity as a new media remained in flux long after radio technology first debuted.[51] Even as radio boosters, radio-electric manufacturers, and station directors used public venues to highlight broadcasting's potential to create a national or even international audience, they did not necessarily envision those audiences as families tuning in at home, but instead promoted a variety of public sites for collective listening.[52] The daily Le Matin, for example, installed loudspeakers outside its offices in 1922 to enable neighborhood residents to hear the 12:30 and 6:00 p.m. news bulletins and the evening concerts broadcast by Parisian stations.[53] Radio listening halls, where customers paid a small fee to listen to programs or dance to music broadcast through loudspeakers, flourished into the mid-1930s. A "Radio Dance-Hall" on the Boulevard de Clichy charged forty francs for its "inaugural gala" and dinner-dance in 1928, but the majority of these establishments, which numbered between 115 and 186 during the 1930s, attracted a more modest clientele.[54] In the southern city of Béziers, a radio listening hall charged a mere one franc fifty for entry.[55]

---

[50] CARAN F12-894. Letter from Le Matériel Radiotechnique to Godefroy, Direction de l'Exploitation technique, Exposition de 1937. December 7, 1936. These events included the *Vrai mystère de la passion*, a medieval passion play staged annually between 1935 and 1937 in front of Notre Dame and rebroadcast over the radio. It attracted crowds of nearly 10,000 from the suburbs and the provinces. For the fiftieth anniversary of the death of Victor Hugo in 1935, the PTT installed loudspeakers across the city to broadcast his poetry. See "Propos d'un parisien," *Le Matin*, May 28, 1935, 2. Rosemary Wakeman, *The Heroic City: Paris, 1945–1958* (Chicago, 2009), 85–92.

[51] Lisa Gitelman and Geoffrey Pingree, eds., *New Media, 1740–1915*, xi–xxi; Gitelman, *Always Already New: Media, History, and the Data of Culture*; and Altman, *Silent Film Sound*, 15–21.

[52] Recent studies have explored collective listening in the context of Nazi Germany. See Lacey, *Listening Publics*, 135–39; Birdsall, *Nazi Soundscapes*, esp. Chapter 2.

[53] Brochand, *Histoire générale de la radio*, 1: 506. "Carnet de la T.S.F.," *Le Matin*, December 1, 1925, 5. The newspaper regularly printed the program for these loudspeakers.

[54] Bibliothèque Nationale de France. Collection Rondel. Invitation for the inaugural gala of "Le Dancing radio." February 11, 1928. Méadel, *Histoire de la radio*, 200–1.

[55] Brochand, *Histoire générale de la radio*, 1: 506.

Nor did radio boosters, who fantasized about filling everyday life with sound, firmly distinguish between radio broadcasting and the sounds (whether live or recorded) broadcast by public address systems. "In the very near future," *L'Antenne* predicted in 1926, "we will very probably see loudspeakers disseminated in the streets of well-administered cities, to bring the public up-to-date on the latest events ... without delay."[56] The engineer and sound entrepreneur Maurice Vinot, who penned France's first radio drama while working for the Radiola station in the early 1920s, developed a scheme for broadcasting radio plays into auditoriums accompanied by special effects such as wind machines.[57] Although this idea never made it off paper, Vinot created a wireless service to provide "sound notices" to factories, schools, universities, and cinemas. A publicity brochure for his Phonex company described how "judiciously placed loudspeakers [will] permit a numerous assembly in any environment to follow word for word" political speeches or radio broadcasts. Phonex installed a loudspeaker in the Gare Saint-Lazare, the train station that funneled suburban residents in and out of the city, but Vinot's company foundered after a few years.[58] However, the advertising cars that conquered Parisian streets during these same years confirm that other firms succeeded where Phonex failed.[59] Another company, Publiphono, contracted with seventy-seven Parisian cinemas, the Vélodrome d'Hiver, the Colombes stadium, and the fairground Luna Park to broadcast advertising jingles, popular music, and radio programs during cinema entr'actes or events.[60]

The postwar vogue for jazz and the accompanying dance craze also propelled café, restaurant, and hotel proprietors to install radios, phonographs, and sound systems in their establishments.[61] Resort hotels on the English Channel advertised wireless as an attraction alongside their casinos, and newspaper announcements for neighborhood street festivals touted the presence of loudspeakers, with the implicit promise of amplified music for dancing.[62] "Music, one recognizes now ... is truly an

---

[56] Mary-Jeanne, "La semaine musicale," *L'Antenne*, March 3, 1926.

[57] Maurice Vinot, pseud. Gabriel Germinet, *Théâtre radiophonique: mode nouveau d'expression artistique* (Paris, 1926), 27; René Duval, *Histoire de la radio en France*, 34–39.

[58] Bibliothèque Nationale de France. Fonds Germinet-Vinot, Carton 3. Manuscript notes and hand-drawn publicity brochure for Phonex. CAC 19950218-9. Maurice Vinot (pseud. Gabriel Germinet), unpublished dossier on the "Oeuvre de Gabriel Germinet," n.d.

[59] A.K., "La publicité parlée," *Vendre. Tout ce qui concerne la vente et la publicité*, February 1927, 195.

[60] A.K., "Publiphono: La voix qui vend," *Vendre*, May 1930.

[61] Jeffrey Jackson, *Making Jazz French: Music and Modern Life in Interwar Paris* (Durham NC, 2003), 40–42.

[62] Advertisement for "Houlgate: la perle de la Côte normande," *L'Antenne*, May 16, 1923; Advertisement in *Le Matin*, April 5, 1935, 10.

indispensable adjuvant" in creating a welcome atmosphere, the trade magazine *Le Monde hôtelier* told its readers in 1930, for clients "seem authentically delivered from their worries. They talk more gaily ... they will come back willingly ... and consume three times more."[63] Both the imposing department stores of Paris's *grands boulevards* and the single-priced chain retailers that catered to working-class shoppers exploited broadcast sound to encourage customers to linger in their aisles. The Audiberts, the couple who founded France's first domestic *prix unique* chain Cinq et Dix, reported an upsurge of nearly one-third of their normal sales after installing a sound system in their stores.[64]

By the mid-1930s, as music, radio broadcasts, and amplified announcements became commonplace in public spaces, businessmen felt compelled to devise more creative strategies for broadcasting sound. The management of the Parc des Princes stadium attempted one such "trial of collective listening" in 1935 in hopes of attracting a larger-than-usual crowd for a Paris–Prague football match by offering a live broadcast of the France–Italy match direct from Rome earlier in the day. Ten thousand spectators flooded the stadium "ready to silence themselves into attentive listeners," the journalist Pierre Descaves recalled in *L'Antenne*, applauding "when the sputtering loudspeakers of the Parc des Princes" started up. Unfortunately, the fans in the stands struggled to hear the commentary of the match, thanks to the cheers of the Roman crowd and the "cascade of sound and the avalanche of bizarre noises," which masked the announcers' voices.[65] The following year, the "radio train" debuted on trunk lines headed from the capital to the south of France. Headsets delivered lectures on regional tourist sites and musical accompaniments to correspond with particular landscapes, while loud-speakers installed in bar cars created *guinguettes* (dance halls) on the rails.[66] The fantasy of being able to "hear voices that you already know announcing the latest news of the day" during a more local trip gave birth to a radio-taxi, which promised to renovate the time-honored Parisian practice of *flânerie* by permitting a "vision of the great city through the windows ... while the accents of distant concerts resound

[63] "Les installations de transmission de musique dans les hôtels, cafés, et bars," *Le Monde hôtelier: revue périodique de documentation et d'informations hôtelières*, October 1930 and November 1930, 710, and Jane Aubert, "La musique," *Le Monde hôtelier*, January 1935, 35.
[64] De Grazia, *Irresistible Empire*, 169; Ellen Furlough, *Consumer Cooperation in France: The Politics of Consumption, 1834–1930* (Ithaca NY, 1990), 267.
[65] Pierre Descaves, "Le haut-parleur au Parc des Princes," *Le Haut-parleur*, February 24, 1935, 104.
[66] "Paris-Orléans-Midi," *Le Petit parisien*, August 31, 1936, 3.

in your ears," according to one traveler. Although the radio-taxi proved to be short-lived, radio trains enjoyed a longer life by attracting sponsorship from tourist associations, youth clubs, and political parties who hired them for holiday excursions.[67]

By 1935, the PTT counted nearly 185 sites across France, most in cities, where customers paid for the privilege of listening to radio broadcasts, as well as another 22,422 public or semi-public spaces where audiences could listen for free, a figure that rose to 53,000 on the eve of the Second World War.[68] Determining whether broadcast sound was destined for "public" or "private" consumption would become increasingly political over the course of the 1930s. When the state instituted an annual radio license fee in 1933, businessmen and café owners contested the elevated fees levied on "public" radio receivers, albeit to little effect.[69] Bar and restaurant owners sought to evade these fees by hiding their "public" radios or phonographs in their kitchens or behind a curtain, while larger establishments sometimes reduced their losses by installing nickelodeon-style radios that played for a half-hour upon the insertion of a coin.[70] Yet this growing *sonorisation* of public and semi-public spaces – whether in department stores and stadiums, cafés and restaurants, or on city streets – enabled people from across the social spectrum to participate in a variety of temporary and overlapping radio publics. More important, the plethora of new listening experiences available to consumers fueled their desire to bring the sounds of live radio broadcasts into their homes.

---

[67] Lucien Lecluc, "D'un micro à l'autre," *Le Petit radio: journal hebdomadaire des sans-filistes*, March 22, 1935, 3; "Pacques avec le Train-Radio-Dancing des 'Amis du Populaire'," *Le Populaire*, March 22, 1938.

[68] *Annuaire de Radio-Télévision 1947. Ouvrage patronné par la Radiodiffusion Française* (Paris, 1947), 106.

[69] CAC 199870714-1. Archives de la Direction de Radiodiffusion. Dossier containing questions posed in parliament to the PTT minister. Question écrite de M. Raymond Susset, December 31, 1936; "Appareil de T.S.F. utilisé dans un lieu public," *Revue générale des industries radioélectriques. Organe mensuel de la Chambre Syndicale des Industries Radioélectriques*, March 1935, 24–25. Judging from the frequent parliamentary questions raised on the subject, businessmen regularly contacted their deputies to lodge protests or question interpretations of the copyright laws that prohibited free "public auditions" of musical works broadcast over the airwaves.

[70] For the nickelodeon-style radios, see *Le Monde hôtelier*, June 1935. See also CAC 19950023-65, Salon des Arts Ménagers Catalogue, 1937. For debates about "public" radio usage, see "La T.S.F. et les petits commerçants," *Radio-Liberté. Bulletin de l'Association des auditeurs de T.S.F.*, January 7, 1938; *La Documentation radiophonique (éditée par la Radio Française)*, 1938. When Léon Blum's first Popular Front government tried to increase revenues for state broadcasting by penalizing tax evaders, PTT inspectors located numerous "private" radios being used for "public" listening.

Buying and selling sound: bringing radio into the home

During the 1920s and early 1930s, radio boosters used public demonstrations of wireless technology to portray broadcasting both as a popular entertainment and an emerging mass media capable of bridging the geographical divides between Paris and the provinces, or France and the wider world, to create potentially vast audiences. However, when manufacturers began marketing radios for domestic use, they faced a dilemma: how to sell devices that many people had come to associate, on the one hand, with the technical culture of *sans-filisme*, and on the other, with urban life and the crowds who flocked to radio demonstrations. To convince consumers that radio technology might be integrated into their homes and quotidian routines, manufacturers turned to the successful model of the gramophone and recording industries, even as they continued to highlight the distinctive features of radio broadcasting.

The immediate postwar years witnessed an explosion in phonograph and record sales. In Paris, the swanky shopping area of the *grands boulevards* became a veritable sound district where customers thronged in search of auditory commodities. Before the war, many consumers had purchased their "talking machines" in bicycle shops or *magasins de bricolage* (hardware stores), but retailers now faced a more discerning clientele in search of high-quality gramophones and records. During the 1920s, Lancel, Ducretet, and Columbia Records all constructed lavish sound palaces near the Paris Opéra, where the Pathé Frères had first opened their famous Salon du Phonographe in 1899, offering shoppers the possibility of stopping in during a Saturday stroll or at the close of a work day.[71] From the comfort of a leather armchair or a soundproofed studio, customers could work their way through a stack of records and imagine themselves listening in the intimacy of their living rooms.[72]

To entice people through their doors, showrooms organized afternoon and evening record "concerts" in which leading musical critics introduced the store's newest selections, sometimes with the accompaniment of slide projections – a practice borrowed by Parisian music hall proprietors to fill their empty afternoon hours.[73] These concerts typically attracted an elite, bourgeois clientele eager to stage their own after-dinner entertainments and develop a record collection that expressed their

[71] Maisonneuve, *L'invention du disque*, 33–38. Maisonneuve suggests that the gramophone, rather than the phonograph, became the preferred instrument for playing recorded sound in Europe.
[72] J.M., "L'épreuve décisive," *L'Antenne*, September 19, 1923.
[73] André Coeuroy, *Le phonographe* (Paris, 1929), 54; *L'Edition musicale vivante. Revue critique mensuelle de la musique enregistrée*, March 1931, 30.

personal style and musical tastes.[74] *Discophilie* was not a cheap hobby, in part because the state taxed phonographs and records, while customs duties elevated the cost of popular foreign jazz recordings. Even after gramophones became affordable, public listening halls, whether they bordered the glamorous nightclubs of Montmartre or humble neighborhoods, remained an important attraction for those unable to afford a music-hall ticket or a record by offering them the chance to hear everything from a "Wagnerian overture . . . to the latest dance . . . or the song in vogue."[75]

Radio manufacturers sought to tap into this growing market for recorded sound by portraying radios as a domestic technology that would rival the phonograph and public listening opportunities by bringing the "magic" of invisible sound waves into the home.[76] The radio-electric firm CSF opened the doors to its multistory Radiola showroom on the Boulevard Haussmann in 1931, offering a wide selection of radio receivers in a luxurious décor modeled on an expensive sitting room. "Architects wielding fairy wands" had constructed a "richly decorated candy box garnished with Radiola receivers, thick carpets, silky fabric, and an oasis of green plants," one brochure boasted, before inviting potential customers to "listen to the music played by the current station broadcasting or one of your choice."[77] The engineer and entrepreneur Lucien Lévy, creator of the Radio LL brand and a short-lived Parisian radio station of the same name, proclaimed his Rue de Cirque emporium, just off the Champs-Elysées, to be the "largest auditorium in France." Like many other manufacturers, Radio LL's staff hosted evening concerts and distributed raffle tickets on the street to draw passers-by into their showroom's glamorous art deco interior.[78]

Contemporary trade periodicals and radio magazines reveal that consumers and music critics alike believed that gramophones offered greater sound fidelity than early radio receivers. Until the invention of the electric pick-up in the mid-1920s, which enabled radio studios to connect gramophones directly to their microphones, playing music over their airwaves proved challenging. This allowed gramophone manufacturers to

[74] Maisonneuve, *L'invention du disque*, 85–89.
[75] Maurice Hamel, "Salles d'auditions phonographiques," *L'Antenne*, February 26, 1933. Sound films contributed to the popularity of public listening halls by allowing cinema audiences to hear their favorite songs repeatedly. See Rearick, *The French in Love and War*, 128–29.
[76] *Le Petit radio*, October 19, 1934, 2.
[77] *Radiola. La grande marque française. Bulletin mensuel*, November–December 1929; January 31, 1931.
[78] *Radio LL revue. Organe mensuel de documentation technique et commerciale*. November–December, 1929.

position themselves as purveyors of high-quality sound reproductions that would satisfy the ears of even the most discerning customers.[79] However, radios delivered thrilling live sounds that a 78-rpm record never could: the applause of concert audiences, the cheers of sports fans, and the noises of city streets. The Crysovox brand promised its customers a loudspeaker that would deliver the "illusion of the orchestra in your home" without "wheezy sounds or disagreeble harmonies." Live retransmissions – from the route of the Tour de France, soccer stadiums, and Parisian theaters – counted among the most popular broadcasts of the late 1920s in the surveys conducted by radio magazines.[80]

At a moment when social conservatives decried the war's disruptions to traditional gender roles and the detrimental effects of the "New Woman" on the sanctity of family life, radio manufacturers emphasized that broadcasting, even as a "public" medium reaching into the "private" sphere, could be reconciled with the family furnishings, inherited traditions, and social conventions of the past. In the catalogue for the 1927 Salon des Arts Ménagers, the state-sponsored home show, the celebrated crime novelist and radio enthusiast Pierre MacOrlan reminded visitors that the "truly modern house must be, for a man of action, a *home* linked by an antenna to all of the prolific waves of his time." However, the "peace of the house" relied upon establishing "equilibrium between the speed of our era, which cannot be escaped . . . and the soft warmth of . . . things that have already witnessed the deaths of generations of men."[81] To this end, industrial designers hid the aesthetically unappealing pieces of radio equipment, from batteries to lamps, in lavishly carved ebonite cases masquerading as furniture. They camouflaged receivers' awkward, horn-shaped loudspeakers by turning them into table lamps or painting them in bold colors to coordinate with household interiors, whether in the style of Louis XVI or art deco.[82] The engineer Pierre Hemardinquer, reviewing a Gaumont loudspeaker modeled on an iron lamp with a crystal shade, assured readers of the popular science magazine *La Nature* that the "wireless amateur can place this accessory among his furnishings without fear of disrupting the harmony and organization of his home."[83]

Of course, advertisements that depicted elegantly dressed couples tuning into the airwaves after dinner or women leisurely smoking cigarettes

[79] Méadel, *Histoire de la radio*, 323, 361; Maisonneuve, *L'invention du disque*, 206–7.
[80] Crysovox advertisement, *Radio-Magazine*, May 16, 1926, 20.
[81] CAC 199850023-65. Pierre MacOrlan, "La maison . . . miroir du temps," *Catalogue du Salon des Arts Ménagers*, 1927, 17.
[82] Pierre MacOrlan, "La maison . . . miroir du temps," 17.
[83] Pierre Hemardinquer, "Un nouveau type de haut-parleur du salon," *La Nature*, May 6, 1925, 147.

during a radio concert presented a fantasy that diverged considerably from the practical realities of listening. Unlike the easy-to-use gramophone, radios demanded skillful tuning maneuvers, and antennas and aerials required constant adjustments. Radio owners without electricity in their homes, still a sizeable proportion of the population, needed to clean and change their batteries on a regular basis – all tasks requiring some rudimentary technical knowledge. For this reason, early radio listeners tended to sit directly in front of their receivers during broadcasts. To conceal the labor involved in tuning and to counter radio's ties with the technical culture of *sans-filisme*, manufacturers also featured female listeners in their advertisements to demonstrate their radio models' facility of use. A 1926 advertisement for "Création Radiomuse" depicted several young women with stylishly bobbed hair and short skirts listening to a receiver that masqueraded as a wall-mounted bookcase [Figure 1.2].[84] The amateur radio press often joked about the very existence of female *sans-filistes* by printing photos of women listening to the radio in a variety of impractical scenarios, from the bathtub to the hair salon. Yet retailers also targeted female consumers, implicitly acknowledging bourgeois women's historic role in selecting household goods that reinforced family reputations and distinguished middle-class lifestyles from those of the working masses.[85]

The radio boosters who envisioned broadcasting's future as a democratic medium of the masses questioned the logic of the radio-electric manufacturers who targeted a bourgeois clientele by producing only expensive and elaborate receivers. In the late 1920s, radio amateurs with technical knowledge could purchase parts to construct their own receivers for a few hundred francs, but a radio receiver with five to seven lamps cost between 5,000 and 7,000 francs, far more than the average family could afford. The largest French radio-electric firms manufactured fewer than 80,000 receivers a year in 1930 – a strategy grounded in longstanding atelier-based production methods and a centuries-old manufacturing tradition of producing luxury commodities for an elite market.[86] "Considering radio only from the point of view of a well-to-do clientele is perhaps, commercially speaking, of a superior interest (though it remains to be proven)," the journalist Alex Virot wrote in *L'Intransigeant* the same year, but "doing so is to ignore its most noble task and duty," for we "live in an era where one cannot deny the rights of

---

[84] Advertisement for Création Radiomuse, *Radio-Magazine*, May 16, 1926.
[85] Cover illustration, *Radio-Magazine*, December 30, 1923. On female consumers, see Lisa Tiersten, *Marianne in the Market: Envisioning Consumer Society in Fin-de-Siècle France* (Berkeley, 2009), 185–231; Auslander, *Taste and Power*, 255–305.
[86] Auslander, *Taste and Power*, 186–224; De Grazia, *Irresistible Empire*, 107–9; Méadel, *Histoire de la radio*, 193–94.

Figure 1.2 Advertisement for Création Radiomuse, *Radio-Magazine* (1926). Image courtesy of the Bibliothèque Nationale de France.

the most humble people to . . . the advantages that power and wealth can procure for them." Modest individuals, he believed, as much as wealthy ones, deserved access to the airwaves.[87]

The onset of the depression and the arrival of multinational conglomerates in the radio market challenged France's traditional production and merchandising methods. In 1930, the cathedral-style "Midget" radio, produced by the American companies RCA and Zenith and the British firm Philco, debuted to enormous acclaim at the Paris *foire*. "America has invaded!" the wireless magazine *La T.S.F. pour tous* proclaimed.[88] The Midget's compact size and comparatively low price of 1,800 francs instantly made French cabinet-style receivers appear cumbersome, inefficient, and anachronistic. Midget models featured electro-dynamic loudspeakers enclosed within the radio case that eliminated the screeching sounds common to older horn-shaped speakers and transmitted a wider range of sound frequencies, which enhanced their musicality and prompted many radio amateurs to put down the headsets they still used for listening.[89] The Midgets also sat unobtrusively on dining room buffets or living room bookcases and could be moved between rooms to accommodate individual family members' listening preferences, further contributing to their popularity. The Syndicat Professionnel des Industries Radioélectrique (SPIR), which represented a conglomerate of small French radio-electric firms, responded to this "foreign invasion" by persuading legislators to impose a hefty tax on imported radio lamps and receivers. They also launched a campaign in favor of home radio construction (*bricolage*) as a guarantor of superior quality in the face of "standardized American cabinets that all look like sisters."[90] This "buy French" campaign won over many experienced *sans-filistes*, for whom *bricolage* remained an important hobby into the late 1930s. However, the lower prices of the Midgets also attracted many first-time radio customers among the lower middle classes and industrial workers.[91]

The internationalization of the radio market in the early 1930s also forced French manufacturers and retailers to seek a more diversified

---

[87] Alex Virot, "La radio humanitaire," *L'Intransigeant*, April 10, 1929, 10.

[88] No author, "L'Amérique nous envahit," *La T.S.F. pour tous*, 1932, 197–200.

[89] Alain Roux, "L'évolution du radiorécepteur domestique en France entre 1931 et 1940" (PhD diss., Ecole des Hautes Etudes en Sciences Sociales, 1987), 188; Pascal Griset, "Innovation and Radio Industry in Europe during the Interwar Period," in François Caron and Wolfram Fischer, eds., *Innovation in the European Economies Between the Wars* (Berlin, 1995), 37–57.

[90] No author, "L'Amérique nous envahit," *La T.S.F. pour tous*, 1932, 197. Christian Brochand, *Histoire générale de la radio*, 1: 83–88. By 1929, France imported more radioelectric material than it exported, primarily from Germany and the United States.

[91] *Radiola*, February 1, 1931; Alain Roux, "L'évolution du radiorécepteur domestique," 158–60, 711.

customer base, with the result that bourgeois social commentators, journalists, and consumers alike linked radio to the arrival of flashy and disruptive "American"-style mass marketing practices. The Dutch-based Philips firm still directed its rural salesmen to employ well-tried sales methods by seeking out their first customers among the "notable persons" of small towns, such as the mayor, doctor, notary, and public school principal. "It will always be possible," the company bulletin *Radio-Phil* instructed its personnel, "to find a pretext to organize little *soirées* . . . which have the great advantage of reaffirming the bonds of friendship that you maintain with your clients, and which permit them to appreciate, through a carefully chosen program, the astonishing musical possibilities of the new Philips models."[92] Still, retailers increasingly portrayed radios as vital necessities for everyday life in the modern world. "Wireless is no longer a luxury," announced the poster for the 1934 Paris Wireless Salon, but had instead become a "utilitarian household good, an instrument for work and evenings of family enjoyment." Retailers even touted radios as a "source of savings" that could replace the costs of newspapers, magazines, and concerts, and indeed, by 1933 radios became a cheaper investment for a modest family than a phonograph and record collection.[93]

No longer the preserve of Parisian palaces of sound, radios began to appear in annual autumn radio salons in regional cities, where consumers could examine a wide variety of models and glimpse their favorite radio stars in live performances.[94] By 1935 all of France's major cities as well as the colonial capitals of Algiers and Saigon boasted retail outlets for the major radio brands, whether French or foreign, including Pathé, Radiola, Ducretet, Thompson-Houston, Philips, and Philco. The Grand Magasins Dufayel and the Bazar de l'Hôtel de Ville even began selling radios and gramophones in their department stores and by mail-order catalogue.[95] Urban consumers could access a flourishing market of used radios and radio parts in flea markets and secondhand shops. In 1936, *Mon programme* reported that the Paris municipal pawnshop (*mont-de-piété*) had received so many radios in exchange for cash that it had

[92] *Radio-Phil. Bulletin d'information et de liaison entre Philips-Radio et ses bons clients,* November 1, 1938, iv.
[93] Advertisement for the 11ᵉ Salon de T.S.F. in *L'Echo de Paris,* September 5, 1934.
[94] *L'Afrique du Nord illustrée,* October 27, 1934, 1–9; *Revue générale des industries radioélectriques,* June 1935, 2–3.
[95] Bibliothèque Fourney. Catalogue for Grands Magasins Dufayel, Palais de la Nouveauté, Eté 1923 and the Catalogue du Bazar de l'Hôtel de Ville, 1935; *T.S.F.-Phono-Ciné de Lyon et du Sud-Est. Annuaire de 1937* (Lyon, 1937). France's second-largest city of Lyon boasted 400 different radio retailers. Nice counted eighty-nine different retailers for its 180,000 residents, while thirty-one radio dealers catered to Dijon's population of 80,000.

established a special showroom to display them to potential purchasers.[96] After the fascist regimes of Italy and Germany turned consumerism into a weapon of their ideological assault on European democracies, the left-wing Popular Front government of 1936–1938 made elevating the purchasing power of the working classes a new political priority.[97] But even after radios began to appear in workers' homes, many people continued to associate them with bourgeois luxury. Rosa Lévy, the daughter of Polish immigrants, recalled with vivid detail in her memoirs the day her widowed mother instructed her to dress up in her best clothes to go shopping for their radio – a gleaming Bakelite model and the first completely unnecessary object her mother had ever purchased.[98]

Innovations in radio design and merchandising techniques demonstrate the reflexive nature of the radio market and the continual dialogue between manufacturers, retailers, and radio listeners that shaped merchandising methods and consumer habits. After 1935, manufacturers faced a discerning public who placed enormous demands on their radios and their suppliers. The trade revue *Machines parlantes et radios* cautioned phonograph and musical instrument dealers considering radio sales to think twice before purchasing stock, for "the public who buys a radio requires of his vendor ulterior services of maintenance ... and repair," making them more likely to purchase from knowledgeable vendors.[99] Technical improvements to radios fueled sales, but retailers still needed to cater to customers' tastes for particular auditory experiences. Radio receivers each produced their own unique sound, but the varied acoustical conditions of showrooms and private homes ensured that the same model might sound very different in each location. Retailers consequently began offering in-home demonstrations to permit customers to test a model for its musicality and amplification before making a final purchase.[100] The musicologist André Coeuroy, always skeptical of popular tastes, believed that the masses lacked the refined ear necessary to distinguish between high and low sound frequencies. Deploring the "veritable menace of the amplifier," he suggested that most people simply wanted radios that would drown out their neighbors' receivers or resonate

[96] Bernard Steele, "Le disque à la foire aux puces," *Radio-Magazine*, November 29, 1936, 6; *Mon programme*, April 10, 1936. Radios first began to appear in the Paris municipal pawnshop in 1931–1932 and were frequently auctioned off before their owners could buy them back. See the records of the Crédit Municipal de Paris in the Archives Municipales de Paris, 1ETP 326–1 ETP 387, November 1931–December 1937.
[97] De Grazia, *Irresistible Empire*, 160–63.
[98] Rosa Claude Lévy, *La T.S.F. ou comment danser avec le Kayser* (Paris, 2009), 121–24.
[99] Roux, "L'évolution du radiorécepteur domestique,"188.
[100] "Marchands, employez de bons appareils," and "La radio est-il profitable?" *Machines parlantes et radio*, March 1930 and July 1931, 621.

through multiple rooms of a residence.[101] The radio enthusiast who believed the "loudspeaker is the soul of his receiver" did so in error, the radio magazine *Le Petit radio* cautioned in 1934, for turning up the volume "simply to make others present hear that his radio is powerful (or better yet, more powerful) than theirs" ultimately distorted a radio's sound. Despite such warnings, consumers continued to prize loud receivers.[102]

Audiences also sought out highly selective radios that could receive a variety of wavelengths. Early receivers required constant adjustment to stay fixed on a single signal, but the introduction of the octode in 1934 enabled listeners to enjoy a station's broadcasts for hours without re-tuning. Selectivity became even more important as the number of radio stations transmitting in Europe increased. Most French stations broadcast on medium waves, but listeners increasingly demanded more expensive multi-wave receivers, often of foreign manufacture, that would enable them to pick up broadcasts from across Europe and around the globe. After 1936, radio designs incorporated backlit dials (popularly known as the "magic eye") printed with the names and wavelengths of European radio stations that made tuning and station selection even easier.[103]

Domestic radio ownership grew rapidly during the mid-1930s, particularly in northern France, thanks to the concentration of radio stations and the dense population of Paris and other industrial hubs, even as regional stations began transmitting in the south and along the western coast. Patterns of electrification further influenced radio ownership, with the result that the number of registered radios in urban areas vastly outstripped those in the countryside. In 1934, France counted 2.5 million licensed receivers to Great Britain's 6.5, a difference that the historian Cécile Méadel attributes to the conservatism of bourgeois families and their reluctance to embrace an "intrusive" modern technology. However, these statistics mask a considerable number of unlicensed radios and the fact that multiple family members often listened around a single receiver, with the result that an estimated twenty million people could access a domestic radio by the middle of the decade.[104] More important, privileging domestic radio ownership as the primary indicator of broadcasting's social or cultural impact obscures how listeners tuned into the radio

[101] André Coeuroy, "La véritable menace de l'amplificateur," *Machines parlantes et radio*, December 1929.

[102] Le Vieux bricoleur, "Le haut-parleur," *Le Petit radio*, September 6, 1934, 4.

[103] "Revue de 1936," *Les Annales des PTT. Revue mensuelle publiée par les soins d'une commission nommée par le Ministre des Postes, Télégraphes, et Téléphones* (Paris, 1936), 622–66.

[104] CAC 19870714-1. Direction du Service de la Radiodiffusion. Question écrite, 1938. Statistics offered in response to a parliamentary question concerning patterns of radio

intermittently from different locations. The diversity of sites in which people listened to the radio – whether in bars and restaurants or the privacy of their homes – shaped how people of all social classes evaluated the potential uses and abuses of broadcasting while contributing to the ever-increasing problem of noise.

Broadcast sound, noise abatement, and the "right to listen"

By the late 1920s, the growing number of people listening to radios and gramophones at home, during street fairs and national celebrations, or in the semi-public spaces of restaurants and bars, posed unprecedented challenges for municipal authorities in Paris and across France, as city residents and public figures alike began to grumble about their cacophonous surroundings. Noise complaints reflected qualitative and quantitative transformations to the urban soundscape produced by the democratization of radios, phonographs, and loudspeakers, but they also betrayed a host of anxieties provoked by recent changes to city spaces and social practices, including an exponential growth in urban populations, increased automobile traffic, and the seemingly frenetic pace of machine-age civilization. Yet broadcast sound, far more than the automobile *klaxon* or the rumbling of the metro, captured people's attention through its ubiquity. Not only did the airwaves separate sounds from their original source, carrying ostensibly "public" messages into the "private" spaces of individual homes, but the shrieking and crackling of loudspeakers, radios, and phonographs resounding from shops, stadiums, bars, and music halls onto city streets turned neighborhoods into nightmarish *fêtes foraines*.[105] Enterprising businessmen and ordinary radio listeners alike soon found themselves in conflict with municipal authorities for control over the urban soundscape, producing an everyday politics of listening that would become increasingly combative over the course of the 1930s.

During the nineteenth century, the Parisian police and municipal authorities typically heard noise as a manifestation of social disorder provoked by the unruly working classes, an association reinforced by the capital's long history as a stage for political protests. The first

ownership. Méadel, *Histoire de la radio*, 198. Although the 1933 license fee required retailers to submit the names and addresses of radio customers to the PTT, many unwittingly assisted in evasion through sloppy bookkeeping, while others engaged in deliberate fraud. Méadel estimates the number of tax evaders to be 15–20 percent of the total number of registered radios.

[105] René Bizet, "La fête foraine des boulevards," *L'Intransigeant*, April 28, 1925, 1.

municipal noise ordinances of the twentieth century prohibited the use of sirens, phonographs, or horns on the public thoroughfare on the grounds that they might disrupt "public tranquility" by clogging sidewalks with crowds of listeners. Fears of Bolshevik agitation amid the wave of industrial strikes that followed the Armistice, followed by the descent of right-wing paramilitary groups into the streets a few years later, only propelled the police to issue further regulations governing the use of sound technologies in public spaces.[106] A 1919 decree mandated that businesses obtain permits for phonograph use – a regulation intended to limit unauthorized political gatherings and prevent wine merchants from creating impromptu *dancings* in their shops. Permits were issued to proprietors who promised to allow no singing or dancing and terminated the music by 11 p.m. A subsequent 1926 ordinance banned "the use of loudspeakers on the public thoroughfare" on the grounds that they threatened "the order and security of the street" as well as inside buildings if their volume was "intended to reach" passers-by on the sidewalk. This latter measure succeeded in eliminating the advertising cars that many Parisians had come to associate with aggressive "American"-style marketing, but did little to halt individual merchants' reliance on phonograph or radio loudspeakers to attract customers. The Paris police force, preoccupied with crime and political surveillance, lacked the manpower and financial resources to enforce noise ordinances in a city with thousands of offenders, particularly when enterprising businessmen and politicians flooded the desks of *arrondissement* police chiefs with requests to employ loudspeakers in public spaces.[107]

The spread of radio challenged these older methods of noise control because the ostensibly "private" sounds of personal radio receivers resonated through buildings into the semi-public spaces of courtyards and gardens as well as onto public sidewalks and streets. After radio amateurs abandoned listening with headsets in favor of domestic receivers with powerful amplifiers and loudspeakers, the sheer density of radios in a city of apartment dwellers produced a veritable cacophony.[108] When people left their windows open during the warm summer months, a mixture of political speeches, sports matches, and music filled the common areas

[106] Clifford Rosenberg, *Policing Paris: The Origins of Modern Immigration Control Between the Wars* (Ithaca NY, 2006), 38–40; Stovall, *Paris and the Spirit of 1919*, 142–81.
[107] Archives of the Paris Préfecture de Police DB143. Ordonnance concernant la mise en usage des haut-parleurs. December 30, 1926; DA460, Camille Marchand, Directeur de la Police Municipale, Note au sujet du 14 juillet pour les Chefs districts, July 11, 1935. Malcolm Anderson, *In Thrall to Political Change: Police and Gendarmerie in France* (Oxford, 2011), 85–88.
[108] Roux, "L'évolution du radiorécepteur domestique," 158–60, 711. Méadel, *Histoire de la radio*, 191, 200–3.

surrounding apartment buildings. Since the 1860s, urban hygienists, architects, and social theorists had defined the home as a sanctuary to which bourgeois families could retreat to protect themselves from the chaos of the streets and the moral corruption of the lower orders, but now private homes, and frequently their respectable middle-class residents, became new sources of sonic disorder.[109] One Parisian chronicler strolling past the new, modern apartment buildings going up in the chic 16th arrondissement heard powerful receivers "picking up" Moscow and Washington through open windows. These sounds, he believed, revealed less about the owners' regular listening habits than it did about their vanity in sounding off an expensive, long-distance receiver that demonstrated their wealth and cultural sophistication to the neighbors.[110]

The amplified volume of Paris, the daily newspaper *Le Matin* confirmed in 1931, resulted as much from the "internal noises" of modern buildings and their residents as it did from industrial racket or the rise in personal automobile ownership. The "hastily constructed buildings of iron and reinforced concrete" that had sprung up in recently razed slum areas proved to be "terribly indiscreet structures," permitting human and mechanical sounds to penetrate through walls and hallways into neighboring apartments.[111] Modern heating and plumbing systems installed in newer buildings carried sounds, while early twentieth-century interior designs emphasizing clean lines and simplicity in home decoration often had damaging acoustic consequences by eliminating noise-reducing materials such as wall hangings and rugs common to earlier Victorian and *art nouveau* interiors.[112] Parisian concierges prevailed upon radio owners with a taste for loud music, whom the radio journalist Paul Dermée cheekily christened "*haut-hurleurs*," to close their windows when listening to the radio, though often with little effect.[113] One concierge reported to the newspaper *L'Oeuvre* that twenty-two out of the twenty-five residents in her building owned radios, but "even the most well-disposed concierges can only with difficulty obtain results when their tenants don't leave their neighbors alone."[114] Some radio enthusiasts gloried in annoying their neighbors by playing loud music or broadcasts that would offend their political sensibilities. The voices of angry

---

[109] Sharon Marcus, *Apartment Stories: City and Home in Nineteenth Century Paris and London* (Berkeley, 1999), 154–60.
[110] Paul-Léon Fargue, *Le piéton de Paris* (Paris, 1939, 2001), 65.
[111] "Une enquête du 'Touring Club' contre les 'bruits' internes de nos habitations," *Le Matin*, December 9, 1931, 1.
[112] Bijsterveld, *Mechanical Sound*, 163.
[113] Paul Dermée, "Pour obtenir du Parlement le vote rapide d'une loi protégeant les citoyens contre les bruits excessifs," *Comoedia*, September 23, 1936.
[114] Lucien Wahl, "On demande une réglementation," *L'Oeuvre*, June 3, 1937, 2.

apartment residents screaming across courtyards "Enough! Turn that off! ... I am at home and please leave me the h*$l alone! ... This is a scandal! Concierge!" only added further to the problem.[115]

While complaints about radio noise reflected city-dwellers' practical concerns, such as the inability to sleep or work, they also proved to be highly subjective, at times revealing more about the social background and political sympathies of those lodging the protests than the sonic qualities of the "noise" itself. "When discreet, wireless is a friend," the psychiatrist Henri Lemesle wrote in the *Mercure de France* in 1931, but "how can one accept ... the Yankee speech, Negro tangos, etc. ... that French stations, reputable but complicit ... furnish all the noise-makers of France?"[116] Intellectuals in Paris and other European capitals had long complained about street noises interrupting their labor, but Lemesle heard radio sound as a foreign invasion tied to the recent influx of African-American jazz musicians as well as immigrants from Eastern Europe and the colonies. Cultural elites frequently described jazz, with its syncopated rhythms and unfamiliar instrumentation, as little more than a "primitive" racket.[117] The right-leaning urban chronicler Paul-Léon Fargue, for his part, worried that broadcasting had homogenized and commercialized the Parisian soundscape by drowning out the unique voices of the street criers and musicians that once defined *quartiers*, replacing them with radio programs that could be heard in every neighborhood. Even in Montmartre, a neighborhood famed for its street singers, the "guys of La Chapelle and the gals on the Rue de Flandre sing like phonographs. Thanks to the radio and the record, the nineteenth *arrondissement* resembles ... [all] other *arrondissements*."[118]

For the conservative essayist Georges Duhamel, however, France's growing noise problem had less to do with the jazz and popular music that people consumed (though he detested both) than the volume of their sound devices and the decisions they made about when and where to listen. This everyday politics of radio listening, Duhamel believed, was indicative of more pressing twentieth-century concerns, such as the fate of the individual in a mass society where the will of the collective predominated. In his 1932 essay collection *Querelles de famille*, Duhamel railed against the "communism of noise" that had destroyed the tranquility of his residences in

---

[115] Clement Vautel, "Radio chronique," *Radio-Magazine*, July 16, 1933.

[116] Henri Lemesle, "Le bruit et les bruiteurs," *Mercure de France*, 1931, 289–302. Lemesle specialized in "sleep cures" for urban dwellers and patented a sleep mask designed to block light and sound.

[117] On urban noise and Victorian intellectuals, see John Picker, *Victorian Soundscapes* (Oxford, 2003), esp. Chapter 2; Jackson, *Making Jazz French*, 31–33.

[118] Fargue, *Le piéton de Paris*, 18–19. See Charles Rearick, *Paris Dreams, Paris Memories: The City and Its Mystique* (Stanford, 2011), 44–81.

Paris and the countryside by forcing him to listen to music or radio programs not of his choosing. People who "nourished the ambition of making their noise triumph over their neighbors" had turned the "war of the *phonos*" into a "veritable aspect of the civil war" emerging between the left and the right, he argued. Although French law still *appeared* to protect "individual property against the most flagrant aggressions," in reality people no longer had the right to quiet or privacy in their homes, for "he who possesses ... a parcel of space does not possess the freedom to silence his space." If partly in jest, Duhamel charged the government with creating a Ministry of Noise to protect citizens from "forced listening" to their neighbors' radios and phonographs, for to "regulate noise would be to treat the symptom and the cause of the harm" undermining French civilization.[119]

Municipal authorities and the Parisian police came under renewed pressure to reign in the capital's burgeoning soundscape when the Touring Club de France, the nation's oldest tourist association, launched a noise abatement campaign under the banner of "La Lutte contre le bruit." The Touring Club's noise commission, whose members included prominent architects and engineers, wanted to standardize anti-noise legislation across France to eliminate "useless" noises, whether the din of traffic or radio loudspeakers.[120] Founded by bourgeois businessmen in the 1890s to promote regional tourism through cycling, Touring Club boasted a membership of several hundred thousand by the 1930s, having expanded its activities to include hiking and camping. Encounters with France's distinctive regional cultures, or *la France profonde*, the club argued, could rejuvenate a socially fractured nation, but only if the provinces retained their unique regional cultures of language and cuisine and preserved their landscapes from disruptive modern incursions such as noise.[121]

Complaints about urban noises polluting the quiet of the countryside, from backfiring automobiles and motorcycles to squawking portable gramophones and radios, abounded in the press. "Thanks to the phonograph and the electro-dynamic loudspeaker," the novelist Lucien Descaves wrote in *L'Intransigeant*, "the countryside is inundated from morning to evening ... with songs rarely French and always with foreign jazz," while the radio completely eliminated the possibility of "finding

[119] Duhamel, *Querelles de famille*, 206–9; Jordan, "Discophile ou Discomanie?" 160.
[120] Touring Club de France, *La lutte contre le bruit. Etudes entreprises sur les matériaux dits insonores, sous les auspices du Touring Club de France, avec la collaboration du Laboratoire d'essais au Conservatoire National des Arts et Métiers* (Rouen, 1934), 3–5, 51–52.
[121] Steven Harp, *Marketing Michelin: Advertising and Cultural Identity in Twentieth-Century France* (Baltimore, 2001), 54–58; Patrick Young, "*La Vieille France* as Object of Bourgeois Desire: The Touring Club de France and the French Regions, 1890–1918," in Rudy Koshar, ed., *Histories of Leisure* (Oxford, 2002), 165–89.

solitude."[122] A nostalgic longing for a calmer, quieter, and less frenetic pace of life informed the slogan for the Touring Club's noise abatement campaign, "each person's silence ensures everyone's rest," which built upon longstanding bourgeois traditions valorizing silence as evidence of respectability and self-control.[123] However, if reformers' primary concern was protecting the countryside from noise, they also sought to attack the problem at its source: in the capital.

Recognizing the inherent subjectivity of noise complaints, the Touring Club adopted strategies already employed by reformers in New York City and London to measure noise and provide objective scientific proof of its harmful effects on human physiology.[124] Engineers, architects, and urban planners took a keen interest in the nascent disciplines of audiometry and architectural acoustics, whose most dynamic practitioners hailed from Germany and the United States.[125] In 1932, the physicist Jean-Fernand Cellerier, the director of the Laboratoire d'Essais at the Conservatoire Nationale des Arts et Métiers and a member of the Touring Club's noise abatement commission, set out to measure in decibels the noise produced by the nearly three million vehicles that traversed Parisian streets. Cellerier's team of researchers also tested the volume produced by a variety of radio loudspeakers and evaluated the sound absorption properties of building materials. To reduce interior noise and resonance, Cellerier recommended that architects combine multiple materials in a single building. He also proposed banning motorcycles and automobile horns at night.[126] His findings provided ammunition for the Touring Club's battle against "useless" sounds and nighttime noise, as did the work of the jurist André Defert, who prepared a legal manual detailing methods for prosecuting offenders of municipal noise ordinances.[127]

[122] Lucien Descaves, "Les vacances aux champs: La faillite du silence," *L'Intransigeant*, September 1, 1929.

[123] Gutton, *Bruits et sons dans notre histoire*, 120–23; Johnson, *Listening in Paris*, 231. Johnson suggests the "golden rule of bourgeois decency was not to bother others."

[124] Thompson, *The Soundscape of Modernity*, 148–58; Bijsterveld, *Mechanical Sound*, 113–17.

[125] Henri Piéron, "Revue générale d'acoustique physiologique," *L'Année psychologique*, 35, 1934, 167–97.

[126] Pierre Hemardinquer, "La sonde phonique pour la mesure des intensités des sons," *La Nature*, March 15, 1932, 269–71. Automobile accidents became an enormous problem in the early twentieth century, prompting the creation of safety campaigns that sought to shame irresponsible drivers. See Jeffrey H. Jackson, "Solidarism in the City Streets: La Société Protectrice Contre les Excès de l'Automobilisme and the Problem of Traffic in Early Twentieth-Century Paris," *French Cultural Studies*, 20, 3, 2009, 237–56.

[127] André Defert, *Le bruit au point de vue juridique* (Paris, 1930); "Les conditions juridiques de la lutte contre le bruit," *Revue municipale. Recueil hebdomadaire d'études édilitaires pour la France et l'étranger*, February 1931, 1565.

More important, the Touring Club's noise abatement campaign attracted significant support from the medical establishment. For decades, physicians had acknowledged the dangers that machine noise posed to the hearing of industrial workers, telephone operators, and train engineers, while fin-de-siècle theorists of degeneration such as Max Nordau targeted noise as a leading cause of neurasthenia.[128] However, the deafening bombardments of the First World War radically transformed physicians' perceptions about the fragility of the human ear. In 1921, Georges René Marage, an otolaryngologist who treated thousands of soldiers with ruptured eardrums, cautioned his colleagues about the pernicious vibrations produced by automobile engines, tramways, household appliances, and above all, radios and phonographs. "In large cities like Paris where noises of all sorts are multiplied to excess," Marage warned, it is "necessary to take precautions to ensure that deaf people do not outnumber the hearing."[129] Sanitary reformers and urban hygienists of the 1920s consequently began to treat noise, much like the insalubrious buildings, dark alleys, and overflowing sewers of the early nineteenth-century city, as detrimental to the physical health of the individual, and thus to the national population as a whole.[130]

René Martial, the physician who served as the municipal director of hygiene for Paris in the early 1930s, argued that traffic and industrial noise, when combined with the "howling loudspeakers of radios and gramophones," inflicted a form of shell shock on city dwellers. Having begun his career in the northern mining town of Douai, Martial was particularly attuned to the impact of sanitary conditions on workers' productivity. Modern cities' constant assault on the ears, he wrote in the *Revue municipale*, could potentially cause the nervous system to collapse, producing a category of invalids "completely unknown to physicians twenty-five years ago." These "*bruités*" suffered from sleep disorders, circulatory congestion, and auditory hallucinations requiring "care in special health centers to return their rattled nervous systems to a normal state," although some unfortunate victims would never recover and became "permanent mental patients."[131]

---

[128] Pierre Petit, *Le bruit et ses effets dans la vie moderne*. Thèse pour le doctorat en médecine, diplôme d'état, Faculté de Médecine de Paris (Paris, 1936); Kern, *The Culture of Time and Space*, 125–26. Reformers across Europe cited noise as a leading cause of nervous disorders. James C. Mansall, "Neurasthenia, Civilization, and the Sounds of Modern Life: Narratives of Nervous Illness in Interwar Campaigns Against Noise," in Daniel Morat, ed., *Sounds of Modern History: Auditory Culture in 19th and 20th Century Europe* (New York, 2014), 278–302.

[129] G. Vitoux, "La lutte contre le bruit," *Le Petit parisien*, November 22, 1921, 5.

[130] "La lutte contre le bruit," *L'Urbanisme*, November 1932, 261–62.

[131] René Martial, "Bruits, T.S.F., et maladies nouvelles," *Revue municipale*, October 1932, 1951–53.

Martial and several of his colleagues feared that listeners' over-exposure to radio waves might have unforeseen physical effects on the body, much like the accidental cases of radiation poisoning that followed the discovery of X-ray technology.[132] Given that Paris was "bathed in a sort of electromagnetic field thanks to the many and very powerful stations operating in the capital," the journalist Olivier Merlin asked in the daily *Le Temps* in 1932, did Parisians face a particular danger? Merlin consulted the renowned psychiatrist Edouard Toulouse, famous for his treatments of shell-shocked veterans, who refuted such myths as little more than unscientific superstition. However, Toulouse warned that broadcast sound "generated an intense excitation of the auditory nerves ... which could cause deprived individuals fatigue and harmful complications, particularly when the sound waves are too powerful." Like Martial, he believed excessive noise to be pernicious for the mentally ill as well as overworked industrial laborers and children, and recommended the creation of "quiet zones" around hospitals, rest homes, and public schools. Listening to the radio too loudly was a "violation of the social contract," Toulouse observed, and given the large number of *déséquilibrés* in postwar society, radio enthusiasts should use caution and consider their neighbors' health before turning up the volume of their wireless.[133]

The Académie de Médecine responded to these concerns by appointing a special committee to study the effects of noise, which in turn advocated "silent" countryside cures for Parisians.[134] With physicians and legislators anxious about the rise of a vigorous and health-obsessed German population across the Rhine, removing working-class children from unhealthy urban environments each summer became a goal of the social reformers and youth advocates on the left and right who animated the *colonies de vacances* (summer camp) movement of the early 1930s.[135] They in turn lent support to the Touring Club's noise abatement campaign and that of its sister society, the Ligue de Légitime Défense Contre le Bruit – the latter founded by the physician Marcel Gommès and backed by a roster of intellectuals.[136]

---

[132] *Ibid.*; René Martial, "Le silence: vertu municipal, urbaine, et éducative," *Revue municipale*, July 1933, 2139–41. On Martial's background, see William H. Schneider, *Quality and Quantity: The Quest for Biological Regeneration in Twentieth-Century France* (Cambridge, 2002), 231–34.
[133] Olivier Merlin, "Trop de bruit nuit. L'influence de la T.S.F. sur l'organisme humain. Une visite au docteur Toulouse," *Le Temps*, August 27, 1932, 6.
[134] P. Portier, "Les méfaits du bruit," *Bulletin de l'Académie de Médicine*, meeting of May 13, 1930, 515–18.
[135] Laura Lee Downs, *Childhood in the Promised Land: Working-Class Movements and the Colonies de vacances in France, 1880–1960* (Durham NC, 2002), 137–39.
[136] C.M. Savarit, "La défense contre le bruit," *L'Echo de Paris*, September 19, 1934.

The Touring Club's noise reformers, however, found their most powerful advocate in the Corsican-born Paris police prefect Jean Chiappe, whose larger-than-life personality made him the subject of both celebrity and vitriol. Chiappe's right-wing political sympathies and hostility toward communists, working-class demonstrators, and immigrants won him support from many bourgeois Parisians. They backed his citywide *épuration* to remove prostitutes from the streets and improve traffic flow and pedestrian safety through the introduction of crosswalks and traffic lights. An enthusiastic modernizer, Chiappe believed that eliminating noise would help to transform Paris into an efficient and ordered modern metropolis.[137] In February 1931, he issued a sweeping noise ordinance that banned the use of automobile horns at night, restricted the operating hours of street fairs and nightclubs, and outlawed a variety of cacophonous practices, such as the beating of carpets from windows. This new ordinance also explicitly targeted radios for the first time. Reiterating the earlier bans on loudspeakers in the "public thoroughfare," Chiappe added provisions to ban "noises made inside properties and residences ... coming from phonographs, loudspeakers, and musical instruments."[138]

Radio clubs in Paris and the provinces immediately rose up in defense of audiences' "right to listen" in any way they chose. Paul Berché, the director of *L'Antenne*, claimed that the authorities were confused about the nature of broadcast sound, for "radio broadcasting cannot be considered ... noise in the same category as the dings of a cash register and the honks of a horn."[139] The newly formed Confédération Nationale des Radio Clubs demanded that the Touring Club formally outline its complaints against listeners, which included playing radios with open windows, excessive volume, and late-night listening – the latter resulting from the fact that radio reception improved significantly after 10 p.m. To rebut these charges, the Confederation declared that "commercial and industrial loudspeakers ... are for the most part responsible for the invention of radio noise," rather than individual radio users. Those who complained about radio noise were either conservatives hostile to modernization or they simply failed to understand what they were hearing, the journalist F. Soulier-Valbert argued in *L'Antenne*, for "listening is an indisputable right that must be protected

---

[137] Brooke L. Blower, *Becoming Americans in Paris: Transatlantic Politics and Culture Between the World Wars* (Oxford, 2011), 131–72.
[138] Archives of the Paris Préfecture de Police DB143. Ordonnance sur le bruit, Paris, February 20, 1931.
[139] Paul Berché, "La T.S.F. et la croisade contre le bruit," *L'Antenne*, November 15, 1931, 1.

under conditions as liberal as music, theater, and public lectures."[140] However, the radio newspaper did prevail upon its readers to discipline their listening habits and demonstrate "respectable" behavior by lowering the volume of loudspeakers, even while backing radio clubs in a coordinated campaign defending the "right to listen." The latter included filing official grievances against businesses whose electrical devices, from hair stylists' dryers and couturiers' sewing machines to physicians' X-ray machines, generated electromagnetic interference (*parasites*) that ruined radio reception.[141] By 1933, listeners' complaints compelled legislators to crack down on radio interference at both the municipal and national level through punitive legislation protecting radio reception.[142]

Chiappe's hostility toward broadcast sound also discomfited radio manufacturers and employees of radio stations, who feared that the noise ordinances would slow broadcasting's expansion. As the radio reporter Alex Surchamp argued in *Vu et lu*, the subjective nature of noise made it almost impossible to determine "at which moment a broadcast leaves a normal state to become a 'noisy' broadcast, with the result that loudspeakers risk being regulated [at the height] of their expansion."[143] Spokesmen for the Parisian entertainment industry also criticized Chiappe's policies. Defending his position before the Paris municipal council in 1932, the police prefect told the delegates that his office had been "fighting the noise of the capital for eighty years." However, the "origin of noise had changed" since the war, in turn demanding more stringent and uniform noise regulations. Addressing the shopkeepers, bar owners, and nightclub proprietors who used broadcast sound to attract a clientele and feared restrictions on their livelihoods, Chiappe insisted that he was "not making war against noises that are an ineluctable expression of Parisian activity," but rather sought to create a sonic equilibrium. "Cities are like children, and doctors and urban planners worry when a child becomes silent or a city mute,"

---

[140] F. Soulier-Valbert, "Le Touring Club et la radio," *L'Antenne*, July 12, 1931, 423.

[141] Paul Roué, "Code de la T.S.F.," *Almanach de T.S.F. et du disque* (Paris, 1934), 45; Pierre Jouvenet, "La suppression des parasites de la T.S.F. intéresse à la fois les usagers, les commerçants, et les médecins," *L'Echo de Paris*, September 17, 1934, 5. Noise abatement campaigners across Europe promoted self-discipline as the key to eliminating noise. Bijsterveld, *Mechanical Sound*, 110–34.

[142] Brochand, *Histoire générale de la radio*, 1: 359–60. The amateur radio press campaigned against "industrial parasites" as early as 1926. In 1931–1932 the Confédération Nationale des Radio Clubs organized conferences on the subject. In April of 1934, new legislation provided guidelines that enabled listeners to sue for damages against disruptions caused by *parasites*.

[143] Fonds Radio France. Carton 280. Alex Surchamp, "Le bruit . . . trop bruyant," *Vu et lu*, 1937.

while a "noisy city is alive and kicking." The policeman's task was to "eliminate useless noises, reduce indispensable noises to a minimum, and seek to obtain absolute silence during the night."[144]

Chiappe's successor Roger Langeron expanded the battle against broadcast sound during the summer of 1935 by offering Parisians additional options for pursuing their complaints against noisy neighbors. Residents disrupted by a loud radio inside their apartment building could now telephone their local police bureau and request the dispatch of a police cyclist. After interviewing witnesses and performing "all the necessary observations to determine the abusive nature of the broadcasts," the policeman would engage the disruptive party in dialogue to make sure they understood the law. Like Chiappe, Langeron insisted that he was not interested in "thwarting the admirable progress of wireless nor attacking the freedom of a radio owner to listen at home, but rather in reconciling that freedom with the right of neighbors to rest and tranquility."[145] Despite the increased severity of municipal policies, however, listeners ultimately had little to fear because the existing legislation did not permit police to prosecute offenders under criminal charges, but only to issue tickets for violations of municipal ordinances.[146] However, between 1935 and 1937, the Parisian police recorded 15,000 noise violations, 1,913 of which involved radios or phonographs played illegally on the "public thoroughfare." They investigated another 1,982 complaints about loud radios and gramophones inside apartment buildings and handed out 558 tickets.[147]

Even in the face of these vigorous interventions, complaints about radio and loudspeaker noise continued to land on the desks of high-ranking police officials, although the severity of penalties levied against salesmen, store proprietors, and individuals remains unclear, for newspapers and municipal reports frequently ignored the details of cases. One file from the police archives stands out. In 1935, the composer Gustave Charpentier, whose brother Victor directed the Radio-Paris station orchestra, wrote to Paul Guichard, the director of the municipal police, protesting the "loudspeakers . . . of an infernal volume and the sales talk of [vendors] with a microphone in their hand" that polluted his Montmartre neighborhood. From 3 to 11 p.m., street performers on the Place

[144] "Le budget de police devant l'Assemblée Municipale," *Le Petit parisien*, December 30, 1932, 2; Procès-verbaux du Conseil Municipal de Paris, December 29, 1937 (Paris, 1932), 757–62.
[145] "La lutte contre le bruit à Paris. Des sévères mesures sont pris par le préfet de police," *Journal des débats politiques*, August 31, 1935, 3.
[146] Paul Dermée, "Pour obtenir du Parlement le vote rapide d'une loi protégeant les citoyens contre les bruits excessifs," *Comoedia*, September 23, 1936.
[147] *Annuaire statistique de la ville de Paris* (Paris, 1943), 558.

d'Anvers shouted "the refrains of their songs into their loudspeakers," Charpentier grumbled, so that "even with the windows shut one cannot have a conversation." Not unlike the radio audiences who complained about electrical *parasites* disrupting their clear radio reception, Charpentier condemned these "parasites of the street" as a "disgrace to Parisian life" – particularly those affiliated with a nearby nightclub whose amplified music violated city ordinances and whose drunken clientele disrupted his sleep.

Charpentier's celebrity compelled Guichard to undertake a full investigation, but the local *arrondissement* commissioner, Sollier, believed that the elderly composer had simply failed to adjust to the city's modern soundscape, a situation not without irony. Referencing the street criers who inspired the libretto for Charpentier's 1900 lyric opera *Louise*, Sollier noted that in his younger days the composer clearly "appreciated nocturnal sounds, which appeared melodious to him." The police eventually promised to move the street performers and their loudspeakers off the square, but reminded Charpentier that they could not shut down the city's profitable entertainment industry, especially when "no one can really say exactly where endurable noise begins or leaves off."[148]

Municipal authorities in provincial cities and villages across France waged their own wars against broadcast sound that mirrored and departed from those in the capital. Edouard Herriot, the radical deputy and mayor of Lyon, made national headlines in 1925 when he banned the use of loudspeakers in his city and threatened the listening habits of local radio amateurs.[149] The mayors of Chambéry and Chagny forbade the use of radios in public and private spaces between 10 p.m. and 8 a.m., while the prefect of the southeastern *département* of Bouches-du-Rhône imposed similar limits across the entire region under his jurisdiction.[150] In the southwestern city of Toulouse, the mayor went so far as to fix the limits of radio listening in public to specific hours of the day – from 11 a. m. to 2 p.m.; 6 p.m. to 7 p.m.; and 9 p.m. to 11 p.m. – hours of high traffic in hotels, cafés, and restaurants.[151] Whether the comparatively smaller size and population of regional cities gave provincial police greater

[148] Archives of the Paris Préfecture de Police DA460. Lettre de Gustave Charpentier à Paul Guinchard, Directeur Général de la Police Municipale, June 27, 1935. Réponse de Sollier, Le Commissaire d'arrondissement, July 1, 1935.
[149] "Herriot contre la T.S.F.," *L'Humanité*, November 26, 1925.
[150] "La campagne contre le bruit s'étend," *Le Matin*, September 8, 1931, 1. Michel Adam, "La lutte contre les parasites," *Revue générale des industries radioélectriques*, November 1937, 11.
[151] Charles Bernardin, *Le Bruit: danger social. Le bruit à Toulouse. Thèse pour le doctorat en médecine* (Toulouse, 1938), 86.

success than their Parisian colleagues in suppressing noise, however, is difficult to determine. Evaluating the penalties imposed on violators of noise ordinances proves equally challenging. When an Amiens shopkeeper named Kahn contested a ticket he received for playing a phonograph on the street in 1934 to raise money for Les Gueules Cassées, an association for First World War veterans with severe facial disfigurements, the presiding judge ordered Kahn to pay only a one-franc fine, a decision that perhaps reflected the judge's sympathy with the cause, or alternatively, his conviction that noise violations constituted a minor offense.[152] Public perceptions of broadcast sound as a form of "noise" clearly varied across France, in keeping with the uneven spread of radio technology and diverse cultural expectations about appropriate public and private behavior. Complaints about radio noise only reached a fevered pitch in regional cities such as Nantes in the late 1930s.[153] However, the tension between some citizens' requests for protection against "forced listening" and others' demands for safeguards to their "right to listen" in the ways they chose would continue to challenge police and public authorities across France as they sought to regulate the soundscape against the rapidly shifting political climate of the mid-1930s.

The politics of broadcast sound

It would be tempting to interpret the concerns raised by the noise abatement campaigns as evidence that many people had come to regard broadcasting as a public medium intended for consumption in the privacy of the home, where responsible listeners would tune into the airwaves discreetly without subjecting their neighbors to shrieking and squealing loudspeakers. But during the very years when domestic radio ownership began to grow exponentially, broadcast sound returned to the streets as an integral component of the mass political demonstrations that overtook Paris and other large cities. Disagreements about who should control the urban soundscape – the police and municipal authorities, politicians, or ordinary citizens – only increased as quotidian disputes about how, when, and where people listened to broadcast sound became entangled in national and even international politics.

In February of 1934, after years of electoral turmoil and rumors of financial scandal within the highest levels of government spurred

---

[152] "La municipalité d'Amiens et la T.S.F.," *Revue générale des industries radioélectriques*, October 1934, 18.
[153] "Sans-filistes, fermez vos fenêtres!" *Ouest-Éclair* (Nantes), April 20, 1938, 7.

widespread distrust of parliamentary politics, several far-right leagues and right-leaning veterans' associations took to the streets to protest the newly elected radical government of Edouard Daladier, unleashing riots at the Place de la Concorde that nearly toppled the Third Republic and sparked a wave of left-wing counter-demonstrations. The years that followed witnessed a dramatic increase in street politics, as politicians on both the left and right looked to "the people" for political legitimation, and party propagandists sought out sophisticated sound equipment and powerful loudspeakers that could enable crowds numbering in the tens of thousands to gather in stadiums or in city squares to listen to propaganda speeches and watch political pageants unfold.[154] The Paris police and the security services, fearful that the amplified voices of orators might rouse angry crowds to violence, sought to restrict the number of demonstrations by requiring organizers to obtain official authorizations for their events as well as for any use of phonographs, loudspeakers, or other sound devices. While approvals for both, subject to the political sympathies of police officials, were not always forthcoming, an estimated 900 political demonstrations took place in Paris alone between 1934 and 1936.[155]

During many of these street demonstrations, large parades of party militants and their affiliate youth and women's organizations marched through city streets to converge in a single square or park where crowds could listen to orators' speeches. The Paris police carefully surveilled these marches, instructing uniformed officers and plainclothes agents mixed in with the crowds to pay particular attention to the "physiognomy of the street" when people halted before loudspeakers to listen to speeches.[156] Political rallies held inside stadiums or indoor arenas such as the Vélodrome d'Hiver permitted party leaders to discipline their militants through chanting or singing, and allowed police, at least in principle, to contain participants within an enclosed space. Yet loudspeakers frequently resonated through walls to reach an even larger audience outside, giving political demonstrations a much greater "acoustic presence" than police or many neighborhood residents would have liked.[157]

Such was the case with a rally organized by the French Communist Party (PCF) at the Stade Buffalo on June 14, 1936, where a crowd of 600,

[154] Wardhaugh, *In Pursuit of the People*, 22–24; Robert W. Lewis, "'A Civic Tool of Modern Times:' Politics, Mass Society, and the Stadium in Twentieth Century France," *French Historical Studies*, 34, 1, 2011, 155–84; Danielle Tartakowsky, "Stratégies de la rue, 1934–1938," *Le Mouvement social* 135, April–June 1986, 31–62.
[155] Wardhaugh, *In Pursuit of the People*, 74.
[156] Archives of the Paris Préfecture de Police BA 1862. Rapport de la Direction des Renseignements Généraux et des Jeux dirigé à M. le Préfet de Police, June 13, 1936.
[157] Lewis, "'A Civic Tool of Modern Times,'" 155–84. On the concept of "acoustic presence," see Birdsall, *Nazi Soundscapes*, 36–39.

unable to fit inside, congregated outside the gates to listen. A few months later, in an attempt to prevent communist voices from reverberating across the city, militants from the far right French Social Party (Parti Social Français, or PSF) attempted to cut the electrical wires controlling the sound system of the Parc des Princes before a PCF rally.[158] Containing the voices of political activists proved especially challenging for the police when the PCF and other parties used sound trucks to announce their upcoming rallies, even after municipalities had banned them for ostensibly apolitical advertising purposes. The police commissioner of Aniche, a commune in the Nord de Calais, arrested the driver of a car belonging to the PCF newspaper *L'Humanité* in 1935 for playing a "subversive phonograph" on the public thoroughfare without prior authorization – in this case a record of the Polish revolutionary anthem "La Varsovienne."[159] By the mid-1930s, the amplified sound broadcast by loudspeakers had ceased to be an innovative, modern attraction for many people, and instead symbolized the rising partisan political tensions in the streets.

The tumultuous international climate of the mid-1930s undoubtedly influenced public reactions to this *sonorisation* of French politics. For years, daily newspapers ranging from the moderate *Le Petit parisien* to the right-leaning *Le Matin* had documented the efforts of fascist parties in Germany and Italy to exploit broadcasting to win the support of the masses for their one-party regimes. In the March 1933 elections that solidified the Nazis' power, one journalist described, the radio speeches of the recently appointed chancellor, Hitler, had been enhanced by the installation of "twenty-four loudspeakers in the most frequented centers" of Berlin. Nazi Party officials later instructed members "in possession of a radio to place it in an open window" on days when Hitler spoke, while the subsequent appearance of loudspeakers in theaters and hotels, on factory floors, and in outdoor parks provided further evidence of Germany's evaporating civil society and the Nazis' efforts to colonize their citizens' ears through broadcast sound.[160] When French legislators voted to open radio microphones to political candidates during the 1936 elections, *Le Matin*'s drama critic Guy Launay professed relief that France was still a

---

[158] Archives de la Préfecture de Police BA 1863. Manifestation organisée par le parti communiste au Parc des Princes, October 5, 1936.

[159] "La fête champêtre de l'Humanité," *L'Humanité*, September 9, 1934, 2; "Un grandiose rassemblement," *L'Humanité*, April 14, 1935, 1; "La camarade Fronsac inculpé de chants et cris séditieux pour un disque de phonographe," *L'Humanité*, April 14, 1935, 2.

[160] "L'Allemagne votera demain," *Le Petit parisien*, March 4, 1933, 2; "Avant le plébiscite allemand, à nouveau, Hitler parle," *Le Petit parisien*, November 11, 1933, 1. See also Favre, "Quand le Führer parle," 108–17.

long way away from "German and American practices of noisy [political] advertising with orchestras, flags, films, and chorales."[161]

However, the introduction of electoral politics into the airwaves during the spring elections of 1936 only exacerbated anxieties about the use of broadcast sound in public spaces. While it had become fairly common for radio salesmen, grocers, and café proprietors to place radios from their businesses on city streets during broadcasts of state funerals or Bastille Day celebrations, individuals could now use their radios to annoy neighbors of opposing political sympathies by turning up the volume of their receiver when a favorite politician came on the air.[162] That October, workers occupying a factory in the 15th *arrondissement* in support of the recently elected Popular Front government did just that, *Le Matin* reported, blaring the "robust loudspeakers of their radios" until the wee hours of the morning and forcing bourgeois residents of the neighborhood to listen to their political propaganda.[163] When the Popular Front's PTT minister Robert Jardillier decided to install loudspeakers in the public squares and gardens of Paris and other regional cities to broadcast radio programs of "national importance," the measure immediately provoked suspicion. Jardillier argued that the loudspeakers would democratize access to the airwaves by allowing people without home radios to listen collectively in public spaces, but city residents disenchanted by the prospect of increased noise claimed that they would be forced to listen against their will. Right-wing critics of the government, of course, feared a much more nefarious strategy at work: one designed to fill cities with the sounds of leftist propaganda.[164] While the loudspeakers broadcast sports matches and orchestral concerts, they also transmitted the fiery speeches of left-wing orators addressing crowds at the Place de la Nation on Bastille Day and the "Oath of Peace" (*Serment de la paix*) pronounced by several thousand French and German veterans of the First World War at the Douaumont memorial in Verdun a few months later. These latter broadcasts only confirmed fears on the right about the government's inappropriate use of broadcast sound in public spaces.[165]

---

[161] Guy Launay, "Publicité électorale," *Le Matin*, April 24, 1936, 2. On radio in the elections, see Méadel, *Histoire de la radio*, 158.

[162] Jean-Richard Bloch, *Naissance d'une culture. Quatre essais sur mon temps* (Paris, 1936), 167.

[163] "Un concert de chants révolutionnaire incommode depuis plus d'un mois les habitants de l'avenue de Suffren," *Le Matin*, October 13, 1936, 1.

[164] "Echos et informations: Concerts publiques par T.S.F.," *Radio-Magazine*, October 18, 1936. "Le scandale de la radio d'Etat," *L'Eclair. Journal du Midi*, July 14 and 19, 1936, 7.

[165] CARAN F12-894. Memo de l'Inspecteur Général adjoint, Chef du Service des installations mécaniques, December 22, 1936; Letter from Le Matériel Radiotechnique to Godefroy, Direction de l'Exploitation technique, Exposition de 1937. See also *Le Populaire*, July 13, 1936, 4.

By the mid-1930s, the everyday politics of listening – or questions about how, when, and where it was acceptable for people to listen to broadcast sound – had become entangled in partisan politics and the growing divide between the far left and the far right. For even as radios and other sound technologies became a common feature of living rooms, cafés, and restaurants across France, broadcast sound generated conflicts between public authorities seeking to monitor or control the soundscape and audiences demanding the "right to listen" in any way they chose. These tensions, as we have seen, owed much to radio's destabilization of the boundaries between public and private life, as well as to the distinctly "modern" qualities of broadcast sound. More importantly, the political context in which radio and other new sound media emerged played a critical role in determining the cultural meanings and political tasks that contemporaries assigned to radio broadcasting and to the act of listening. To what extent should the government protect audiences' "right to listen?" Who should have access to the airwaves? What should be the "state of the ear" in France? As we shall see, these questions would continue to preoccupy and divide audiences throughout the interwar decades.

2 Disabled veterans, radio citizenship, and the politics of national recovery

During broadcasting's first decade, when many people were encountering radio for the first time in the streets of Paris and other large cities, wireless boosters and radio station directors eager to cultivate audiences for the new media regularly touted its humanitarian benefits for a nation still struggling to recover from the physical destruction and emotional ravages unleashed by the First World War. "Light to the blind and hearing to the deaf," the radio magazine *T.S.F. Programme* proposed in 1931, "this double miracle, which only the heroes of holy legends accomplished in the past, is achieved in our time by the modern miracle of radio." Describing the recent formation of Radio aux Aveugles (Radio for the Blind) and T.S.F. à l'Hôpital (Wireless at the Hospital), two national charities that distributed free radios to the blind and "infirm," the journalist René Bruyez highlighted radio's advantages for blind veterans, the war's most pitiable victims, whose reliance on sighted guides limited their independence and restricted their movement in society.

Broadcasting could provide a constant stream of sound to brighten their dark worlds, Bruyez proposed, but even more miraculously, it could aid the deaf, who "perceive nothing of the voices of the world, but whose hearing is sometimes sensitive to the vibrations of the microphone." Referencing the sensory disruption many listeners experienced the first time they heard disembodied voices emerging from a radio loudspeaker or a burst of static explode in their headsets, Bruyez insisted that listening offered even greater advantages to the blind and disabled than it did to able-bodied audiences. Broadcasting would advance disabled veterans' physical and psychological rehabilitation by granting them access to the wider world outside their homes and sanatoria, permitting them to rejoin civil society through the airwaves. But until hertzian waves' remarkable cure for deafness propelled a "magician of science" to develop a non-metaphorical cure for blindness, he wondered, would it not be possible for us to "procure radios for all those who are waiting?"[1]

[1] René Bruyez, "Un miracle qui peut en faire d'autres," *T.S.F. Programme*, January, 25–31, 1931.

64

Bruyez's appeal to the readers of *T.S.F. Programme* for donations to the radio charities coincided with significant transformations to the airwaves in France. In the late 1920s, both state-run and commercial radio stations began expanding their daily programs from a few hours of evening music and news into full daily schedules. Although some people still considered radio listening to be a purely technical hobby, bourgeois housewives could now tune into talks about cuisine or the latest fashions before switching on a children's program for their families. Sports fans thrilled to live reportages from stadiums while classical music enthusiasts enjoyed broadcasts direct from Parisian stages and European opera houses. "If it is necessary to underline the benefits we can look forward to with radio," the reporter Alex Virot wrote in the right-leaning daily *L'Intransigeant*, "it suffices to highlight its essentially democratic value." Although radio had thus far remained an "amusing little luxury toy" for elites, it could provide vital services to enhance the lives of people across social classes. "How many isolated people already owe to it the comfort of less solitary evenings," he wondered, and "how many blind people find in it the means to escape the sort of cruel night that surrounds them?" It was precisely for this "modest clientele" that French broadcasters should strive to create a "national domain" of high-quality radio programming, Virot argued, before calling upon manufacturers to produce more affordable receivers.[2]

Virot's conviction that broadcasting should play a greater role in French society resonated with a growing number of politicians, state bureaucrats, and cultural commentators, who feared that radio's potential as a mass media would be squandered unless it could be harnessed for public and political ends. They called for the state to reinforce the PTT's legal monopoly over the airwaves by ending the regime of non-intervention that had enabled commercial stations to begin transmitting alongside state-run PTT affiliates. In 1928, lawmakers voted to ban the creation of any future commercial stations and, shortly thereafter, began debating the institution of an annual radio license fee (*redevance*) to fund the construction of a state network of regional stations across the country.[3] Marcel Pellenc, the energetic young engineer who took the reins of the PTT's first dedicated broadcasting administration in June of 1927, vigorously promoted this concept of radio as a media that should serve the nation's citizens. Radio had an obligation to "enlighten and instruct, promote a taste for order and a respect for physical and moral health," the radio journalist Yvane Arthaud confirmed a few years later in the 1933

---

[2] Alex Virot, "La radio humanitaire," *L'Intransigeant*, October 4, 1929, 10. Virot used the expression "propriété nationale."
[3] Méadel, *Histoire de la radio*, 26–39; 232–38; Ulmann-Mauriat, *Naissance d'un média*, 57–120.

Annuaire de la radiodiffusion nationale. Although traumas of the war years and the "uprooting of individuals and economic migration" that had followed threatened to destroy "old notions of friendship, solidarity, and all that those words mean," broadcasting promised to forge new bonds of community through shared listening experiences, drawing even the most isolated and alienated citizens into a collective national radio audience.[4]

In this chapter I examine how broadcasting shaped postwar debates about national recovery by mediating the renegotiation of citizenship for disabled veterans of the First World War, in the process transforming the political and social tasks that contemporaries assigned to the airwaves and to radio listening. Long after the war's end, disabled veterans begging on city streets or processing in Armistice Day parades remained an all-too familiar sight for many, serving as daily reminders of the war's permanent legacies and the practical challenges of reconstruction.[5] France had drafted approximately two-thirds of its adult male population during the conflict, and of the 3.4 million soldiers wounded in combat, approximately one million returned to civilian life facing limb loss, sensory impairment, or debilitating long-term illnesses, resulting in their categorization as *mutilés de guerre*, or "war disabled."[6] Far from signifying any real medical pathology, Catherine Kudlick suggests, the label "disabled" has long been used to deny the benefits of citizenship to those failing to meet contemporary standards of "independence, strength, and self-mastery," in turn revealing more about how "Western societies determine hierarchy and maintain order" than any individual impairment.[7] The First World War, far more than previous conflicts, raised troubling questions about the social and political status of people with physical disabilities in France.

Not since the Napoleonic Wars had the nation faced caring for such a large number of disabled veterans, and despite an 1831 law granting them the right to a military pension, a succession of nineteenth-century regime changes ensured that no organized system existed to distribute monies or provide medical services. Disabled veterans of the Franco-Prussian War

---

[4] Yvane Arthaud, "L'influence sociale de la radiophonie," *Annuaire de la radiodiffusion nationale 1933* (Paris, 1933), 180–81. See the biography of Arthaud in Prot, *Dictionnaire de la radio*, 628.

[5] Seth Koven, "Remembering and Dismemberment: Crippled Children, Wounded Soldiers, and the Great War in Great Britain," *American Historical Review*, 99, 4, 1999, 1167–202; David Serlin, "Disabling the Flâneur," *Journal of Visual Culture*, 5, 2, 2006, 193–208.

[6] Prost, *In the Wake of War*, 38–45.

[7] Catherine J. Kudlick, "Disability History: Why We Need Another 'Other,'" *American Historical Review*, 108, 3, 2003, 765.

of 1870–1871 were fortunate to obtain any benefits for their wartime service, and despite Red Cross campaigns on their behalf, they disappeared from public view during the early years of the Third Republic as relics of a discredited imperial conflict.[8] Similarly, only a minority of France's disabled civilians attracted the haphazard attentions of state-run and private benevolence institutions such as the Parisian Quinze-Vingts Hospital for the blind or the specialized blind and deaf schools founded during the French Revolution. These establishments offered limited health care, employment, and education while segregating populations associated with vagrancy, contagious diseases, and mental instability from civil society.[9] The progressive medicalization of disability at the turn of the century also produced ambiguous outcomes for people with disabilities: physicians' "cures" of physical ailments at times enabled their assimilation to able-bodied norms, but the medical preoccupation with identifying bodily pathologies marked individuals with permanent disabilities as irrevocably different.[10]

However, after the First World War, disabled men who had displayed heroism and self-sacrifice on the battlefields of the Western Front could not be easily relegated to hospitals and asylums like civilians, even when some veterans displayed physical or emotional weaknesses that rendered them less like independent, autonomous men and more like disenfranchised women whose supposed dependency justified the paternalist interventions of the state in their private lives.[11] When the historic model of the republican citizen relied upon balancing assertions of individuality with assimilation to collective norms, how would disabled men ever be able to regain their prewar social and political status?[12] For the men seeking to reestablish their prewar careers and family life and for the politicians anxious to rebuild France's labor force and promote demographic

---

[8] Isser Woloch, *The French Veteran from Revolution to Restoration* (Chapel Hill, 1979); Bertrand Taithe, *Defeated Flesh: Welfare, Warfare, and the Making of Modern France* (Manchester, 1999), 181–206; Gregory N. Thomas, *Treating the Trauma of the Great War: Soldiers, Civilians, and Psychiatry in France, 1914–1940* (Baton Rouge, 2009), 95–123.

[9] Catherine J. Kudlick and Zina Weygand, *Reflections: The Life and Writings of a Young Blind Woman in Post-Revolutionary France* (New York, 2001); Zina Weygand, *The Blind in French Society: From the Middle Ages to the Century of Louis Braille* (Stanford, 2010); Anne T. Quartararo, *Deaf Identity and Social Images in Nineteenth-Century France* (Washington DC, 2008).

[10] Henri-Jacques Stiker, *Corps infirmes et sociétés* (Paris, 1982), 127–45, Paul K. Longmore and Lauri Umansky, eds., *The New Disability History: American Perspectives* (New York, 2001), esp. 1–57.

[11] David Gerber, ed., *Disabled Veterans in History* (Ann Arbor, 2000), 1–25.

[12] Judith Surkis, *Sexing the Citizen: Morality and Masculinity in France, 1870–1920* (Ithaca NY, 2006) 3–16; and Joan W. Scott, *Only Paradoxes to Offer: French Feminists and the Rights of Man* (Cambridge MA, 1997).

recovery, rehabilitating the bodies and minds of disabled veterans through prostheses, physical therapy, and vocational rehabilitation became a priority. In 1919, legislators voted in a new pension law that codified compensation and eliminated the onerous requirement that veterans prove their injury or illness was sustained in combat. Yet disabled veterans' associations, whose membership numbered in the tens of thousands, continued to pose formidable challenges to the state into the 1930s by demanding pension increases and improvements to the medical and therapeutic services coordinated by the newly created Office National des Mutilés et Réformés de Guerre. Whether martyred by politicians on the left as victims of capitalist war profiteers or celebrated on the right as battle-hardened heroes, disabled veterans' voices could not be ignored in the postwar quest for social and political stability.[13]

At the same time, the war unleashed widespread anxieties about the vitality of the French population that were only exacerbated by the loss of an entire generation of young men. Army physicians' scrutiny of soldiers' bodies had uncovered high rates of tuberculosis and syphilis, spurring the creation of France's first cabinet-level ministry of health in July of 1920 and a network of urban dispensaries to screen, segregate, and treat people infected with contagious diseases.[14] Medical professionals, politicians, and wealthy businessmen from the Michelin brothers to the perfumer François Coty concluded that France had better care for its human capital lest the nation falter in the face of international competition, prompting them to fund campaigns to increase France's birthrate, combat alcoholism, and improve physical fitness. These concerns took center stage in print media and over the airwaves, where physicians corralled radio microphones for talks on preventative hygiene and the famous Dr. Henri Diffre took audiences through a home calisthenics course to the sounds of a military band.[15] When staged against this backdrop of health-related propaganda, debates about whether disabled veterans could, or

---

[13] Bruno Cabanes, *The Great War and the Origins of Humanitarianism, 1918–1924* (Cambridge, 2014), 24–81; Laura Frader, *Breadwinners and Citizens: Gender in the Making of the French Social Model* (Durham NC, 2008), 15–49; Millington, *From Victory to Vichy*, 3, 37, 41–43.

[14] Olivier Faure and Dominique Dessertine, *Combattre la tuberculose, 1900–1940* (Lyon, 1988), 25–31; Pierre Guillaume, *Du désespoir au salut: les tuberculeux aux XIXe et XXᵉ siècles* (Paris, 1986).

[15] Timothy B. Smith, *Creating the Welfare State in France, 1880–1940* (Quebec City, 2003), 97. On the importance of physical culture, see Joan Tumbelty, *Remaking the Male Body: Masculinity and the Uses of Physical Culture in Interwar France and Vichy* (Oxford, 2012), 17–56. For radio programs about physical health, see the *Cahiers de Radio-Paris*, 1930–1936, and "Dr. Diffre," *Mon programme*, May 27, 1932. The magazine *Guérir* regularly sponsored talks about preventative hygiene on Radio LL in the early 1930s.

even should, be reintegrated into civil society had the potential to become politically divisive.[16]

Radio broadcasting, which bridged the divide between public and private life and promised to draw individual listeners into a collective national audience, appeared to many people to be a perfect solution to the dilemma of disabled veterans' citizenship. Wireless already bore numerous cultural ties to the war as a "heroic" technology first exploited by the army, and veterans flooded the ranks of amateur radio clubs. The conceptual ties linking radio to disability also drew upon a discourse of sensory impairment that surfaced in early radio theory. The historical synchronicity of cinema, photography, and typewriting, as the German media theorist Friedrich Kittler proposed, "separated optical, acoustical, and written data flows" in ways that appeared to isolate the sensory mechanisms of seeing and hearing to render "eyes and ears autonomous."[17] The physician-turned-radio dramatist Paul Deharme summarized the difference between silent film and radio accordingly: "we had mute art, here is blind art."[18] This "blindness" of the sighted listener vis-à-vis the disembodied voice of the radio announcer quickly became a trope for explaining the complex sound décor required to guide audiences during radio plays, which contemporaries branded "theater for the blind."[19] Radio receivers, like earlier sound technologies such as the telephone or phonograph, even appeared to replicate human sensory organs, with the ear-like microphone collecting sounds to be transported through the airwaves to the horn-shaped mouth of a loudspeaker, the latter a persistent reminder of how amplified sound might aid the deaf and hard of hearing.[20]

---

[16] Schneider, *Quality and Quantity*, 116–69. On rehabilitation and the welfare state, see Kristen Stromberg Childers, *Fathers, Families, and the State in France, 1914–1945* (Ithaca NY, 2003); Deborah Cohen, *The War Come Home: Disabled Veterans in Britain and Germany, 1914–1939* (Berkeley, 2001).

[17] Friedrich Kittler, *Gramophone, Film, Typewriter*, trans. Geoffrey Winthrop-Young and Michael Wutz (Stanford, 1999), 3, 14.

[18] Paul Deharme, "Proposition d'une art radiophonique," *La Nouvelle revue française*, 174, March 1, 1928, 415.

[19] For examples, see André Coeuroy, *Panorama de la radio* (Paris, 1930), 14; Tristan Bernard, "Pour les aveugles invisibles," *Annuaire de la radiodiffusion nationale 1933*; Georges Barbarin, "Dans le domaine des sons, les aveugles sont rois," *Le Quotidien*, January 14, 1930; Carlos Larronde, *Théâtre invisible. Le douzième coup de minuit. Le chant des sphères* (Paris, 1936).The German theorist Rudolph Arnheim titled a chapter in his radio treatise "In Praise of Blindness: Emancipation from the Body." See Arnheim, *Radio*, trans. Margaret Ludwig and Herbert Read (London, 1936), 133–203. The blindness trope has persisted into the twentieth century, as evidenced by Andrew Crisell's *Understanding Radio* (London, 1986), 3–11.

[20] Sterne, *The Audible Past*, 31–86.

When René Bruyez appealed to the readers of *T.S.F Programme* for donations to the charities Radio for the Blind and Wireless at the Hospital, he identified two groups of veterans – the war blind and the war "deaf" – who he believed might especially benefit from broadcasting. While less iconic than the men with severe facial disfigurements known as *gueules cassées* ("smashed faces"), blind and "deaf" men comprised a significant proportion of France's population of disabled veterans. Approximately 10–15 percent of battlefield injuries resulted in severe head traumas that produced blindness or deafness as their counterpart.[21] Soldiers endured disorienting gas attacks and exploding shrapnel attacked their eyes and left their ears ringing. Medical diagnoses of shell shock or "war neuroses" frequently identified aphasia, stuttering, visual or auditory hallucinations, and temporary hearing loss as common symptoms.[22] Radio broadcasting, a modern sound media that disrupted conventional modes of sensory perception, now promised unique solutions to veterans of a conflict that many had experienced as a veritable war on the human senses.[23]

Between 1928 and 1934 a series of debates unfolded in radio clubs, medical circles, parliament, and the pages of the mass press over how to facilitate disabled veterans' access to radio technology and the degree to which radio listening could reintegrate them into civil society. The radio charities portrayed broadcast sound as a "prosthesis" that could replace blind veterans' absent vision, arguing that listening would facilitate their social inclusion by incorporating them into a national radio audience. But as we shall see, blind and deaf veterans exploited radio in very different ways to navigate the norms of republican citizenship and determine the terms of their participation in national life. Some blind people embraced radio for offering them new ways to participate in civil society, but they repudiated the passive model of listening promoted by the radio charities, instead embracing active forms of listening that allowed them to engage meaningfully with the world. "Deaf" and hard-of-hearing veterans, in contrast, used radios as hearing aids to demand greater recognition of

---

[21] Delaporte, *Les gueules cassées*. Prost, *In the Wake of War*, 39. Blind veterans' organizations were among the largest disability-specific veterans' associations. The Fédération des Mutilés de l'Oreille claimed that 16,000 ex-servicemen received pensions for hearing loss. Robert Morche, *Guide du mutilé de l'oreille et des personnes sourdes, demi-sourdes, et dures d'oreille* (Paris-Asnières, 1927), 71.

[22] Thomas, *Treating the Trauma of the Great War*, 21–70; Joanna Bourke, *Dismembering the Male: Men's Bodies, Britain, and the Great War* (Chicago, 1996), 107–23; Eric Leed, *No-Man's Land: Combat and Identity in World War One* (Cambridge, 1979), 164; Marc Roudebush, "A Battle of Nerves: Hysteria and its Treatments in France during World War I," in Paul Lerner and Mark S. Micale, eds., *Traumatic Pasts: History, Psychiatry, and Trauma in the Modern Age, 1870–1930* (Cambridge, 2001), 254–75.

[23] Schwartz, *Making Noise*, 559–90.

their wartime injuries, drawing on medical studies of auditory rehabilitation to reinforce their claims, even as they rejected the label of "disabled" in their effort to rejoin hearing society. A careful analysis of the arguments deployed by these two groups illustrates how broadcasting transformed the dynamics of French politics by privileging radio listening as a new form of social and political engagement. More importantly, that debates about radio and disabled veterans surfaced at the very moment when broadcasting first began to acquire a national audience helped to solidify public perceptions of the airwaves as a "radio nation" to which all citizens should have access. To understand how radio first became tied to the fate of disabled veterans, we turn now to examine the fundraising campaigns launched by the radio charities.

"A Ray in their Night": radio charities for the blind and "infirm"

In the late 1920s the charities Radio for the Blind and Wireless at the Hospital first drew the public's attention to radio's potential benefits for disabled veterans by inaugurating national campaigns to donate free radio receivers to the blind and "infirm." Although the charities' precise origins are unknown, they developed out of longstanding bourgeois philanthropic traditions, and more recently, from the thousands of wartime *oeuvres* founded to assist displaced refugees, wounded soldiers, war widows, and orphans.[24] Radio for the Blind co-hosted its first fundraiser in May of 1929 with the blind veterans' association Amitié des Aveugles, and counted among its founding members General Augustin Mariaux, the governor of the Invalides veterans' hospital, and the playwright Eugène Brieux, the director of a number of wartime rehabilitation schools and the editor of the blind veterans' newspaper *Le Journal des blessés des yeux*.[25] Two early Radio-Paris personalities, the announcer Marcel Laporte, and the station's orchestra director, Victor Charpentier, served as the public faces of Wireless at the Hospital.

Later that year Radio for the Blind and Wireless at the Hospital debuted weekly radio variety shows for the blind and hospitalized – the very targets of their fundraising efforts – as well as for a wider radio audience. Taking advantage of their personal connections with the staff of several Parisian radio stations, the charities conducted a series of experimental broadcasts on the commercial stations Radio-Vitus and Radio LL before

---

[24] Cabanes, *The Great War and the Origins of Humanitarianism*, 42–43.
[25] "La bienfaisance," *Journal des débats politiques et littéraires*, May 25, 1929, 2. The Amitié des Aveugles exists today as the Fédération des Aveugles et Handicapés Visuels de France.

finding a permanent home on the state-run station Paris PTT. Over the course of the next decade, the charities' shows would become a weekly staple of state broadcasting, retransmitted from Paris PTT to the nascent network of regional stations that grew to include Lyon PTT, Marseille-Provence, Rennes-Bretagne, Limoges, Montpellier, and Bordeaux-Lafayette.[26] The charities' collective project of "eliminating boredom, creating joy, and bringing life to sites of lamentation and despair" appealed to PTT *fonctionnaires* eager to define a greater civic role for broadcasting, but it resonated with audiences as well, spurring the creation of local chapters of the charities across France and in the colonial capital of Algiers.[27]

When the charities first began their campaigns in 1928, the cost for a multi-lamp radio far surpassed the reach of many laborers, and particularly veterans living on pensions regularly devalued through inflation. To raise funds for radio donations, charity volunteers organized raffles and mounted stands at the annual autumn radio salons, while Parisian galas featuring recording sensations such as Georges Chepfer, Max Régnier, Suzy Solidor, and the comic duo Gilles et Julien offered audiences the opportunity to see their favorite stars perform live while opening their pocketbooks for a worthy cause.[28] Wireless at the Hospital also sought out donations from businesses to support the installation of networked "central" radios in hospitals that delivered broadcast sound into common room loudspeakers for collective listening or to individual bedside headsets for patients requiring bed rest.[29] Municipalities eager to modernize their hospital facilities lent their support to the charities as well. Between 1932 and 1936, the Paris municipal budget provided an annual subsidy of 5,000 francs to Wireless at the Hospital, permitting the introduction of approximately 400 radios in the city's hospitals.[30]

---

[26] Brochand, *Histoire générale de la radio*, 1: 105. These stations were completed in 1927.
[27] Victor Charpentier, "La T.S.F. à l'hôpital," *Annuaire de la radiodiffusion nationale 1933*, 185–87.
[28] Jean Antoine, "T.S.F. Entre deux ondes. Le bal de la T.S.F.," *L'Intransigeant*, October 27, 1929; C.M. Savarit, "L'inauguration du salon de T.S.F.," *L'Echo de Paris*, September 8, 1934, 2; "2ᵉ Gala de la radio française," *Mon programme*, March 13, 1936; *Mon programme*, January 27, 1937.
[29] CARAN F12-894. Letter from the Société des Etablissements Homo-Beaugez, December 22, 1936. The Ste des Etablissements Homo-Beaugez installed loudspeakers for twenty-five rooms of a Parisian suburban hospital and headsets for the chalets of the army-run Saint-Gobain sanatorium on behalf of the charities. See the *Journal des mutilés et combattants*, March 5, 1932, 2.
[30] Christian Chevandier, *L'hôpital dans la France du XXᵉ siècle* (Perrin, 2009), 145. Archives de Paris Série D4K3 53–56. Délibérations du Conseil Municipal de Paris, 1932–1936, 113.

While the charities distributed free wireless receivers to both disabled veterans and civilians, the presence of General Mariaux as the leading spokesmen for Radio for the Blind tied their activities directly to the fate of the war blind. Mariaux commanded enormous public sympathy as an amputee and a grieving father who had lost a son on the Western Front. His own deteriorating eyesight contributed to his interest in the war blind, "those men deprived of the most precious of our senses," and whose disability he believed to be more debilitating than his own. He also served as the honorary president of the Association des Mutilés des Yeux, one of France's largest associations of blind veterans, with an estimated membership of 10,000.[31] Moreover, by soliciting small subscriptions from individuals rather than large sums, Radio for the Blind obtained the support of broad sectors of French society. When the post office issued a surtaxed Radio for the Blind stamp in 1938, it sold over a half a million to raise 200,000 francs for the charity, a testimony to the success of the group's decade-long fundraising campaign.[32]

Radio for the Blind clearly drew much of its inspiration from an earlier radio club created in 1923 by the Association Valentin Haüy (AVH), a blind advocacy organization dedicated to providing education and vocational training to the blind.[33] Having launched a crusade on the eve of the war to train blind telephone operators, the club secretary told *Radio-Magazine*, the AVH had wasted no time in "seeking out how our blind members could take advantage of the new science [of wireless]." For the club's first meetings, the AVH invited sighted members of the Société Française d'Etudes de T.S.F., France's oldest radio amateur association, to instruct its blind members in the principles of radio construction. Blind advocates hoped the radio club would generate a sense of "common destiny" among blind civilians and veterans who had only recently lost their sight – two groups that often perceived their rights and interests to be very different. The AVH radio club, which counted "former military wireless operators and blind war veterans" among its 140 members,

---

[31] SHD 13ydd444. Personnel dossier for Général Augustin Mariaux. Procès-verbal de la Commission de réforme, 5ᵉ région du corps de l'Armée, June 24, 1936. Mariaux lost his leg in October 1918 following a front-line injury. The medical board that reevaluated his pension in 1936 commented on his progressive vision loss. For his family history, see "Le Général Mariaux est mort," in *Le Mutilé des yeux* (June, 1944?).

[32] *Catalogue des timbres-poste de France et des colonies* (Paris, 2005) and *Le patrimoine du timbre-poste français* (Paris, 2004), 244. The post office produced 1,500,000 stamps and sold 751,000, more than any other surtaxed stamps produced that year.

[33] Pierre Henri, "Un groupement des sans-filistes aveugles: le radio-club Valentin Haüy," *Le Valentin Haüy: revue française des questions relatives aux aveugles*, April–June, 1923, 2, 41. Founded in 1888, the AVH took its name from the eighteenth-century blind educator. Pierre Villey, *Maurice de la Sizeranne: aveugle, bienfaiteur des aveugles* (Paris, 1932), 32–44.

would also facilitate blind people's entry into the *sans-filiste* community, whose members cultivated a distinctive masculine technical identity grounded in Morse code proficiency and expertise in radio construction and tuning.[34]

The AVH clearly regarded the radio club as an opportunity to showcase the intelligence, self-sufficiency, and manual dexterity of blind people.[35] At a moment when legislators and the staff of the Office National des Mutilés et Réformés de Guerre were debating how best to rehabilitate blind veterans for remunerative employment, the very existence of the club proved that blind people could work in higher-paying, modern industrial jobs, rather than the manual trades of basket-weaving or cobbling for which they often received training. That so many blind radio amateurs built their own receivers, the club boasted, only proved that "fabrication work in radio-electric plants could be undertaken by the blind."[36] This goal of generating employment for the blind paralleled the AVH's campaign to place blind musicians within the house orchestras of several Parisian radio stations. Since the 1830s, the Institut National des Jeunes Aveugles (National Institute for Young Blind People) had trained many of its students as professional musicians, but blind advocates now worried that the popularity of recorded and broadcast sound would eliminate the demand for live music, even as others saw new opportunities for blind musicians in radio.[37] Jean Pergola, the blind organist at the Saint-Germain l'Auxerrois church, became a veritable celebrity on Paris PTT after performing piano improvisations on themes telephoned in by listeners during the interval of the nightly news broadcasts, while the blind violinist Jean Nocetti could regularly be heard on air in solo and orchestral concerts.[38]

Radio for the Blind initially adopted many of the same goals as the AVH radio club, from the publication of radio construction manuals in Braille

---

[34] Charles Avron, "Les aveugles aussi s'adonnent à la T.S.F.," *Radio-Magazine*, October 25, 1923. References to the club also appear in "Pour les aveugles," *L'Antenne*, June 13, 1923. On *sans-filiste* culture see Méadel, *Histoire de la radio*, 186–87, and Haring, *Ham Radio's Technical Culture*, 37–48.

[35] "Concerts de T.S.F.," *Le Valentin Haüy*, July–September, 1924, 3, 57; October–December, 1924, 4, 89.

[36] Avron, "Les aveugles aussi s'adonnent à la T.S.F."; "Courrier des amateurs de T.S.F.," *Le Petit parisien*, March 10, 1923, 4.

[37] "Concerts de T.S.F.," *Le Valentin Haüy*, July–September, 1924, 3, 57, and October–December, 1924, 4, 89; Louis Vierne, "Rapport général sur les travaux de l'AVH pour l'année 1930," Association Valentin Haüy pour le bien des aveugles. Assemblée générale, April 28, 1929, and April 26, 1931.

[38] Duval, *Histoire de la radio en France*, 84. Pergola performed on the radio through the Second World War; "Les musiciens aveugles au poste radiophonique du Petit Parisien," *Le Petit parisien*, July 4, 1925.

to the inclusion of blind musicians in its weekly variety show. However, the charity's focus on distributing radios soon eclipsed these other activities, while the AVH radio club disappeared from public view. More important, Radio for the Blind's focus on creating blind listeners rather than stimulating independent *sans-filiste* activity informed its portrayal of disability and the rhetoric of pity it deployed to solicit funds for its coffers. Charity spokesmen, in their myriad appeals to sighted radio audiences, invited them to consider the blows to masculine virility, physical strength, and personal independence suffered by the war blind, predicating the latter's psychological and physical rehabilitation directly on their access to the airwaves. During the inaugural Radio for the Blind broadcast of 1929, General Mariaux enjoined audiences to "imagine the horrible situation of being plunged into eternal darkness ... [of] depending constantly on a guide for the scheduled activities of life."[39] Though Mariaux occasionally linked veterans' diminished physical status to their wartime sacrifices for a "glorious cause," he invoked longstanding tropes about the supposed "interiority" of the blind dating to the Enlightenment, when the *philosophes* proposed that blind people, while not lacking in intelligence, remained emotionally and morally detached from their surroundings.[40]

Echoing these misconceptions about the psychology of the blind as well as contemporary debates within radio theory, Radio for the Blind's fundraising campaigns emphasized how the invisibility and simultaneity of radio waves, their defiance of the perceived boundaries between public and private life, and broadcasting's exclusively auditory form provided even greater benefits to blind listeners than to sighted audiences. A continuous stream of broadcast sound, General Mariaux explained to the weekly radio magazine *Le Haut-parleur*, would penetrate the psychological and physical barriers separating the blind from "exterior life" while granting them access to concerts, theater performances, and live news reporting.[41]

Other charity representatives pointed to radio's virtual splitting of mind and body, or the sensation of disembodiment many people experienced while listening to radio, as especially advantageous for those with physical impairments.[42] "Think of the importance radio presents for the blind," journalist Charles Avron rhapsodized in *Radio-Magazine*, "it permits those who like music ... to listen to beautiful music without the

[39] "La radio aux aveugles," *Le Haut-parleur*, April 8, 1928.
[40] Jessica Riskin, *Science in the Age of Sensibility: The Sentimental Empiricists of the French Enlightenment* (Chicago, 2002), 20–67; Weygand, *The Blind in French Society*, 57–79.
[41] "La radio aux aveugles," *Le Haut-parleur*, April 8, 1928.
[42] Jeffrey Sconce, *Haunted Media: Electronic Presence from Telegraphy to Television* (Durham NC, 2000), 27, 65.

inconvenience of going to a recital or a concert hall ... which they cannot attend without someone to accompany them." If sighted wireless neophytes sometimes decried the unsettling impression of bodily dislocation they experienced when listening to the radio, a phenomenon the Frankfurt School theorist Theodor Adorno would later term "aural flânerie," this "armchair travel" allowed disabled listeners to defy the constraints of their infirm bodies by visiting distant locales without "the discomfort of physical displacements."[43] General Mariaux likewise acclaimed radio's "liveness" for offering comfort to "our unfortunate compatriots, plunged into the eternal night [and] deprived of the sweetness of seeing the faces of their fellow men."[44] Radio announcers of the 1920s typically addressed their audiences directly as "dear listeners" in an effort to establish an interpersonal connection with them. Listening through a headset enhanced this sensation of intimate contact, René Bruyez concluded, and "it is this individual character of radio that must make it one of the most precious elements of the blind man's patrimony."[45]

These unique features of radio together contributed to what journalists hailed as the technology's prosthetic function, whereby broadcast sound replaced the absent vision of blind veterans and substituted for the active lives they purportedly missed.[46] As the radio reporter F. Soulier-Valbert explained in *L'Antenne* in 1933, radio's "sound décor returns to [the war blind] the sensation of living and participating in the activities around them, which is a curative *par excellence*." Though deprived of the sight upon which they had long relied, through an "adaptation ... vision has become auditory for them ... and it suffices for them to hear to evoke different images based on their former memories."[47] Soulier-Valbert's description of listening replacing an absent vision reinforced the slogan adopted by Radio for the Blind – a "Ray in their Night" – and the image featured on the charity's postage stamp of a blind man reaching out to touch sound waves emanating from a distant source [Figure 2.1].

---

[43] Charles Avron, "Les aveugles aussi s'adonnent à la T.S.F." For the Adorno reference, see Serlin, "Disabling the Flâneur," 193–208.

[44] Général Mariaux, "La radio aux aveugles," *Annuaire de la radiodiffusion nationale 1933*, 188–90.

[45] Bruyez, "Un miracle qui peut en faire d'autres."

[46] Stiker, *Corps infirmes et sociétés*, 139–40. Stiker identifies an interwar "prosthetic" logic geared toward the replacement and substitution of aberrant bodies and their respective parts. For a survey of the theoretical uses of "prosthesis," see Ott, Serlin, and Mihm, eds., *Artificial Parts, Practical Lives*, 3–8; Sarah Jain, "The Prosthetic Imagination: Enabling and Disabling the Prosthesis Trope," *Science, Technology, and Human Values*, 24, 1, 1999, 31–54.

[47] F. Soulier-Valbert, "La radio pour aveugles," *L'Antenne*, May 14, 1933, 354.

Figure 2.1 Radio for the Blind postage stamp (1938). © Jules Piel/La Poste.

However, if Radio for the Blind focused on reintegrating blind people into civil society through the intermediary of the airwaves, the charity's not infrequent press coverage alongside Wireless at the Hospital ensured that its representatives frequently collapsed the blind into a larger, amorphous category of invalids. Despite postwar improvements to lighting, ventilation, and sanitation in hospitals, they remained overcrowded and inhospitable spaces, often housing in a single ward adult patients with chronic illnesses, young people with physical disabilities, and the indigent elderly. The radio charities' equation of blind veterans' condition with this broader experience of confinement suggested that successful rehabilitation required psychological rejuvenation in order to eliminate the depression produced by disability – a recurring theme in contemporary treatises about rehabilitation.[48]

The Algerian-born *chansonnier* and humorist Dominus, a frequent performer on Wireless at the Hospital broadcasts, invoked the combined benefits to mental stability and physical health that radio provided to the "sick, the crippled, the immobilized, the disinherited ... patients of hospitals [and] hospices." When "radio comes to snatch them from their boredom, their sadness, and their distaste for their pitiful asylums, is it not a marvelous thing for them?" he asked in the weekly *Le Petit radio*. The tuberculosis patients who sometimes spent years forcibly immobilized on a *chaise longue* would "no longer become worked up by their immobility," Dominus asserted, but would "live the life that comes to them through the loudspeaker," while those "whose appalling illnesses

---

[48] Axelle Brodiez-Dolino, *Combattre la pauvreté: vulnérabilités sociales et sanitaires de 1880 à nos jours* (Paris, 2013), 133–50. This mixing of ages and sexes in hospital wards and hospices became a frequent complaint among hospital reformers and disability advocates.

have cut them off from other human beings . . . will no longer be the most isolated people in the world, because the world comes to them with its voices, its sounds." Former sanatorium patients would be able to imagine just "how much music and words traveling through the hertzian waves put merry gleams into dull eyes and smiles onto clenched lips," even curing some patients' "obsession with suicide." Every citizen should be able to support this cure of broadcast sound, Dominus concluded, and he begged the public to "give a small mite to offer to the most unhappy of humankind something better than an ephemeral sensation of smell, sight, or taste – the joy of listening, constantly renewed."[49]

Dominus's appeal to the radio public exposes the multiple contradictions imbedded in the charities' strategy of reintegrating veterans into civil society through the airwaves, for how could ostensibly passive radio listening stimulate active, engaged citizens? What would distinguish disabled veterans from another prominent image circulating in the radio press – that of the female listener, seduced and mesmerized by the "warm and colorful voices" of male radio announcers?[50] René Bruyez explained this "paradox" as the product of a modern broadcast media encountering the experience of disability, writing in *T.S.F. Programme* that "the [blind] person has never been more himself than in the moment when . . . already isolated from the world," he donned a radio headset and "appears to isolate himself even more [as] the only means of coming closer to exterior life." Radio listening demanded a certain disengagement from one's surroundings, Bruyez proposed, but when coupled with the social and psychological alienation already experienced by the blind, it facilitated their inclusion into a community of listeners.[51]

General Mariaux similarly sought to divorce radio listening from associations with malingering or neurasthenia, charges that physicians sometimes leveled upon disabled veterans, by arguing that listening promoted active engagement with the world. Without precisely detailing how radio would permit blind veterans to triumph over poverty, Mariaux argued that listening reduced veterans' quotidian dependency on spouses and friends, which robbed many of the initiative to seek employment. "The blind man does not beg," he told one journalist, but "wants to work in spite of it all . . . Alas, those who work, with rare exceptions, receive only paltry wages or earn a famine salary." However, Radio for the Blind had "undertaken to help them in their task, in giving them free individual wireless sets. It will permit them, once the headset is on their heads, to escape the miseries

[49] Dominus, "La T.S.F. à l'hôpital," *Le Petit radio*, April 11, 1931.
[50] "Radiolo Don Juan," *L'Antenne*, May 9, 1923.
[51] Bruyez, "Un miracle qui peut en faire d'autres."

of daily life by listening to the broadcasts of all the large stations."[52] The promotional photograph accompanying adjacent articles on the radio charities in the 1933 *Annuaire de la radiodiffusion nationale* reproduced the ambiguities in their construction of both disability and radio listening. The photo depicted a blind man wearing a radio headset while reclining in a bed at the Parisian Quinze-Vingts Hospital for the blind. With a blanket pulled up to cover his hands (or possibly his stumps) and dark glasses shielding his eyes, he appeared completely dispassionate or sedated, displaying no evidence of mental activity [Figure 2.2].

Moreover, even as Radio for the Blind and Wireless at the Hospital portrayed radio listening as critical to disabled veterans' participation in civil society, the charities' broadcasts did little to facilitate their social integration. Between 1928 and 1940, the charities' variety shows aired on the state PTT network on Wednesdays and Saturdays from 2 to 3:30 p.m. This placement corresponded perfectly with hospital schedules, according to the radio critic Paul Roux, where the "long" afternoon hours remained empty after patients' morning therapies.[53] The variety shows often shared casts and consistently featured short, lighthearted skits by the Fernand Cazes dramatic troupe interposed between instrumental music and performances by the sopranos Adrienne Gallon and Suzy Solidor, the Montmartre cabaret stars Dominus and René Devilliers, and the clown René-Paul Groffe, the latter primarily known to radio audiences for his children's programs.[54] In a 1932 survey conducted by *Le Petit radio*, the magazine published by the Fédération Nationale de la Radiodiffusion, which represented the interests of public radio, listeners ranked the Groffe and Cazes troupes among their favorite radio acts.[55] However, the programs were clearly designed for listeners with short attention spans, and rarely included informational talks, otherwise a staple of state broadcasting. These programming choices, made by the charities' staffs, bureaucrats in the state radio administration, and the advisory board of Paris PTT,[56] echoed the conclusions aired in the radio

---

[52] Mariaux, "La radio aux aveugles," 188–90. For a similar statement, see "Pour les aveugles," *Le Petit radio*, September 29, 1934, 6.
[53] Paul Roux, "La T.S.F. à l'hôpital," *Le Petit radio*, March 22, 1930.
[54] Dominus, "La T.S.F. à l'hôpital," *Le Petit radio*, April 22, 1931; "La Troupe Cazes," *Le Petit radio*, November 12, 1932. The two variety shows counted among the more expensive shows of the Paris PTT, although the performers earned smaller salaries for performing in the afternoons. See CARAN F60-573. Memos from the conseil de gérance de Paris PTT, November 1938 and April 1939.
[55] Brochand, *Histoire générale de la radio*, 1: 466.
[56] CAC 19870714-2. Projet de procès-verbal de la séance du conseil de gérance de Paris PTT, March 18, 1938. Memos from the Paris PTT conseil de gérance, November 1938 and April 1939. Paris PTT spent approximately 17,000 francs monthly on *T.S.F. à l'hôpital* and *Radio aux aveugles*.

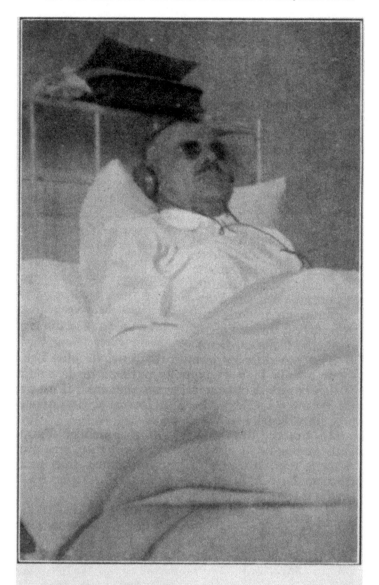

A L'HOPITAL DES QUINZE-VINGTS. — UN AVEUGLE A L'ÉCOUTE.

Figure 2.2 Blind hospital patient listening to the radio, *Annuaire de la radiodiffusion nationale* (1933). Image courtesy of the Bibliothèque Nationale de France.

press by cultural critics and audiences alike, that programs for the infirm should be morally uplifting and contain no news bulletins or "serious" content, but only "sound waves of well-chosen harmonies."[57] By the early 1930s, as we have already seen, the spread of radios, phonographs, and other electro-acoustical technologies stimulated a new interest among physicians and social hygienists in the effects of broadcast sound on the human body. In the literary journal *La Revue de France*, the poet Lucie Guillet now proposed that poems recited over the airwaves could provide a panacea for depression by exerting "powerful suggestions through their rhythms" to instill "serenity, hope, resignation, gaiety, strength, and courage," depending on a particular patient's psychological profile.[58] The pseudo-medical Institut Coué, dedicated to psychotherapeutic self-help via "autosuggestion," translated these ideas into practice through its widely advertised 78-rpm records featuring repetitions of its pharmacist founder's famous mantra: "Every day, in every way, I am getting better and better."[59] Some critics dismissed these sound cures as unscientific bunk, but since the pioneering research of Jean-Marie Charcot in the 1860s, French neuropsychiatry had dictated that powerful suggestions could ameliorate a wide variety of symptoms associated with "hysteria," claims reinforced by army physicians' research with shell-shocked soldiers.[60] The trade magazine *L'Edition musicale vivante* reported in May 1931 that the celebrity psychiatrist Edouard Toulouse was employing "sound treatments" as a form of "psycho-medical" therapy for mental illness at the Maison Blanche asylum, one of France's first outpatient psychiatric clinics. However, given Toulouse's contributions to the contemporary noise abatement campaigns that proclaimed the capital's burgeoning soundscape to be dangerous to public health, one wonders how reliable he found such treatments.

Despite *Mon programme*'s claims that the French medical establishment universally recognized wireless as a "remarkable means of healing nerves," Dr. Louis Mourier, the director of public assistance for the city of Paris, worried that excessive exposure to radio static would alarm patients with mental illnesses. Mourier believed the phonograph to be the more appropriate technology for use in the capital's hospitals, not only because records provided better fidelity of sound reproduction, but also because

---

[57] Germaine Blondin, "En pensant aux malades," *Radio-Magazine*, March 26, 1933; "L'Intermède," *Choisir la radio, le cinéma ...*, July 13, 1937; Henry de Forge, "La poésie et la musique: moyens nouveaux pour guérir!" *Mon programme*, March 13, 1936.
[58] Lucie Guillet, "Psychothérapie. L'alliance poético-médicale," *La Revue de France*, September 1934, 184–89.
[59] "Le phonographe guérisseur," *Machines parlantes et radio*, October 15, 1933.
[60] Thomas, *Treating the Trauma of the Great War*, 33–43.

physicians could stop and start a phonograph and control its speed.[61] Careful to avoid taking a firm position in this debate over the merits of sound cures, *Le Petit radio* told its readers that the rehabilitation of sanatorium patients relied on cultivating a balance between activity and sedation. The Parisian "chapter of Wireless at the Hospital has received numerous proofs" of the radio programs' efficacy in that domain, Paul Roux asserted, for "tubercular patients must maintain the most rigorous rest but nevertheless be overfed, and listening to the radio assures patients' immobility while not leaving them lifeless."[62]

This last account of Wireless at the Hospital exposes the complex – if at times contradictory – politics undergirding the charities' distribution of radio receivers, for inasmuch as they promised to reintegrate veterans into civil society through the airwaves, they also hoped to keep those same men contented with their fates. Piping cheerful music into hospitals partly served to pacify unruly patients while securing the integrity of the social body by keeping contagious invalids from circulating freely. Relegating men with facial disfigurements to sanatoria or to their homes also masked everyday reminders of the horrors of war, while diverting veterans from dwelling on their injuries or from making demands for additional services upon the scarce resources of the state.[63]

The charities' staffs saw themselves as advocates for disabled veterans and the chronically ill, but the rhetoric of their fundraising campaigns told a very different story. Dominus repeatedly highlighted Wireless at the Hospital's goal of distracting discontented invalids from their poverty, physical pain, and emotional isolation. "We know the sadness … [and] the moral desolation of hospital boarders, the dull and painful hours that weigh on the guests," he wrote. "Suffering only aggravates the boredom that emanates from despair." Yet the "facility of listening [and] diversity of programs brings a healthy distraction; cheerfulness is sometimes a powerful curative."[64] This dual goal of distracting invalids while reforming their "negative" attitudes surfaced in a 1928 Radio for the Blind broadcast featuring a "theatrical piece written especially for the blind" entitled "The Blind Soul." One reviewer described the play, set in a "rest home for the blind," as a "lesson of profound philosophy" in which an elderly worker blinded in an industrial accident taught a younger blind

---

[61] Henry de Forge, "La poésie et la musique: nouveaux moyens de guérir!" *Mon programme*, March 13, 1936, 6; Paul Allard, "Le disque à l'hôpital, à l'école, et à l'étranger," *L'Edition musicale vivante*, May 1931, 9.

[62] Paul Roux, "La T.S.F. à l'hôpital," *Le Petit radio*, March 22, 1930.

[63] Millington, *From Victory to Vichy*, 36–37, 43; Prost, *In the Wake of War*, 94.

[64] "La T.S.F. à l'hôpital en Algérie," *Le Petit radio*, April 2, 1932. On the goal of distracting veterans and the infirm, see Paul Dermée, "Il faut que les malades, les aveugles, et les vieillards indigents puissent écouter la Radio," *Comoedia*, September 14, 1936.

veteran to cope with the "moral suffering" of disability.[65] Precisely how blind listeners responded to this "uplifting" drama or to "humorous musical sketches" with titles such as "Pierrot's Suicide" or "Let's Commit Suicide" performed live during Radio for the Blind shows of 1931 and 1933 is more difficult to discern.[66]

The blind radio amateur Paul Rémy, however, immediately perceived contradictions between the charities' claims to promote social integration and their disabling rhetoric. He believed the charities offered blind people only proxy citizenship through the airwaves by encouraging passive listening, while still denying them the benefits of full participation in civil society, a conviction informed by his personal history. Blinded at eighteen by a laboratory explosion in his chemistry class at the Ecole Lavoisier, Rémy abandoned his engineering studies but maintained an interest in technology. After learning Braille, he patented a Braille writing tablet and began lobbying in the Chamber of Deputies for a number of special privileges to be granted to the blind – from reduced postage on Braille correspondence to free travel for blind people and their sighted guides on public transit. In 1904, he founded a Union of Blind Workers with the support of the AVH, and during the war, managed several rehabilitation schools that trained blind veterans in massage therapy.

During the 1920s, Rémy became active in several Parisian radio amateur clubs and clearly enjoyed tinkering with his radio receiver to pick up distant stations from across Europe, an experience that solidified his political commitments to pacifism and socialism. As an officer of the Radio-Club Espérantiste de France, he promoted the international language by teaching correspondence courses to fellow radio amateurs and organized a letter-writing campaign to convince French stations to introduce "Esperanto hours" into their daily schedules. More important, Rémy believed that broadcasting's auditory form made it the perfect medium through which to provide practical information about employment, education, and support networks to blind people that would enhance their participation in national life.[67] In May of 1927 Rémy drafted an elaborate proposal for a "Radio-Newspaper for the Blind" that he hoped would "create a sense of

[65] "A l'écoute," *Le Haut-parleur,* April 15, 1928. Reviews of the Radio for the Blind broadcast on April 1, 1928. See a similar review of the play in *Le Valentin Haüy,* January–March, 1928, 2, 41–42.

[66] Program listings in *L'Ouest-Éclair,* April 15, 1931, 13, and *Le Haut-parleur,* January 4, 1933. No transcripts for these plays are available.

[67] CARAN 94AP 396. Manuscript, "Biographie de Paul Rémy, 1879–1948." Rémy believed that blind people, once liberated from their reliance on national languages, would be able to participate in an international blind community.

community and common sort among the blind," inform "blind people about technologies that could benefit them," and educate sighted people about the experience of blindness. He envisioned a permanent staff of five to six to prepare broadcasts, write press releases, and cultivate relationships with regional radio stations and newspapers.[68] To obtain time on the air, he solicited the support of veterans' associations and the leaders of Radio for the Blind, but without much success.

Some of Rémy's closest friends even questioned his agenda. The blind veteran Eugène Guilbot, the former president of the AVH's radio club, believed that specialized programming for the blind undermined the universality of radio listening, and the charities' broadcasts at least claimed to address a heterogeneous national audience. "I don't know if all blind people are like me," Guilbot wrote to Rémy, "but if a quarter hour *for the blind* were announced, I would look for another program. I desire, in my position as a blind person, to live as much as possible like sighted people, and I am happy to listen to news and broadcasts designed for everyone."[69] Rémy's friend Dr. Pierre Corret, a fellow Esperantist and the president of the Société des Amis de T.S.F., concurred with Guilbot.[70] Corret believed the radio charities' broadcasts to be useless for invalids and the blind, even if they succeeded in raising money for radio donations. "I have never understood what the [programs] done in the name of Radio for the Blind or Wireless at the Hospital have of special interest for blind and hospitalized people," Corret wrote to Rémy in October of 1931, and "being myself in treatment for the past two and a half years at the Saint-Louis Hospital, it is principally the *ordinary* broadcasts of Radio-Paris, PTT, Petit Parisien, etc. that I listen to with a simple crystal receiver that I *built specially for myself*. If I was blind, I am convinced I would do the same, and that I would not listen specifically to programs with the label *Radio for the Blind.*"

By constructing his own receiver, Corret argued, he displayed his independence and able-bodiedness by navigating the airwaves on his own terms, rather than remaining part of a circumscribed public of sick people. For these reasons, he told Rémy, "I think it *without interest* to transmit by a powerful station the current broadcasts, *said to be* for the blind. They must certainly want to listen to *ordinary* broadcasts, and that corresponds well ... with their general desire to live as much as possible

[68] CARAN 94AP 397. Paul Rémy, "Project pour le Radio-Journal des Aveugles" (handwritten note), May 4, 1927.
[69] *Ibid.* Letter from Eugène Guilbot to Paul Rémy, January 23, 1926. Guilbot's emphasis.
[70] Pierre Corret, "L'hôpitodyne et quelques bavardages à son sujet," *L'Almanach de la T.S. F. pour tous* (Paris, 1932), 137–43, 187–92. Corret published his own design for a "hospital radio."

the *life of everyone.*[71] Radio permitted blind people's inclusion into the emerging national radio audience, Guilbot and Corret determined, but specialized programming only marked them as "disabled" listeners rather than able-bodied, "normal" citizens, reproducing in the airwaves the very social exclusion the charities claimed to eliminate through their distribution of radio receivers. Even General Mariaux rejected Rémy's attempts to have his "radio-newspaper for the blind" included in the Radio for the Blind broadcasts, and given the charity's claims to be a "neutral organization," he likely disapproved of Rémy's vocal socialist sympathies.[72]

After several rejections, Rémy turned for assistance to his friend Albert Thomas, a socialist politician and former minister of munitions. In 1920, Thomas became the head of the International Labor Office (ILO), a transnational agency attached to the League of Nations and charged with investigating global labor conditions. The ILO took a particular interest in the fate of Europe's disabled veterans, sponsoring a series of international conferences that showcased the latest developments in prostheses and orthopedic surgery.[73] Thomas agreed to sponsor two talks by Rémy on the Eiffel Tower station in 1932–1933 that examined the work of blind laborers as personal masseurs and assembly-line technicians in a Ford automobile plant and a Thompson-Houston radio-electric factory. In his first talk, Rémy expressed his hope that broadcasting would "bring out of their sad isolation a considerable number of people who do not know how to reach the rare ... revues published by blind charities." He also emphasized blind people's technical aptitudes and their rapid adaptation to new environments, and thus implicitly, their potential for successful careers.[74] These subtle critiques of the Radio for the Blind broadcasts may ultimately have persuaded the state

[71] CARAN 94AP 398. Letter from Dr. Pierre Corret to Paul Rémy, October 28, 1931. Corret's emphasis.
[72] CARAN 94AP 397. Letters from Henri Favrel to Paul Rémy, October 22, 1934, and July 8, 1935. For the organization's declaration of political neutrality, see "La radio aux aveugles," *T.S.F. Tribune*, April 12, 1936, 5.
[73] Cabanes, *The Great War and the Origins of Humanitarianism*, 50–62. These conferences were boycotted by some left-wing veterans' groups distrustful of the Treaty of Versailles as well as by right-wing nationalist veterans' groups unwilling to cooperate with former enemy nations. CARAN 94AP 397. Letter from Albert Thomas to Paul Rémy, December 22, 1931; Letters from Dr. Pierre Corret to Paul Rémy, November 8, 1931, and November 20, 1931. Corret cautioned Rémy that his Eiffel Tower broadcasts should not "kindle any idea of rivalry with the current artistic broadcasts of *Radio for the Blind.*"
[74] CARAN 94AP 396. The first two talks appeared in print as *Une oeuvre de justice sociale à accomplir: le retour des travailleurs infirmes à la vie normale. L'emploi des travailleurs aveugles – première série de communications radiophoniques faites sous les auspices du Bureau International du Travail par Paul Rémy, secrétaire du comité technique et parlementaire pour les aveugles.* Collection of the Bibliothèque Valentin Haüy. Review in Soulier-Valbert "La radio pour aveugles," 354.

broadcasting administration to amend the programs' content and style. In 1935, the postal minister Georges Mandel instructed Paris PTT to make a more concerted effort to employ blind musicians, and program descriptions from the mid-1930s reference several talks by physicians and lawyers on "subjects of interest to the blind."[75]

In the short term, however, disagreements persisted among blind advocates about how broadcasting might best facilitate the social integration of blind people. Pierre Corret wondered if Rémy's time could be better spent reinforcing the radio charities' distribution drives rather than organizing radio programs for and about the blind. "Listening to the radio is more precious for the blind than for other people," he wrote to Rémy, and "they can profit from it more than others, as visual entertainments are forbidden to them." However, there was no need to create special broadcasts exclusively for the blind. As Corret argued, "I often happen to listen to *Radio for the Blind*, precisely because I have recommended to readers to construct a radio like my own in order to ... donate it to Wireless at the Hospital, and I thus had the intention of attracting people to *Radio for the Blind* for the same reason." But "I never heard anything special that could merit a wide broadcast. They are broadcasts completely similar to others."[76] The integration of blind and disabled listeners in national life relied upon access to a radio receiver, and "in my opinion, all blind-friendly radio activity should be taken in this direction." Disability advocates' most critical task, Corret concluded, "was to procure for the blind the means of listening to the same broadcasts as everyone else," and equipping blind veterans and civilians with radios remained a question of fundraising and distribution.[77]

Citizenship through the airwaves: disabled veterans and the radio tax

If Radio for the Blind and Wireless at the Hospital first politicized veterans' access to broadcasting by claiming that radio listening could advance the psychological and physical rehabilitation of veterans and reintegrate them into civil society through the airwaves, the subsequent parliamentary

[75] *Le Haut-parleur*, January 9, 1935, 2. A 1936 article identified the goals of Radio for the Blind as producing work for blind musicians, editing a Braille radio revue, maintaining a "laboratory" for the construction of radio receivers, and conducting "propaganda for blind workers." See A.P., "La radio aux aveugles," *T.S.F. Tribune*, December 4, 1936, 5. Program listings show a series of "talks for the blind" hosted by a Dr. Baconnet and the lawyer Louis Lespine. See listings for *Radio aux aveugles* in *Mon programme* for August 12, 1936; September 30, 1936; November 25, 1936; December 2, 1936.
[76] CARAN 94AP 396. Letter from Dr. Pierre Corret to Paul Rémy, October 31, 1931.
[77] CARAN 94AP 398. Letter from Pierre Corret to Paul Rémy, October 28, 1931.

debates about exempting listeners with disabilities from a proposed radio license fee (*redevance*) further tied radio listening to the dilemma of veterans' citizenship and France's successful postwar recovery. The *redevance*, which would impose an annual tariff ranging from fifteen francs for home-built receivers to fifty francs for more powerful, multi-lamp radios, signaled legislators' growing recognition of broadcasting as a public service for which all citizens should contribute. Opponents of the license fee, who included the French Communist Party and commercial broadcasters, countered that it would discriminate against working-class audiences and ultimately slow the democratization of radio. As Cécile Méadel has shown, the license fee, together with an affiliated tax on radio lamps, became a significant factor in determining audiences' access to radio, even figuring into consumers' budgets when they selected a model for purchase. However, the PTT would only agree to exempt hospitals, public schools, and other "public assistance" establishments from the fee, arguing that its proceeds would fund the programs audiences enjoyed, thus ensuring a vigorous debate about any further exemptions.[78]

These legislative efforts to expand the state's control over radio broadcasting coincided with another series of parliamentary debates about the structure of France's postwar welfare state and the pensions, family allowances, and medical benefits to be allotted to the population. Under pressure from pronatalists and social hygienists, lawmakers in April of 1928 voted in France's most comprehensive social welfare legislation to date, which provided limited insurance coverage for illness, disability, maternity, and old age to all citizens.[79] Debates about the health insurance scheme gave veterans' associations the opportunity to press for increases to their pensions, which seemed to lose their value daily through inflation. Disability advocates exploited these concurrent debates to demand the exemption of blind people and deaf veterans from the license fee. If, as the charities' campaigns suggested, the airwaves had become a virtual extension of civil society, disabled veterans now argued that access to radio constituted a social right of citizenship equivalent to a pension that should be guaranteed by the state. In an era of rising unemployment and economic hardship, the exemption of disabled veterans would confirm the state's commitment to providing for those who had

---

[78] Méadel, *Histoire de la radio*, 39–41. After the passage of the finance law of May 31, 1933, the license fee provided a consistent source of income for public broadcasting. The tax on lamps weighed more heavily on consumers with expensive, multi-lamp radios or those who listened for longer periods of time and needed to regularly replace their lamps. Brochand, *Histoire générale de la radio*, 1: 476–82.

[79] Smith, *Creating the Welfare State*, 125–38, and Susan Pedersen, *Family, Dependence, and the Origins of the Welfare State: Britain and France, 1914–1945* (Cambridge, 1993), 357–409.

suffered for the nation. Yet far from rallying disabled veterans behind a common cause, the campaign for exemptions from the license fee instead unleashed fierce competition between different veterans' groups for recognition of their wartime injuries.

Paul Rémy's political connections proved especially useful to him when he began campaigning to have blind people exempted from the *redevance*, at the very moment when lawmakers began working in committee to draft the finance law. In January of 1927, he wrote to his friend André Fribourg, a radical deputy from the Ain, to demand the exemption of blind people in the initial drafts of the law.[80] In his letter, Rémy situated radio among a series of existing state concessions to assist blind people, from free postage on Braille correspondence to free travel for the blind and their companions on public transit. However, Fribourg cautioned Rémy that PTT bureaucrats, as well as his fellow legislators, would resist the exemption on the grounds that multiple family members, rather than a single blind person, frequently used the same radio receiver. For the exemption to even be introduced for debate in the Chamber, Fribourg suggested, Rémy and other blind advocates would need to demonstrate that radios were not merely a source of domestic entertainment, but that they had become vital to the everyday existence of the blind.[81]

Rémy then approached Maurice Privat, the director of the state-run Eiffel Tower station, to defend the exemption for blind people during his evening news program, the *Journal parlé*, "where the large public that listens to the Tower would certainly respond to your call." Given that France "always liked the blind and offered them sympathy," Rémy wrote, "why has it not yet been thought of to give them a wireless receiver? With it they would have familiar companions, they would learn ... they would cultivate their minds ... to endow [the blind] with radio receivers, which would be so precious to them, would be a veritable window opened to intelligence."[82] Impressed by Rémy's eloquence, Privat published the letter together with his own appeal to radio listeners in the station's weekly newspaper *La Libre parole T.S.F.*, echoing the radio charities' prosthetic

---

[80] CARAN 94P397. Letter from Paul Rémy to Maurice Privat, January 3, 1927. Rémy served as secretary of the Comité technique et parlementaire pour les aveugles, which he founded with Albert Thomas in 1919 to promote blind-friendly legislation. After Thomas moved to Geneva to work for the International Labor Office, the deputy André Fribourg led the committee.
[81] CARAN 94AP396. Letters from André Fribourg to Paul Rémy, August 5, 1926, and January 13, 1927. Attached letter from the minister of public works to the deputy, Jean Loquin, May 3, 1930.
[82] *Ibid.*, Letter from Paul Rémy to Maurice Privat, January 3, 1927. Reprinted in *La Libre parole T.S.F.*, January 8, 1927. Privat's emphasis. *La Libre parole T.S.F.* took the name *Mon programme* in 1934.

logic by urging audiences to consider "why it has not yet been thought of to give [the blind] a radio receiver ... For them, *wireless is practically light.*" Calling for audiences to support an "indispensable" national radio drive, Privat argued that "every blind person in France must be able to listen comfortably at home to the voices of the entire world."[83]

Blind advocacy groups and veterans' associations rallied behind Rémy's campaign, rejecting the rhetoric of pity deployed by the radio charities by linking the radio tax exemptions directly to veterans' wartime sacrifices and to their future participation in national life. The members of the AVH organized a letter-writing campaign to legislators defending radio ownership as vital to securing the citizenship of the blind. In "Germany, where the tax is 24 marks per year ... 144 francs of our money," *Le Valentin Haüy* reported, "blind people were exempted from the very beginning. In England, where they were first subject to a common tax of ten shillings, a law ... has just exonerated them."[84] Although the Union des Aveugles de Guerre (Union of the War Blind) had already committed significant financial resources to the development of a phonograph-based "talking book," the group's leaders pressed its members to support the exemption campaign. To avoid offending the diverse political sympathies of its' broad constituency, the Union's *Bulletin* appealed to readers' patriotic and republican sensibilities by emphasizing how radios would help them fulfill their civic responsibilities, describing recent fundraising drives overseas that provided free radios "so that their War Blind can recover a little liberty."[85] In a letter to the radio magazine *L'Antenne*, the blind veteran Octave Champonnier even demanded that the state furnish all blind veterans with free radios. "We must, as much as possible, live the existence of those who have the invaluable happiness of seeing," Champonnier argued, and "for that, we should all be given a radio receiver."[86] For Champonnier, radio sound directly replaced the eyesight he lost in service to France and facilitated his personal independence and participation in civil society, and the state should guarantee his right to listen by providing him with a radio receiver. These arguments clearly succeeded, for when the first published drafts of the radio license fee appeared in committee in 1931, they included exemptions for both blind veterans and civilians.

---

[83] CARAN 94AP 397. M.P., "C'est presque la lumière," *La Libre parole T.S.F.* (January 1, 1927?).
[84] No author, "La T.S.F. aux aveugles," *Le Valentin Haüy*, January–March, 1927.
[85] H.A., "En Angleterre," *Bulletin de l'Union des Aveugles de Guerre*, January 1933, 15. See *Le Valentin Haüy*, April–June, 1933, 44. Asa Briggs, *The History of Broadcasting in the United Kingdom, Vol. 2: The Golden Age of Wireless* (Oxford, 1965), 205, 235. The BBC produced Braille manuals for its adult education programs.
[86] Champonnier cited in Soulier-Valbert, "La radio pour aveugles," 354.

However, when a group of deaf and hard-of-hearing veterans – represented by the Bordeaux dentist Robert Morche, the president of the
Fédération des Mutilés d'Oreille (Federation of the War Deaf) – began
to demand their own exemption from the license fee later that year, they
did not receive the same friendly reception. Morche's association
assembled men rendered completely deaf by wartime injuries with those
who experienced varying degrees of hearing loss resulting from shell
shock, head wounds, and illnesses such as typhoid or meningitis contracted during military service. If broadcast sound could substitute for the
lost vision of the war blind as the radio charities proposed, Morche now
argued that radios could serve as hearing aids (auditory prostheses) to
literally replace the damaged ears of the war deaf. In contrast to the blind
advocates who embraced radio technology for allowing them to defy the
label of "disabled," Robert Morche viewed the parliamentary discussions
over the impending radio tax as the opportune moment to legitimize
deafness, and particularly hearing loss resulting from the war, as a disability requiring physical and vocational rehabilitation, increased pensions, and the provision of hearing aids.[87] Although revisions to the
pension scale in 1928 had increased the amounts awarded to the "war
deaf," Morche charged that the sums deaf men received remained paltry
compared to those granted for more visible injuries, such as blindness or
amputation.[88] Approximately 16,000 ex-servicemen received pensions
for hearing loss, but an additional 100,000 "half-deaf" veterans suffered
from hearing disorders not recognized by the state, simply because they
could not "prove that their otitis, half-deafness, or hearing difficulty was
really contracted or aggravated during the war or as a result of wounds or
illnesses" contracted during the six-month period surrounding their service. Morche counted himself among this latter group, having experienced partial hearing loss before shell explosions and the 1918 influenza
epidemic destroyed his residual hearing.[89]

---

[87] Matthew Price, "Bodies and Souls: The Rehabilitation of Maimed Soldiers in France and
Germany during the First World War" (PhD diss., Stanford University, 1998), 63–76.
[88] Soldiers automatically received a pension for any injury resulting in amputation or
blindness. Amputees received an 80 percent pension. Vision loss in a single eye (without
any corresponding "facial deformity") resulted in a 65 percent compensation. Pensions
awarded for hearing loss ranged from 508 francs for a 10 percent hearing loss to 5,000
francs for "total deafness," with supplements for persistent earaches, vertigo, and ringing
or buzzing noises in the ear. See Charles Louis Valentino, *Militaires blessés et infirmes.
Réformes, gratifications, et pensions* (Saintes, 1916), 25–27; Jean Souquet, *Code des anciens
combattants et des victimes de la guerre* (Paris, 1932), 45, 88; A. Bonain, *L'oreille et ses
maladies. L'audition et ses troubles. Les organes de l'équilibre* (Paris, 1933), 261–65.
[89] Morche, *Guide du mutilé de l'oreille*, 114, 118, 128–31. Veterans could obtain one hearing
aid and one free battery per month from their regional Centre d'Appareillage, but only for
those receiving 40–60 percent on the pension scale.

Morche's medical background undoubtedly influenced the campaign he launched in favor of the "war deaf," whom he defined in opposition to France's civilian deaf population, as evidenced by his careful choice of the terms *mutilé d'oreille* ("war deaf") and *sourd* (deaf) to reference the members of his Federation. Hearing people frequently identified congenitally or early deafened people by their use of French sign language and classified them as *sourds-muets* (deaf-mutes) – a label that privileged hearing and speaking as the defining features of bodily "normality" and marked deaf people, even while not mute, as cognitively impaired.[90] Although Western deaf education began in eighteenth-century Paris, where the Abbé de l'Epée developed a sign language pedagogy to teach deaf students to communicate in their "natural" language, deaf people struggled to gain acceptance among a hearing majority during the nineteenth century. French sign language flourished for several decades in religious and secular deaf schools and in Parisian and provincial deaf civic associations, but progressively came under assault from physicians who defined deafness as a physical pathology demanding a medical cure.

By the 1880s, a majority of educators and physicians embraced oralism, or teaching the deaf to speak, as the only legitimate deaf pedagogy. The educational reforms of the early Third Republic, which sought to impose French over regional languages, reinforced oralists' efforts to formally abolish sign language in deaf schools. Deaf advocates who considered themselves a cultural minority of non-French speakers subsequently risked marginalization as recalcitrant protestors who deliberately defied the norms of hearing society by refusing to relinquish their use of sign language, in turn threatening the republican project of cultural and linguistic assimilation.[91] By the start of the First World War, a medicalized view of deaf people as sick, neurasthenic, or mentally ill predominated in France. Morche consequently sought to distance the *mutilé d'oreille* from negative stereotypes of the *sourd-muet*, particularly as veterans deafened later in life sustained fewer alterations in speech patterns and showed little interest in learning sign language. The "war deaf," Morche argued, not only *wanted* to hear and speak, but *could* hear with proper medical treatment and prostheses, an outcome hindered only by contemporaries' conviction that hearing loss affected work and everyday life less than the loss of vision or a limb. This hierarchy of disability was

[90] See Jan Branson and Don Miller, *Damned for Their Difference: The Cultural Construction of Deaf People as Disabled* (Washington DC, 2002), 20–25.
[91] Nicholas Mirzoeff, *Silent Poetry: Deafness, Sign, and Visual Culture in Modern France* (Princeton NJ, 1995), and Anne T. Quartararo, *Deaf Identity and Social Images in Nineteenth-Century France* (Washington DC: Gallaudet University Press, 2008), 139–92.

inscribed in the state's pension codes and contributed to legislators' disregard of deaf veterans' demands.[92]

Members of the Federation of the War Deaf consequently adopted the tenuous political strategy of claiming recognition of their war-induced disability by demanding tax-free radios in order to use those same devices to pass, if only partly, as non-disabled, hearing citizens. As Morche's friend Commander Jourdy confirmed in *La Revue de l'ouïe*, the bulletin of the Federation of the War Deaf, "today [a] deaf person in France [is] in the situation where a cripple was twenty years ago, who had to take on life with a coarse wooden leg . . . in a society that appeared scornful or hostile to amputees . . . no one imagined that we could methodically search for a profession compatible with this or that mutation." Modern science had produced reliable hearing aids that permitted hearing loss to become a temporary impairment, rather than a permanent disability. Yet these "eyeglasses for the deaf," as Jourdy called them, remained unavailable to many veterans. By failing to provide the "war deaf" with rehabilitation equivalent to that offered to the war blind or to those "who learned to use an amputated or deformed member," the state treated deaf veterans as second-class citizens.[93] The physician Foveau de Courmelles, the president of the amateur-based Confédération Nationale des Radio Clubs, concurred with Jourdy that "the *blind person* is privileged over the deaf. His infirmity is seen: it is sympathetic."[94] The problem facing deaf veterans, he claimed, was that symptoms of hearing loss remained largely invisible except to the most discerning eye, whereas contemporaries could easily identify blindness as a common wartime injury. Obtaining an exemption for deaf veterans from the radio license fee would consequently render their invisible hearing disorders visible to the state.

Morche's repeated failures to obtain the radio tax exemption through letter-writing campaigns in 1929 and 1931 are striking given the tenor of the debates that unfolded in the Chamber of Deputies in 1933 over the first written drafts of the license fee legislation. When the law was introduced for discussion, two blind deputies from the Seine region, Georges Scapini and Albert Nast, intervened to draw their colleagues' attention to the fate of blind radio listeners. Scapini, the president of the Union des Aveugles de Guerre, who later that year published his own

[92] Price, "Bodies and Souls," 42–44. Rehabilitation for hearing loss was not a priority for the Army's Service de Santé.
[93] Commander Jourdy, "Opinions," *La Revue de l'ouïe*, July 1928, 5–7.
[94] Dr. Foveau de Courmelles, "Les cruautés inconscientes," *La Revue de l'ouïe*, July 1936, 21. For background on Foveau de Courmelles, see "Enquête chez les auditeurs: Le docteur Foveau de Cormelles," *L'Antenne*, September 14, 1930, 484.

memoir of wartime disability, *L'apprentissage de la nuit*, initially sought the exemption for veterans like himself who had lost their eyesight in the trenches. However, Albert Nast, a physician whose personal experience of progressive vision loss followed by complete blindness had exempted him from front-line service, requested that a more inclusive definition of "blind" be cited in the exemption clause.[95] "It is well understood," Nast told his fellow deputies, "that the blind themselves do not make any distinction between blind civilians and veterans, and you want to exonerate all those who do not see." Moreover, "you know the word 'blind' has two meanings ... that which you find in the dictionary: 'no longer has a sensation of light.'" Yet the term blind also "includes those 'partially sighted' people ... who need a guide, and yet who have the sensation of light, see the sun, and even perceive objects in a chaotic fashion." Many of these people "could no longer read after illnesses that attacked the retina, the cornea, or other eye tissues, and they too must be exonerated," Nast argued, invoking the definition of blindness (or 20 percent of "normal" vision) endorsed by several blind advocacy groups. He appealed to the Chamber to "give this relief to all those unfortunates whose fate is so sad" and to those for whom "too often in the shadows, there is a single sun: a soul that knew how to struggle ... and who finds in the charm of exterior things ... a sufficient reason for continuing to live." Nast's speech drew unanimous applause from the deputies present and a cordial response from the postal minister Laurent-Eynac, who promised to enforce "the most liberal interpretation of the law possible."[96]

In contrast, Morche obtained little support from the legislators he lobbied, such as the right-leaning republican Edouard Soulier, who privately promised to support the exemption but judged it inopportune to intervene publicly in parliament.[97] Albert Nast also spoke up for the "war deaf," but in the end Morche only obtained his exemption through the intervention of the senator Georges Portmann, a renowned

---

[95] *La Revue de l'ouïe*, April 1931, 29, and May 1931, 18. Jean Jolly, *Dictionnaire des parlementaires français. Notices biographiques sur les ministres, députés, et sénateurs français de 1889 à 1940* (Paris, 1960), 7: 2554–55. Nast served in the auxiliary medical corps during the war. He lost his remaining vision in 1931, the same year as his election to the Chamber. Scapini was blinded in 1915. Back from the front, he learned Braille and studied law before running for office in 1921. Both men participated in the parliamentary Groupe des indépendants in the Chamber, though Scapini moved toward the far right, later serving as the ambassador to Berlin under the Vichy regime.

[96] *Journal officiel de la République Française. Débats-Chambre des Députés*, 1ᵉʳ séance, April 13, 1933. My emphasis.

[97] Letter from Edouard Soulier to Robert Morche cited in "La taxe de T.S.F. et les sourds de guerre. Une intervention du Sénateur Portmann. Exemption des mutilés d'oreille," *La Revue de l'ouïe*, July 1933, 6.

otolaryngologist and the dean of medicine at the University of Bordeaux.[98] When the Senate moved to vote on the law, Portmann introduced a revision designed to "repair a great injustice" in the exemption clause by adding the words "veterans with wounds to the ear." To neglect the "war deaf" would be a grave mistake, Portmann charged, because "wireless devices serve a double purpose for those with defective ears: first as amplifying devices to hear better and also as therapeutic devices to rehabilitate their hearing." From this perspective, it "would thus be illogical for the state, which cares for its war wounded free of charge, to levy a tax on devices that are therapeutic agents of the first order."[99] Portmann's amendment passed through the Senate with little debate, although the final exemption included only deaf veterans and no civilian deaf. The exemption signaled senators' recognition of Portmann's medical authority, but the inclusion of the "severely disabled" (disabled veterans or civilians with vocational disabilities receiving 100 percent on the pension scale and classified as *grands mutilés*) and all blind individuals (whether veterans and civilians) exposed legislators' doubts about the legitimacy of Morche's demands. While many senators could imagine how broadcast sound might benefit blind people or paraplegics, few understood the utility of radio technology for deaf people. However, by presenting radio as both an auditory prosthesis and as a medically authorized "therapeutic device" that could potentially cure deafness, Portmann situated the deaf veterans' demands firmly within the politics of national recovery. As a result, senators could scarcely deny the exemption to the war deaf, whether in acknowledgment of their wartime sacrifices or their rights to a full physical recovery.

Still, considerable skepticism about the exemptions persisted among some legislators and PTT bureaucrats. In the Catholic daily *La Victoire*, the anti-Semitic and right-leaning deputy Xavier Vallat, who would go on to become one of the chief architects of the Vichy regime's discriminatory racial legislation, expressed his astonishment that deaf people "who couldn't use radios" had been released from paying the license fee, particularly when state broadcasting desperately needed funds.[100] Over the next few years, Morche collected complaints from deaf veterans reporting that local post office agents denied them their promised

---

[98] In 1940, Portmann joined the Vichy government as Undersecretary for Information. Portmann was condemned in post-Second World War purges but resumed his seat in the Senate in 1955. Jolly, *Dictionnaire des parlementaires français*, 7: 2734–735.

[99] *Journal officiel de la République Française. Débats-Senat.* May 20, 1933.

[100] Vallat cited in "Les mutilés de l'oreille et la taxe de T.S.F.," *La Revue de l'ouïe*, September 1933, 18; B. Yvert, *Dictionnaire des ministres de 1789 à 1990* (Paris, 1990), 698.

exemption. As the veteran Jean Ducret protested in 1936, "my agent argues that by receiving only a 30 percent pension, I don't have a right to exoneration from the tax ... which requires 100 percent." Morche instructed Ducret to file a complaint with the PTT, noting that it was "above all the disabled receiving 20 to 80 percent pensions for whom auditory rehabilitation by wireless is recommended; the completely deaf alas, have no need for it!"[101] Morche also encouraged veterans to obtain clear proof of their hearing loss before applying for the exemption. While the post office required blind and deaf veterans to submit annual medical certificates detailing the severity of their disability, its staff frequently appeared unfamiliar with medical terminology and seldom understood that "otitis" signified "deafness." It was up to individuals, Morche argued, to advocate for themselves and force the state to protect their rights to tax-free radio receivers and their inclusion in the French nation.[102]

Training deaf ears to hear: radio and the rationalization of hearing

Legislators' discomfort with exempting deaf people from the radio *redevance* exposed their lack of knowledge about modern electro-acoustical technologies as well as the persistence of deeply rooted stereotypes about deaf people as asocial and cognitively impaired. Yet Robert Morche's defense of radio as an auditory prosthesis and the root of modern rehabilitation therapy also situated deaf veterans' fate within competing scientific discourses about the human ear. In the 1920s and 1930s, discoveries in electro-acoustics and audiology revolutionized knowledge about human hearing, but many physicians continued to draw upon much older physiological conceptions of the ear when treating deaf and hard-of-hearing patients. A closer examination of these competing scientific and medical narratives about hearing, in which radio technology featured prominently, further illuminates the complex strategy adopted by the "war deaf" for achieving assimilation and recognition of their wartime injuries. However, it also reveals how France's emerging auditory culture posed new challenges for the nation's diverse deaf and hard-of-hearing population by valorizing hearing and speaking as vital to the exercise of citizenship.

Senators' eventual support for the exemption of the "war deaf" from the radio tax illustrates how the progressive medicalization of disability during the First World War coalesced with technocratic visions for

[101] *La Revue de l'ouïe*, May 1936, 32.
[102] "Taxes sur les appareils de T.S.F.," *La Revue de l'ouïe*, January 1934, 34.

streamlining the minds and bodies of the nation's citizenry. As Roxanne Panchasi has shown, the war's destruction, whether inscribed on the ravaged landscape of northern France or the bodies of disabled veterans, generated a widespread cultural fascination with the possibilities of an "artificial and synthetic future." Engineers and physicians embraced machines' ability to enhance the physical power of the human body, both through Taylorist-inspired industrial management schemes to increase workers' productivity and domestic appliances designed to rationalize women's housekeeping.[103] Journalists fueled bourgeois consumers' fantasies of improving their physical health and appearance by promoting home exercise machines and electrotherapy devices in glossy photo spreads in popular science magazines, even touting the potential health benefits of radio waves. A 1926 *Radio-Magazine* feature titled "The Effects of Currents on the Human Body" invited readers to experiment with using their bodies as electrical conductors, while a *Je sais tout* article of 1936 explained how the application of radio waves to the body could cure maladies as diverse as rheumatism, eczema, and insomnia under the headline "Wireless that Heals."[104]

Radio boosters and journalists for the specialized wireless press, always keen to demonstrate that broadcasting offered more than domestic entertainment, regaled readers with tales of radio's miraculous cures of deafness, repeating many of the claims made decades earlier about telephones and phonographs.[105] In 1931, *Radio-Magazine* published the personal account of a PTT agent in central France, E. Digo, who had constructed a homemade device comprised of a wireless amplifier, headset, and two microphones that permitted his voice to be heard by a "deaf-mute" child.[106] *L'Echo du Studio*, Paris PTT's weekly newspaper, similarly described how a "deaf-mute" teenager heard sounds for the first time during a broadcast of Johann Strauss's *Blue Danube*: "a headset was placed ... behind the left ear, as close as possible to the auditory nerve. The deaf-mute emitted a hoarse sound, his face lit up, and his hands began to follow the rhythm and dance to music ... his eyes shone and he

[103] Roxanne Panchasi, *Future Tense: The Culture of Anticipation in Interwar France Between the Wars* (Ithaca NY, 2009), 10–42; Marjorie Beale, *The Modernist Enterprise: French Elites and the Threat of Modernity, 1900–1940* (Stanford, 1999), 71–103; Robert Frost, "Machine Liberation: Inventing Housewives and Home Appliances in Interwar France," *French Historical Studies*, 18, 1, 1993, 109–30.
[104] Carolyn Thomas de la Peña, *The Body Electric: How Strange Machines Built the Modern American* (New York, 2005), 89–136; "Effets des courants sur le corps humain," *Radio-Magazine*, October 3, 1926, and October 17, 1926; B.L. "La T.S.F. qui guérit," *Je sais tout*, April 1936.
[105] Sterne, *The Audible Past*, 32–85.
[106] No author, "Pour vaincre la surdité," *Radio-Magazine*, May 31, 1931, 10.

experienced an intense joy."[107] Claims that sound reproduction technologies could restore hearing to the deaf were not entirely new, but the
rapturous description of the young deaf man's transfigured visage
reminded readers how little they understood about the physics of sound
or the emerging discipline of audiology.

Judging from the hundreds of articles that appeared in technical
magazines devoted to the mechanical components of sound technologies, educated audiences took an interest in the latest discoveries in
acoustical science and engineering. Although the conceptual foundations of hearing sciences dated to the eighteenth-century experiments
conducted by physicians on the ears of deaf people and the attempts of
the inventors Alexander Graham Bell and Edouard-Léon Scott de
Martinville in the 1870s to replicate the mechanisms of human hearing
and speech, interwar studies about hearing thresholds challenged conventional medical practices.[108] "All the processes permitting [us] to
amplify, record, reproduce, and transmit wireless music have been
perfected in a remarkable manner in recent years, thanks particularly
to the use of radio-technical procedures," the engineer J. Lefebvre
explained in the *Annales de prothèse auriculaire* in 1934, provoking a
"deeper study of the physical characteristics of hearing" that made
"possible the completion of auricular prosthetic devices of an unima-
gined quality."[109] The engineer Pierre Hemardinquer concurred. "Even
in the current century of noise," he marveled in *La Nature*, "it was just a
short time ago that we could determine in a rational and scientific
fashion the acoustical qualities of hearing."[110]

In 1923, the American engineer Harvey Fletcher designed an audiometer for the Western Electric Company that permitted otologists in the
United States to test the hearing ranges of thousands of schoolchildren
and industrial workers. Physicians could access American audiometers,
but French radio-electric firms did not begin producing them until 1934,
rendering the technology something of a novelty in medical circles and a

---

[107] "La T.S.F. et la surdité," *L'Echo du studio: revue de T.S.F. artistique, littéraire, technique*,
January 1, 1930; "La radiophonie et la surdité," *Radio-Magazine*, November 4, 1923.
For more examples of this discourse, see "Pour les sourds-muets," *Le Petit radio*,
February 22, 1930; "Pour vaincre la surdité," *Radio-Magazine*, May 31, 1931; "Le
problème de la surdité et la T.S.F.," *L'Antenne*, April 16, 1933; Ed. Dalebrac, "La radio
pour les sourds et les aveugles," *Alger-Radio*, January 22, 1939, 2.
[108] Sterne, *The Audible Past*, 32–85; Robert T. Beyer, *Sounds of Our Times: Two Hundred
Years of Acoustics* (New York, 1999), 177–211.
[109] *Les Annales de prothèse auriculaire*, June 1934, 3.
[110] Pierre Hemardinquer, "Les recherches physiques récentes sur l'ouïe," *Les Annales de
prothèse auriculaire*, June 1934, 6. Hemardinquer published widely on the subject of
sound technologies, hearing, and acoustics, collecting his numerous essays in *La surdité
et l'acoustique moderne* (Paris, 1934?).

reminder of American technological superiority.[111] Pierre Hemardinquer praised the audiometer, which shared its technical core – "the small, marvelous wireless lamp" – with the radio, for permitting physicians to measure "in the most simple and exact manner the characteristics of the human ear."[112] By determining the precise sound frequencies individuals could hear, this modern device exposed the frailties of the human ear, an organ subject to "many more pathological deformations than the eye itself," in turn revealing the "multiple and frequent malformations of hearing ... that render a great number of people deaf, or at least half deaf."[113] These large-scale audiometric surveys evaluated hundreds of individuals to produce a statistically averaged "normal" hearing, Hemardinquer explained, revealing that the "distinction commonly expressed between the *normal hearing person* and the *deaf* person is over-simplified ... there are only a few people among those with 'good hearing' who enjoy perfect hearing, just as there are a relatively small number of completely deaf people." On the scale of hearing to deaf, Emmanuel Gauthier concluded in *Le Tympan*, the majority of people possessed a hearing range somewhere "between the two extremes."[114] Even more important, radio headsets and telephone receivers permitted certain "formerly deaf" and hard-of-hearing people to detect sounds for the first time, whether by transmitting particular ranges of sound frequencies or by facilitating bone conduction to concentrate sound pressure on the eardrum more directly than through natural listening.[115]

In a peculiar analytical twist, Hemardinquer and fellow engineers constructed radio as a liberating technology with a double advantage for the deaf. While permitting certain deaf people to hear again, radios also exposed the prevalence of partial hearing loss among a wider population, overturning historic perceptions of deafness as an incurable disability. Any individual, they suggested, even those without significant hearing loss, could exploit sound technologies to rationalize their hearing and put their ears to more effective daily use. "From this point forward," argued Emmanuel Gauthier, "the question of hearing better is posed; everyone

[111] Thompson, *The Soundscape of Modernity*, 146–48; Henri Piéron, "Revue générale d'acoustique psycho-physiologique," *L'Année psycho-physiologique*, 35, 1934, 167–97. French physicians rarely used audiometers before the mid-1930s, instead relying upon spoken word tests to measure the distance at which an individual could hear a "loud" and a "whispered" voice. See A. Bonain, *L'oreille et ses maladies*, 264.
[112] *Ibid.*, Pierre Hemardinquer, "La radiotechnique, l'ouïe, et la surdité," *La Nature*, July 1, 1930, 21.
[113] Hemardinquer, "Les recherches récentes sur l'ouïe," 5.
[114] Emmanuel Gauthier, "Mieux entendre," *Le Tympan*, November 1, 1934, 1.
[115] Pierre Hemardinquer, "Surdité et audition dans les salles de cinématographe sonore," *Annales de prothèse auriculaire*, June 1935, 1.

does his best to improve his hearing, consciously or unconsciously, just as he tries to overcome his myopia."[116] For these acousticians, the interwar "sound revolution" promised to diminish the stigma of hearing loss, if not entirely eliminate deafness. This conclusion betrayed their assumption that every deaf person not only *wanted* to hear but *could* hear with appropriate treatment, a conviction that ignored what little auditory prostheses offered to profoundly deaf people. Precisely how the different sectors of France's diverse deaf population, and particularly those people whose used French sign language, responded to this promise of a technological cure for deafness is difficult to discern, although deaf advocates' fin-de-siècle campaign against the state's imposition of oralism in deaf schools suggests that many would have been disconcerted by their hearing compatriots' growing interest in broadcast sound.[117]

However, many hard-of-hearing people who did not consider themselves "deaf" did embrace the potential amelioration of hearing promised by modern electro-acoustical technologies. The Association des Durs d'Oreille de la Région Parisienne (Parisian Association for the Hard of Hearing) pressured cinemas and theaters to install listening devices with hand-held speakers or headsets in their auditoriums.[118] The abundant advertisements in the mainstream press for devices claiming to cure even the "oldest and most rebellious cases of deafness" and suppress "ringing, whistling, and other noises of the ear" testify to a competitive consumer market for hearing aids. However, the first mass-produced auditory prostheses of the 1930s remained prohibitively expensive, many selling in the range of 2,000 francs. Nor were the most reliable hearing aids the "invisible," miniature, and wearable devices advertised by manufacturers and desired by consumers, but instead were large appliances containing vacuum tubes and electromagnetic receivers that could be placed at the center of a room to detect sounds.[119] Some hard-of-hearing people consequently began

---

[116] Gauthier, "Mieux entendre," 1.
[117] J.R. Presneau, "Les sourds face à l'hégémonie des oralistes après le Congrès de Milan," in Florence Paterson, Catherine Barral, Henri-Jacques Stiker, and Michel Chauvière, eds., *L'institution du handicap. Le rôle des associations. XIXe–XXe siècles* (Rennes, 2000), 105–16. Deaf educators contested the imposition of oralism in deaf schools during the 1880s, making it unlikely that France's vibrant deaf associations would have ignored the arrival of hearing aids in the consumer market.
[118] *Entendre. Organe de l'Association des Durs d'Oreille de la Région Parisienne*, May 1935, 12. *Entendre* provided a list of Parisian establishments equipped with assistive hearing devices.
[119] "La surdité," Advertisement for Etablissements Novaphone, *La Semaine radiophonique*, February 20, 1938, 23; Hemardinquer, "La radiotechnique, l'ouïe, et la surdité," 22–23. Morche, "Les divers genres de microphones," 9; Leland Watson, *Hearing Aids and Hearing Instruments* (Baltimore, 1949), 280. Portable vacuum tube hearing aids, first marketed by Thompson-Houston in 1934–1935, did not become widely available in France until the late 1930s. Consumer demand for invisible and miniature hearing

to convert their radio receivers into stationary hearing aids, reconfiguring manufacturers' original designs to produce a cheaper and more effective alternative to commercial prostheses. *La Nature* even published detailed schemas for conversions that instructed readers how to attach a microphone to the "pick-up" jack in most radios before replacing the loudspeaker with a headset. This simple adaptation, one "how-to" article of 1930 explained, could transform a radio receiver into an "excellent device against deafness" that "when placed on a table … permits a deaf [person] to hear everything that people in the room are saying without having to approach them" [Figure 2.3].[120]

Veterans in the Federation of the War Deaf and civilians in the Parisian Association for the Hard of Hearing became active *bricoleurs*, circulating Hemardinquer's wireless schema widely among friends and in their respective associational bulletins. Much like the blind radio amateurs who cultivated technical knowledge in radio construction in order to become active listeners, deaf veterans tinkered with their receivers in order to redefine themselves as normal, hearing citizens rather than permanently disabled deaf men. Given veterans' wartime exposure to radio, many Federation members would likely have possessed the skills required to complete the tasks, but for those who were less technically inclined, *La Revue de l'ouïe* offered advice on how to instruct radio vendors or repairmen in the procedure. "Go to any *good* merchant of wireless devices and ask him to adapt your five- or six-lamp receiver." With a "pick-up on the receiver, add a headset – that's to say a radio or telephone receiver – and place an ordinary loudspeaker in the place of the antenna sockets." With a headset, the "deaf person with some remaining hearing can easily hear all that is said in the room, the office, or the shop."[121]

Some deaf veterans testified to their personal successes in using converted receivers as a "listening set for conversations" or to enjoy radio broadcasts. Gabriel Limoges claimed he could once hear only a "raised voice near my ear," but thanks to "headphones and a modified wireless set," he could now hear clearly without "my interlocutors having to raise their voices."[122] These testimonies reinforced Morche's campaign to demonstrate how radio receivers doubled as prostheses that could transform the lives of deaf veterans. The Federation even launched a campaign

devices drove innovation and marketing elsewhere. See Mara Mills, "Hearing Aids and the History of Electronics Miniaturization," *IEEE Annals of the History of Computing*, 33, 2, April–June, 2011, 24–45.

[120] Pierre Hemardinquer, "Les illusions d'acoustique, la radiophonie, et la surdité," *La Nature*, September 1, 1931, 222.

[121] "La T.S.F. et les sourds," *La Revue de l'ouïe*, October 1931, 9.

[122] Gabriel Limoges, "Distraction et rééducation: mon appareil de T.S.F." *La Revue de l'ouïe*, July 1931, 34.

sition; aussi, dans ce cas particulier, peut-on fort bien utiliser un amplificateur à lampes à vide, d'ailleurs très simple, et comportant au maximum une ou deux lampes.

Un tel appareil comportera ainsi un microphone qui peut être d'ailleurs du type ordinaire, ou réalisé par des moyens de fortune, un amplificateur à fréquence musicale à une ou deux lampes avec ses organes d'alimentation, et un casque téléphonique ou un écouteur d'un type spécial pour personnes sourdes (fig. 12).

Les étages basse fréquence d'amplification peuvent être ceux du poste de T. S. F. lui-même.

COMMENT RÉALISER UN APPAREIL AMPLIFICATEUR CONTRE LA SURDITÉ

On trouve dans le commerce des microphones à grenaille avec plaque en charbon qui donnent d'excellents résultats et qui ne sont pas d'un prix élevé. Il existe en particulier des microphones de ce genre qui sont utilisés pour l'enregistrement phonographique d'amateur. On peut se procurer ces accessoires dans la plupart des maisons de fournitures de T. S. F., et plus spécialement dans celles

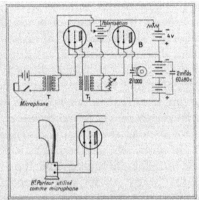

Fig. 13. — Un amplificateur simple pour réaliser un appareil microphonique pour sourds.

En employant un haut-parleur électromagnétique comme microphone, il est inutile de recourir à un transformateur d'entrée.

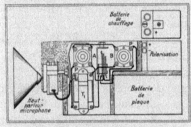

Fig. 14. — Plan d'un bloc portatif d'amplification pour sourds (d'après The Wireless World).

qui vendent des appareils d'enregistrement phonographique.

Ces microphones, étant donné leur faible résistance, ne peuvent être reliés directement à la lampe d'entrée de l'amplificateur à fréquence musicale, et on adopte un transformateur d'entrée T à noyau de fer et de rapport élevé dont le primaire est placé dans le circuit microphonique en série avec une pile qui est généralement de quatre volts, et dont le secondaire est connecté au circuit de grille de la première lampe. Cette première lampe A est reliée à la lampe de sortie par l'intermédiaire d'un transformateur T, de type courant de rapport 1/3 par exemple. On relie les écouteurs téléphoniques à la plaque P de cette lampe de sortie B (fig. 13).

L'appareil est donc très simple, et il est facile de modifier l'intensité sonore, soit en agissant sur l'amplificateur, soit en montant un rhéostat dans le circuit primaire du microphone.

Rien de plus simple que d'utiliser les étages basse fréquence d'un amplificateur pour obtenir un tel résultat. D'ailleurs, la plupart des radiorécepteurs actuels compor-

tent une fiche avec jack destinée à l'utilisation d'un pick-up; il suffit de connecter le secondaire du transformateur microphonique à la place du pick-up et de placer les écouteurs à la place du haut-parleur pour obtenir un excellent appareil contre la surdité.

Il va sans dire que le microphone ne doit pas être placé près de l'amplificateur, de façon à éviter les sifflements désagréables qui pourraient se produire. D'autre part, il faudra qu'il soit suspendu élastiquement ou placé sur un bloc de caoutchouc mousse afin d'éviter toutes les vibrations parasites.

Un tel ensemble est extrêmement sensible, et, placé sur une table dans une pièce, il permet à un sourd d'entendre tout ce que disent les personnes qui se trouvent dans la pièce sans qu'il ait besoin d'approcher

Fig. 15. — Le montage du Radiophon du Dr Eichhorn dans le circuit plaque d'une lampe de sortie.

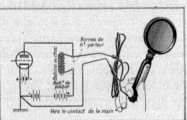

Figure 2.3 Schemas for converting radios into hearing aids, *La Nature* (1932). Image courtesy of the Bibliothèque Nationale de France.

to convince manufacturers to produce radios with high-powered amplifiers specifically for the hard of hearing.[123] "The device we're waiting for," implored M. Gabriel, "it's a wireless device, simple [and] easy to manipulate, that can be placed in any location or transformed on site by a simple maneuver into a powerful and clear amplifier, permitting even the most hard of hearing to follow a conversation with several people, without them having to raise their voices." This wireless-amplifier combination would immediately find a consumer base among "deaf people, and would permit them to undertake with wireless an entirely agreeable rehabilitation."[124]

However, veterans' enthusiastic defense of radios as prosthetic devices and tools for auditory rehabilitation ultimately undermined the demands of the "war deaf" for greater recognition of their combat-induced disability, for otologists judged many cases of deafness to be the product of a patient's psychological instability or poor hygiene. Out of 24,000 estimated cases of "deaf-mutism" in France, the physician Max-Albert Legrand argued in 1921, nearly 70 percent could have been cured with proper treatment.[125] Gérard de Parrel, a prolific interwar otologist and a leading physician at the Institut National des Sourds-Muets (Paris Deaf Institute), believed it was imperative to liberate the nation from the maintenance of people with "psychic deficiencies," including many deaf people, given the heavy financial burden deaf schools and rehabilitation centers imposed on the state.[126]

Parrel's views corresponded with those of Justin Godart, the minister of health under the radical-socialist Herriot government, who in 1932 introduced a bill backed by the French Eugenics Society to require mandatory premarital examinations to prevent the hereditary transmission of contagious diseases and disabilities. However, social hygienists also embraced a neo-Lamarckian intellectual tradition dictating that physical improvements in the population could be passed on to subsequent generations, and thus lent their support to campaigns to improve the biological stock of the French population by restoring the health of the disabled or chronically ill.[127] Despite the eugenic undertones of

---

[123] "La T.S.F. et les sourds," *Guérir*, August 1932, 5; "Le problème de la surdité et la T.S. F.," *L'Antenne*, April 16, 1933, 300; "La T.S.F. et les sourds," *Le Petit radio*, April 28, 1934, 6.

[124] Gabriel's article appeared in several newspapers. See "L'appareil qu'attend les mutilés d'oreille," *L'Antenne*, April 29, 1929, 343; and M. Gabriel, "L'appareil que nous attendons," *La Revue de l'ouïe*, April 1929, 20. Multitone manufactured converted radios during the mid-1930s. See *Entendre*, May 1936, 43.

[125] Max-Albert Legrand, *L'oreille et la surdité. Hygiène, maladies, traitement* (Paris, 1921), 7.

[126] Gérard de Parrel, *La rééducation de la voix parlée* (Paris, 1932), vi. Parrel headed the Clinique André Castex at the Institut National des Sourds-Muets.

[127] Schneider, *Quality and Quantity*, 146–69.

Parrel's publications, he also argued that many deaf people, particularly late-deafened individuals such as the war deaf, could with proper medical treatment and auditory rehabilitation "be recuperated for the Collectivity and ... participate like others in the general effort of society."[128]

Auditory rehabilitation – the treatment for deafness cited during the 1933 parliamentary debates over the radio license fee – united otologists' longstanding oralist preoccupations with modern rehabilitation techniques honed during the war.[129] Army physicians treating deaf servicemen in hospitals and rehabilitation clinics viewed instruction in sign language as an impractical solution and lip reading as a palliative, and instead focused their efforts on restoring wounded soldiers' hearing.[130] As Joanna Bourke has shown, shell shock blurred the boundaries between the organic and psychological causes of illness, as well as between "neurasthenic" men and malingers, for servicemen whose visible wounds had healed continued to complain about physical symptoms associated with their original conditions.[131] This ambiguity particularly complicated diagnoses of deafness, as enlisted men sometimes simulated deafness to escape front-line duty, while shell shock frequently induced temporary hearing loss.[132]

In 1917, Georges René Marage, the physician managing auditory rehabilitation for the army, reported the difficulty of determining which servicemen had truly sustained hearing loss, for if "measurements for visual acuity are well-determined, those for auditory acuity are experimental and not very scientific." As a result, many discharged men should have been sent back to the front while "inversely, men whose deafness is absolutely certain are maintained in the regiment and treated as fakers." Marage observed identical symptoms in soldiers whose outer ear had been destroyed and those who had been near battlefield bombardments, but not directly hit by shrapnel. The difficulty of visually assessing damage to the internal ear further obscured the origins of many patients' deafness.[133]

[128] Gérard de Parrel, *La rééducation de l'ouïe chez les sourds, les sourds-muets, et les durs d'oreille* (Paris, 1932), 2.
[129] Robert Jouet, *Etudes sur les sourds-muets* (Paris, 1917), 67–68.
[130] Albert Maurice, *Surdité et rééducation auditive: traitement de surdité chronique par les exercices acoustiques* (Paris, 1924), 120–23; Dr. Emile Galtier-Boissière, dir. *Larousse médical illustré de guerre* (Paris, 1917), 15–26.
[131] Bourke, *Dismembering the Male*, 116–19. On deafness in shell-shock diagnoses, see also Schwartz, *Making Noise*, 581–84.
[132] A. Bonain, *L'oreille et ses maladies*, 261–55.
[133] Georges René Marie Marage, *Contribution à l'étude du sens de l'ouïe, surdités vraies et simulées consécutives à des blessures de guerre* (Paris, 1917) 1–10.

Rather than challenging physicians' correlation of deafness with emotional distress or cognitive impairment, the war only advanced their conclusion that many deaf people were psychologically unstable. The army medical corps consequently treated deafness as the product of wartime "hysteria" – a moral disease of the will rather than the psychological product of trauma – resulting in the classification of numerous deaf veterans as neurasthenics, or even worse, as shirkers (*embusqués*).[134] Wounds to the ear "might make hearing difficult," the physician Albert Maurice wrote in 1924, but deaf people often furthered their "affliction" by isolating themselves from hearing society. As Maurice described, the "weakening of hearing makes listening tedious; the sick person … becomes tired of listening, and little by little he loses the train of conversation; he isolates himself …" He concluded that "sick people of this category" were weak individuals for whom "it requires too much intellectual work to listen," while others simply feared hearing "like an agoraphobic person dreads crossing the street." Restoring the ability of deaf veterans to hear, and perhaps even more importantly, to speak, constituted the only means to reestablish their membership in society.[135] The "war deaf" consequently became the perfect candidates for rehabilitation, which treated nervous disorders and bodily ailments as intertwined conditions requiring mechanical therapy and powerful "suggestions" to "restore the harmony between volition and action" in the body.[136]

After 1918, physicians like Gérard de Parrel began applying auditory rehabilitation therapies streamlined on the "war deaf" to civilian populations, from deaf children schooled at the Paris Deaf Institute to adults seeking to improve their hearing loss or correct speech impediments. Parrel's therapy combined experimental phonetics, electrotherapy, and auditory training with the goal of "awakening hearing by the excitation [throughout sound] of the labyrinth, the regeneration of ear tissues by circulatory and therapeutic action, and the improvement of the functions of accommodation" in the ear.[137] He drew heavily on a mechanical conception of the ear developed by nineteenth-century physiologists

---

[134] Roudebush, "A Battle of Nerves," 254–77.
[135] Maurice, *Surdité et rééducation auditive*, 9–10. For similar views see M. Fourcade, "La Phobie de la surdité," in *La rééducation auditive, vocale, respiratoire. Revue trimestrielle*, February–March 1914, 5–12; and Gérard de Parrel, *La surdité et son traitement: manuel de rééducation auditive à l'usage du sourd et de son entourage* (Paris, 1927), 9–12.
[136] Galtier-Boissière, *Larousse médical illustré de guerre*, 15–26; Price, "Bodies and Souls," 54.
[137] De Parrel, *La rééducation de l'ouïe*, 14. Parrel built directly on Emile Tillot's *Le réveil de l'ouïe par les excitations fonctionnelles coup sur coup. Manuel de l'auxiliaire ou rééducateur de l'ouïe* (Rouen, 1930). Tillot's text, winner of the Prix Itard from the Académie de Médecine in 1921, detailed the use of acoustic tubes to train the ear to hear particular syllables.

that Jonathan Sterne has termed the "tympanic model," whereby the ear appeared as a distinct organ operating independently of other sensory mechanisms. This tympanic model of the ear coalesced with the prevailing conceptual framework of the human body as an organism whose individual parts could be trained to achieve maximum efficiency.[138] "A normal sense is perfectible by an appropriate education and professional training," Parrel wrote in *La rééducation de l'ouïe*, just as "a sense diminished by a pathological lesion and not by use is perfectible by exercise … Rehabilitation can everywhere play an effective role in the development or recuperation of sensory and functional activity." Invoking an economic metaphor to emphasize the productive value of auditory rehabilitation, Parrel argued that deaf ears could regain their "auditory capital" through a combination of mechanical exercises (physical therapy) and training (pedagogy).

Parrel's treatment of deaf patients centered on creating "attention," or the physical and mental preparation required for the ear to accommodate sounds. Such attention was "not as we once believed," he wrote, "a pure act of the mind, an imperceptible mechanism, but an essential motor act." To achieve the state of attention required for hearing, the "entire muscular mass of the ear must put itself into action, both in the middle and the outer ear."[139] Parrel's two-pronged therapy included an initial "passive" stage comprised of external head massages to restore blood flow to the ear and the application of a "sound wave massage" to the patient's ear. Using a device resembling a radio and a headset, to which Parrel assigned the pseudo-scientific label of "phono-pneumatic massager," he bombarded his patients' ears with a range of sound frequencies selected to vibrate differently against the eardrum and stimulate varied patterns of muscular movement along the ossicular chain. This treatment proved effective, Parrel claimed, when patients felt a "warming sensation" in their ears that signaled increased blood flow and wax production. The second and "active" portion of Parrel's treatment consisted of speech therapy with an acoustic tube designed to train the ear to distinguish particular "sound zones" of consonants or vowels. The goal of this latter training, Parrel confirmed, was to teach the deaf person to "put forward his ear and his mind."

Most importantly, these repetitive auditory exercises would rid the body of poor motor habits and "inhibitory phobias" that prevented good hearing and intelligible, refined speech. "We know the tyranny that our motor habits, which are the elements of our daily activity, impose on us," Parrel wrote, and "it is against these habits that psycho-motor

[138] Sterne, *The Audible Past*, 34.   [139] Parrel, *La rééducation de l'ouïe*, 20.

rehabilitation must intervene" by training patients to try to listen at all times. In between periodic six-week long treatment sessions, Parrel instructed his patients to undertake regular auditory practice with radios and phonographs to acclimate their ears to hearing conversations or other environmental sounds.[140] Such "sessions of auditory work should only be suppressed under extraordinary circumstances," Parrel noted, and he urged patients to "seek out all occasions to train [their] ears with ... the wireless. It is only through this mental-auditory activity that he will obtain practical results."[141] Parrel admitted that his treatments worked only with certain types of partial deafness: middle ear disorders, hearing loss produced by illness or infection, and progressive forms of deafness resulting from aging.

Other rehabilitation specialists, however, proved far less circumspect in their claims to cure patients. Advertisements for auditory rehabilitation offered by physicians and non-medical practitioners alike abounded in newspapers, promising astounding cures for all varieties of hearing loss. Patients seeking auditory rehabilitation therapy could follow a course at the Clinique Rousselot, an experimental phonetics laboratory at the Sorbonne, or at the Ecole psycho-médico-pédagogique, where Parrel's wife, the soprano Louise Matha, turned her background in diction and vocal training into work with deaf children.[142] The physician Albert Hautant even touted the virtues of auditory rehabilitation over the microphones of Radio-Paris in 1933.[143]

Robert Morche was not immune to the ways auditory rehabilitation pathologized deafness and further excluded the profoundly deaf, whether civilians or veterans, from hearing society by marking them as permanently different. He acknowledged the long history of medical experimentation on deaf people that began during the 1830s with the physician Jean-Marc-Gaspard Itard's application of astringents, injections, and hot irons to deaf patients' ears.[144] For this reason, Morche first judged Parrel and other rehabilitation physicians to be little more than charlatans. *La Revue de l'ouïe* published numerous testimonies from deaf veterans

---

[140] *Ibid.*, v, 15–20, 31–33. Abbé Rousselot developed these methods of speech pathology during the 1890s in his Laboratoire de Phonétique at the Sorbonne. Katherine Bergeron, *Voice Lessons: French Mélodie in the Belle Epoque* (Oxford, 2011), 29–120, and Enrica Galazzi, *Le son à l'école: phonétique et enseignement des langues* (Brescia, Italy, 2002), 63–80.
[141] Parrel, *La rééducation de l'ouïe*, 115.
[142] *La Revue de l'ouïe*, January 1929, 27, September 1933, 14, and March 1936, 1–2; Louise Matha, "La voix enregistrée," *Machines parlantes et radio*, December 1931.
[143] Albert Hautant, "Le traitement de la surdité," *Les Cahiers de Radio-Paris*, August 15, 1933, 752–59.
[144] Mirzoeff, *Silent Poetry*, 93–98.

describing how unscrupulous physicians sold them expensive but worth-less devices to "train" their ears to hear.[145] *Le Tympan* likewise discour-aged its readers from using "devices that have as their goal the 'rehabilitation' of the eardrum and hearing organs and that pretend to achieve this by 'vibratory massages.'" Regardless of the "intensity or frequency of sound they emit," the journal surmised, they are "frankly harmful."[146] Nor did Morche ignore contemporary eugenic debates that sought to restrict the reproductive rights of the deaf.[147] However, his desire to distance deaf veterans from charges of malingering (and thus psychological instability) and his own desire to reenter normative hearing society compelled him to endorse auditory therapy by licensed physicians and the use of radios for self-treatment. In 1937, he invited Parrel to write a short article in the *La Revue de l'ouïe*, and Parrel composed the preface to the second edition of Morche's *La lutte contre la surdité*.[148]

Several Federation members also testified to successes in using their radios for auditory rehabilitation. Gabriel Limoges recommended daily training sessions with a high-quality receiver, describing how his headset served as a "marvelous tool for massaging and awakening my sleeping ears. My right ear, dead for eight years, has begun to live and wax reappeared," a sure sign of good health. Yet he cautioned his readers against listening to the radio too loudly for fear of harming their ears: "choose a good headset of a reputed manufacturer that is not too heavy. Try to avoid *dazzling* the ear." Several months of regular auditory train-ing, he claimed, resulted in a "light improvement" in his hearing that "even while imperceptible to strangers . . . translates above all . . . into the fact that my hearing is more regular and that the 'holes' – days when I heard much less – are less frequent."[149]

---

[145] Henri Rebière, "Les charlatans," *La Revue de l'ouïe*, July 1929, 13; April 1928, 28; and April 1929, 10–12. Robert Morche, *La lutte contre la surdité. Encyclopédie des mutilés d'oreille* (Sanary, 1930) 60–64; "Avis," *Le Tympan*, May 1937. Rehabilitation physicians sought to distinguish their treatments from negative associations with "quackery" by defining rehabilitation therapy as a distinctive medical discipline. The professionaliza-tion of audiology and speech pathology shaped Parrel's vocabulary, which emphasized the "modern" (and by implication, scientific) characteristics of his particular treatment methods. On these points, see Ott, Serlin, and Mihm, eds., *Artificial Parts, Practical Lives*, 15–16; Watson, *Hearing Aids*, 2–22; Raymond H. Hull, ed., *Rehabilitative Audiology* (New York, 1982), 4.

[146] "Avis," *Le Tympan*, May 1937.

[147] Morche, *Guide du mutilé*, 43. Morche commented that every "completely deaf person free from any contagious illness had the right . . . to create a family."

[148] Robert Morche, "Les centres de rééducation auditive et de lecture labiale," *La Revue de l'ouïe*, March 1936, 1–4.

[149] Gabriel Limoges, "Distraction et rééducation: Mon appareil de T.S.F." *La Revue de l'ouïe*, July 1931, 334.

For this reason the deaf were "better off than the [blind]," Morche's friend Commander Jourdy concluded in *La Revue de l'ouïe*, for the "hard-of-hearing person can 99 times out of 100 recover part of his diminished hearing. Like the partial arm amputee, he can, with appropriate gymnastics, rehabilitate his diminished organ."[150] For Emmanuel Gauthier, this personal effort remained the most important factor in regaining hearing. "Recovering the joy of hearing is not as simple as one thinks," he wrote in *Le Tympan*, and the "deaf person who wants to hear and not only perceive sounds must . . . through constant effort . . . help his own hearing aid." This process resembled learning a foreign language, requiring deaf people to reform their "sound vocabulary" in order to be successful.[151] But by attempting to regain their lost hearing, the deaf veterans in Morche's Federation demonstrated their capacity and their desire to participate in the norms of hearing society and leave behind the trauma of the war years, even as their activities reinforced the importance of hearing and speaking. Above all, their claims remind us how normative models of citizenship have historically been grounded in particular modes of sensory perception. With the expansion of auditory culture in the twentieth century, participating fully in national life would not only require the ability to hear, but the desire to listen.

"Light to the blind and hearing to the deaf"

The radio charities' efforts to distribute free radios to disabled veterans and the blind, followed by the parliamentary debates over the radio license fee, illustrate how the emerging mass media of broadcasting began to transform the dynamics of politics by privileging radio listening as a quotidian practice of citizenship. During their fundraising campaigns, charity spokesmen cast the airwaves as an extension of civil society – a "radio nation" – by arguing that access to radio technology was critical to veterans' reintegration into national life. However, Paul Rémy's subtle critique of the charities exposed their reformist tendencies: namely, that their vision of social reintegration relied upon disabled men adopting "positive" attitudes toward their disability, even if they remained physically isolated at home or in hospitals or sanatoria. A similar tension surfaced in deaf veterans' embrace of auditory rehabilitation, a treatment that privileged hearing as critical to physical and psychological "normality," but which marginalized profoundly deaf

[150] Ct. Jourdy, "Opinions," *La Revue de l'ouïe*, July 1928, 7.
[151] Emmanuel Gauthier, "Le rôle de l'habitude," *Le Tympan*, March 1935, 1–2.

people from hearing society and from membership in France's emerging "radio nation" in the airwaves.

Yet even as Rémy and other disability activists criticized the radio charities for promoting a passive model of radio listening, they did not reject the notion that broadcasting could advance the social integration of blind, disabled, or chronically ill people, and thus continued to demand access to the airwaves. Their requests for tax-exempt radios and, on occasion, free receivers, ensured that listening gradually came to be seen by many people as an important form of participation in public and political life. That the *Radio for the Blind* and *Wireless at the Hospital* broadcasts became a fixture of state broadcasting further cemented audiences' perceptions of the airwaves as a "radio nation" – a distinctive space in which citizens could come together to debate and negotiate the boundaries and membership of the of the body politic.

Assessing the success of the charities' campaigns to distribute free radios remains challenging, however. In 1936, the Paris PTT advisory board, which monitored and evaluated the station's programs, deemed it inappropriate for the charities to make direct appeals for donations on air, since listeners indirectly supported them through the payment of their radio license fees.[152] However, radio newspapers and the mainstream press continued to celebrate the charities' victories. The blind veterans' newspaper *Le Mutilé des yeux* reported in July 1934 that Radio for the Blind had donated over 700 individual receivers to blind veterans, while General Mariaux claimed in 1936 that the number had increased to 1,000.[153] *T.S.F. Tribune* announced the same year that Wireless at the Hospital had overseen the installation of radio equipment in thirty-four hospitals and sanatoriums across France, ranging from nursing homes to rehabilitation clinics and asylums for veterans with mental illnesses.[154] While these donations served only a small proportion of France's population of disabled veterans, organizations including the Union des Aveugles de Guerre and the French Red Cross brokered deals with manufacturers such as Philips and Philco to obtain discounts for disabled men.[155]

Veterans likely began purchasing their own receivers in the early 1930s after radios became more affordable, though many in less favorable

---

[152] CAC 19870714–2. Projet de procès-verbal de la séance du conseil de gérance de Paris PTT, March 18, 1938.
[153] *Le Mutilé des yeux*, July 1934; A.P. "La radio aux aveugles," *T.S.F. Tribune*, April 12, 1936, 5.
[154] Géo Charles, "La T.S.F. à l'hôpital," *T.S.F. Tribune*, March 13, 1936, 5.
[155] *Bulletin de l'Union des Aveugles de Guerre*, May 1934, 31. The UAG sought discounted radios for its members and obtained price reductions from the manufacturers Philips and Philco, as did the Société de Secours aux Blessés Militaires (a branch of the French Red Cross).

economic circumstances longed for access to the airwaves, while numerous sanatoria and asylums remained underserved.[156] In 1937, one patient
who had spent two years in a tuberculosis sanatorium wrote to Radio-
Liberté, an association affiliated with the newly elected Popular Front
coalition, to encourage the government to put the installation of hospital
radios at the forefront of its political platform. "Workers who are alive and
kicking have been able to improve their condition of life, thanks to the
Popular Front," F. Auclair wrote, and "it would only be just for those who
have lost their health, most of the time at work, to enjoy for themselves the
right to a little well-being."[157] Questions about precisely which sectors of
the population could access the airwaves as well as what programs they
could hear would become increasingly pressing in the years to come,
particularly after state bureaucrats, politicians, and diplomats began
working to carve out a distinct space for the French "radio nation" in
the airwaves over Europe.

[156] Jean-Yves Le Naour, *The Living Unknown Soldier: A Story of Grief and the Great War*,
trans. Penny Allen (New York, Holt, 2005), 128.
[157] F. Auclair, "La T.S.F. aux malades hospitalisés," *Radio-Liberté*, December 31, 1937.
My emphasis.

3 Cosmopolitanism and cacophony
Static, signals, and the making of a "radio nation"

In January of 1936, an editorial in the radio magazine *Mon programme* contemplated broadcasting's impact on French society over the course of the previous decade. Far more than any other modern media, the author "Scaramouche" proposed, radio had challenged people's provincial mentality by exposing them to the wider world outside their local communities. For much of the nineteenth century, the "typical Frenchman did not focus his attention on more than a tiny part of the planet. The local news was enough to satisfy his curiosity." Parisian sophisticates imagined the capital as the "only region of the universe worthy of their attention" and the rest of France as a "vague extension of land inhabited by people who would assuredly spend the rest of their lives regretting not being born between the Seine and boulevards." The rural farmer, for his part, appeared "little enthralled by the sounds outside of the country-side." Even on the eve of the First World War, the "great majority of Frenchmen displayed a total indifference to events taking place overseas, unless they were in Germany, England, or the United States." Four years of total war in Europe and the colonies had brutally thrust people into a greater awareness of global affairs, as soldiers in the trenches and their families waiting at home for news of their fate suddenly took an interest in distant battles unfolding around the globe. But it was only now, thanks to the airwaves, that "we could say that the earth has contracted . . . shriveled up . . . the distance between continents is diminished."[1]

While exaggerating France's prewar provincialism for effect, *Mon programme* celebrated radio waves' ability to transcend conventional boundaries of space, time, and distance and incorporate listeners into a common national radio audience, while simultaneously promoting intimate quotidian contact with foreign populations. Radio had both contracted and expanded the size of the earth, the magazine suggested, permitting audiences to tune into French and foreign stations alike from the comfort of their living room or the corner café. Through the airwaves, "we hear breathing, right up against our ears, men separated from us by a day of

[1] Scaramouche, "La radio et la terre," *Mon programme*, January 3, 1936.

111

train travel," Scaramouche rhapsodized, an experience that only fueled a desire for travel and cultural exchange. "There is not a radio amateur among us who has not sensed awakening in him the desire to run across the world after hearing Hungarian czardas, Bavarian choirs, or the bells of England. Our sensibility has been enriched and complicated by its infinite contributions." Although this daily exposure to foreign voices, particularly after the rise of authoritarian regimes in neighboring Germany and Italy, may have stirred nationalist pride in many listeners, for others radio's cosmopolitan allure remained undiminished. "The roars of Hitler may deepen our love of our native soil," the editorial suggested, but "they do not keep us, while under the influence of our radios, from forgetting in spite of ourselves our qualities as children of Montmartre or Palavas-les-Flots, to become, for several minutes each evening, citizens of the world."[2] That the author saw no contradiction in this statement highlights one of the salient features of France's interwar auditory culture: audiences' desire to tune in regularly to both French stations and foreign stations from across Europe and around the globe.

Radio waves fascinated wireless audiences of the 1920s because they called into question the very concept of the nation ratified just a few years earlier at the Paris Peace Conferences of 1919: that of a community of common language speakers inhabiting a bounded and defined territory. Although the conservative *bloc national* that took power after the Armistice sought to reassert France's position on the world stage by promoting nationalism at home and enforcing the Versailles Treaty's punitive measures against Germany, by the mid-1920s Weimar politicians' willingness to sign non-aggression treaties and Germany's subsequent admission to the League of Nations spurred a wave of internationalist sentiment in France.[3] Radio boosters, cultural commentators, and audiences alike hailed wireless as the technological embodiment of the spirit of Locarno and a modern media with the potential to forge an *entente* between former enemies as well as distant populations around the globe. "Hertzian waves have no borders," asserted Pierre Descaves, an early foreign affairs correspondent on the Eiffel Tower station and a proponent of Franco-German rapprochement. "One word over the microphone and that word encircles the globe." If world leaders exploited radio appropriately, Descaves predicted, broadcasting would "one day find the voice that will carry the words of peace to the world" by creating a "universal public" in which

[2] *Ibid.*
[3] Sally Marks, *The Illusion of Peace: International Relations in Europe, 1918–1933* (Basingstoke, 1976, 2003).

the "the Londoner, the Berliner, the Romanian, and the Spaniard all compose an immense public of one mind."[4]

Yet even as many radio listeners embraced broadcasting's internationalism by tuning into radio programs from outside of France, others began to worry about the cacophony of interference and foreign voices that drowned out the signals of French stations and impeded their clear reception, contributing to what the journalist Paul Dermée described as a "state of anarchy" in the airwaves.[5] Both problems increased as European nations began building powerful radio networks whose stations could be heard at vast distances. By the early 1930s, listeners' inability to hear French voices within this wider "concert of Europe" compelled them to demand greater state intervention in the airwaves, both to "decongest and unblock the ether" and to create equivalent listening conditions for radio listeners across France.

During the very same years that the radio charities were redefining the airwaves as an extension of civil society by promoting listening as a means for disabled veterans to participate in public and political life, politicians and bureaucrats began to imagine constructing a different "radio nation" – a distinctive space filled with French radio signals and inhabited by French voices – in the airwaves over Europe. In 1930, legislators endorsed a plan for the construction of a "democratic" broadcasting network that they hoped would harmonize France's national and regional interests while reinforcing its international prestige. But to do so, bureaucrats in the state radio administration had to negotiate with neighboring countries to obtain the right to use particular wavelengths at a series of international conferences designed to partition the European radio spectrum. Radio audiences came to regard these conferences, which occurred several times in the 1930s, as a direct corollary to the more serious diplomatic discussions unfolding at the League of Nations over the fate of peace in Europe. For radio listeners, the quotidian act of turning the radio dial and the results it produced became a gauge by which they evaluated their status within the emerging "radio nation" as well as France's evolving geopolitical status.

Examining debates about the future of France's state radio network and its status on the world stage as a "radio power," this chapter

---

[4] Pierre Descaves, "La T.S.F. et la paix," *Lumière et radio*, June 10, 1930, 7. On Descaves's career in broadcasting, see Prot, *Dictionnaire de la radio*, 201–2. For his political views, see Elana Passman, "Civic Activism and the Pursuit of Cooperation in the Locarno Era," in Carine Germond and Henning Turk, eds., *A History of Franco-German Relations in Europe: From "Hereditary Enemies" to Partners* (New York, 2008), 101–12.

[5] Paul Dermée, "La course aux kilowatts," *T.S.F. Programme*, September 25–October 25, 1932.

uncovers how a combination of listeners' demands and top-down state initiatives together shaped interwar broadcasting policies. Radio's internationalism, as we shall see, consistently challenged lawmakers' efforts to employ broadcasting as a tool of nation building, for even after hostile foreign propaganda reached French radios, audiences continued to defend their "right to listen" to overseas stations, while simultaneously calling for the state to reinforce France's "borders" on the radio spectrum. More important, by uncovering how audiences' everyday listening habits became entangled in a local, national, and international politics of radio reception, or what Pierre Descaves described as a "new genre of sound conflicts," this chapter contributes to a growing body of scholarship demonstrating how historical developments within France have been shaped by transnational forces.[6] But to understand how French radio listeners first began to conceive of themselves as "French" citizens and as cosmopolitan "citizens of the world" by navigating the airwaves, we turn now to examine the technical features of early radio listening as well as the ever-shifting geography of the European radio spectrum.

The poetry of space: navigating the radio spectrum

Reflecting on postwar vogue for wireless, the writer and radio dramatist Fernand Divoire highlighted what he believed to be the airwaves' most distinctive feature: their reduction of distance and their reconfiguration of geographical space. Radio's originality as a sound media resided in its "poetic base," Divoire commented, a quality that could be "defined in a single phrase: wireless is communion between men. That is why there is a great difference between wireless amateurs and record enthusiasts. Deep down, those who love Radio are poets." Where the "record amateur thinks about sounds, of beautiful sounds preserved," Divoire claimed, the "wireless amateur thinks about space, for he loves the noise of life."[7] In the early 1920s, audiences could access this "noise" by tuning into three Parisian stations – Radio-Paris, Paris PTT, and the Poste Parisien. By 1931, a host of new regional stations, both public and commercial, had

---

[6] Pierre Descaves, "La guerre des ondes est pour demain," *T.S.F. Programme*, January 10–16, 1932. For the historiography of transnationalism, see Akira Iriye, *Global and Transnational History: The Past, Present, and Future* (Basingstoke, 2013), 1–18. Recent works examining French history through a transnational lens include Stovall, *Paris and the Spirit of 1919*; Cabanes, *The Great War and the Origins of Humanitarianism*, 6–23; Blower, *Becoming Americans in Paris*, 1–14; Daniel Lacqua, ed., *Internationalism Reconfigured: Transnational Ideas and Movements Between the Wars* (London, 2011).

[7] Fernand Divoire cited in Coeuroy, *Panorama de la radio*, 13.

begun broadcasting in France, bringing the total number of stations to twenty-five.[8] Yet listeners could also hear stations transmitting from nearby Germany, Italy, Great Britain, and Belgium. Europe counted 170 different radio stations in 1926, a figure that increased to 238 by 1930 and an estimated 2,000 by 1936.[9]

The cultural, linguistic, and above all, geographical range of these sonic offerings fueled a "craze for distance" among radio amateurs, who sought out distant signals and the widest possible array of foreign voices, including stations from as far away as Prague, Bratislava, and even Moscow. Listeners began to describe the airwaves as a distinctive, if amorphous, space with the ability to simultaneously contract and expand the globe. Writing in *Lumière et radio* in 1929, Divoire captured the excitement many listeners experienced during their initial explorations of the airwaves, as they detected stations closer to home before locating others outside France's borders: "You first 'caught' the Eiffel Tower, Radio-Paris, or Paris PTT. You then searched for something else and came upon Daventry, so you turned triumphantly toward your family and proclaimed 'I am in England!'" Crossing the English Channel "appeared as absolutely miraculous to you," spurring further "travels" to Germany and beyond.[10] Since the early nineteenth century, bourgeois readers had fueled a flourishing market for armchair travel, in the form of illustrated travelogues and popular ethnographies of "exotic" populations, but radio broadcasting offered something that even the latest glossy travel magazines could not deliver: immediate, live contact with a distant voice.[11] Some listeners might content themselves with the sounds of café-concerts or jazz bands broadcast by a Parisian station, Divoire claimed, but the true "wireless amateur is an insatiable Don Juan," always seeking a new auditory experience in the sounds of an unknown, distant station.[12]

Although international listening began as the hobby of the predominantly male *sans-filistes* who animated radio clubs of the early 1920s, the proximity of national stations in Europe ensured that tuning into foreign

---

[8] Brochand, *Histoire générale de la radio*, 1: 97–98.
[9] Arno Huth, *La radiodiffusion: puissance mondiale* (Paris, 1938), 39, 111, 126, 193. The principal European stations on the borders of France included: Berlin (1923); Leipzig, Frankfurt, Munich, Stuttgart, and Breslau (1924); Langenberg (1927); London, Birmingham, and Newcastle (1923); Daventry (1925); Rome and Milan (1924); and Turin (1927).
[10] Fernand Divoire, "Le Don Juan des ondes," *Lumière et radio*, October 1929, 1–2.
[11] Philip Stern, "Exploration and Enlightenment," in Dane Kennedy, ed., *Reinterpreting Exploration: The West in the World* (Oxford, 2014), 54–79; C.W. Thompson, *French Romantic Travel Writing: Chateaubriand to Nerval* (Oxford, 2012). Susan Douglas describes this "exploratory listening" in *Listening In*, 38–39.
[12] Fernand Divoire, "Le Don Juan des ondes," 1–2.

programs became commonplace as radios made their way into homes across France.[13] Determining precisely which foreign stations audiences listened to remains challenging, however, because reception – of French or foreign stations – relied upon a complex constellation of factors including the weather, the time of day, a radio station's transmitting power, and its frequency or wavelength. Listeners' own technical skills, the type of receiver they used, and their topographical location (near bodies of water or mountains, or in urban versus rural settings) could also affect what they heard. As the engineer and radio industrialist Paul Brenot explained to *La Nature* in 1932, a distinction should made between listening to radio programs and merely receiving signals, for there are a "number of stations that one hears but does not listen to. This applies for the most part to those that can only be heard at night, but with such variations that listening is without interest."[14] When readers of *Radio-Magazine* wrote to the editorial page to boast that they "regularly picked up" stations in Barcelona, Langenberg, or Milan, it is unclear whether they were describing regular listening habits or merely indicating the stations their radios could receive.[15]

Channeling what the popular mystery novelist Pierre MacOrlan hailed as the "bazaar of Europe" through one's radio further demanded the cultivation of special tuning and listening skills.[16] To receive radio stations near and far, radio amateurs had to navigate a vast, amorphous, and seemingly infinite "ocean" of airwaves – a voyage fraught with thrills and perils for the ears. Early listeners frequently invoked this metaphor of the "etheric ocean," Jeffrey Sconce suggests, because it captured the "seeming omnipresence, unfathomable depths, and invisible mysteries of both radio's ether and its audiences – mammoth, fluid bodies ... that were boundless and unknowable."[17] On the spectrum below Hilversum, according to Fernand Divoire, he entered a "storm zone" of static and encountered a "crowd of demons that whistle, sing, and scream," sometimes imitating "sirens and sometimes the whistles of a locomotive," before being startled by a burst of harmonics or the whispers of a human voice.[18] Nor was the method for distinguishing a radio broadcast

[13] On international listening as a technical pursuit, see Susan Douglas, *Inventing American Broadcasting 1899–1922* (Baltimore, 1987), Chapter 6, and Haring, *Ham Radio's Technical Culture*, 19–48.
[14] Paul Brenot, "L'organisation de la radiophonie en France," *La Nature*, September 15, 1932, 202.
[15] *Radio-Magazine*, January 19, 1930, 6.
[16] Pierre MacOrlan, "Le chasseur des ondes à l'écoute dans la nuit mystérieuse," *Mon programme*, December 2, 1932.
[17] Sconce, *Haunted Media*, 63–64.
[18] Fernand Divoire, "En écoutant ... le zone des tempêtes," *Lumière et radio*, February 10, 1930, 4.

from the "frying sounds" of static or the "ta, tagada ... ta, tsoin, tsoin" of Morse code signals always self-evident.[19] The engineer Michel Adam offered to "unmask the secret of the airwaves" for readers of *Radio-Magazine* in 1927. "Music, which is an international language" provided the befuddled listener few clues about a station's origin, he admitted, but "even without being a polyglot, it is not impossible to distinguish ... the particular timbre of the whispered English tongue, the stressed and aspirated German, the musical and vocalized Italian, the sonorous and guttural Spanish, and the hard and chopped Scandinavian. It is a question of ear and of habit." The more precise identification of a radio signal required one to distinguish its wavelength (or frequency) and its intensity, the latter an indication of the station's distance from the listener. Radio stations typically identified themselves by their names and precise location on the spectrum: "This is Paris PTT wavelength 450 meters." But station identifications often came only at the beginning and end of each day's broadcasts, which placed the burden of distinguishing station signals on listeners themselves.[20]

Perhaps even more challenging for the wireless neophyte, navigating the airwaves required listeners to master the unique and ever-shifting geography of the airwaves – no small task in the 1920s, when new stations began transmitting every month, including many based in the "young" countries of Central and Eastern Europe created by diplomats' division of the "old" multinational empires at the Paris Peace Conferences, as well as others in Europe's overseas colonies.[21] With many people still adjusting to the recently redrawn map of the Continent, radio listeners now encountered a radio spectrum filled with stations whose placement – in long, medium, or short waves – bore little relation to their actual geographical location and whose "voices" extended far beyond their national borders. Recalling his nightly "travel circuit" in his memoirs, the journalist and radio dramatist Georges Armand-Masson listed the cities he visited by ascending wavelength: Budapest to Hanover, followed by Fribourg, Ljubljana, Lausanne, Geneva, and Basel via Moscow and Leningrad; then Hilversum, Eindhoven, Kalundborg, and finally the Eiffel Tower, Daventry 5XX, and last but not least, Radio-Paris.[22] In

---

[19] Scaramouche, "Etude sur les Morses," *Mon programme*, December 23, 1932.
[20] Michel Adam, "Pour dévoiler le secret des ondes: comment reconnaître une émission," *Radio-Magazine*, April 10, 1927. Radio waves are typically described either as a wavelength (distance from peak to peak) or frequency (how many peaks move through a point at a given time). Interwar authors used the terms "wavelength" and "frequency" interchangeably, with "frequency" gradually more common, partly because frequencies were easier to measure.
[21] Lommers, *Europe on Air*, 51–63.
[22] Georges Armand-Masson, *Radio, quand tu nous tiens* (Paris, 1932), 52–53.

1932, the station Radio Normandie/Fécamp (222.1 m) could be found between Cork (224.4 m) and Königsberg (217 m), while Radio-Toulouse (385 m) appeared between Glasgow (376.4 m) and Frankfurt (390 m). Traveling the distant reaches of the radio spectrum required listeners to simultaneously manipulate several controls on their radios to first detect a station's signal, and then again to increase its volume or clarity in their loudspeakers. Radio-electric manufacturers consequently prioritized the development of automatic tuning mechanisms. Critical to the emergence of calibrated radio dials and user-friendly tuning instruments was engineers' exploitation of the superheterodyne circuit (or "superhet"), which mixed two sound waves of different frequencies to generate a third frequency that could be more easily processed by a receiver and adapted for operation through a single dial.[23] The radio-electric firm CSF introduced its Radiola SFER 20 model in 1925 with a poster by the celebrated graphic artist Leonetto Cappiello, featuring a young woman with bobbed hair and chandelier earrings dreamily turning a radio dial "with a single maneuver" to receive a variety of European broadcasts – an image so popular that several small retailers copied it for their own print advertisements [Figure 3.1].[24]

Yet even after the introduction of calibrated radio dials, any new station that began transmitting could disrupt listeners' reference points for tuning, prompting the radio press to supply their subscribers with regularly updated "maps" of the spectrum detailing stations' placement on the radio dial [Figure 3.2].[25] Not until the mid-1930s did manufacturers produce radios with backlit station scales, popularly known as the "magic eye" (*oeil magique*), that listed the major European stations by name, allowing audiences to easily turn their dials to the station (or city) of their choice. One precondition for the emergence of these visual station scales, as we shall see, was the regulation and stabilization of the radio spectrum. By presenting distant stations as just a turn or two away on the dial, Andreas Fickers suggests, radio station scales became "early atlases of globalization," providing radio listeners with a daily reminder of the airwaves' ability to contract and expand the globe, while encouraging them to interpret the sounds they heard through a geospatial framework.[26]

---

[23] Andreas Fickers, "Visibly Audible: The Radio Dial as Mediating Interface," in Bijsterveld and Pinch, eds., *The Oxford Handbook of Sound Studies*, 411–39; Griset, "Innovation and Radio Industry in Europe during the Interwar Period," 37–57.
[24] For one example, see the advertisement for Pierre De Gialluly Radio, *L'Antenne*, June 26, 1929, 604.
[25] "Pour repérer les stations sur vos cadrans," *Mon programme*, April 8, 1932, 24.
[26] Fickers, "Visibly Audible," 411–39. Ulmann-Mauriat, *Naissance d'un média*, 14–15. Fickers emphasizes the complex mechanical construction and design required for the creation of station scales to ensure that stations appeared at an equal distance from one another on the radio dial.

Figure 3.1 "A Single Maneuver with the SFER Radiola 20," *Radio-Magazine* (1926). Image courtesy of the Bibliothèque Nationale de France.

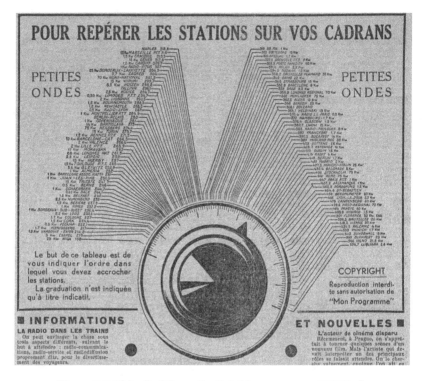

Figure 3.2 "Map" of the radio dial, *Mon programme* (1932). Image
courtesy of the Bibliothèque Nationale de France.

Memoirs, newspaper accounts, and letters from listeners published
regularly in the radio press suggest that tuning into foreign broadcasts
encouraged audiences to imagine themselves as cosmopolitan citizens of
an increasingly interconnected world. For Pierre MacOrlan, traveling
through the seemingly boundless ether as a "wave hunter" (*chasseur des
ondes*) delivered "an entire European festival into the headset that covers
my ears … Englishmen, Poles, Dutchmen, Italians, Spaniards, and
Germans are all at my house this evening."[27] Georges Armand-Masson
similarly described how the "oriental music" played by Radio-Alger
transported him to the Arab Cafés of the Casbah, while Milan conjured
up the glittering opera house of La Scala and the English station Daventry
permitted him to become a London *bon vivant* across the Channel in the

---

[27] Pierre MacOrlan, "Le chasseur des ondes à l'écoute dans la nuit mystérieuse," *Mon
programme*, December 2, 1932.

"Grand Hall Cecil, amid the drops of music that fall on the bare shoulders of beautiful English women on Saturday nights."[28] Radio listeners' embrace of cosmopolitanism reflected the prevailing optimism of the mid-to-late 1920s, when diplomatic accords from the Dawes Plan to the Treaty of Locarno offered real hope of Franco-German rapprochement, and with it, the prospect of a permanent peace in Europe.[29] Intellectuals including the communist novelist Romain Rolland, the poet Paul Valéry, the philosopher Henri Bergson, and the Catholic liberal Marc Sangnier repudiated the chauvinistic nationalism they blamed for the outbreak of the First World War in favor of transnational communication and exchange as part of a movement that the historian Akira Iriye has termed "cultural internationalism."[30] For the novelist Victor Marguerrite, the author of the 1925 pacifist manifesto *Appel aux consciences*, wireless was a "magnificent discovery, that overturning the narrow limits of the world, opens our astonished dreams to the perspective of a new *cité*, a New Society."[31] Such fantasies of international exchange were not, however, the exclusive preserve of literary elites or journalists. Martial Barraud, a public schoolteacher from the Vanves region, wrote to *Le Petit radio* that when listening to the Rome station, "I see myself seated beneath orange trees in the bay of Sorrento, shaking hands with the beautiful female announcer."[32]

Much in the way that radio boosters highlighted broadcasting's social benefits for a nation still grappling with the traumas of the First World War, wireless magazines portrayed radio as an inherently international media that could heal longstanding hatreds by facilitating intimate contact between radio listeners of former "enemy" nations. "Numerous times we have heard Germans and Frenchmen say 'if different peoples knew one another better, they would appreciate each other more and points of friction could be eliminated,'" *L'Antenne*'s editor Henry Etienne proposed in 1928. "Radio now offers us an admirable means to make ourselves known to one another."[33] *Radio-Magazine* published maps of

---

[28] Masson, *Radio, quand tu nous tiens*, 53.
[29] J.B. Duroselle, "The Spirit of Locarno: Illusions of Pactomania," *Foreign Affairs*, 50, 4, 1972, 752–64.
[30] Akira Iriye, *Cultural Internationalism and World Order* (Baltimore, 2000), 54–58; Gearoid Barry, *The Disarmament of Hatred: Marc Sangnier, French Catholicism, and the Legacy of The First World War, 1914–1945* (Basingstoke, 2012), 104–27.
[31] Victor Marguerite, "Devant le micro," *Lumière et radio*, April 8, 1930; Norman Ingram, *The Politics of Dissent: Pacifism in France, 1919–1939* (Oxford, 1991), 43–46.
[32] "Un auditeur provincial à Paris," *Le Petit radio*, December 26, 1931.
[33] Henry Etienne, "Les relais internationaux, instrument du paix," *L'Antenne*, October 7, 1928, 1. Etienne was the pseudonym of Henri-Georges Steffen, who was involved in the creation and management of the international commercial broadcaster Radio-Luxembourg in the early 1930s. Brochand, *Histoire générale de la radio*, 1: 257.

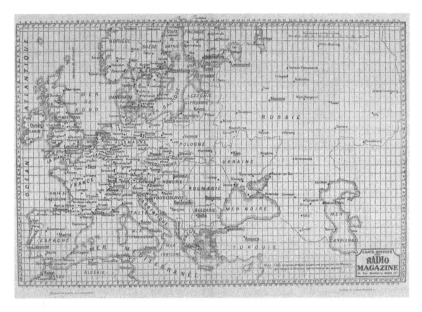

Figure 3.3 Map of Europe marked with the principal radio stations,
Radio-Magazine (1930). Image courtesy of the Bibliothèque Nationale
de France.

the Continent with dots marking the principal stations, urging listeners to
hang them on their walls, plot out the signals they received with pushpins,
and compete with other *sans-filistes* by boasting about their tuning and
detection skills [Figure 3.3].[34] Radio newspapers published international
program listings that directed their subscribers to foreign programs of
interest, whether news reports, music, or theatrical performances.
Foreign station listings were initially sparse in detail, filling a single
column in *Radio-Magazine* in 1923, but a decade later they occupied
multiple pages in the weeklies *Le Petit radio* and *Mon programme*, which
offered daily schedules for as many as twenty to fifty different overseas
stations.[35]

    Lest this promotion of international listening appear purely disinter-
ested, French radio-electric manufacturers such as the Compagnie
Générale de T.S.F (CSF) and its subsidiaries Société Française de

---

[34] *Radio-Magazine*, April 6, 1930, 24–25.
[35] Méadel, *Histoire de la radio*, 270; "Horaire des principales émissions radiophoniques
françaises et étrangères," *Radio-Magazine*, October 27, 1923, 7.

Radioélectricité and Radio France relied heavily on overseas markets for sales of their radio transmitters in the late 1920s.[36] Small-scale ateliers and larger radio-electric firms also capitalized on audiences' interest in armchair travel to market their products. In 1930, the Paris-based Etablissements Adrien Beausoleil advertised a model called "The Polyglot" that promised to deliver "foreigners into your loudspeaker."[37] A few years later, Radiola began advertising short-wave models that could receive "Uncle Sam and his orchestra" from across the Atlantic, even as the fantasy of cross-cultural interaction through the airwaves gradually became an advertising cliché.[38]

French radio stations further encouraged audiences to tune into foreign broadcasts by offering an array of on-air foreign language lessons, casting bilingualism as a vital survival skill in a twentieth century that would be defined by international travel and business. In the immediate postwar years, Paris began to rival London as Americans' preferred center of business operations in Europe, and American companies from Frigidaire to Atwater Kent opened up branches across the capital.[39] A French subsidiary of the US-based Berlitz Academy introduced courses in English and German on the commercial station Radio-Paris in 1924, exploiting radio's auditory form to teach pronunciation and basic conversational skills that could assist store clerks and business executives.[40] High-school teachers and university professors also volunteered courses in English, Spanish, and Italian on regional state stations.[41] Judging from the ubiquitous print advertisements that appeared in mass dailies for Linguaphone, a phonograph-based foreign language learning system, these free radio lessons likely found an eager audience.[42]

The commercial stations Poste Parisien, Radio-Toulouse, and Radio Côte d'Azur even designed broadcasts for listeners overseas, albeit less in the spirit of internationalism than their directors' desire to make a profit.

---

[36] Griset, "Innovation and Radio Industry in Europe during the Interwar Period," 37–57; Méadel, *Histoire de la radio*, 28–29. France's radio-electric industry competed well in international markets until competition from foreign multinational corporations outstripped their markets in the early 1930s.
[37] "Le polyglotte," *Radio-Magazine*, November 2, 1930, 26.
[38] Radiola advertisements in *Mon programme*, January 31, 1936, and February 14, 1936. For more on transatlantic short wave, see Vaillant, "At the Speed of Sound," 888–921.
[39] Blower, *Becoming Americans in Paris*, 27–30.
[40] CAC 19870714-2. 68e leçon d'anglais par un professeur de l'Ecole Berlitz. Cours de perfectionnement, August 24, 1924.
[41] "Horaire des cours des langues vivantes," *Radio-Magazine*, May 28, 1933; *L'Antenne*, January 3, 1933. On the introduction of the Berlitz method into France, see Christian Puren, *Histoire des méthodologies de l'enseignement des langues* (Paris, 1998), 110.
[42] Linguaphone advertisements, *Radio-Magazine*, September 28, 1930, 50, and November 2, 1930, 26.

Taking advantage of the BBC's ban on commercial advertising, the stations signed contracts with Selfridge's department store and Philips radio to sponsor evening "concerts" of jazz and dance records. The coastal station Radio-Normandie went so far as to import radio announcers from England on the weekends, when it played light music that rivaled the BBC's religious programming. Of course, French audiences tuned into these programs as well, which introduced them to an entirely new English vocabulary that crept into some listeners' everyday parlance, a phenomenon that did not go unnoticed by right-leaning cultural critics fearful that French might soon be eclipsed as a global language of diplomacy and trade.[43]

More deliberate efforts to exploit broadcasting as a tool of European rapprochement came from the Radio-Club Espérantiste de France, which counted a membership of approximately 1,500 adepts of the invented international language. France had been a stronghold of Esperanto before the war, but the right-wing politicians who took power after the Armistice banned its teaching in public schools in favor of a more overtly nationalist curriculum. After the radical-socialist *cartel des gauches* coalition government overturned the prohibition in 1924, Esperanto found new converts within socialist circles and in radio clubs.[44] The physicians, public school teachers, and engineers who filled the ranks of the Radio-Club Espérantiste saw themselves as the vanguard of a truly international community forged in the borderless airwaves, and eagerly tuned into the Czech station Brno, which boasted its own Esperanto dramatic troupe. They also petitioned the advisory boards of several state-affiliated stations (including Lille, Marseille-Provence, Paris PTT, Limoges, Alpes-Grenoble, Nice-Juan-les-Pins, Lyon-la-Doua, and the Eiffel Tower) to broadcast on-air Esperanto language courses, and even persuaded the undersecretary of state for tourism to host a short-lived series of Esperanto talks advertising France's tourist destinations to audiences overseas.[45] One Esperantist, boasting to the Paris PTT magazine *Echo du studio* about his rapid fluency in the language, insisted that his radio lessons had permitted him to become a "good worker for the rapprochement of peoples and the spread of universal peace."[46]

---

[43] Briggs, *The History of Broadcasting in the United Kingdom*, 2: 324–26; Sean Street, *Crossing the Ether: Pre-War Public Service Radio and Commercial Competition in the U.K.* (Eastleigh UK, 2006), 137–54; Paul Crouzet, "La défiguration du français à la radio," *La Grande revue*, October 1936, 564–71.

[44] Mona Siegel, *The Moral Disarmament of France: Education, Pacifism, and Patriotism, 1914–1940* (Cambridge, 2004), 174–75; Panchasi, *Future Tense*, 135–69.

[45] "Les émissions en espéranto au Tour Eiffel," *L'Antenne*, June 11, 1933, 422.

[46] "Boîte aux lettres d'espéranto," *L'Echo du studio*, September 13, 1930.

But given that Esperantists represented only a minority of French radio listeners, what did others hear when they tuned into foreign stations? Musical programs attracted many French listeners, to be sure. Live jazz from London hotels such as the Savoy garnered rave reviews in the radio press, and Jack Payne, the director of the Hotel Cecil Orchestra, became a celebrity across Europe.[47] Serious music lovers favored Berlin for symphonic concerts and Milan for operas, but France's leading musical critics also endorsed the German and Italian stations for the superior technical quality of their transmissions.[48] France's burgeoning immigrant population clearly took comfort in hearing broadcasts from "home." The Polish station Katowice created a "Letter Box" program especially for Polish immigrants living in France, featuring an elderly "Papa Stéphane" who read letters from Poles working overseas in both Polish and French.[49] Yet for most French audiences, foreign talk radio programs – whether news reports or conferences on artistic, scientific, or medical topics – were difficult to understand. Elites and middle-class audiences who had attended a *lycée* (high school) often mastered the rudiments of a foreign language, and a significant number of veterans returned from the war with a smattering of English or German, but few French people spoke another language fluently.

Tuning into foreign stations could thus provoke ridiculous dinner-table speculations about the national origins of stations, the journalist Georges Armand-Masson recalled: "under the name of London all the English stations are grouped, from Sheffield to Daventry. 'Spain' includes different stations whose *speaker* (announcer) rolls their 'r,' like Poznan, Katowice, Brno, Rome, and also, to be just, Madrid. As for the 'Fritzes,' they are the Germans, the Dutch, the Danish, and the Swiss."[50] Yet for some listeners, even if they could not follow a broadcast word for word, simply encountering foreign sounds proved to be a thrilling experience. The blind radio amateur Jacques Lusseyran, a teenager in the 1930s, remembered himself as a "veritable Tower of Babel in miniature" when he conducted his "evening tour of Europe" via the airwaves. As he recalled in his memoir, he always stopped his dial on German cities because the "German language appeared to have an exceptional sonic beauty; it appeared to me to be gifted with a marvelous power." He also recalled listening to an entire BBC production of *Hamlet* during which he "understood nothing," even though he "remained fascinated" by the accents of a foreign tongue. From these listening sessions, he learned

[47] James J. Nott, *Music for the People: Popular Music and Dance in Interwar Britain* (Oxford, 2002), 61.
[48] See *L'Edition musicale vivante* for March 2, 1935, and May 11, 1935.
[49] Prot, *Dictionnaire de la radio*, 335.   [50] Masson, *Radio, quand tu nous tiens*, 38.

enough German to understand Hitler's speeches, a skill that would later serve him well as a member of a Parisian resistance cell during the German occupation of the Second World War.[51]

But for all those listeners who embraced the cosmopolitan culture of early radio, many others worried that Europe's linguistic diversity would ultimately undermine broadcasting's ability to facilitate lasting rapprochement. Wireless technology had created the possibility of global interconnection, *Radio-Magazine* observed, but as a purely auditory media it also exposed the "barriers and difficulties that separate poor humanity" far more than the telegraph, the telephone, or the airplane. If the "story of the Tower of Babel was only a fable, had it not become reality" in the airwaves?[52] Audiences are "interested in international stations and listen to them willingly to the degree that they can understand them," the journalist Maurice Bex concurred, and few people could resist the "pleasure of hearing La Scala or the Savoy." But "there is always a limit to polyglotism," and the time would come when "even the best disciples of Berlitz will flunk out in the face of a broadcast in Hindustani or Eskimo."[53] One *Radio-Magazine* cartoon of 1930 suggested that some listeners would always hear foreign languages as little more than noise. The artist depicted a man struggling with his malfunctioning radio to locate a station, only to conclude that the crackling and distorted voices pouring forth were "surely Moscow."[54] The cartoon's deliberate conflation of foreign broadcasting with static signaled the end of the optimistic 1920s, when so many listeners embraced radio's potential to facilitate international exchange, presaging a decade of conflicts over the European radio spectrum.

Border accidents: interference and the congested airwaves

Radio-Magazine's cartoon of a befuddled and frustrated radio listener tinkering with his defective radio pointed to the emergence of a serious problem that began to plague the airwaves in France by the end of the 1920s: interference, or as listeners referred to it, *brouillage*. As early as 1926, one listener complained "we can hardly use our receiver because of interference."[55] *Brouillage*, one radio newspaper explained to its subscribers, was a sonic affliction produced by spatial disorder on the radio spectrum. When two stations happened to broadcast on the same or

[51] Jacques Lusseyran, *Et la lumière fut* (Paris, 2005), 105–8.
[52] Général Cartier, "Radiophonie rurale," *Radio-Magazine*, April 13, 1930, 13.
[53] Maurice Bex, "En guise de plaidoirie," *Radio-Magazine*, February 15, 1931.
[54] *Radio-Magazine*, April 13, 1930, 11.
[55] "Comment éliminer une station gênante," *Radio-Magazine*, August 22, 1926.

adjacent wavelengths, their signals clashed, producing "noise" as the more powerful signal disrupted the reception of the weaker one.[56] Interference had increased exponentially alongside the growing number of radio stations in Europe, as stations were forced to transmit too close together on the radio spectrum. This practice made tuning difficult and hindered audiences' ability to locate and maintain a steady signal. Even worse, radio stations compounded the problem by switching their wavelengths to create better reception for their audiences. "There is not a single radio listener who does not complain of the incessant changes that European stations make to their wavelengths," the musicologist André Coeuroy remarked in 1930. The ether, which many people had once imagined as a vast, infinite "ocean" of sound waves, now appeared incapable of containing the hundreds of voices clamoring to be heard.[57] "Space is too small for the human adventure . . . colonized by the invasion of the airwaves," the radio dramatist Suzanne Malard wrote a few years later in her poem "Interferences," for "already there are border accidents between invisible adjacent walls. Madrid disrupts Rabat, Zurich covers Saint-Sebastien, and Stockholm denounces Rome."[58] Listeners and journalists for the radio press echoed Malard's spatial adjectives in describing the state of the airwaves: overcrowded, congested, colonized, and incapable of containing the "multiplicity of stations that send out radio signals."[59]

Radio interference was a Europe-wide problem, but France suffered acutely thanks to its mountain ranges and sea borders, and particularly after its neighbors Germany, Great Britain, and Italy began expanding their radio networks. Audiences frequently complained about the powerful British station Daventry disrupting their reception of Radio-Paris, but French stations contributed to the problem as well. Six public and commercial stations were transmitting from the capital and its suburbs by 1930, including Radio-Paris, Tour Eiffel, Paris PTT, the Poste Parisien, Radio LL, and Radio-Vitus.[60] The physical proximity of these stations' transmitters sometimes made clear reception impossible. The Eiffel Tower and Paris PTT had turned the airwaves in the capital into a "cacophonous hell," *L'Antenne*'s Henry Etienne protested, and the squeals of radio loudspeakers only exacerbated other forms of urban

---

[56] E.H. Weiss, "La nouvelle répartition des longueurs d'ondes. Le plan de Bruxelles," *Radio-Agricole française*, February 1929, 9. See also Lommers, *Europe on Air*, 75.
[57] Coeuroy, *Panorama de la radio*, 98.
[58] Suzanne Malard, "Interférences," *Radiophonies* (Paris, 1931).
[59] E.H. Weiss, "La nouvelle répartition des longueurs d'ondes. Le plan de Bruxelles," *Radio-Agricole française*, February 1929, 9.
[60] Brochand, *Histoire générale de la radio*, 1: 97–98.

noise. "It is absolutely certain that if the Eiffel Tower had not already been there, no one would have thought of putting a powerful wireless station" on the Champ de Mars.[61] City dwellers also suffered from electrical static (*parasites*) generated by appliances, tramways, and elevators that produced a whole "lexicon of crackling noises" in their receivers: ringing bells, purring motors, firecrackers, and other loud explosions.[62] Although Parisians should have had access to the greatest variety of programs, they had instead become the "true pariahs of wireless," *L'Echo du studio* claimed, because the "majority of listeners who live in the capital, particularly those who live in the center, have a great difficulty picking up foreign stations, the provinces, and even their own Parisian stations."[63]

By the end of the 1920s, a sharp disjuncture had emerged between the radio reception enjoyed by rural and urban audiences, as well as between listeners of different social classes. The staff of *L'Echo du studio*, seeking scientific confirmation for the litany of complaints that flooded their mailbox, dispatched a technician into the streets of Paris to investigate. He tested several multi-lamp radios in buildings of different shapes and sizes across the city. "With the exception of several privileged persons on the upper floors, or those living in spacious squares, or perhaps still the happy Montmartre resident" on the hill overlooking the capital, he concluded, "the Parisian listener is forced to hear poorly and to possess an expensive radio." Moreover, wealthy individuals with more powerful radio receivers could better combat *parasites*, while those with cheaper radios or home-built receivers were deprived of the privilege of listening. Parisians might live near France's most important radio stations, but only "country and provincial folk" could "listen to them comfortably and affordably."[64]

An anonymous provincial listener who moved to the capital from the Limousin confirmed these impressions in a 1931 letter to *Le Petit radio*, comparing the relative purity of rural listening with the "congestion" of the urban airwaves. In the countryside, he easily tuned into sixty stations and enjoyed foreign broadcasts in the evenings, because "the English are excellent to put you to sleep [and] the warm voices of the German singers make you dream." Yet picking up his favorite foreign stations was impossible in the capital, thanks to the commercial stations Radio LL and the

[61] Henry Etienne, "L'enfer parisien," *L'Antenne*, January 27, 1929, 1.

[62] Georges Armand-Masson, "La vie des ondes. Dictionnaire des bruits," *Le Haut-parleur*, August 14, 1932, 431.

[63] No author, "Les parias de la T.S.F. postes parisiens et d'ailleurs," *L'Echo du studio*, October 14, 1929.

[64] *Ibid.*

Poste Parisien. While the weaker "Paris PTT, at 417 m, doesn't keep me from hearing Rome at 441 m or Beromünster at 459 m," Radio LL produced "explosions of sound when the index passed 35, 40, and then 72." His friends were "better positioned to listen in their village than in Montrouge or Ménilmontant," he noted. Why did the state allow these commercial stations to "bully a city of four million inhabitants?"[65]

The growing problem of radio interference revealed another pressing concern: namely, that many listeners could hear foreign stations more clearly than French ones. *L'Antenne*'s editor Paul Berché summed up the situation succinctly in December of 1929: "our loudspeakers vibrate in German, in English, in Spanish, in Italian, in Polish, in Czech, in Hungarian, and even in Esperanto," with two notable exceptions. "In Paris, listeners could complain of being saturated, except for the PTT station covered by Langenberg," while listeners in the southwest could only hear Radio-Toulouse. Radio-Paris was the only station capable of covering all of France, but "that's if the majority of listeners have sensitive receivers."[66] A survey conducted by another radio magazine the following year revealed that twenty foreign stations could be heard more clearly in the capital than their French counterparts, while rural audiences could only hear foreign stations, rather than the Parisian broadcasts they longed for.[67]

Radio listeners, amateur radio clubs, and the wireless press together began calling for the state to impose order in the disorganized and chaotic airwaves in France. They demanded the creation of a "radio nation" – or a distinctive space composed of French radio signals and voices in the airwaves – and suggested that their inability to hear French stations constituted a form of exclusion from national life. "French radio waves do not reach certain regions such as the Alps; other regions, like Alsace, hear only German voices," the businessmen and future Radio-Luxembourg administrator Jacques-Lacour Gayet lamented, while "on the coasts of the English Channel and in the Finistère, there is permanent interference between stations."[68] Georges-Jean Guiraud, the president of the Association Radiophonique de la Côte d'Argent, the listeners' asso-ciation that managed the Bordeaux PTT station, called for the creation of a broadcasting network to "assure programming across all points of

---

[65] "Un auditeur provincial à Paris," *Le Petit radio*, December 26, 1931, 3. Méadel discusses this phenomenon in *Histoire de la radio*, 203–4.
[66] Paul Berché, "Les allemands se plaignent," *L'Antenne*, December 1, 1929.
[67] H. Mathis, "Le salon de T.S.F. vu par un agriculteur," *Radio-Agricole française*, November 1928, 2.
[68] Jacques Lacour-Gayet. *La grande pitié de la radiodiffusion. Extrait du Correspondent du 25 janvier 1930* (Paris, 1930), 7–8.

[French] territory." He insisted that the "working and peasant classes" should be able to tune into French stations with inexpensive radios, permitting radio listening to become a "democratic" practice rather than remaining a bourgeois pastime.[69] At the same time, these critics concluded, French radio signals could barely be heard beyond the nation's borders, offering proof that France had failed to establish a sufficient presence in the "concert of Europe."[70] France's history had long been shaped by its geography, Léon de la Forge argued in L'Antenne, but if this made France well disposed to receive foreign broadcasts, why did the state not exploit France's strategic placement on the Continent to ensure that French voices could be heard overseas?[71]

More important, because interference was a European, rather than an exclusively national problem, France needed to establish a "precise border, complete with quarantine and customs lines," to protect its own airwaves from the invasion of foreign radio signals.[72] The "encumbered and lawless" nature of the European airwaves posed unprecedented challenges for lawmakers and diplomats, André Coeuroy admitted in 1930, but "only a single international regulation, complete with sanctions, can remedy this anarchy."[73] Growing nationalist concerns about the international status of French broadcasting thus converged with audiences' demands for the state to protect their "right to listen" by constructing a "radio nation" and by entering into agreements with neighboring countries that could guarantee stable listening conditions across France, permitting citizens of all social classes to participate in national life through the airwaves.[74]

Building a "radio nation": the Ferrié Plan for state broadcasting

The years between 1929 and 1931 marked a significant departure in the ways that audiences, state bureaucrats, and politicians alike conceived of the airwaves. Although many listeners continued to tune into foreign

---

[69] Georges-Jean Guiraud, président de l'Association Radiophonique de la Côte d'Argent et président du Conseil d'administration de la Fédération Nationale de Radiodiffusion. *Pour un statut démocratique et rationnel de la radiodiffusion* (Rennes, 1930), 30, 43–45, 46–47.
[70] Jacques Lacour-Gayet. *La grande pitié de la radiodiffusion*, 7–8.
[71] Léon de la Forge, "La radiodiffusion française écoutée de l'étranger," *L'Antenne*, November 5, 1930, 613–14.
[72] Scaramouche, "Etude sur les Morses," *Mon programme*, December 23, 1932.
[73] Coeuroy, *Panorama de la radio*, 98.
[74] Michel Adam, "Le droit des auditeurs de radiodiffusion et l'élimination des parasites en T.S.F.," *La Nature*, September 1, 1932, 215.

broadcasts, they now began to demand that the state carve out a space for the "radio nation" in the airwaves to ensure that French voices could be heard across the country as well as throughout Europe. Lawmakers responded by voting in 1928 to reaffirm the state monopoly and prohibit the construction of any new commercial stations, a gesture aimed partly at reducing interference. In 1930, the Tardieu government appointed a commission to develop a comprehensive plan for a state radio network, and selected the aging General Ferrié, the "father" of French radio and the symbolic head of France's vocal *sans-filiste* community, to head it.[75] Ferrié boasted significant scientific expertise, but he was also a regular contributor to wireless magazines and the popular scientific press, whose appointment signaled to audiences that their complaints had been heard. Marcel Pellenc, the recently named director of state broadcasting, the Sorbonne physicist Henri Abraham, and Camille Gutton, the director of the National Radio-Electric Laboratory, joined Ferrié on the commission.[76]

One the eve of the commission's first meeting, PTT minister Charles Guernier charged Ferrié with creating a "continuous spiritual current across the Nation," so that "next to our great national works, which Paris and several of our other large cities have at their disposal, their innumerable precious and fecund works produced in so many different places will be broadcast over the entire territory." To this end, Guernier tasked the commission with designing a system so that "the most modest fellow citizens can, with the most modest of radios, hear a broadcast wherever he happens to be."[77] Every French citizen should be able to hear an equal balance of "regional" and "national" (i.e., Parisian) broadcasts on the most basic and inexpensive radio receiver, he insisted. While solidifying the state's commitment to creating a democratic "radio nation" by creating equivalent listening conditions across France, these ideological and technical priorities also reflected to a broader conversation unfolding in the mass press and in political circles about the relationship of France's cities to its rural provinces.

Since the 1880s, politicians from across the political spectrum had shared the view that a stable economy and harmonious civil society required an equilibrium between industry and agriculture. The industrial rationalization introduced during the First World War appeared to have

[75] Ulmann-Mauriat, *Naissance d'un média*, 160–62. Mallarmé, the PTT minister under the Tardieu government, first created the Ferrié Commission.
[76] Prot, *Dictionnaire de la radio*, 29, 241, 293.
[77] Charles Guernier, quoted in Ulmann-Mauriat, *Naissance d'un média*, 61, 187–88. Marcel Pellenc, who distrusted commercial broadcasting, had already called for artistic decentralization through the airwaves.

disrupted this balance, however, as agricultural laborers fled the country-side in search of higher wages in factories, with the result that France's urban population outstripped its rural regions for the first time in 1931.[78] Social reformers and economists feared that rural depopulation would destroy France's agricultural sector while fueling urban crime and political disorder. "The problem is as much psychological as material," Georges Reynauld, a former senator from the Ariège, explained to *L'Echo du studio* in 1930. The "farmer has the feeling of being isolated; the rhythm of his life is slower and gives him the impression of monotony ... he wants not to be severed from the pleasures the city provides, and this desire is most vivid among young people." Regular infusions of music and news delivered through the airwaves, he believed, could "render the youth of the countryside more cheerful and recover their favor."[79]

Reynauld's fantasy of reconciling rural traditions with the demands of modern life inspired him, along with several other prominent politicians, to join the lobbying group Radio-Agricole Française (RAF), which dedicated itself to promoting "progress and joy" in the countryside through the democratization of radio.[80] Founded in 1927 by Joseph H. Ricard, a colonial lobbyist and one-time minister of agriculture, the group's members included Paul Brenot, the industrialist and vice-president of the Syndicat Professionnel des Industries Radioélectriques; Maréchal Hubert Lyautey, and General Ferrié himself. Radio-Agricole Française promoted radio listening as the ideal means for isolated farm families and the residents of small villages to "participate at will in the life of cities and in their economic, artistic, literary, and scientific life." While educating children and rendering rural homes more "gay and lively," the RAF argued, broadcasting also offered practical benefits to farmers.[81] To demonstrate radio's value to countryside, the RAF sponsored a series of nightly agricultural broadcasts on Radio-Paris that began with meteorological and market reports and concluded with talks on modern cultivation techniques.[82]

---

[78] Shanny Peer, *France on Display: Peasants, Provincials, and Folklore in the 1937 Paris World's Fair* (Albany NY, 1998), 7–11; Lebovics, *True France*, 24–26.

[79] Georges Reynauld, "La radiodiffusion dans les communes," *L'Echo du studio*, March 15, 1930.

[80] General Cartier, "La radiophonie: remède à la dépopulation de la campagne," *Le Petit radio*, April 30, 1927. The RAF drew support from the Société des Agriculteurs de France and the Union Coloniale Française. *Radio-Agricole française*, May 1928, 10.

[81] "Programme officiel de Radio-Agricole Française," *Radio-Agricole française*, May 1928, 19; and André Pavié, "La radiodiffusion et la diffusion de la pensée française," June 1928, 7. The RAF took no formal position in the ongoing battle between "monopolists" and "liberals," and defended both the expansion of the state network and commercial stations' right to broadcast.

[82] R.V., "Radiophonie et météorologie agricole," *Radio-Agricole française*, June 1928, 10; William G. Clément, "A propos du communiqué agricole quotidien de Radio-Paris,

Yet if the RAF hoped to modernize rural life, its members proved to be less interested in promoting regional diversity than in imposing their own views on the countryside. The group's magazine depicted France's provinces, not unlike its overseas colonies, as isolated outposts in need of the capital's civilizing mission, replicating decades-old stereotypes about the backwardness of rural populations.[83] In advocating a democratized geography of radio sound that would allow rural listeners to receive both Parisian and regional broadcasts with simple and cheap receivers, however, the RAF proved sensitive to the fact that many farmers lacked electricity in their homes and could not afford the expensive multi-lamp receivers required to pick up Parisian broadcasts. The construction of regional radio stations, the RAF concluded, would allow them to enjoy many of the same auditory experiences as listeners in the capital.[84]

The RAF's political program clearly informed the work undertaken by the Ferrié Commission and its analysis of the technical requirements necessary for a "democratic broadcasting network," such as station placement and transmitting power, the physical properties of wavelengths, and France's unique topography – all factors that would affect the density and reach of the network. The Commission divided France into eleven different "listening zones" with the goal of "assuring reception of broadcasts from one long-wave and one medium-wave station at every hour and at every point in French territory." One long-wave Parisian station, broadcasting at 100 kW, would serve as a "national" station reaching all eleven zones, while each individual zone would be served by one or more regional stations transmitting at 60 kW. In regions where PTT-affiliate stations already existed, the Commission called for an augmentation of their transmitting power, in many cases from 12 to 15 kW, while new transmitters would be built in regions where none existed. These new 60-kW regional stations, the Commission calculated, would be heard with a simple radio at a distance of 150–200 km, and the national station,

---

rédigé par les membres du Comité-directeur de la RAF," *Radio-Agricole française*, August 1928, 6.
[83] E.H. Weiss, "La T.S.F., organe de liaison de la métropole et colonies," *Radio-Agricole française*, May 1928, 10. The RAF, alongside the Institut Colonial and the Association Colonies-Sciences, played an active role in petitioning legislators to construct a short-wave transmitter that could reach France's colonies overseas. Their efforts resulted in legislators voting funds for the construction of the short-wave Poste Colonial, inaugurated at the 1931 Colonial Exposition at Vincennes. On French perceptions of the peasantry, see Eugen Weber, *Peasants into Frenchmen: The Modernization of Rural France, 1870–1914* (Palo Alto, 1976).
[84] H. Mathis, "Le salon de T.S.F. vu par un agriculteur," *Radio-Agricole française*, November 1928, 2, and G.L., "En T.S.F. que demande un auditeur rural," *Radio-Agricole française*, November 1928, 6.

transmitting at 100 kW, would be audible across France during the day and outside France's borders at night.[85] The final proposal put forward by the Ferrié Commission and sent to the Chamber of Deputies for a vote on June 30, 1931, demonstrates that the bureaucrats and engineers involved had listened to audiences' complaints about interference and poor reception. Creating a single "national" station would reduce the possibility of interference between several powerful transmitters, while limiting regional stations to one per zone would reduce the "troubles profoundly altering reception" that resulted from geographically proximate stations transmitting simultaneously. The Ferrié Plan also insisted that the new regional stations be constructed outside municipalities to reduce interference with those already in existence. Finally, with the global economic depression already wreaking havoc in the economy, the plan was financially practical. Constructing one national station would cost less than building several, while exploiting the current PTT infrastructure would limit spending. The Ferrié Commission called for the full implementation of the plan within three years, and lawmakers voted in eighty million francs to cover the cost of the transmitters and to install the telephone lines necessary to link the stations together for relays. This structure was designed to permit broadcasts of "federal" radio programs that originated in Paris (or occasionally in the provinces) via multiple regional stations. In 1934, the state took the first step toward completing the plan by purchasing the commercial station Radio-Paris to become France's flagship national station, while legislators voted in additional funds to increase the transmitting power of regional stations from 60 to 100 kW.[86]

The Ferrié Plan transformed the expectations that successive governments and radio audiences placed on the airwaves by establishing that there should be a firm correlation between the shape of the "radio nation" in the airwaves and the physical geography of France, making the complete "coverage" of national territory with French signals and voices a

---

[85] CAC 19870714-1. Rapport de la commission constituée par la décision du 10 février 1931 en vue de dresser le plan d'organisation de la radiodiffusion, n.d., 6. The eleven zones outlined in the Ferrié Plan and their corresponding stations were North (Lille/PTT Nord), East (Strasbourg PTT), West (Rennes PTT), Center (Radio-Paris, Paris PTT), Lyon (Lyon-la-Doua), Bordeaux (Bordeaux-Lafayette PTT), Toulouse (Toulouse PTT), Marseille (Marseille-Provence PTT), Monaco/Nice-Corsica (Nice-Côte d'Azur PTT), and a twelfth zone later added to serve the Alps (Grenoble PTT).

[86] Méadel, *Histoire de la radio*, 63–68, 149–51. Lawmakers voted in a budget of eighty million francs for the completion of the Ferrié Plan, which was the total of the revenues generated by the license fee in 1934. The number of commercial stations remained consistent into the 1930s: Radio-Lyon, Poste Parisien, Ile de France, Radio-Cité (purchased from Radio LL in 1935), Nice-Juan-les-Pins, Radio-Agen, Radio-Toulouse, Radio-Béziers, Radio-Montpellier, and Radio-Normandie.

political priority. Shortly thereafter, the state introduced additional measures to protect audiences' "right to listen." Radio clubs and the wireless press, as we have already seen, launched a campaign to protect listeners from the electrical appliances that generated *parasites* and disrupted their radio reception, resulting in the first Congress for the Defense of Radio Amateurs Against Static in 1931. Two years later, the PTT opened a consultation service that allowed radio owners with reception problems to request investigations by one of its technicians. Legislators also voted to require businesses to install *anti-parasite* devices on their machines to limit electric interference. Unfortunately, the PTT could do little to eliminate the *parasites* caused by public services, such as electric tramways or telephone and telegraph lines, that caused the majority of problems in cities.[87]

Even more problematic for listeners, the Ferrié Plan did not acknowledge the existence of commercial radio stations, their transmitting power, or the reach of their broadcasts, all of which would pose significant challenges to state broadcasting in the future.[88] The general chaos of the European airwaves, however, did factor into the Ferrié Commission's plans for creating a "radio nation" in the airwaves. Marcel Pellenc proved to be especially forward-looking with regard to France's international position, and worried constantly about foreign radio signals dominating French radios. The "English station Daventry is approximately 200 to 250 km [sic] away from Paris as the crow flies," he told fellow Commission members, and the "sound waves coming from this station follow a considerable maritime trajectory despite the current feeble power of the station (around 40 kW)," permitting it to be heard in Paris with the simplest of receivers. France needed to ensure that "Daventry's auditory effect in Paris will not be greater than that produced by Radio-Paris," he argued, for it was psychologically important that listeners in the capital to be able to hear the station bearing their city's name – a factor that contributed to an increase in its transmitting power a few years later.[89] When PTT minister Charles Guernier appealed to legislators for additional funding for state broadcasting, he similarly asked "should I leave France to be invaded by these wavelengths which no person can resist?"[90] This new concern with France's international status as a "radio power"

---

[87] *Radio-Magazine*, October 11, 1931. *Bulletin de l'Union Internationale de Radiodiffusion*, April 9, 1934, #4158. Anti-parasite devices were required for washing machines, coffee grinders, hair dryers, sewing machines, elevators, printing machines, and x-ray machines.

[88] Méadel, *Histoire de la radio*, 64.

[89] CAC 199870714-1. Procès-verbal de la commission chargée de dresser le plan national de la radiodiffusion française, November 11, 1931.

[90] Ulmann-Mauriat, *Naissance d'un média*, 175, 188.

would subsequently manifest itself in the form of a unique preoccupation with where French radio stations could be heard and whether France occupied a greater space on the radio spectrum than its neighbors.

The regional, national, and international politics of radio reception

The successful implementation of the 1931 Ferrié Plan and the creation of a "radio nation" in the airwaves did not rely solely upon the efforts of politicians, technicians, and engineers, but also on European cooperation in resolving the growing problem of interference in the airwaves. By the late 1920s, radio audiences and governments alike had begun to recognize the necessity of regulating the radio spectrum. Even before legislators endorsed the Ferrié Plan, France had signed a number of international agreements delimiting the wavelengths at its disposal. Regional, national, and international radio reception thus became embroiled in a new diplomacy of the airwaves, as audiences' radio reception and the proportion of French to foreign signals that they heard through their radio receivers now hinged upon the ability of diplomats and PTT bureaucrats to maneuver in the international arena.

To resolve the problem of radio interference, policymakers found themselves obliged to negotiate with other European nations through the International Broadcasting Union (IBU), a non-governmental regulatory agency established in Geneva in 1925 with the goal of facilitating international cooperation in broadcasting. Founded by a coalition of radio-electric manufacturers, state radio administrations, and scientific "experts" from several nations, the IBU's mandate developed out of traditions of cartel capitalism and international scientific cooperation. Eliminating interference, the IBU's founders believed, would fulfill important regulatory tasks ignored by national governments, while simultaneously promoting the economic well-being of the global radio-electric industry by making radio tuning easier and listening more pleasurable.[91] Although commercial interests predominated during the IBU's early years, its staff began gradually presenting the organization to European

[91] Lommers, *Europe on Air*, 60–65; Briggs, *The History of Broadcasting in the United Kingdom*, 2: 316–18; Brochand, *Histoire générale de la radio*, 1: 623. Brochand claims that the IBU was dominated by a CSF-Telefunken-RCA cartel eager to protect its financial interests. Briggs suggests BBC bureaucrats pushed the IBU to become a more neutral organization. Lommers suggests that both factors contributed to the emergence of a public service model of broadcasting on the Continent. On the history of France's international cooperation in telecommunications, see Léonard Laborie, *L'Europe mise en réseau: la coopération internationale dans les postes et télécommunications, années 1850–1950* (Brussels, 2010), 249–412.

publics as a "League of Nations" of the airwaves: a supposedly neutral arbiter whose duty was to establish and reinforce the "borders" between stations of different national origins on the radio spectrum. The IBU regarded radio interference as a uniquely European problem resulting from the "proximity of nations which each make large use of broadcasting." Radio was "essentially an international question," one 1930 IBU brochure asserted, and its "problems, which increase incessantly in importance and number, cannot find a happy solution in independent or isolated efforts."[92] To this end, the IBU hosted a succession of international conferences in the 1930s that brought together delegates from different nations to partition the airwaves.

Wireless boosters and the specialized radio press praised the IBU as an institution that might preserve radio's early international potential by ensuring "each radio signal a free path through the ether."[93] The IBU represented a "serious effort of European organization," Pierre Descaves told *Lumière et radio* in 1930, without which would be the "clogging of the ether, the monopolizing of wavelengths, and the practical impossibility of powerful or weak stations to make themselves heard."[94] For these reasons, the IBU's conferences, hailed by another journalist as the "complete and total union of Europe," generated a significant amount of coverage both in radio newspapers and in the mainstream press, which presented them as a direct parallel to the contemporary disarmament conferences that so preoccupied diplomats, even leaking details of closed-door IBU meetings to their readers.[95] However, if the IBU's multi national staff presented the organization's goals as expressly internationalist in orientation, the solutions it devised for regulating the radio spectrum were decidedly nationalist and informed by the principles of self-determination.[96] "The fundamental problem on which all others depends is to assure each authorized station

---

[92] Union Internationale de Radiodiffusion, *Les problèmes de la radiodiffusion: éxposé en français et anglais des études entreprises depuis cinq ans par l'Union Internationale de Radiodiffusion* (Chambéry, 1930), 6–9, 14–15, 42–43. In keeping with their goal of promoting "entente" between European nations, the IBU's "Commission for Social and Artistic Rapprochement" organized "national nights" in the early 1930s in which member countries broadcast programs from a particular European country on their state networks. The IBU coordinated the use of telephone lines for this purpose. Europe did experience unique patterns of radio interference, but the problem of frequency allocation plagued governments across the world. On this point, see Hugh Aitken, "Allocating the Spectrum: The Origins of Radio Regulation," *Technology and Culture*, 35, 4, 1994, 686–716.
[93] Léon de la Forge, "Les longueurs d'onde," *L'Antenne*, January 8, 1929, 1.
[94] Pierre Descaves, "La T.S.F. et la paix," *Lumière et radio*, June 10, 1930, 7.
[95] H. d'Orvillers, "Les décisions de la Conférence de Prague," *Radio-Agricole française*, June 1929, 5.
[96] Jennifer Spohrer, "Ruling the Airwaves: Radio-Luxembourg and the Origins of European National Broadcasting, 1929–1950" (PhD diss., Columbia University, 2008), 93–157. Spohrer also employs the term "maps" to describe frequency protocols.

the freedom to broadcast without disturbances in the territory for which it was constructed," one IBU publication asserted. Moreover, "each of the nations represented by the IBU" had the right to a designated space on the radio spectrum and a "sufficient number of wavelengths to ensure the functioning of a national broadcasting service covering its physical territory."[97] That this "national" model for dividing the radio spectrum prevailed owed much to the fact that most European states had already claimed a monopoly over the airwaves, as well as to the IBU's deliberate exclusion of representatives from commercial broadcasting stations, who lost their right to participate in IBU conferences in 1929.[98]

During the first two IBU conferences in Geneva (1925) and Brussels (1928), the organization's technical staff worked with delegates to develop a "map" of the radio spectrum that assigned specific frequencies to individual nations and their stations. Engineers at the IBU's control center in Brussels regularly monitored European stations and maintained records of their radio frequencies, transmitting power, and modulation – all factors that determined a station's reach. Their studies suggested that a separation of 9–10 kilohertz (kHz) would create a sufficient "border" between stations to prevent interference. Using this measurement, IBU technicians then calculated the number of available wavelengths on the spectrum and developed a formula for dividing them up between nations.[99] Each IBU member country would receive at least one exclusive wavelength (if not several) as well as the use of several common wavelengths. The number of wavelengths assigned to each country would be weighted according to a variety of factors: a nation's geography, its population, its degree of economic development, and its existing telecommunications infrastructure. This formula, while intended to be "scientific," clearly left room for subjective assessments of a nation's needs. Countries with older radio stations could claim sovereignty over particular wavelengths, a strategy that Britain and Belgium both manipulated to their advantage. Each conference produced a final "map" that assigned specific wavelengths to stations based on their predicted

[97] Union Internationale de Radiodiffusion, Les problèmes de la radiodiffusion, 14.
[98] Ulmann-Mauriat, Naissance d'un média, 70–71, 132–33. Representatives from the commercial stations Radiola, Petit Parisien, Radio-Toulouse, and Radio-Lyon attended. Marcel Pellenc refused to participate in the IBU in 1927 until the organization prevented private stations from being officially represented.
[99] Brochand, Histoire générale de la radio, 1: 635. The IBU used specific bands of wavelengths allocated to radio broadcasting by the International Telecommunications Union (ITU), which partitioned wavelengths between the broadcasting, telegraphy, military, and marine services of its participants. ITU conferences held in Washington (1927), Madrid (1932), and Cairo (1938) established these boundaries.

radius.[100] Stations that subsequently deviated from the map, either by increasing their transmitting power or by switching their frequency, would receive an official reprimand from the IBU. Of course, the IBU's protocols, not unlike the diplomatic agreements signed at the League of Nations, had no binding authority, but relied upon the spirit of cooperation and goodwill among member countries for their effectiveness.

These initial conferences brought some order to the radio spectrum, with Germany, France, and Great Britain respectively emerging as Europe's leading "radio powers" in possession of the largest number of wavelengths. However, the years that followed saw significant changes to the airwaves and to European geopolitics, as the enthusiasm surrounding the Treaties of Locarno and the 1928 Kellogg-Briand Pact renouncing war evaporated alongside the Nazis' ascension to power in Germany in 1933. In the meantime, not only did more stations begin broadcasting in Europe, but many ignored the 9–10-kHz "border" mandated by the IBU, while others progressively increased their transmitting power to ensure that their "voices" could be heard. A station broadcasting at 5 kW was considered a "star" in 1925, the journalist Arno Huth commented, but several stations had already begun transmitting between 100 and 192 kW.[101] By 1933, the collective transmitting power of Europe's 237 radio stations totaled 3,200 kW, *Radio-Magazine* reported. Was it any wonder, in this era of rising nationalism and international competition, that "national prestige" was now being computed in kilowatts?[102] The increasing number of radio stations would "not have been as disastrous for the listener," the journalist Paul Dermée concluded in *T.S.F. Programme*, had not "various nations launched themselves headfirst into a race for kilowatts, with the same frenzy as the arms race ... There is not a single small country that does not plan to construct stations at 100 or 120 kW."[103]

By the time the IBU organized its third and most important conference in Lucerne in May of 1933, French policymakers and radio audiences alike recognized that there were an insufficient number of individual wavelengths to supply all the radio stations on the Continent, and that

[100] Lommers, *Europe on Air*, 77–80. CAC 19870714-23. Union Internationale de Radiodiffusion, Bruxelles, Document 145. Projet de plan de répartition des ondes établi en vue de la Conférence de Lucerne; Union Internationale de Radiodiffusion, *Les Problèmes de la radiodiffusion*, 14.

[101] Huth, *La radiodiffusion, puissance mondiale*, 40–41.

[102] Jean Royer, "Diplomatie des ondes: Politique d'abord," *Radio-Magazine*, July 2, 1933.

[103] Paul Dermée, "La course aux kilowatts," *T.S.F. Programme*, September 25–October 25, 1932.

the complicated nature of this new domain of international politics could potentially incite hostilities between rival nations.[104] IBU technicians had already determined that a policy of "shared wavelengths" would have to be instituted by assigning stations at significant physical distances from one another to the same frequency. Any station not assigned a specific frequency would be asked to operate on a series of "common international wavelengths" where their transmitting power would be restricted. Raymond Braillard, the IBUs' chief technical officer, also wanted to limit the transmitting power of stations above 300 m – the most "clogged" portion of the spectrum.[105] Countries typically took "exclusive" wavelengths for their long-wave stations and assigned their regional stations to medium wavelengths.[106] The goal of most nations attending the Lucerne Conference, including France, was to obtain high-quality frequencies and have as many of their stations as possible named specifically in the final protocol.[107]

In preparing for the Lucerne Conference, PTT minister Laurent-Eynac conferred with the prime minister Edouard Daladier for the first time to determine the composition of the French delegation, signaling broadcasting's new importance as a matter of state. Heading the French delegation to Lucerne was Jules Gautier, an agronomist and radio enthusiast known for his international negotiating experience. It also included Marcel Pellenc, several PTT engineers, and representatives from the Ministries of Defense, Public Works, and Foreign Affairs. The group

[104] CAC 19870714-23. Union Internationale de Radiodiffusion, Document 116, Procès-verbal de la 25ᵉ réunion de la commission technique, February 8–18, 1933. Premier séance, February 8, 1933; Union Internationale de Radiodiffusion, Document 145, Projet de plan de répartition des ondes établi en vue de la Conférence de Lucerne. Even before the conference officially opened, radio technicians representing different nations gathered for a preliminary "technical" meeting where they established a "theoretical" plan for the division of the European airwaves that took account of the desiderata presented by different national delegations.
[105] Prot, *Dictionnaire de la radio*, 119. The Frenchman Raymond Braillard was appointed president of the Technical Commission of the IBU in 1925, and later became the director of the Brussels Control Center. In 1942, Braillard became the director of technical services for broadcasting under the Vichy regime.
[106] Brochand, *Histoire générale de la radio*, 1: 632–38. The Lucerne Conference limited broadcast power to 150 kW for frequencies below 300 kHz (wavelengths above 1,000 m); 100 kW for frequencies between 550 and 1,100 kHz (wavelengths between 545 and 272.7 m), 60 kW for frequencies between 1,100 and 1,250 kHz (wavelengths between 272.7 and 240 m), and 30 kW for frequencies between 1,250 and 1,500 kHz (wavelengths between 240 and 200 m).
[107] CAC 19950218-1. Union Internationale de Radiodiffusion, *Conférence de Lucerne. Protocol final annexé à la Convention Européenne de Radiodiffusion* (Lucerne, 1933), 11. The broadcast power for "common international wavelengths" was limited to 2 kW (type 1) and 0.2 kW (type 2), and the broadcast power for "common national wavelengths" was limited to 5 kW.

took as its charge obtaining a sufficient number of wavelengths to ensure the proper functioning of the Ferrié Plan.[108] But even formulating a strategy became difficult when the army and navy representatives attending the pre-conference planning meetings contested the Ferrié Plan's placement of future stations along France's coastlines. Defending radio's origins as a military technology, the naval captain Paul Bion demanded that the projected stations be moved at least 100 km inland to reduce interference between their transmitters and naval vessels. In contrast, Pellenc asserted that broadcasting was becoming vital to national prestige in the twentieth century and that the "applications of such strict rules would, for reasons of the geographical configuration of France, force the renunciation of any effective broadcasting system in the maritime regions . . . to the benefit of Italian, English, and German stations."[109]

Employing the newly militaristic language of the early 1930s, Pellenc painted an image of France "invaded" by foreign voices. Without constructing new radio stations along France's coastlines and borders, he argued, citizens living on the nation's peripheries would be "abandoned" with no possibility of hearing French voices clearly. Moreover, the government had already approved the funds for the new transmitters' construction. PTT minister Laurent-Eynac backed Pellenc, instructing the delegation to "try and obtain the best possible situation" for France on the radio spectrum. We "must arrive [at Lucerne] with the possibility of making our rights known and obtaining a partition of the airwaves in favor of our interests," he declared, and told Gautier to refuse any decisions that would "weaken the interests of national broadcasting." Despite protests from the military, delegates made their way to Switzerland in May of 1933 determined to secure a strong position for French broadcasting in the "concert of Europe."[110]

[108] *Ibid.* Préparation de la Conférence de Lucerne au Ministère des PTT, April 11, 1933, 10. As the president of the Confédération Nationale des Associations d'Agriculteurs, Gautier participated in discussions at the League of Nations about Europe's food supplies. See Luciano Tosi, "The League of Nations, the International Institute of Agriculture, and the Food Question," in Maria Petricioli and Donatella Cherubini, eds., *Pour la paix en Europe: institutions et sociétés dans l'entre-deux-guerres* (Brussels, 2007), 117–40. Gautier also served on the administrative boards for the Eiffel Tower station and Radio-Paris during the 1920s. See Brochand, *Histoire générale de la radio*, 1: 291–92.

[109] *Ibid.* Préparation de la Conférence de Lucerne au Ministère des PTT, April 11, 1933, 3. Bion argued that his services had not been adequately represented at the 1932 telecommunications conference in Madrid, where delegates divided up the radio spectrum between military and civilian services. He wanted navy representatives at the Lucerne Conference to negotiate for the defense services.

[110] *Ibid.* Note de Laurent-Eynac, Ministre des PTT à la Délégation de Lucerne, May 4, 1933; Préparation de la Conférence de Lucerne au Ministère des PTT, April 11, 1933, 9.

At the beginning of the Lucerne Conference, France had held fourteen "exclusive" wavelengths (two long, twelve medium) shared between twenty-five public and private stations.[111] In 1931, the Ferrié Commission had judged it "indispensable" to maintain one "exclusive wavelength" for each of the eleven listening zones in the plan, and believed it would "always be possible to satisfy these conditions."[112] Once the delegation arrived, it asked only for "sensible modifications" to earlier IBU protocols in order to portray France as a good negotiator.[113] One of the most divisive issues at Lucerne would be the division of long wavelengths – by far the most important commodity on the radio spectrum thanks to the distance they traveled – of which France held two, used respectively by Radio-Paris and the Eiffel Tower station. The French delegates declared themselves ready to "abandon" the Eiffel Tower's wavelength for the sake of international cooperation, despite its venerable history as France's first radio station, but wanted to ensure that it went to a "friendly" country.[114] This gesture made a good impression on other national delegations, but in reality France could do little to control which country obtained the wavelength.[115] Faced with a Europe-wide shortage of wavelengths, the French delegation simply tried to obtain an attribution for each of the state stations contained in the Ferrié Plan, whether existing or under construction.

Throughout the Lucerne Conference, France found its bargaining power compromised by the activities of its commercial stations, as other national delegations complained that the private broadcasters violated earlier international conventions. The British delegate Noel Ashbridge insisted that Radio-Vitus (operating on an unauthorized wavelength)

---

[111] CAC 19870714-9. Considérations techniques pour l'établissement d'un projet de radiodiffusion. Rapport de la sous-commission constituée de MM Abraham, Gutton, Le Corbellier, Veaux, Baize, and Pellenc. March 19–20, 1930/1931(?).

[112] CAC 19870714-1. Rapport de la commission constituée par la décision du 10 février 1931 en vue de dresser le plan d'organisation de la radiodiffusion française, n.d., 4–5.

[113] CAC 19870714-23. Union Internationale de Radiodiffusion. Document 145, Projet de plan de répartition des ondes établi en vue de la Conférence de Lucerne.

[114] *Ibid.* Report on the "Etablissement des stations de radiodiffusion dans les petits états limitrophes de la France" n.d. (1937–1938?). See also CAC 19950218-1. Note de Laurent-Eynac, Ministre des PTT à la Délégation de Lucerne, May 4, 1933. The "friendly country" in question was Luxembourg, which had constructed a powerful 200-kW transmitter in 1932. Radio-Luxembourg targeted a multi national audience and broadcast popular programs in multiple European languages, with generous support from commercial advertising. Radio-Luxembourg's directors refused to employ the medium wavelengths assigned to the station at IBU conferences throughout the 1930s. BBC representatives declared the station to be an "outlaw" because of this "illegal" wavelength use. See Duval, *Histoire de la radio en France*, 265.

[115] *Ibid.* Jules Gautier, Président de la Délégation de Lucerne à M. le Ministre des PTT, August 18, 1933, 4.

produced interference with Cardiff, as did Radio-Toulouse – a particular problem because both French stations continued to broadcast advertising in English, long after it had been banned in Great Britain. BBC representatives formally requested that Radio-Toulouse restrict "its coverage to French territory." At least one French delegate defended the commercial stations, arguing that they had only augmented their transmitting power to escape the "disturbance caused by foreign stations," but others feared that the private stations' "illegal" activities were beginning to threaten France's international position.[116]

In the end, France came away from Lucerne with a greater number of attributed frequencies than it had previously held (twenty rather than sixteen) but now possessed fewer "exclusive" wavelengths (three instead of fourteen), with its single long-wave frequency assigned to Radio-Paris. The bulk of France's remaining fifteen state stations (including the colonial station Radio-Alger) shared wavelengths with distant transmitters in the USSR and Finland. None of France's commercial stations received dedicated wavelengths in the plan, forcing them to transmit on common national or international wavelengths. However, France did receive two medium wavelengths without station designations. In the interest of carving out the largest space possible for French "voices" on the radio spectrum, the PTT temporarily assigned them to the Poste Parisien and to Radio-Toulouse, stations that operated two of France's most powerful radio transmitters.[117] Marcel Pellenc also managed to convince other IBU delegates that the "generally poor conductivity of French soil" limited the radius of its stations, and thus obtained permission for Paris PTT, Toulouse PTT, and Rennes PTT to transmit at 120 kW, which vastly surpassed the power permitted to other stations in their region of the radio spectrum.[118] France now possessed fewer frequency attributions than the USSR, but more than Germany, Great Britain, or Italy, leaving the delegation pleased with the outcome.

However, before the ink had dried on the final Lucerne protocol, French politicians, PTT bureaucrats, and journalists expressed concerns that the agreement might prove insufficient to stabilize the spectrum. The Lucerne Conference represented an "original effort to return to a

---

[116] CAC 19870714-23. Union Internationale de Radiodiffusion, Document 120. Procès-verbal de la 25e réunion de la commission technique; CAC 19950218–1. Jules Gautier, président de la Délégation de Lucerne à M. le Ministre des PTT, May 30, 1933.

[117] CAC 19950218-1. Union internationale de radiodiffusion. *Conférence de Lucerne. Protocol final annexé à la Convention européenne de radiodiffusion. Plan de Lucerne annexé à la Conférence européenne de radiodiffusion* (Lucerne, 1933), 15–23.

[118] CAC 19870714-23. Union Internationale de Radiodiffusion, Document 119, Procès-verbal de la 25e réunion de la commission technique. Première séance, February 8, 1933.

technical certitude the lawless principle of national sovereignty" in the airwaves, the right-leaning journalist Jean Royer wrote in *Radio-Magazine*, but "what must one think of this limitation of transmitting power from above that hardly resembles ratification?" Although "everyone, without exception, condemns the race to large-caliber hertzian armaments that the majority of European nations have indulged in for the past two years," diplomatic censure had done little to stop the expansion of Soviet, German, and Italian broadcasting networks or limit their reach. "Radio was born in liberty," Royer argued, but "with the liberty of usage came the temptation for abuse ... No more borders! Nor more customs controls ... the opportunity was too good. Politics grabbed hold ... certain countries systematically encroached ... upon their neighbor."

By the spring of 1933, the Nazis had already conducted a purge of the German Rundfunk and had begun transmitting speeches by "rough and blaring orators in the 'Führer' style" defending the nation's claims to Alsace and Lorraine, the Saar protectorate, and Upper Silesia. "Whether we like it or not, a broadcast in a foreign language, reaching foreign ears, is an attack on national sovereignty," Royer argued. Yet even as he worried about the possibility of foreign radio propaganda reaching France, he remained fixated on the technical capacities of French radio transmitters, rather than on the content of the possible German broadcasts, a concern shared by many of his contemporaries. If the "universal increase in kilowatts" is at the "origin of a new radiophonic chaos," he wrote, "France should not bear the responsibility. The fetishism of power comes with a German, Soviet, and British stamp. It was perhaps this moderation, this *innocence* of French radio that permitted it to return with its hands full."[119]

French delegates to Lucerne shared Royer's concerns about the overall increase in stations' broadcasting power and signed the final protocol only after issuing a statement of official "reserves" regarding the proximity on the spectrum of Radio-Paris (transmitting with a power of 75 kW) to Moscow (transmitting at 500 kW). "One of the questions that appeared the most worrying," Gautier reported after the conference, "was the power of stations in kilowatts and the general tendency to increase that power." He insisted "the Moscow station ... is an object of constant fear

[119] Jean Royer, "Diplomatie des ondes: sur les pied de guerre," *Radio-Magazine*, May 14, 1933. My emphasis. Royer, "Diplomatie des ondes: fétichisme de puissance," *Radio-Magazine*, July 16, 1933; "Diplomatie des ondes: vers un nouveau statut quo," *Radio-Magazine*, May 7, 1933; Thyll, "Ce que nous réserve le plan de Lucerne," *Mon programme*, March 10, 1933; "Aux écoutes de la radio," *Aux écoutes*, April 21, 1934.

for neighboring nations."[120] In fact, Radio-Moscow had been directing communist radio propaganda in English, German, and French toward audiences in Western Europe for several years. The French security services already listened in to Radio-Moscow regularly in order to uncover possible links between foreign propaganda and communist agitation in France.[121] "From the point of view of European peace," Gautier claimed, it was imperative to force a "necessary disarmament" of Radio-Moscow's powerful transmitters, nor did the inadequate separation between Radio-Paris and Radio-Moscow "provide sufficient guarantees for the functioning of the French station to compensate for the loss of the Eiffel Tower." Of course, there was little acknowledgement on his part that France's commercial stations had violated international accords before Lucerne or that France had obtained exemptions to increase the transmitting power of some of its own stations.[122]

* * *

Looking forward to January of 1934, when the Lucerne protocol would take effect, audiences anticipated immediate improvements to their radio reception, even though most understood that IBU protocols would be effective only insofar as the countries that signed them heeded the final decisions. Radio journalists dramatized the impending frequency changes that would "force transmitters on a walk through the entire band of wavelengths." At 11 p.m. on January 14 and 15, stations went off the air while their technicians adjusted their transmitters, and then returned to announce their names, countries, and new wavelength. Toulouse PTT moved from 255 to 386.6 m and Radio-Alger from 365 to 318.8 m, while Limoges moved from 294.7 to 328.2 m, forcing listeners to recalibrate their radios [Figure 3.4].[123] The results proved to be jolting to the mental maps of the radio spectrum internalized by audiences. "Where one once went looking for a French *speaker*, now an Italian *speakerine* has taken his place," one listener described. "The English have permutated the Germans

---

[120] CAC 199870714-1. Rapport de Jules Gautier à M. le Ministre des PTT, August 18, 1933, 4.
[121] CAC 20010216-280. Ministre de l'Intérieur, Sûreté Général, Police de l'Air et de T.S. F. Renseignements. March 10, 1931.
[122] CAC 199870714-1. Note sur la situation des postes français au regard des accords européens réglant la répartition des fréquences, n.d. Several countries refused to sign the final protocol, signaling their rejection of their wavelength assignments and their refusal to adopt the terms of the Lucerne plan. See "Du plan de Prague au plan de Lucerne," *Mon programme*, December, 1, 1933.
[123] Jean Royer, "Diplomatie des ondes: vers un nouveau statu quo," *Radio-Magazine*, May 7, 1933; François de Tessan, "Emissions de T.S.F. Aux écoutes de la radio...," *Le Bavard-Marseille*, April 7, 1934.

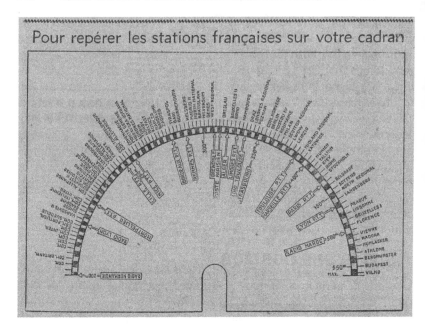

Figure 3.4 Post-Lucerne Conference "map" of the radio dial, *Mon programme* (1934). Image courtesy of the Bibliothèque Nationale de France.

and the Polish fight against the Czechs by intermediary of the loudspeaker. And protests everywhere! No one is content with his place."[124]

Audiences felt the effects of the Lucerne agreement keenly, for some could no longer hear their favorite stations. The change that provoked the most discussion was the transfer of the Eiffel Tower station from 1,145 to 206 m, a dramatic reduction in wavelength ensuring that the "doyen of French stations" could no longer be heard in some rural areas. The Eiffel Tower's history as a wartime wireless transmitter for the French army and its ties to General Ferrié had turned the station into a national symbol of technological prestige, and few listeners received the news of its impending demise "without a certain emotion and a legitimate pang of anguish," *Mon programme* reported. But did France's oldest station merit this "sacrificial death"?[125] Letters from individual listeners and from the Fédération Nationale Radiotéléphonique de la Tour Eiffel, the listeners' association

[124] "Après l'application du plan de Lucerne," *Mon programme*, February 16, 1934.
[125] Georges de Flins, "Avant une disparition. Contribution à l'histoire de la Tour Eiffel," *Mon programme*, July 21, 1933, 3–4.

that managed the station's programming, flooded the desk of the newly appointed PTT minister André Mallarmé with demands that the station be assigned a better wavelength, though he could do little to resolve the situation without violating the Lucerne protocol.[126]

The Lucerne Conference did bring some stability to the European radio spectrum, permitting radio-electric manufacturers to begin producing the visual station scales that would become so prized by consumers. Yet it did not, unfortunately, resolve the many "border accidents" that it had been intended to eliminate. French stations sharing wavelengths with other European transmitters continued to experience interference: the commercial station Radio-37 created problems in Romania and Radio-Normandie disrupted a Portuguese station. Radio-Paris and the Finnish station at Lahti, both operating at 167 kHz, disrupted one another, as did Radio-Toulouse and Helsinki, and Marseille PTT and Viipuri.[127] Nor did the 9-kHz "border" separating Radio-Paris and Moscow eliminate their mutual interference, prompting PTT bureaucrats to brand Moscow as a hostile "aggressor."[128]

Moreover, a number of the commercial stations excluded from the Lucerne protocol refused to transmit on France's common national wavelengths, arguing that to do so would reduce their audience base. In fact, the only commercial stations to adhere to the agreement were Radio-Nîmes, Radio-Lyon, and the Poste Parisien, and even then they generated interference.[129] Listeners in northern and eastern France complained they could not hear the Poste Parisien (959 m) because of interference with the neighboring Breslau station (950 m). The BBC complained to the PTT that the Poste Parisien disrupted reception of the West Regional station (977 m).[130] By 1935, just two years after the Conference, many listeners across France and Europe were calling for a revision of the Lucerne agreement, forcing the IBU to acknowledge that it had failed to resolve many of the problems plaguing the airwaves.[131]

However, whereas audiences had five years earlier blamed interference on the general chaos of the airwaves, the Ferrié Plan and the Lucerne

---

[126] Paul Campargue, "La Tour Eiffel veut vivre … mais son sauvetage est-il utile?," *Le Populaire*, April 18, 1934; "Aux écoutes de la radio," *Aux écoutes*, April 21, 1934.
[127] CAC 19870714-23. Union Internationale de Radiodiffusion. Tableau de brouillages. February 26, 1934.
[128] CAC 19870714-24. Rapport au conseil sur la réunion de la commission technique à Berlin, May, 1937.
[129] Brochand, *Histoire générale de la radio*, 1: 650.
[130] CAC 19870714-10. Communication interministérielle, March 21, 1934.
[131] CAC 19870714-25. Union Internationale de Radiodiffusion. Fonctionnement du Plan de Lucerne, Document 369, February 13, 1937. Twenty-two medium-wave stations failed to obey the rules.

protocol had established precedents regarding the geographical distribution of transmitters, their broadcasting power, and their position on the radio spectrum. Audiences could now direct their complaints about reception to the PTT by demanding that the state protect their "right to listen," and thus their full inclusion in the "radio nation." Listeners frequently targeted commercial stations as the source of their reception problems, arguing that they disrupted the democratic distribution of stations promised in the Ferrié Plan by "usurping" wavelengths that did not belong to them.[132] One disgruntled Parisian *rive droite* resident, a Lieutenant Chanteaud, protested that the "harmonics and interference caused by the Parisian station Radio LL" would not occur if the station "scrupulously respected the wavelength and the power assigned to it at the Lucerne Conference." Since the transfer of the Eiffel Tower to 206 m, "Radio LL transmits with an increased power ... on essentially phony wavelengths. Even with the most modern and selective of radio receivers, it sometimes becomes impossible to separate this station from Parisian, French, and foreign broadcasts." If the government allowed Radio LL to continue, he complained, it should "choose an immutable wavelength and restrict its power to 300 watts!"[133] Equally striking in listeners' letters to the PTT was their insistence that interference restricted their ability to clearly hear foreign stations. The *parisienne* Mlle Dermanouk protested that Radio LL's uneven modulation "provokes considerable disturbance in ... the Milan and Berlin stations, which are placed next to Radio LL and are almost entirely covered by its broadcasts. Briefly, these stations are rendered inaudible because of the broadcasts of Radio LL." She wondered whether "it would not be possible to relegate this station to the place that it is assigned to ... or oblige to diminish the power and range of its broadcasts in order not to disturb reception of foreign broadcasts."[134]

The PTT's response to the commercial stations' activities suggest that few bureaucrats saw the need to put an end to the regime of "controlled freedom" that had allowed commercial stations to flourish in France, in part because some audiences clearly enjoyed listening to them. Moreover, despite their unauthorized activities, the commercial stations contributed to France's overall presence in the airwaves, and for this reason they enjoyed a certain leniency. When they violated international agreements, the PTT typically ordered the offending station to move, but never took steps to shut down those that failed to comply. When Radio-Normandie

[132] Alex Surchamp, "Chevauchements, brouillages, pagaie!" *Le Petit journal*, October 28, 1937; No author, "Cacophonie et injustice," *Radio-Magazine*, March 6, 1938.
[133] CAC 19870714-10. Letter from Lieutenant Chanteaud, Paris, April 9, 1935.
[134] *Ibid.* Letter from Mlle Dermanouk to the Director of Radio Broadcasting, April 5, 1934.

began transmitting on 269.9 m, a wavelength assigned to a Czech station, the Ministry of Foreign Affairs received complaints from Prague.[135] After the station was ordered to move, it adopted a wavelength shared by Portuguese and Romanian stations, provoking reactions from their respective governments and forcing diplomats to issue formal apologies, even as Radio-Normandie continued to switch its frequency.[136]

However, by the mid-1930s the phenomenon that provoked the most alarm among politicians and audiences alike was not interference, though it remained a significant problem, but rather the fact that many French radios continued to receive foreign signals more clearly than French ones.[137] Anecdotal reports by listeners in the radio press as well as state-commissioned studies of radio reception demonstrate this clearly. In 1936, an anonymous listener from the Indre reported to *Radio-Magazine* that even with a powerful seven-lamp radio he only received the Eiffel Tower, Radio-Lyon, Radio-Alger, Radio-Agen, Paris PTT, and Marseille stations poorly and with considerable fading. He could clearly hear Radio-Paris, Grenoble, and Lyon-la-Doua, as well as the commercial stations Poste Parisien and Radio-Normandie, but he also described his "good" reception of Königsberg, BBC Midland, Brussels, BBC Scottish, Rome, Sottens, BBC North, Cologne, Florence, and the "very good" signals of Milan, Berlin, Leipzig, Vienna, Stuttgart, Beromünster, Budapest, Luxembourg, and BBC Droitwich.[138]

In the summer of 1936, following the elections that ushered into power Léon Blum's left-wing Popular Front government, the first to establish a clear agenda for the "radio nation" in the airwaves, postal minister Robert Jardillier dispatched regional PTT inspectors to investigate listening conditions across France.[139] In the Pyrénées-Orientales, inspectors noted the presence of "clearly defined zones of silence" resulting from the region's mountains that "made the propagation of radio waves vary considerably." The stations Marseille-Provence PTT and Nice PTT could be heard during the day, but Radio-Paris and Paris PTT could only be heard during the evening hours.[140] An inspector reporting from the Morbihan

---

[135] CAC 19870714-9. M. le Ministre des Affaires Etrangères à M. le Ministre des PTT, June 5, 1936.

[136] *Ibid.* M. le Ministre des PTT à M. le Ministre des Affaires Etrangères, March 5, 1938; Note pour M. le Ministre des PTT de l'Inspecteur Général chargé de l'Administration des Services de Radiodiffusion, December 5, 1938.

[137] Franz de Beville, "La T.S.F. en vacances," *Radio-Magazine*, August 16, 1936, 16.

[138] "Comment on entend les postes français et européens dans le centre de la France," *Mon programme*, July 17, 1936, 2.

[139] CAC 19950218-1. Rapport sur la mission effectuée dans les régions de Lyon et de Grenoble par M. Viaux, ingénieur en chef et M. Casals, ingénieur, n.d.

[140] CAC 19950218-9. Rapport de M. Martin, Inspecteur Général du Département des Pyrénées-Orientales, n.d. 5–7.

in southern Brittany noted that picking up Radio-Paris required a receiver with five or six lamps, a prohibitive cost for many in the countryside.[141]

Although the Ferrié Commission had made the creation of an inclusive, democratic "radio nation" a national priority, in 1937 the plan's goals had only been partly achieved. The PTT had completed much of the technical work prescribed by the plan, but only after a delay of nearly three years, brought on by the frequent ministerial turnover and economic turmoil of the depression years. Moreover, PTT bureaucrats had discovered that even 100–120 kW of transmitting power was insufficient to ensure clear reception in certain regions, which meant that a number of regional stations could only be heard at night.[142] Many of the same patterns of interference and reception experienced by listeners in the mid-1920s persisted a decade later. France's "radio nation," far from inhabiting a fixed location on the European radio spectrum, remained an amorphous and ever-shifting auditory space.

To remedy the situation, the PTT sought legislative authorization for funds to increase the broadcasting power of Radio-Paris to 200 kW, and finally, to construct a powerful new 450-kW transmitter in Allouis, just outside of the capital, with a projected completion date of 1938.[143] However, there was a growing sense among listeners and politicians alike that France's needs in the domain of broadcasting could not be met unless it survived as an international "radio power," something that would only be achieved by shoring up its "borders" in the airwaves and dominating a greater physical space on the European radio spectrum. Many of the problems plaguing France's airwaves were domestic in origin – the product of political turnover, insufficient funding, and competing agendas for the airwaves— but as the left-leaning magazine *Radio-Liberté* concluded in 1938, it is "only on the diplomatic and international level that our imperiled radio can be saved."[144]

The diplomacy of the airwaves: propaganda, borders, and the radio spectrum

Undergirding audiences' growing anxieties about the space occupied by France's "radio nation" on the European radio spectrum was a dramatic

---

[141] *Ibid.* Rapport de l'Inspecteur Chautant du Morbihan, June 3, 1937.
[142] CAC 19950218-9. Rapport de l'Inspecteur du Contrôle Labbé, August 11, 1938.
[143] CAC 19870714-1. Etude sur l'état actuel de la radiodiffusion nationale, February, 1937. The new Radio-Paris transmitter would not be completed until 1939, just before the outbreak of the Second World War.
[144] No author, "Deux périls de la radiodiffusion: interférences et parasites," *Radio-Liberté*, June 17, 1938.

increase in foreign radio propaganda. In addition to Radio-Moscow's broadcasts, Italy's Radio-Bari and Germany's Zeezen station began bombarding France's North African colonies and Middle Eastern protectorates with Arabic-language propaganda in late 1934. Although neither of the fascist regimes transmitted propaganda in French before 1938, French audiences could easily hear their German- and Italian- language domestic radio programs vaunting their leaders' expansionist goals and discriminatory racial policies.[145] After Franco's coup launched the Spanish Civil War in the summer of 1936, both the Spanish nationalists and republicans took to the airwaves to win over European audiences to their respective causes. French newspapers provided readers with instructions for tuning into Spanish stations on both medium and short waves as well as tips on how to avoid the jamming signals (*brouillage*) deployed by each side.[146] Given the facility with which audiences could easily hear these foreign broadcasts, why did successive French governments of the 1930s do so little to shore up France's "borders" in the airwaves by jamming the signals of foreign stations? This reluctance to jam hostile propaganda broadcasts is all the more curious given military elites' fixation with the security of France's territorial borders, which took concrete form in the construction of the defensive Maginot Line along the Franco-German frontier.[147]

Bureaucrats within France's expansive state security apparatus had long acknowledged radio's potential to become a dangerous medium of propaganda and developed multiple techniques of aural surveillance over the course of the interwar decades. These included a Listening Center staffed by the PTT that monitored, transcribed, and recorded the radio speeches of foreign political leaders for analysis, as well as the Police de l'Air, founded by the Interior Ministry in 1929.[148] Yet as Derek Vaillant's research on the Police de l'Air has shown, the agency focused its efforts more on the control of clandestine radio transmissions within France than it did on the surveillance of foreign radio broadcasts. During the First World War, France had outlawed amateur radio communications to

---

[145] Michael Nelson, *War of the Black Heavens: The Battles of Western Broadcasting in the Cold War* (Syracuse NY, 1997), 1–9; Lommers, *Europe on Air*, 140–43; Bergmeier, *Hitler's Airwaves*, 22–34.

[146] Alan Davies, "The First Radio War: Broadcasting in the Spanish Civil War, 1936–1939," *Historical Journal of Film, Radio, and Television*, 19, 4, 1999, 473–513; "Voix d'Espagne," *Courrier du Centre* (Limoges), July 16, 1936.

[147] On the interwar cultural fixation with borders, see Panchasi, *Future Tense*, 77–110.

[148] CAC 19950218-2. Rapport sur le fonctionnement du Centre d'écoute, Direction Générale de Radiodiffusion, n.d.; Derek Vaillant, "La Police de l'Air: Amateur Radio and the Politics of Aural Surveillance in France, 1921–1940," *French Politics, Culture, and Society*, 28, 1, 2010, 1–25.

prevent espionage and protect the airwaves for military use, but a 1926 law allowed amateurs to broadcast provided they obtained permission from the post office. Not wishing to alienate France's vocal *sans-filiste* community, which included many veterans, the PTT typically granted their requests. As a result, the Police de l'Air focused much of its early activity on monitoring amateurs whose signals accidentally interfered with radio stations or defense signals.

The rising political tensions of the mid-1930s, however, tempted some radio amateurs to begin using their personal transmitters to broadcast political propaganda. Right-wing militants of the Parti Social Français hostile to the left-wing Popular Front coalition government as well as sympathizers of the Spanish republicans briefly took their cause to the airwaves before being shut down by the Police de l'Air. The security services also maintained detailed lists of foreigners who sold radio equipment or worked in the radio-electric industry, fearing that radio sales might serve as a cover for espionage, enabling spies to broadcast illicit propaganda or employ clandestine jamming stations to disrupt French radio broadcasts. Only rarely, however did the information gathered by the Police de l'Air result directly in surveillance of listeners, even though the security services showed little reluctance about violating citizens' civil liberties in other domains.[149] Worried that Radio-Moscow's French-language broadcasts would incite political agitation, the Interior Ministry dispatched policemen to meetings of the French Communist Party and its affiliated radio club to assess the reactions provoked by the broadcasts. Yet the security services never tried to jam Radio-Moscow's signal, in stark distinction to both the British and German authorities.[150]

Although some radio amateurs criticized the Police de l'Air for interfering in their activities, the radio and scientific press frequently presented aural surveillance as a service designed to protect listeners. In "certain totalitarian countries ... there is an effort to keep listeners from receiving certain foreign broadcasts," the engineer Pierre Hemardinquer told readers of *Je sais tout* in 1938, but in France the Police de l'Air worked to guarantee audiences' right to tune into any programs of their choice, regardless of their origin.[151] This "liberty" of French audiences to receive

[149] ANOM 15H32. J. Berthoin, le Directeur de la Sûreté Nationale pour M. le Ministre de l'Intérieur, à MM. les Préfets, September 27, 1934. Clifford Rosenberg, *Policing Paris: The Origins of Modern Immigration Control Between the Wars* (Ithaca NY, 2006).
[150] CAC 20010216-280. Police de l'Air et de T.S.F. Dossier Radio-Moscou, 1931–1933; Vaillant, "La Police de l'Air," 1–25.
[151] Roger Simonet, "Comment fonctionnent les services de 'Radio-police'," *Mon programme*, January 24, 1936; Pierre Hemardinquer, "La police de l'éther: est-elle impuissante?" *Je sais tout*, January 1938, 392–94.

foreign stations became a common refrain in the radio press of the mid-1930s, where journalists of all political stripes juxtaposed France's broadcasting policies favorably against the fascist dictatorships' restrictions on international listening.[152] In fact, bureaucrats in the security services and the postal administration never seriously considered jamming foreign broadcasts in metropolitan France until the *drôle de guerre*, revealing a distinctive French attitude toward radio propaganda. French policymakers understood by the late 1920s that radio's internationalism would pose unprecedented challenges for European *rapprochement*, as did the IBU, which persuaded its members to adhere to a "Gentleman's Agreement" in 1925 promising that their stations would deliberately avoid transmitting any broadcasts that might offend other nations, including those destined for a domestic audience but which could be heard overseas. From Geneva, the IBU's staff also lobbied to put radio propaganda on the agenda at the League of Nations, obtaining support from the International Institute for Intellectual Cooperation, a Paris-based think tank affiliated with the League, which produced a report in 1933 exploring radio's potential for promoting "moral disarmament."[153]

However, the League did not introduce an International Convention on the Use of Broadcasting for the Cause of Peace until 1936. The agreement required signatories to deliberately avoid inciting conflict through the airwaves, to refrain from the transmission of false news reports, and to avoid constructing transmitters along their borders that would disrupt radio signals (whether intentionally or accidentally) in neighboring countries. Twenty-three countries signed the convention in 1936, but only seven governments ratified the agreement to make its provisions binding. Germany and Italy, perhaps unsurprisingly, did not sign the convention, but France's Popular Front government did, signaling its willingness to forego aggressive, fascist-style propaganda in the interest of being a "good citizen" of the international airwaves.[154] The existence of this agreement explains in part why the French state refrained so long from developing counterpropaganda and why bureaucrats in the

---

[152] Georges Armand-Masson, "La vie des ondes: contact permanent," *Le Haut-parleur*, August 22, 1937, 456.

[153] Lommers, *Europe on Air*, 184; Institut International de Coopération Intellectuelle, *La radiodiffusion et la paix. Etudes et projets d'accords internationaux* (Paris, 1933). French policymakers took the 1926 Geneva agreement seriously and cited it in later discussions about France's counterpropaganda strategies. See ANOM 10 APOM 830, Centre des Hautes Etudes sur l'Afrique et l'Asie Moderne (CHEAM), M. Delahaye, "Les émissions de langue arabe du poste Radio PTT-Alger." Exposé fait par M. Delahaye au cours de perfectionnement des Affaires Indigènes, February, 1937.

[154] Lommers, *Europe on Air*, 209–14; Spohrer, "Ruling the Airwaves," 318–48.

PTT and Ministry of Foreign Affairs focused so much of their efforts on collecting data about where and under what conditions French broadcasts could be heard.[155] The only notable exceptions to these policies, as we shall later see, emerged in North Africa, where French colonial bureaucrats proved much more willing to create propaganda and limit their colonial subjects' access to the airwaves.

* * *

By 1938, listeners and politicians across Europe were once again demanding revisions to the Lucerne plan. With another war looming on the horizon, French policymakers knew that they needed to secure France's status as an international "radio power" and looked forward to the next IBU conference, scheduled for the summer of 1939 in Montreux.[156] Although the decisions enacted at the Montreux Conference were never implemented, France's preparations for the conference reveal policymakers' persistent preoccupation with the space occupied by French voices and signals on the radio spectrum, which in turn drove France's domestic and international broadcasting policies. They also reveal a misplaced reliance on diplomacy as the solution to France's vulnerable international position that mirrored some politicians' appeasement policies toward Germany. That French officials even took seriously their preparations for the conference is remarkable, given that virtually every European nation had violated earlier IBU agreements about wavelength usage and transmitting power, as well as Geneva's "recommendations" concerning propaganda.

PTT bureaucrats were divided over the best strategy to employ at Montreux, and debated whether the *quality* of wavelengths should take precedence over the *quantity* of frequency attributions assigned to France. Should they be willing to sacrifice the nation's single long wave (assigned to Radio-Paris) to obtain a better overall distribution of wavelengths? Léon Mulatier, the PTT engineer who headed the French delegation to Montreux, argued that France should try to maintain all of its "exclusive" wavelengths, including two common national wavelengths and three attributed to individual stations.[157] Others believed France might have

---

[155] CAC 19870714-1. Rapport de la Commission de Radiodiffusion auprès du Comité d'action artistique à l'étranger," April 7, 1932. This Commission included staff from the radio broadcasting administration and the Ministry of Foreign Affairs. See also CARAN F60-574. Dossier indicating where French stations could be heard abroad, n.d. (1938/9)?
[156] Brochand, *Histoire générale de la radio*, 1: 648–50.
[157] CAC 19370714-24. Commission des longueurs d'onde. Procès-verbal de la 2ᵉ séance, June 9, 1938.

to compromise to maintain Radio-Paris's exclusive wavelength, an attribution that they determined was vital to national security. In the case of a future war, France would require a single, powerful transmitter that could be heard across Europe.

Equally central to preparations for the Montreux Conference was an internal debate about the role of commercial stations in determining France's stature as a "radio power." Faced with renewed complaints from the BBC and other European broadcasting administrations about the commercial stations' "illegal" use of wavelengths, PTT minister Jules Julien argued that private radio posed a serious risk to France. "In the interest of French broadcasting itself, the interference caused by the functioning of certain private stations on frequencies not attributed to our country should be suppressed before ... the Conference," he asserted. Restraining commercial radio stations' "irregular" activities would permit the French delegation to avoid "the possibility of hostile votes by the representatives of nations whose services are disrupted by the irregular functioning of certain French stations."[158] During the winter of 1938, Julien invited the directors of the private stations to a meeting, urging them to respect international conventions or risk jeopardizing France's bargaining power. But the Fédération des Postes Privés, which represented the majority of France's commercial stations, proved to be much less interested in national security than in maintaining contact with their audiences, in turn demanding that the private stations be assigned specific wavelengths in the Montreux protocol, something that had been denied to them at Lucerne.[159]

Whether Julien saw fit to heed the commercial stations' requests or changed his mind before the Montreux delegation left for Switzerland, he arrived with the goal of obtaining as many individual wavelengths as possible. Julien's last-minute appeal to the commercial stations should also be read in light of the state's earlier ambivalence toward enforcement, for some policymakers clearly viewed the private stations as vital to France's overall status as a "radio nation." In 1939, the Poste Parisian possessed a transmitter whose reach was rivaled only by Radio-Paris, a status the private station celebrated by proclaiming itself "The French

[158] CAC 19870714-24. Commission des longueurs d'onde. Procès-verbal de la 1ᵉʳ séance, May 24, 1938. For complaints about the private stations, see CAC 19870714-9. Note pour M. Jean-Luc, Chef-adjoint du cabinet from the Services de Radiodiffusion, April 29, 1938. Radio-Normandie and Radio-Toulouse provoked complaints as early as 1933. Lettres du Ministère des Affaires Etrangères au Ministre des PTT July 12, 1933 and August 17, 1933.
[159] CARAN F60-571. Lettre de la Fédération des Postes Privés à Jules Julien, Ministre des PTT, n.d.

Station the World Listens To."[160] Nor could the state deny that the Poste Parisien was heard in French colonies in Africa, as well as across Europe, in stark comparison to many of the state stations. Consequently, when a PTT engineer prepared a report in 1939 outlining France's broadcasting needs, he argued that the nation required twenty-nine designated wavelengths – to be divided evenly between public and commercial stations – even as he acknowledged the impossibility of such concessions.[161]

In the end, the Montreux Conference produced outcomes that left few national delegations content and many listeners irate. The protocol called for the synchronization of radio stations within national borders, introduced a policy of "directed antennas" (designed to limit a station's radius), and reduced the number of attributed frequencies assigned to each IBU member nation. News of the conference decisions provoked immediate protests in the right-wing press, where journalists criticized the relegation of French stations to lower wavelengths on the spectrum. "If technical necessities demand a revision of the wavelengths, it is particularly annoying that ... it should be to the detriment of France," the conservative Catholic radio periodical *Choisir* complained, pointing to the close proximity of Soviet and French stations on the spectrum.[162] *Documentation radiophonique*, another right-leaning publication, claimed that the conference protocol had endangered national security.[163] While some newspapers offered more measured assessments of the "small concessions" required to maintain the long wave for Radio-Paris, press coverage of the IBU's final conference of the 1930s predicted nothing but doom. France had become a "radio nation of second rank" within the concert of Europe, Pierre Descaves lamented, and was "grossly wounded in its prestige by the progressive diminution of French wavelengths in the ether."[164]

[160] Fonds Radio France Carton 85. Brochure "*Le Poste Parisien. Le poste français que le monde écoute*" (1936?).
[161] CAC 19870714-24. Note de Scholtes pour l'Inspecteur Général de radiodiffusion, May 6, 1938.
[162] André Forèze, "La France va-t-elle perdre des longueurs d'onde?" *Choisir*, February 12, 1939.
[163] "Partirons-nous battu à la Conférence de Montreux?" *La Documentation radiophonique*, February 1939. "La Conférence internationale de radiodiffusion de Montreux," *La Documentation radiophonique*, n.d. (after June 1939?); *La Documentation radiophonique's* "press release" was reprinted in Carlos Larronde, "La radio française en péril à la Conférence de Montreux," *L'Intransigeant*, April 4, 1939. For similar concerns, see "A la Conférence de Montreux. La radio française est menacée ... au profit des stations allemandes et italiennes ..." *Excelsior*, April 3, 1939, and "La conférence radiophonique de Montreux? Une catastrophe française," *Le Jour-Echo de Paris*, April 12, 1939.
[164] Pierre Descaves, "Les succès de la radio française à la conférence de Montreux. Nos longueurs d'onde sont accrus en nombre et en quantité," *Radio-Magazine*, April 9, 1939.

The persistent preoccupation of bureaucrats, diplomats, and politicians with radio reception during the interwar decades illustrates the critical role that audiences played in shaping the cultural and political tasks assigned to broadcasting. Radio cultivated a new geographical imagination of Europe defined by stations' location on the radio bandwidth, which in turn determined where or how clearly they might be heard. For many listeners, a simple turn of the radio dial and the sounds it produced – whether static, French signals, or foreign voices – became a gauge by which they evaluated France's geopolitical status and their own inclusion in the emerging "radio nation." Long before a state radio network even existed, listeners imagined a distinctive space in the airwaves filled with French radio signals and sounds, and demanded that the state provide consistent listening conditions across national territory. France's "radio nation" consequently emerged through the interaction of state initiatives and listeners' demands.

Yet many listeners so embraced the cosmopolitan culture of interwar radio that they continued to conceive of themselves as "citizens of the world" until the eve of the Second World War. Even as journalists and politicians called for the reinforcement of France's "borders" on the radio spectrum, audiences' desire for unencumbered access to foreign stations constrained on the state's ability to jam hostile foreign propaganda broadcasts or adopt more aggressive counterpropaganda strategies. Whether radio audiences tuned into foreign broadcasts as nationalists, socialists, or communists, they demanded access to sounds from across Europe and from around the globe. In doing so, they fueled the persistent tensions between nationalism and cosmopolitanism, and between the protection of individual rights and the promotion of collective national interests, that defined French politics in the 1930s. More important, their insistence that the French "radio nation" belonged, at least in part, to them only exacerbated the fierce battles over listening that unfolded as politicians sought to harness radio listening for particular political agendas.

4   Learning by ear
School radio, partisan politics, and the pedagogy of listening

In October of 1938, Parisian literati, academics, and journalists gathered at the Institut de France for the annual session of the five academies, crowned by a lecture on radio broadcasting and intellectual culture by the physician-turned-essayist Georges Duhamel. That the academicians judged radio to be a worthy subject for the event spoke to their fascination with broadcasting, as well as to their anxieties about its impact on French society in the previous decade. In Duhamel's address, which would be reprinted and analyzed repeatedly in the mainstream press for weeks to come, he decried the intellectual depravity of the airwaves, declaring that broadcasting could never appeal to "literate listeners" or truly educated individuals. "From the moment they turn on the radio," Duhamel asserted, listeners became "indisposed by the weak amount of truly nutritious intellectual substance contained in the diluted torrent of noise" emerging from their loudspeakers. Few in the room would have been surprised by this vigorous condemnation of broadcasting. In his 1918 Goncourt prize-winning essay *Civilisation*, penned at the close of the war, Duhamel lamented humanity's over-reliance on technology, a theme he reiterated in his 1930 *Scènes de la vie future*. In the latter text, he denounced wireless (which he mockingly called *la téhessef*) as an insidious modern invention that threatened to mechanize body and mind while producing a soulless, materialist mass culture like the one he had observed, and abhorred, in his travels to the United States.[1] Similar complaints resurfaced in his 1934 *Querelles de famille*, where Duhamel argued that broadcast sound constituted little more than earsplitting noise.[2]

From the podium beneath Le Vau's iconic cupola, Duhamel excoriated the directors of France's commercial radio stations for dispensing nothing but "superficial notions, easily acquired and easily forgotten," in the form

---

[1] Georges Duhamel, *Radiophonie et culture intellectuelle. Séance publique des cinq Académies présidées par Petit-Dutaillis, président de l'Académie des Inscriptions et Belles-Lettres*, Institut de France, October 25, 1938 (Paris, 1938), 63–73. For more on Duhamel's attitudes toward radio, see Christopher Todd, "Georges Duhamel: Enemy-cum-friend of the Radio," *Modern Language Review*, 92, 1, 1997, 48–59.
[2] Duhamel, *Querelles de famille*, 203–9.

of advertising jingles, crime dramas, popular melodies, and talk shows, while transmitting with only "negligible interruptions" for eighteen out of the twenty-four hours of the day. This continued exposure to broadcast sound would cause listeners to "lose, little by little, the habit and even active sense of brain work," Duhamel warned, perpetuating a "form of intelligence known as elementary intelligence" at the very moment that "education reformers are striving to open up intelligence to the greatest chances for growth and escape." Was it any wonder, he asked, that certain well-meaning politicians resorted to "intellectual demagoguery" in an effort to tame the airwaves? Under such circumstances, listening "could never contribute to liberating the citizen ... but only to oppressing him."[3] Duhamel's speech electrified the audience, *Le Figaro* reported, provoking a wave of applause and nodding heads, though the moment proved not without irony, given that the state PTT network transmitted the session live to listeners across France.[4] Many outside the académies dismissed Duhamel's criticisms as those of a conservative intellectual discomfited by modernity, for he clearly disapproved of commercial broadcasting and its "American"-inspired advertising. Yet his reference to demagoguery in the airwaves also directed a pointed jibe at a recent state broadcasting initiative targeting the very heart and soul of French society: the school classroom.

In January of 1937, the state radio network began transmitting hundreds of radio lessons – in singing and music appreciation, diction, French and foreign languages, as well as philosophy, history, and science – to primary and secondary students across France. Launched by Léon Blum's first Popular Front government and continuing to September 1939, the school radio initiative (*radio scolaire*) promoted collective radio listening as a tool of citizen formation and civic engagement among France's youth. The program synthesized the government's efforts to democratize culture, reform the public education system, and exploit broadcasting for political ends – all measures the Popular Front deemed necessary to fight the rising tide of fascism at home and across Europe. In fact, the Popular Front was the first interwar political movement to make the reform of state broadcasting a central component of its platform. As Jean Zay, the Popular Front's education minister, told schoolchildren in the inaugural *radio scolaire* broadcast, classroom listening would provide them with an apprenticeship in citizenship through the "radio nation" in the airwaves – that "French community where personal fantasies ... and a diversity of individual wills and temperaments come

---

[3] Duhamel, *Radiophonie et culture intellectuelle*, 63–73.
[4] Louis Chauvet, "M. Duhamel se plaint de la T.S.F. devant les cinq Académies réunies," *Le Figaro*, October 26, 1938, 2.

together." In a country fractured by partisan politics and struggling to survive the depression, the school broadcasts would suspend temporarily, if not permanently, differences of class, confession, and regional identity to unite students through a "fraternity of listening."[5]

Yet, far from reconciling individual prerogatives with collective interests, as Zay intended, the *radio scolaire* broadcasts instead unleashed a series of virulent debates between politicians and cultural critics on the left, who celebrated radio as a medium of cultural democratization, and others on the right, who condemned the Popular Front for permitting mass culture to invade the classroom, or even worse, for exploiting the airwaves to indoctrinate France's youth with left-wing propaganda. Since the French Revolution, politicians had regarded the public school as the preeminent institution for shaping the political and moral values of the nation's youth, pitting republican proponents of secularism against Catholics in a battle for control over the classroom. Republican legislators of the early Third Republic hoped to end this century-long ideological battle with the passage of the Ferry Laws of 1881–1882, which instituted free, mandatory, and secular primary schooling across France.[6] However, in the aftermath of the war, France's declining birthrate and its rapidly aging population ensured that young people once again moved to the forefront of political discourse.[7] The right accused republican teachers of replacing patriotic classroom lessons glorifying France's "victory" in 1918 with "pacifist" teachings touting the virtues of internationalism and collective security, while communists and Catholics alike looked to adolescents as the vanguard that could save France from moral and political decadence.[8] Rising diplomatic tensions only further exacerbated the national debates over educational reform, with *radio scolaire* at their center, that unfolded in the airwaves, the mass press, and in educational circles, where teachers, parents, and politicians evaluated the merits and vices of classroom radio listening with the knowledge that school broadcasting already existed in Germany, Italy, and Great Britain.

---

[5] Jean Zay's speech reprinted as "La radio scolaire. Discours d'ouverture du ministre de l'E. N.," *L'Ecole libératrice. Organe hebdomadaire du Syndicat National des Institutrices et Instituteurs de France et des Colonies*, January 9, 1937, 332–33.

[6] Weber, *Peasants into Frenchmen*, 67–94; Jacques and Mona Ozouf, *La république des instituteurs* (Paris, 1992); Olivier Loubes, *L'école et la patrie: histoire d'un désenchantement, 1914–1940* (Paris, 2001).

[7] Susan B. Whitney, *Mobilizing Youth: Communists and Catholics in Interwar France* (Durham NC, 2009), 3; Jackson, *The Popular Front*, 133–36.

[8] Siegel, *The Moral Disarmament of France*; Whitney, *Mobilizing Youth*, 3; Olivier Loubes, "L'école et les deux corps de la nation en France, 1900–1940," *Histoire de l'éducation*, 126, 2010, 55–76.

The debut of *radio scolaire* also provoked the first sustained discussion in France about the impact of mass-reproduced and broadcast sound on the intellectual capital of the nation's citizens. During these same years the German Frankfurt School theorists began formulating their now-canonical critique of the "culture industry" by arguing that the repetitive and mundane sounds of radio and records lulled listeners into passivity and political complacency, in turn contributing to the rise of fascism. Conservatives such as Duhamel likewise condemned broadcasting as a distraction that threatened to "modify our entire system of culture" for the worse.[9] In contrast, an emerging cadre of pedagogical reformers began to argue that sound technologies could play a vital role in culti-vating human intelligence and self-expression. Collective auditory and vocal training, now made possible for the first time on a mass scale, might be harnessed to develop the critical capacities of France's youth. The "multiplication of radio receivers will not engender stupidity any more than the multiplication of books," the socialist essayist Jean Guéhenno concluded in 1938, for active radio listening could only enable the "general mobilization of intelligence and the human spirit . . . among a national population."[10]

The tense political climate of the mid-to-late 1930s exacerbated the tenor of the debates about the intellectual merits of *radio scolaire*, which centered on questions about radio listening and its relationship to the exercise of citizenship. Historians have long regarded this period as one of near civil war, when "two Frances" – one deeply conservative, Catholic, and authoritarian, and the other secular and republican – threatened to tear one another apart. Profound ideological convictions divided French people, to be sure, but the boundaries between left and right shifted almost daily as politicians competed to win the support of the masses, often adopting rhetorical positions that resembled those of their political opponents.[11] In the battle over *radio scolaire*, far right critics of the Popular Front positioned themselves as defenders of individual liberty and listeners' rights against a "tyrannical" left-wing state seeking to manip-ulate the nation's ears, even as they partly accepted the premises behind the program. But to understand how debates about radio listening became embroiled in a larger partisan political battle between the left and the right, we turn first to examine the evolution of state

---

[9] Theodor Adorno, "On the Fetish Character in Music and the Regression of Listening," *The Culture Industry: Selected Essays on Mass Culture* (London, 1991), 29–60. For the impact of the Frankfurt School argument in radio studies, see Hendy, *Radio in the Global Age*, 134–43.
[10] Jean Guéhenno, "La radio et l'esprit," *Radio-Liberté*, February 1938, 39–40.
[11] Wardhaugh, *In Pursuit of the People*, 16.

broadcasting policy and mass politics in the mid-1930s, as well as contemporary efforts to develop a modern pedagogy of the ear.

Mass politics and the media of the masses

Radio's expansion as a mass media coincided with the rise of partisan politics between 1932 and 1935, when a succession of governments collapsed in failure as legislators struggled to combat the economic depression through a series of largely unsuccessful deflationary measures. Direct attacks on parliamentary democracy, once aired only by parties of the far right, now began to appear in the mainstream press, as voters grew distrustful of backroom legislative wrangling and demanded greater popular participation in politics. In January of 1934, after the arrest and apparent suicide of the Jewish financier Alexandre Stavisky fueled charges of financial corruption in the highest circles of government, the radical-socialist premier Camille Chautemps resigned in disgrace. A month later, when the newly formed Daladier government dismissed the Paris police prefect Jean Chiappe, a man widely known for his right-leaning political sympathies and hatred of communists, members of the far right extra-parliamentary leagues – including the Croix de Feu, the Camelots du Roi, and Jeunesses Patriotes – launched a violent protest on February 6 at the Place de la Concorde that left fifteen dead and wounded nearly 1,500 demonstrators. The ensuing street fighting rallied together anti-fascist intellectuals, left-wing politicians, and labor unions, paving the way for the eventual political alliance of socialists, radicals, and communists known as the Rassemblement du Front Populaire.[12]

Between the February 6, 1934, demonstrations at the Place de la Concorde and the May 1936 elections that ushered into power the first Popular Front government under the socialist Léon Blum, the number of registered radios in France jumped from 1.5 to 3.2 million. This exponential growth, even amid rampant inflation that reduced the purchasing power of the middle classes, resulted from the growing professionalization of broadcasting and the increased number of stations transmitting across Europe. When the indefatigable (and many argued, dictatorial) Georges Mandel assumed the direction of the PTT in November 1934, he hoped to advance his own political career and France's international prestige by building up its "radio nation" in the airwaves. To this end, he presided over the inauguration of the new 200-kW Radio-Paris transmitter and worked to eliminate whatever commercial advertising remained on public

[12] Wardhaugh, *In Pursuit of the People*, 24–52; Kennedy, *Reconciling France Against Democracy*, 15–49.

stations. To replace the listeners' associations that managed many regional PTT stations, Mandel introduced advisory boards (*conseils de gérance*) in February 1935 to which registered radio owners could elect representatives. Although he maintained the right to nominate half the members of each station's advisory board, the measure cast the sheen of democratization over the state's growing control of the airwaves by promising listeners a voice in shaping their local PTT station's programs.[13] Thanks to the radio elections, France possessed the "only example in Europe of broadcasting with a democratic character," the director of radio broadcasting Marcel Pellenc boasted to a crowd later that year at the Salon de T.S.F., making the airwaves into an expression of the nation's will through the "universal suffrage of listeners," or at the very least, those who had paid their license fees.[14]

The opening of public radio microphones to political candidates during the 1936 elections further encouraged audiences to imagine the airwaves as a "radio nation" by drawing direct parallels between the airwaves and the vagaries of electoral politics. Although state bureaucrats had tried to restrict formal political speeches from the airwaves, listeners had grown accustomed to hearing politicians' voices emerging from their radio loudspeakers.[15] President Gaston Doumergue turned to the radio to calm middle-class anxieties in the wake of the February 1934 riots, deploying a confidential and familiar tone that drew comparisons to the "fireside chats" of the American president Franklin D. Roosevelt. By the spring of 1935, politicians from both the left and right had begun to demand access to radio microphones in order to reach voters. Léon Blum, then secretary of the French Socialist Party (Section Française de l'Internationale Ouvrière, SFIO), obtained this concession after making an impassioned plea in the Chamber of Deputies that only the use of state broadcasting for electoral speeches could counter the influence of corporate interests, which already dominated the print media, in politics.[16]

Audiences could hear the capitalist ethos Blum decried every day in the programs of the new commercial stations Radio-Cité and Radio-37, which joined the older private stations Poste Parisien, Radio-Toulouse, Radio-Normandie, and Radio-Luxembourg in the skies over France. The Poste Parisien already enjoyed a sizeable audience cultivated from the

---

[13] Méadel, *Histoire de la radio*, 55–78.
[14] CAC 19070147-1. Speech by Marcel Pellenc at the Salon de T.S.F., June 21, 1935.
[15] Derek Vaillant, "La Police de l'Air," 9. In 1932, the industrialist Lucien Lévy granted the right-wing nationalist Henri de Kérillis permission to use his station Radio LL, while a host of minor government ministers employed the radio for speeches on national holidays.
[16] Méadel, *Histoire de la radio*, 93–95.

readership of the daily *Le Petit parisien*, but the advertising entrepreneur Marcel Bleustein-Blanchet revolutionized commercial broadcasting in 1935 when he purchased the lackluster Parisian station Radio LL and rechristened it Radio-Cité. Backed by the right-leaning *L'Intransigeant*, Radio-Cité pioneered innovative programming based on the American model of corporate sponsorship, including quiz shows, the soap opera *La famille Duraton*, police dramas, and variety hours featuring celebrities such as Maurice Chevalier, the actress Mireille, and the dance-band Ray Ventura et ses collégiens. Radio-Cité's on-air amateur talent show *Le crochet radiophonique* invited listeners to participate in broadcasts, as did its game shows offering prizes of furniture and household appliances. Bleustein-Blanchet's own firm Publicis quickly acquired a monopoly over radio advertising by hiring talented creative staff to produce memorable jingles and sketches touting the virtues of Monsavon soap and the health benefits of Lustucru pasta, the breakfast drink Banania, and the fortified table wine Vin de Frileuse. These advertising spots aired regularly on Radio-Cité and the other commercial stations in the widening Publicis advertising "network," including Radio-Alger and the multilingual Radio-Luxembourg. Bolstered by advertising revenues unavailable to state stations, commercial radio promised larger salaries to France's most talented radio dramatists and reporters, and thus began to pose formidable competition to public radio.[17]

This rapid expansion of commercial broadcasting after 1935 has led some scholars to conclude that state radio lost its audiences as people sought refuge from everyday anxieties in the comforts of popular music or comedy sketches. Certainly, the radio press filled its pages with a litany of complaints about the quality of state broadcasting. Listeners and professional critics alike juxtaposed the fast-paced news and humorous dialogue of commercial stations with the officious tones of state radio announcers or the dry subject matter of the infinitesimal lectures aired by the PTT stations. Yet these frequent condemnations of state broadcasting also reflected a common trend, shared among voters on the left and the right, of criticizing the status quo as a form of political protest.[18]

Moreover, audiences could regularly hear foreign broadcasts through their radios, while newspapers documented in detail the strategies deployed by the National Socialist and Italian fascist regimes to install radios in school classrooms, churches, and village halls.[19] The dramatic

---

[17] Neulander, *Programming National Identity*, 23–44.
[18] Nord, *France's New Deal*, 241–46.
[19] *Radio-Magazine* ran a regular "Chronique d'Italie" during the early 1930s that charted the expansion of radio broadcasting in fascist Italy and chronicled Count Ciano's rural and school broadcasting initiatives.

success of commercial broadcasting, combined with this knowledge of foreign radio policies, only convinced many politicians, cultural critics, and radio listeners that the state should do more to develop the "radio nation." Now that "the declaration of the three millionth French listener is about to be registered by an unknown post office," the right-leaning radio critic Pierre Domène argued in *Radio-Magazine* in September of 1936, the government should "organize listening" so France could better compete with Germany and Italy.[20] Chastising audiences who dodged paying their annual radio license fee, often with the complicity of their local wireless salesman, Domène reminded his readers that the *redevance* constituted a "radio duty analogue to a civic responsibility."[21] Paul Campargue, a one-time editor of *Mon programme* and the radio columnist for the socialist daily *Le Populaire*, concurred. "In our century of collective mystiques where propaganda plays a premier role," cultivating a distinctive identity for broadcasting constituted a "radiophonic necessity as much as a political one."[22]

That voices from both the left and right called for the state to develop what Domène termed a "national politics of reception" owed much to the rapidly shifting domestic political landscape of the mid-1930s. The street fighting that erupted in February 1934 reminded politicians and their constituents that the masses in the street conferred political legitimacy, producing what the historian Jessica Wardhaugh has identified as two rival images of the "people." For the far right, the crowds who challenged the Third Republic at the Place de la Concorde represented an honest people united against parliamentary inefficacy and the corruption exposed by the Stavisky Affair. For the left, and the alliance of socialists, communists, and radicals who joined the Popular Front coalition, the masses represented a rational and optimistic working people joined against the threat of fascism.[23] Harnessing the power of mass culture and the "radio nation" would henceforth become central to the claims of both the left and right to represent the interests of the people, and in turn, to mobilizing them for political action.

[20] Pierre Domène, "La politique des ondes. Nous sommes trois millions," *Radio-Magazine*, September 27, 1936.

[21] Pierre Domène, "La politique des ondes. L'instrument des loisirs," *Radio-Magazine*, July 26, 1936.

[22] Paul Campargue, "La radio doit se faire 'sa' propagande," *Le Populaire*, October 14, 1936.

[23] Wardhaugh, *In Pursuit of the People*, 23.

The fraternity of listening: Popular Front politics and the radio

When Jean Zay invoked the "fraternity of listening" in his radio address inaugurating *radio scolaire*, he pointed to the recent efforts of left-wing parties to develop an auditory politics that would rally the working people of France. Since the early 1920s, the French Communist Party (PCF) had used broadcasting to attract supporters through its radio club and at party meetings, where members tuned into the short-wave broadcasts of Radio-Moscow. Both the PCF and SFIO published their own labels of 78-rpm records that recreated the auditory atmosphere of political meetings for listeners at home.[24] Dropping a needle on the grooves of these records released the voices of orators addressing audiences of "dear comrades," followed by the "spontaneous" cheers or applause of a crowd, and on occasion, a rendition of the socialist anthems "Le temps des cerises" or the "Internationale".[25] Broadcast sound, as we have already seen, transformed the mass urban political demonstrations of the mid-1930s by gathering tens of thousands on city streets to listen to political candidates or cheer their parties. "The loudspeaker, principally used outdoors," the teacher René Maublanc opined in the communist newspaper *L'Humanité*, "has given an oratory a hitherto unknown scope."[26] Although scholars have long privileged the left's propensity for cultural innovation, recent scholarship suggests that parties on the right embraced modern media. Colonel de La Rocque's Croix de Feu and Pierre Taittinger's Jeunesses Patriotes employed films and glossy magazines to reach constituents, while the novelist Robert Brasillach and the journalist Lucien Rebatet, both contributors to the right-wing, anti-Semitic newspaper *Je suis partout*, celebrated radio's ability to magnify the persuasive power of the human voice.[27]

Candidates from across the political spectrum consequently looked to the May 1936 elections as an opportunity to recreate in the airwaves

[24] Advertisements for *La voix des nôtres* records in *Le Populaire*, July 27, 1936, 7, and January 17, 1937.
[25] Méadel, *Histoire de la radio*, 98. See, for example, Bibliothèque Nationale de France, Maurice Thorez, "Le Front Populaire vaincra," Piatileka Records, 1936, 78-rpm recording.
[26] René Maublanc, "Destin de la poésie," *L'Humanité*, September 4, 1937, 8.
[27] Simon Dell, *The Image of the Popular Fron: The Masses and the Media in Interwar France* (London, 2007); Dudley and Ungar, *The Popular Front and the Poetics of Culture*; Wardhaugh, *In Pursuit of the People*, 153–57, 174–82; Alice Kaplan, *Reproductions of Banality: Fascism, Literature, and French Intellectual Life* (Minneapolis, 1986), 133–35; Paul Mazgaj, *Imagining Fascism: The Cultural Politics of the French Young Right, 1930–1945* (Newark DE, 2007), 186–88.

the momentary sensation of consensus experienced during street demonstrations and political rallies. However, if "all the representatives of the larger parties could make themselves heard" on Radio-Paris, *Le Populaire* reminded its readers, voters owed this "demonstration of equity" to the SFIO.[28] The "people" had in turn rewarded the Popular Front with their votes, giving the Blum government a mandate to restructure the "radio nation," much to the chagrin of its right-wing critics, who feared their impending disenfranchisement in the airwaves, in a direct extension of the government's dissolution of the right-wing extra-parliamentary leagues that June. In the warm summer months that followed, café patrons, industrial workers, and families clustered around radios to listen to news of the post-election industrial unrest – the largest wave of strike activity in the Third Republic's history – that halted work in automobile plants, mines, and department stores. With the printing and delivery of newspapers slowed, broadcasting provided direct access to the festival atmosphere that reigned on city streets and factory floors – sounds welcomed by the lower classes, but feared by the *bourgeoisie*.[29]

The Blum government confronted one of its central dilemmas during these turbulent first weeks in power: how best to exploit mass media in the struggle against fascism. Faced with the success of Nazi and fascist programs to enhance leisure and boost consumerism, Blum's advisors turned their backs on the left's historical asceticism and the deflationary policies of earlier governments. They instead looked to the American New Deal for inspiration, announcing an expansive public works program to stimulate employment and introducing reforms to empower workers on the shop floor and in the marketplace. The June 1936 Matignon Accords and subsequent labor legislation legalized collective bargaining and the right to strike, while instituting universal wage increases, a forty-hour work week, and mandatory two-week paid vacations.[30] The socialist lawyer Léo Lagrange, appointed to head a new Under-secretariat of State for the Organization of Sport and Leisure, launched a host of state-sponsored schemes, from free museum entries and circulating libraries to summer camps, to give the working masses access to French culture and fill their newly acquired weekend and summer holidays. Many of these programs, as Julian Jackson and Susan

---

[28] Paul Campargue, "La grande espérance des auditeurs français," *Le Populaire*, May 5, 1936, 4.

[29] Méadel, *Histoire de la radio*, 158.

[30] Jackson, *The Popular Front*, 113–15, 120, 125–28; De Grazia, *Irresistible Empire*, 121–23, and Pascal Ory, *La belle illusion: culture et politique sous le signe du Front Populaire* (Paris, 1994), 61.

Whitney have shown, directly targeted young people – a key political constituency for a government eager to demonstrate democracy's vitality in the face of the fascist threat.[31]

Repudiating the far right's vision of a France composed of socially conservative Catholics rooted in regional traditions, the Popular Front instead cultivated a populist French culture that would unite industrial workers, agricultural laborers, and the urban bourgeoisie. The banner of the Rassemblement veiled considerable class and cultural differences among its leaders, who sometimes disagreed over economic and foreign policy. Yet the socialist and communist cultural groups that rallied behind the Popular Front typically displayed less interest in importing Stalinist aesthetics than in democratizing access to France's preexisting cultural heritage, whether regional folklore or the fables of La Fontaine.[32] Even Jacques Duclos, the head of the PCF's propaganda section, maintained that French represented the "universal language of intelligence," making broadcasting an ideal medium through which to advance the government's political agenda.[33]

The Popular Front consequently made increasing workers' access to the airwaves a central component of its political platform, given that working-class families still spent approximately 50 percent of their incomes on food, and a domestic receiver cost upwards of two months' wages for a day laborer. If *bricolage* remained an inexpensive option for the technically inclined, many workers listened to the radio in the semi-public spaces of cafés, greasy spoon restaurants, labor union headquarters, or in public listening halls.[34] It would be "childish to maintain that radio receivers constitute an exclusive privilege of a posh and self-righteous bourgeoisie," *Le Populaire* argued, but "it is a social and political duty for the Popular Front and its government ... to popularize wireless and make it sink in among the laboring classes."[35] Robert Jardillier, the bespectacled high school (*lycée*) history teacher and amateur musicologist appointed to run the PTT, tackled this problem in June 1936 by instructing staff to install loudspeakers in the public squares and parks of sixteen cities across France to broadcast music and "great demonstrations of

[31] Whitney, *Mobilizing Youth*, 190–96.
[32] Ory, *La belle illusion*, 61; Lebovics, *True France*, 137–57.
[33] Jackson, *The Popular Front*, 120.
[34] Furlough, *Consumer Cooperation in France*, 265. Furlough cites a 1936 study from Toulouse which found that workers and employees spent between 41.7 and 56.4 percent of their incomes on food.
[35] Paul Campargue, "Pour une radio populaire," *Le Populaire*, March 17, 1936, 6, and Campargue, "Pour une radio populaire: le problème du prix et de la qualité," *Le Populaire*, March 21, 1937, 6.

national importance." The loudspeakers, he believed, would create live-lier urban spaces and facilitate the "collective education of the masses."[36]

Government propagandists sought to infuse collective listening with a renewed significance by developing a sonic aesthetic that united individuals with the collective, and which borrowed from both Soviet and fascist models.[37] Jardillier's loudspeakers debuted on Bastille Day, when the government's media strategist, the socialist Marceau Pivert, hoped to reclaim the holiday from the right, which had dominated commemorations since the early 1900s. Pivert collaborated with SFIO and PCF affiliates to stage a vast "victory" parade of trade unions, youth organizations, political clubs, and cultural associations across Paris, culminating in a massive assembly at the Place de la Nation. From the stage, Victor Basch (head of the national Rassemblement committee), the Radical party leader Daladier, PCF secretary Léon Jouhaux, and the new premier Léon Blum addressed the crowd, while Paris PTT transmitted their speeches and the cheers of crowds to audiences across France via the state radio network. In the capital, the PTT mounted loudspeakers in the Cours de Vincennes and along the Faubourg St. Antoine and Boulevard Diderot to permit those who could not fit into the square to listen, as did loudspeakers installed in Lille, Toulouse, Nantes, Lyon, Marseille, Avignon, and Nîmes.[38] In Jardillier's native Dijon, supporters gathered in three parks and squares to listen to the Paris rallies and to a retransmission of Romain Rolland's 1902 play *Le quatorze juillet*, a dramatic reenactment of the storming of the Bastille staged specially for the occasion at the Alhambra theater in Paris.[39]

Perhaps unsurprisingly, the installation of the loudspeakers provoked a heated public discussion about the government's motivations in encouraging collective listening. *Le Populaire* praised the loudspeakers for permitting "an entire nation to communally celebrate the triumph of its will" and allowing residents of provincial cities to participate in Parisian street politics. "The broadcasts of the popular celebrations of July 14, [and] the speeches of Léon Jouhaux, Maurice Thorez, and Léon Blum reveal to us a new aspect of radio art that is only beginning," the newspaper argued, calling upon radio dramatists to develop new artistic works specifically for collective listening.[40] Other observers, however,

---

[36] CAC 19870714-2. Archives de la Direction de la Radiodiffusion. Exposé de M. Jardillier, October 30, 1936.
[37] Favre, "Quand le Führer parle," 108–17.   [38] *Le Populaire*, July 13, 1936, 4.
[39] *Le Progrès de la Côte d'Or* (Dijon), July 15, 1936, and July 13, 1937; See also "Ce que sera la manifestation du Front populaire," *L'Eclair. Journal du midi*, July 14, 1936, 6. For a detailed description of *Le quatorze juillet*, see Wardhaugh, *In Pursuit of the People*, 165–67.
[40] Paul Campargue, "La radio et le peuple," *Le Populaire*, July 22, 1936, 4.

proved to be far less enthusiastic. "When anyone can receive wireless at home," *Radio-Magazine* wondered, why did the government want to "add several decibels to the level of urban noise?"[41] The Montpellier daily *L'Eclair* conflated the loudspeakers with Nazi propagandists' assaults on German citizens' ears, so that "even in their promenade, and in the name (well understood) of liberty, modest French citizens" were subjected to "official opinion" imposed on them from above.[42] Despite these protests, the loudspeakers continued to operate in several cities until 1939, where they broadcast classical concerts, political speeches, the opening ceremonies of the 1936 Berlin Olympics, and news reportage of state funerals and Armistice Day commemorations.[43]

Radio-Liberté, a lobbying group formed in late 1935 to promote the election of left-wing candidates to the state radio advisory boards, approached the problem of workers' access to radio differently, launching a campaign in the spring of 1937 to produce an inexpensive *poste populaire*, or people's radio, modeled on the German *Volksempfänger*.[44] Bourgeois critics were already accusing Blum of inciting irresponsible consumerism among the working class that threatened to obliterate social distinctions, but Radio-Liberté insisted that the production of affordable radios would not involve the "totalitarian methods that permitted Hitler to dictate his imperatives on the German radio electric industry. The nationalization of radio manufacturing is *not* on the agenda."[45] Moreover, where the design of the *Volksempfänger* (with a small number of lamps) restricted international listening by limiting reception to Germany's national long-wave and regional stations, Radio-Liberté insisted that French wireless enthusiasts would accept no such restrictions.[46] "The *poste populaire* must capture all the local and regional stations as well as the great European transmitters," *Radio-Liberté* magazine argued, for in a democratic nation such as France, international radio reception represented a political right and not just a privilege of the wealthy.[47] The

---

[41] "Le haut-parleur sur la place publique," *Mon programme*, November 20, 1936; "Echos et informations: Concerts publiques par T.S.F.," *Radio-Magazine*, October 18, 1936.

[42] "Révoltez-vous! Le scandale de la radio d'état," *L'Eclair. Journal du midi*, June 19, 1936, 1.

[43] CAC 19950218-8. L'Inspecteur du Contrôle Durant à M. le Ministre des PTT April 7, 1939. Municipalities eventually controlled the programs the speakers broadcast. For program listings of the public broadcasts in Dijon and Limoges, see *Le Bien public*, July 31 and August 29, 1936, and *Le Courrier du centre*, July 12 and August 23, 1936.

[44] "Le poste populaire," *Radio-Liberté*, May 21 and October 22, 1937.

[45] Paul Campargue, "Pour une radio populaire," *Le Populaire*, March 17, 1936, 6.

[46] Bergmeier, *Hitler's Airwaves*, 8–10.

[47] "Le poste populaire," *Radio-Liberté*, May 21, 1937. By October, Radio-Liberté had constructed a four-lamp radio that allowed listeners to "capture, with ease, more than 60 stations between 200 m and 500 m, and 7 on the long waves: Huizen, Radio-Paris,

association's plans for a *poste populaire* never materialized further than the construction of a model, but several manufacturers embraced Radio-Liberté's scheme as a marketing strategy. Radio-Sfar advertised its 1,150-franc Orchestral model as a receiver "in the reach of all workers – available in twelve monthly installments of ninety francs" that promised easy access to "Moscow, Madrid, Barcelona, New York, and all the powerful broadcasts of the globe" – at a cheap price.[48] From Radio-Liberté's perspective, listening would give a political voice to people who might not otherwise have the opportunity to participate in national or international affairs. The communist playwright Jean-Richard Bloch echoed this view in his 1936 essay *Naissance d'une culture*, arguing that the airwaves had "enlarged to the size of nations the little Athenian agora or the Roman forum."[49]

However, the Popular Front's broadcasting policy contained a tension between the desire to democratize access to the radio and the conviction that only firm state control over the airwaves could ensure that they fulfilled their social and political potential. Blum's cabinet briefly entertained proposals to create a ministry of propaganda to coordinate state policy in education, media, and the arts, reflecting an integralist view of French culture shared by many left-wing intellectuals, but many on the right as well.[50] Although the government never implemented this project, Jardillier further expanded state control over the "radio nation" by restructuring the advisory boards to contain even more political appointees. He also reorganized the Paris-based Conseil Supérieur des Emissions de la Radiodiffusion, charging the members he appointed with overseeing the content and quality of state broadcasting. He named to the council's first roster a number of public school teachers, civil servants, and Parisian artistic and intellectual luminaries, including the composer Darius Milhaud, the cinema pioneer Louis Lumière, the novelist Jules

Droitwich, Warsaw, Motala (Sweden), Luxembourg, and Oslo." On the short waves, it picked up New York, Tokyo, Prague, Moscow, and multiple English, German, and Italian stations.

[48] Advertisement for Radio-Sfar, *Le Populaire*, February 2, 1937, 5; Advertisement for the Coopérative de la T.S.F., *Le Populaire*, January 6, 1938, 3. The Coopérative de la T.S.F. sold models called the "Democrat" and the "Global" in the largely working-class 18th arrondissement of Paris.

[49] Jean-Richard Bloch, "Nous sommes au commencement de tout," *Europe*, May 15, 1936, 89–96; *Naissance d'une culture*, 158–65.

[50] Ory, *La belle illusion*, 178–79. Zay's wartime papers contained a proposal for a "ministry of cultural life" devoted to education and forms of "national expression." The right-wing Parti Social Français proposed a similar "super-ministry of education, responsible for overseeing radio, the press, fine arts, scientific research, technical and physical education, child protection, health and hygiene, and the defense of morality against 'immoral propaganda.'" See Kennedy, *Reconciling France Against Democracy*, 178, and Kalman, *The Extreme Right in Interwar France*, 171.

Romain, and that ever-peevish critic of radio, Georges Duhamel.[51] Keen
to avoid accusations of bias, the government granted its political opponents periodic access to the airwaves, although speeches by left-wing
politicians and performances by leftist cultural organizations, such as
the socialist and communist theater collectives Mai 36 and Art et
Travail, would henceforth be heard with greater frequency. By 1937 the
Popular Front possessed greater control over the "radio nation" than any
previous government, a fact that few of its far right, or even moderate
political critics, could forget. These tensions in turn shaped audiences'
reaction to *radio scolaire*, which encapsulated the Popular Front's efforts
to transform education by harnessing the power of radio listening.

Learning to listen: defining a modern pedagogy of the ear

When Jean Zay wrote to Léon Blum in July 1936 to announce his intentions for creating a national school radio program, he intended to capitalize on a decade of haphazard experimentation with educational
broadcasting, from the Berlitz company's foreign-language radio correspondence courses of the 1920s to the broadcasts produced by the
Syndicat National des Instituteurs, France's powerful national teachers'
union, on several regional stations in 1932.[52] These early efforts had
foundered for want of coordination and funding, but introducing modern
technologies like radio into the classroom was imperative, the *lycée*
instructor André Ravizé argued in a 1934 teachers' manual, for "given
the sensitivity of young people in this third decade of the twentieth
century ... we must be of our time."[53] In 1935, the Paris-based
International Institute for Intellectual Cooperation, a think tank affiliated
with the League of Nations, lent further impetus to school broadcasting
by arguing that radio would elevate the cultural level of students in rural
and working-class milieu and foster international *rapprochement*.[54] When

[51] Méadel, *Histoire de la radio*, 135–36; Nord, *France's New Deal*, 247–49. This renamed
committee replaced and modified the membership of the Conseil Supérieur de la
Radiodiffusion created by Georges Mandel a year earlier.
[52] CARAN F21-4699. Administration des Beaux-Arts. Le Ministre de l'Instruction
Publique à M. le Directeur des Beaux-Arts, January 7, 1928. The radical education
minister Edouard Herriot organized a short-lived school radio commission in 1928. For
the Berlitz radio programs, see *L'Echo du studio*, January 1, 1930, and June 15, 1929. For
the trial broadcasts on Alpes-Grenoble PTT, *Le Petit radio*, January 22, 1932, and July
23, 1932, and *Annuaire de radiodiffusion nationale 1933*, 158–59.
[53] André Ravizé, *Répertoire des disques de langues étrangères enregistrées et éditées sous les auspices
du Comité Français du Phonographe dans l'Enseignement et l'Association des Professeurs de
Langues Vivantes* (Paris, n.d. 1934 ?), 6.
[54] Institut International de Coopération Intellectuelle, "Rôle social et international de la
radiodiffusion. Enquête sur la radiodiffusion et l'éducation du grand public par l'Institut

a group of Parisian primary school teachers subsequently organized a series of trial broadcasts on Paris PTT in 1936, they garnered the support of the Société Française de Pédagogie and the government.[55] Blum's undersecretary of state, Jules Moch, told Zay that their initiative encapsulated "our common ideas in the matter of modern techniques of education," and Zay immediately convened a school radio commission of classroom teachers and pedagogical experts at the Centre National de Documentation Pédagogique, the state's pedagogical research center.[56]

The Blum government planned to democratize education by creating an *école unique* (mixed-ability school) that would reduce the historic gap between working- and middle-class students' learning opportunities by reforming classroom spaces and pedagogy. Even after the passage of the Ferry Laws of the 1880s, many working-class families could not afford the secondary school fees required for their children to continue their schooling. A 1937 law reduced the school leaving age to fourteen and created an intermediate *classe d'orientation* (orientation class) to evaluate students' intellectual aptitude independently of their social status or family background and guide them toward appropriate training in a technical school or *lycée*.[57] To redesign school curricula, Zay assembled a team well-versed in contemporary educational trends, appointing the veteran teacher Marcel Abraham to head his cabinet. Together they proposed new teaching methods that synthesized the secular humanism of the republican tradition with "active" pedagogy inspired by the New Education movement – the latter intended to cultivate critical thinking skills and teach students to reason, argue, and resist the social homogenization undergirding fascism.[58] Renovating schools and equipping classrooms with film projectors, scientific instruments, and above all, phonographs and radios, would provide the teaching corps with a modern infrastructure through which to achieve these goals. Zay's staff calculated that 72,000 radios would be required to equip every school with at least one receiver, at a cost of sixty-five million francs. Given the government's other

International de Coopération Intellectuelle," *Revue générale des industries radioélectriques*, December 1934, 8–10, and January 1935, 4–6.
[55] Mme Bessan, Mlle J. Barre, et M. Martini, "L'enseignement musical et la T.S.F.," *Bulletin de la Société Française de Pédagogie*, September 1936, 72–86.
[56] CARAN F60-427. Jean Zay, Ministre de l'Education Nationale à M. le Président du Conseil, July 6, 1936, and the response from Jules Moch, Présidence du Conseil à M. le Ministre d'Education Nationale, September 17, 1936. The Centre National de Documentation Pédagogique succeeded the Musée Pédagogique, a pedagogical research and documentation center dating to the early the Third Republic.
[57] David L. Hanley, A.P. Kerr, and Neville H. Waites, *Contemporary France: Politics and Society Since 1945* (London, 2005), 234–35; Loubes, *L'école et la patrie*, esp. Chapter 3.
[58] Antoine Prost, "Les instructions de 1938," in Antoine Prost, ed., *Jean Zay et le gauche du radicalisme* (Paris, 2003), 191–208.

financial commitments, however, the Ministry of Education invited municipalities, school cooperatives, and student associations to purchase radios on the promise of a subsidy for half the cost of the receiver, lowering the state's burden to thirty million francs.[59]

In designing the *radio scolaire* broadcasts, Zay turned to a group of pedagogical reformers whose classroom experimentation with sound technologies had already earned them a reputation in educational circles. Even before the Popular Front took power, these teachers had been working to transform France's visually oriented school curriculum through a new focus on auditory and vocal training. Nineteenth-century republican educators had distrusted oral culture, which they associated with Catholic religiosity and peasant superstition, prompting them to create a curriculum focused on teaching literacy and rational observation through the *leçon de choses*.[60] Modern sound technologies offered a "new means of expression" that would revolutionize education, Margueritte Rocher told teachers during a demonstration of radio pedagogy in 1937. Given radio's influence on the "public's comprehension of global and national affairs," educators had an obligation to train their students to listen attentively and critically. How would students ever learn to distinguish between poor- and high-quality sounds when radios, phonographs, and public address systems distributed political speeches, jazz bands, and crime dramas indiscriminately into public and private spaces?[61] Reformers thus targeted for renovation two areas of the school curriculum where the cultural impact of broadcasting had already been felt and where they believed it might best be exploited in the classroom: music education and language training. In doing so, they inserted the Popular Front's *radio scolaire* initiative into a much broader conversation about the psychology of listening and its effects on individual and collective behavior.

* * *

"The word 'crisis' is the order of the day," the composer Maurice Emmanuel told *La Musique à l'école* in 1932, and while the economic *crise* struck fear in the hearts of many, most people ignored the national crisis of the ear. "Wireless and records introduce music everywhere, distributing the best and worst to listeners who are little capable of discerning the difference," while the public, "gorged with sound ... has

[59] CARAN F60-427. Jean Zay, Ministre de l'Education Nationale à M. le Président du Conseil, July 6, 1936, and the response from Jules Moch, Présidence du Conseil à M. le Ministre d'Education Nationale, September 17, 1936.
[60] Jacques and Mona Ozouf, *La république des instituteurs*; Bergeron, *Voice Lessons: French Mélodie in the Belle Epoque*, 72–118.
[61] Marguerite L. Rocher, "La radiodiffusion scolaire," talk presented at the IIIe Congrès internationale des professeurs de langues vivantes (Paris, 1937), 342–52.

begun to believe that music ... is an indispensable pleasure." The "evil is that it does not know anything about how music is made or that most of it is sung and played 'falsely.'"[62] The pedagogical theorist Maurice Chevais agreed. As the inspector of singing for Paris city schools, Chevais had ample opportunity to observe the phenomenon Emmanuel described, but rather than place the blame solely on the popularity of "mechanical music," he pointed to inadequacies in the public school curriculum. In his 1937 treatise *L'éducation musicale de l'enfance*, Chevais argued that listening remained underdeveloped in most children because schools historically privileged vision as the critical sense in shaping rationality, in turn creating a false hierarchy of sensory perception in children.[63] Although politicians had long recognized the value of music to civic socialization, teachers introduced classroom singing only when called upon by the state to elevate patriotic sentiment, such as during the Franco-Prussian War or the First World War.[64]

Modern sound technologies now offered teachers a simple way to restore equilibrium to the human sensorium, according to Chevais, and he challenged teachers who viewed listening as peripheral to learning by arguing that exposure to music, or the "echo of the soul," was essential to individual psychological and physiological development because it trained the sensory mechanisms of young children to prepare them for more advanced learning. As the core of the "governing faculties of memory, imagination, and auditory attention," Chevais claimed, learning to listen properly would help the "child profit from the most diverse oral teaching" and serve as a base for all future learning.[65] Building off the theories of Maria Montessori, Jacques Dalcroze, and Ovide Decroly, Chevais advocated active, experiential learning adapted to individual students' needs that contrasted sharply with the rote memorization demanded by older school curricula.[66]

---

[62] Maurice Emmanuel, "Les principes de l'éducation musicale," *La Musique à l'école*, April 1932, 121–22.

[63] Maurice Chevais, *L'éducation musicale de l'enfance, Vol. 1: L'enfant et la musique* (Paris, 1937), 106–8.

[64] Michèle Alten, "L'introuvable identité disciplinaire de la musique scolaire en France sous la IIIe République," *Paedagogica Historica*, 40, 3, 2004, 279–91; Michèle Alten, "Un siècle d'enseignement musique à l'école primaire," *Vingtième Siècle*, 55, July–September 1997, 3–15; Claire Fijalkow, *Deux siècles de musique à l'école: chroniques de l'exception parisienne, 1819–2002* (Paris, 2003); and Regina Sweeney, *Singing Our Way to Victory*, esp. Chapter 1. The state-run teachers' training colleges (*écoles normales*) provided no formal training in musical pedagogy to their students.

[65] Maurice Chevais, *L'éducation musicale de l'enfance*, 1: 50–53.

[66] Antoine Prost, *Histoire de l'enseignement en France: 1800–1967* (Paris, 1968), 226, 286–87.

During the early 1930s, Chevais collaborated with the Comité Français du Phonographe et de la Radio dans l'Enseignement, a pedagogical reform group based at the Centre National de Documentation Pédagogique, whose members included university professors, public school inspectors, linguists, phoneticians, and rehabilitation therapists. Together they published hundreds of articles touting vocal and auditory training in educational revues such as *La Musique à l'école*, *L'Ecole et la vie*, *Le Phonographe à l'école*, and *Langues modernes* and conducted public demonstrations of phonographic and radio pedagogy for teachers.[67] The primary school inspector Charles L'Hôpital used Chevais's theories to develop lessons that exposed young ears to the sounds, movements, and meanings of symphonic music, operas, and folk songs. To cultivate active listening and auditory comprehension, L'Hôpital asked students to evaluate conceptual themes (such as the weather, the seasons, or emotions) evoked by a musical selection, identify individual instruments, or create physical gestures to accompany sounds.[68] Chevais and L'Hôpital touted *do-re-mi* scale-singing (*solfège*), or the counting of intervals on a numbered scale to replace the reading of musical notes, as a method that privileged the ear over the eye and repudiated traditional musical instruction focused on theory and visual notation. Music should address itself to children "first in a sensory form, then an affective form," Chevais argued, rather than appealing strictly to their intelligence. Phonographs and radios promised to liberate teachers from the "tyranny" of a written score and provide students with beautiful sounds and vocal models they could imitate.[69]

This commitment to training the *ear* and the *mouth* aligned Chevais and L'Hôpital with other Committee members who privileged auditory training, rather than grammar, memorization, or written exercises, in the acquisition of language. "To speak a language correctly," argued

[67] Jules Lallement, "Le Comité Français du Phonographe dans l'Enseignement," *Bulletin du Musée Pédagogique*, 10, 1933, 285–90. Music publisher François Hepp, president of the Union Syndicale de Commerce de Musique, founded the Comité Français du Phonographe dans l'Enseignement in 1928, inviting representatives from France's major recording firms to participate. In May 1936, the Committee added "radio" to its name. See "Comité Français du Phonographe et de la Radio dans l'Enseignement," *La Musique à l'école*, March 1936.
[68] Charles L'Hôpital, "Le disque et l'explication musicale," *L'Ecole et la vie*, November 25, 1933, 9–10. See also Mme Desmettre and Mlles B. and J. Auroy, *Les beaux disques expliqués aux enfants* (Paris, 1935), 6, 11. Teachers used this same method in the experimental school radio broadcasts conducted on Alpes-Grenoble PTT in 1934. Paul Pitton, "Radiophonie," in *La Musique à l'école*, December 1934.
[69] Maurice Chevais, "La radiophonie au service de l'éducation nationale," *Bulletin de la Société Française de Pédagogie*, 64, June 1937, 34–38; Fijalkow, *Deux siècles de musique à l'école: chroniques de l'exception parisienne*, 62–64.

Théodore Rosset, the director of the Institut de Phonétique at the University of Grenoble, "is not simply to articulate isolated words without fault, it is to pronounce phrases with an accent, its adaptations, its rhythms, and the intonation that a native gives them spontaneously, but which a foreigner must learn, and sometimes with difficulty."[70] The emerging disciplines of phonetics and acoustics had first spurred academic interest in the sounds of the French language during the 1880s, fueled by the republican dream of forging a monolingual nation. In the research of the phonetician Abbé Pierre-Jean Rousselot and the linguists Michel Bréal and Paul Passy, French emerged as a uniquely musical language, making the ear and the mouth into powerful agents of civilization responsible for producing "correct" pronunciation, accents, and expression.[71] Techniques drawn from Rousselot's experimental phonetics – including the physical manipulation of the vocal cords, lips, tongue, and teeth to produce particular sounds – inspired both French-language pedagogy and the "direct method" of foreign language teaching introduced in universities in the early twentieth century.[72]

The First World War only accelerated scholarly and medical interest in phonetics, which physicians like Gérard de Parrel used in rehabilitation therapy for disabled veterans, in the process further pathologizing speech irregularities and confirming reformers' convictions that vocal training was vital to human development.[73] The vocal capacities of France's youth weighed on the nation's very survival in a twentieth century defined by global communication and international competition, the Parisian otolaryngologist and celebrity voice coach Alexis Wicart argued in his 1935 treatise *L'Orateur*. The current "corporative and trade union movement ... the public and private meetings of all kinds, [and] local, national, or international political agitation will inundate the entire world with a rising flood of speech that can submerge civilization or carry it to summits." Radio's contributions to the rise of Mussolini and Hitler demanded that "the most clever and far-sighted parties and peoples strive to follow their lead in this domain, by founding schools of oratory to train educated and solidly armed propagandists."[74] Such convictions transcended the cloistered world of academe to resonate in popular culture, as illustrated in a 1934 article in *Je sais tout*

[70] Théodore Rosset, *Exercices pratiques d'articulation et de diction composés pour l'enseignement de la langue française aux étrangers*, cited in Enrica Gallazi, *Le son à l'école*, 80.
[71] Bergeron, *Voice Lessons*, 72–118.
[72] Gallazi, *Le son à l'école*, 24–25; Puren, *Histoire des méthodologies de l'enseignement de langues vivantes*, 94–209.
[73] Gérard de Parrel, "Chronique médicale: la voix et la parole dirigées," *Education*, May 1939, 8–10.
[74] Alexis Wicart, *L'Orateur*, (Paris, 1935), 1: 3–5.

touting the virtues of experimental phonetics and mechanical devices designed to eliminate "faulty" accents.[75]

Yet if broadcasting fueled fantasies of creating a nation of like speakers, the "Babel" of the European airwaves also provided radio audiences with a quotidian reminder of the linguistic and cultural diversity of the Continent, as did the steady flow of immigrants into France from Eastern Europe and the far reaches of the empire. At the Sorbonne's Institut de Phonétique, the linguist and Greek scholar Hubert Pernot used the phonograph to rid provincial and foreign students of their heavy regional or national accents and teach them "correct" (and thus bourgeois Parisian) articulation, diction, and pronunciation. The properly trained ear provided a "remarkable facility for the acquisition of correct pronunciation," Pernot wrote in Le Phonographe à l'école, for if "one pronounces badly, ordinarily one hears badly." But when a "student hears accurately, he is close to being able to correct his own mistakes in articulation." Pernot encouraged classroom teachers to employ phonetic records containing individual vowel and consonant sounds in their classrooms, assuring them that "several weeks of work and the ability to learn by heart one side of a record will often suffice to modify an intonation entirely."[76]

In the corpus of pedagogical treatises produced by the French Committee for the Phonograph and Radio in Education, listening emerged – whether for musical education or language training – as a fundamentally *active* process tied to the cultivation of individual self-development, self-expression, and critical thinking. The success of this modern pedagogy of the ear, however, relied upon establishing a productive equilibrium between active listening (as the generator of individual motor and mental processes) and passive listening (as the source of imitative movements and behaviors) – a balance mirrored in the ideal republican citizen, who maintained his individuality while embracing cultural behaviors similar to those of his countrymen. Teachers should encourage originality and personal growth by teaching students to listen critically, Maurice Chevais argued, while simultaneously harnessing the "instinct of imitation" to encourage impersonation of the recorded

[75] Marcel Hervieu, "La machine à rectifier la prononciation," and "Pour apprendre par les yeux à bien parler," *Je sais tout*, April 1934, 690–91.
[76] Hubert Pernot, "Phonographe, phonétique, et langues vivantes," *Le Phonographe à l'école: revue critique des enregistrements convenant aux discothèques scolaires*, October 1931 (Reprinted from the *Bulletin de la Société pour la Propagation des Langues Etrangères en France*, November–December 1930). Bibliothèque Nationale de France, Archives de l'Audiovisuel, DAV 16. Brochure for the Université de Paris, Institut de Phonétique de la Sorbonne. Année Scolaire 1932–1933. CARAN F17-24694. Personnel dossier for Hubert Pernot.

voices. Repetition would awaken the subconscious to relieve students of their inhibitions, facilitating "valuable automatisms [and] corporal, intellectual, and artistic" habits. Yet Chevais also cautioned against the "dangers of dependency," which came from distracted or "inattentive listening to radio broadcasts outside of class hours," when children, whether unconsciously or deliberately, imitated the voices of "pernicious singers" they heard over the radio.[77]

Even before *radio scolaire* debuted, teachers across France had been experimenting with broadcast sound in their classrooms. Urban schools, supplemented by talented faculty and larger municipal budgets, typically invested more in music education than their rural counterparts.[78] The Paris city councilman Léon Riotor collected donations to install phonographs and radios in the capital's schools in 1932, where teachers used records of diction, theater, and classical music in their classrooms.[79] However, radio and record salesmen saw rural schoolteachers, who held considerable prestige in their communities, as valuable allies in selling gramophones and radios in the provinces, prompting the Ministry of Education to issue repeated warnings about marketing gimmicks promising free radios in exchange for displaying the newest models in classrooms or assigning student compositions on the history of the wireless.[80]

Rural teachers sometimes followed the lead of Parisian pedagogues and embraced auditory training to eliminate "peculiarities" of local speech habits that persisted even after classroom instruction had eradicated them from students' writing. The director of a girls' school in Brittany told *La Musique à l'école* that she used the phonograph to combat the Breton accent and cultivate much-needed skills of articulation and expression.

---

[77] Chevais, *L'éducation musicale de l'enfance*, 1: 287, and *Vol. 2: L'art d'enseigner*, 99–103. See also Louis-André Fouret, "Le phonographe auxiliaire de l'enseignement," *Langues modernes. Bulletin de l'Association des Professeurs de Langues Vivantes*, January–February 1936, 3–5.

[78] Alten, "L'introuvable identité disciplinaire de la musique scolaire en France sous la IIIe République," 279–91. BNF Archives de l'audiovisuel DAV 16. Léon Riotor, Proposition tendant à l'utilisation du phonographe dans les écoles publiques pour l'enseignement du chant, de la lecture expressive, et de la récitation en français, pour l'étude pratique de la prononciation dans l'enseignement des langues vivantes et pour l'étude historique et esthétique des grandes œuvres musicales. Compte-rendu du Conseil Municipal de Paris, Conseil Général de la Seine, July 1932.

[79] Archives Municipales de Paris. 39W 96-39W 101. Inventories of the Lycée Molière for 1934–1939.

[80] CARAN F17-16007. Théodore Rosset, Directeur de l'Enseignement Primaire, Ministère de l'Education Nationale à MM. les Inspecteurs l'Académie, June 19, 1934. See also BNF DAV 16. Théodore Rosset, Directeur de l'Enseignement Public, Ministère de l'Education Nationale à Monsieur le Recteur de l'Académie, July 6, 1932. The Couesnon firm donated one hundred phonographs to the Ministry of Education for distribution in schools around France in 1932. See Union Française des Organismes de Documentation. Extrait du procès-verbal de la séance plénière. February 22, 1934.

After playing a recording several times, Mme Treussart directed her
students to imitate the voice on the record, permitting a "mechanical
regularity" to take over as the "child who had the monotonous delivery of
a schoolgirl corrects herself." As a result, students' speech "becomes
more alive, and the children acquire the habit of articulating, punctuat-
ing." Did such activities constitute "servile imitation," she wondered.
"No more than in the interpretation of a poem or song." Thanks to the
phonograph, the "local accent is combated, at least in the degree to which
it was exaggerated."[81] This imposition of an "elite" mode of speech in a
region where even some teachers doggedly maintained their regional
accents, one school inspector reported, only proved that auditory pedagogy would provoke important cultural transformations when adopted
nationwide.[82]

The flexibility of this modern pedagogy of the ear, which encouraged
spontaneity and standardization, also adapted itself readily to the varied
personalities and political prerogatives of classroom teachers. The members of Célestin Freinet's anticlerical Coopérative de l'Enseignement Laïc
(CEL), who promoted "active," child-centered learning, embraced sound
technologies in their efforts to break away from tired, "bourgeois" instruction. The CEL bulletin *L'Educateur prolétarien* offered discounts on sound
equipment to schools, while its columnists Yvette and Antonin Pagès
recommended the French Socialist Party's ERSA record label, explaining
how one could teach diction and pacifism simultaneously with recordings
titled "March 18, 1871: The Proclamation of the Commune" and "The
Bloody Week: Vision of Horror."[83] In contrast, the primary school teacher
Jean-Jules Roger Ducasse employed the phonograph for an "aural geography lesson," teaching folklore and popular songs that he believed would
reinforce regional identities and instill a "deep sentiment of unity" in
children, practices that propagandists for the collaborationist Vichy regime
would later appropriate to promote their own conservative policies of rural
organicism during the Second World War.[84]

[81] V. le Noach, "Chant, diction, gymnastique à l'aide du phonographe," *La Musique à l'école*, May 1933, 145.

[82] M. Mahaux, "Le phonographe et la diction," *La Musique à l'école*, May 1933, 147.

[83] *L'Educateur prolétarien. L'imprimerie à l'école. Le cinéma. La radio. Les techniques modernes d'éducation populaire*, October and November 1932, November 1934; Luc Bruilart et Gerald Schlemminger, *Le mouvement Freinet: des origines aux années quatre-vingts* (Paris, 1996). A flourishing interwar school cooperative movement used small donations from students, parents, and municipalities to purchase phonographs and radios. See "L'école en fête," October 14, 1933, and "Coopérative scolaire de Noailles (Corrèze)," *L'Ecole et la vie*, March 31, 1934.

[84] Roger Ducasse, "L'emploi du phonographe dans la présentation des chefs d'œuvre de l'art musical dans les écoles," *Machines parlantes et radio*, March 1930, 117–18; Christian Faure, *Le project culturel de Vichy: folklore et révolution nationale* (Lyon, 1989), 199–275.

Faced with this diversity of classroom listening practices, Parisian reformers reminded teachers that the goal of auditory pedagogy lay not only in disciplining the ear, but in equipping students with the auditory skills necessary to make responsible listening choices outside of class, whether they went shopping for records on their way home from school or listened to a family radio in the evening.[85] Distracted listening at home posed a particular danger, given that the youngest students' virginal ears might already be corrupted by over-exposure to broadcast sound before they arrived at school. The Parisian teacher Camille Sicard observed first hand the effects of such "musical saturation" in his classroom. After playing several record selections, Sicard ranked the students in two categories: those "who listened passively, without effort and without profit, and those for whom music was alive and who knew how to express it." These divergent reactions, Sicard concluded, resulted from the fact that the second group had "'new' ears, whereas for many of the other students, the session we just heard appeared simply as family radio." These findings only confirmed his view that proper musical instruction should begin at a young age, so students "will later know how to choose from among the numerous [radio] programs those which merit listening to."[86]

This modern pedagogy of the ear became the basis for the *radio scolaire* curriculum adopted by the Ministry of Education in 1936, and Zay defended auditory training as a remedy for the public school system's failure to train students in elocution, diction, and spoken French. "Whoever examines the educational program in France and the means of action with which it equips students for the future struggles of life is startled by the following fact: almost no part is reserved for the teaching of speech," Zay wrote in his memoirs *Souvenirs et solitudes*, but "it is in speaking, above all, that he must defend his interests, support his thoughts, convince his interlocutors." For Zay, the pedagogy of the ear was vital to France's struggle against fascism. Students "must possess the art of persuading men," he wrote in his official instructions to the teaching corps in 1937, for "in the life of the future, in the encounters between different races and civilizations, filled with passionate and greedy

[85] Henry-Vasseur, "Le phonographe à l'école," *Machines parlantes et radio*, March 1931, 199. The Committee commissioned its own series of foreign language and diction records to respond to this dilemma, featuring the teachers A. Ravizé, Louis-André Fouret, and Sébastien Camugli. See Charles L'Hôpital, *Disques de divertissement sélectionnés spécialement par le Comité Français du Phonographe dans l'Enseignement à l'usage des écoles, établissements d'enseignements, et œuvres postscolaires* (Paris, 1934), and Maurice Chevais, *Liste de disques d'initiation à la musique et de formation du goût musical* (Paris, 1933).
[86] Camille Sicard, "La musique mécanique et l'art d'écouter," *La Musique à l'école*, October 1936.

interests, one will not survive without speaking." Public school instructors had the duty to teach students how to "handle the French language well," for a "living language – and French is for French people the most living of languages – is an instrument of exchange between men" and the primary link binding citizens together.[87]

Radio scolaire and the battle over classroom listening

The Popular Front's school broadcasts debuted on January 4, 1937, after several months of trial broadcasts on Parisian stations. Addressing teachers and students from the studio of the Eiffel Tower station, Zay outlined how *radio scolaire* would reinforce several of the government's political objectives: uniting individuals with the collective, democratizing access to culture, and modernizing education. "Children of France," he began, "I am addressing you across space as will shortly the teachers chosen to address you and supplement your education ... this is wonderful news that I announce and I am more than a little proud to bring you these gifts." To those worried that classroom listening would encourage intellectual standardization, Zay insisted "it is up to man to dominate the machine and make it ... into an expression of his personal liberty," reiterating a recurring theme in Popular Front propaganda. Nor should audiences fear that the government would use the airwaves to indoctrinate students, for "we have banned partisan political battles from our school establishments ... [and] we are not going to reintroduce them with the complicity of the airwaves."[88]

The press greeted Zay's speech and the first *radio scolaire* broadcasts with a combination of trepidation and excitement. The right-leaning *Radio-Magazine* columnist Clément Vautel, a future contributor to the anti-Semitic *Je suis partout*, praised the initiative but wondered whether the state airwaves could broadcast anything other than an "official truth." It "remains to be seen," he quipped, "whether an insidious politics – today of the left, tomorrow perhaps of the right, will not be undertaken with this radio that diffuses lessons to all the pedagogical establishments underwritten by the government."[89] The communist daily *L'Humanité* printed a photograph of forty-odd schoolgirls in the working-class

[87] Jean Zay, *Souvenirs et solitudes* (Le Roeulx, Belgium, 1987), 351–52.
[88] Jean Zay, "La radio scolaire. Discours d'ouverture du ministre de l'E.N.," *L'Ecole libératrice*, January 9, 1937, 332–33. Jean-Richard Bloch's *Naissance d'une culture* emphasized the need for man to dominate the machine and exploit it for his benefit, a theme he translated into the political pageant *La naissance d'une cité*, one of the first dramatic performances sponsored by Blum's first Popular Front government.
[89] Clément Vautel, "Radio chronique," *Radio-Magazine*, January 17, 1937, 2.

Parisian suburb of Saint-Ouen looking eagerly from their wooden benches toward an enormous radio perched atop a pedestal in anticipation of the first broadcast, while *Le Figaro* dispatched a reporter to interview students about one of the first broadcasts, a lecture by the poet and essayist Paul Valéry. "Wireless will make our classes more lively," one young man told the journalist, and "I was very happy to hear [Paul Valéry] because ... it seems to me ... that I would have understood him better than if I read him first." His *lycée* principal conceded that *radio scolaire* constituted a "minor revolution" still in its infancy, but cautioned that its future remained uncertain.[90] Few commentators would remain so circumspect in the coming weeks, as debates about classroom radio listening became entangled in larger partisan battles between the Popular Front and its political opponents.

Three series of programs, each designed for a specific subset of the student population, debuted on the Eiffel Tower station during the winter months of 1937. Music education and language training held pride of place, but the school radio commission created broadcasts that teachers could use in every class. The primary school curriculum, which aired from 3:00 to 3:45 p.m. on Wednesdays and Saturdays, opened with a fifteen-minute current affairs report, followed by sessions on "musical initiation" and "songs learned by ear" taught by three Parisian *institutrices*.[91] For secondary students, the curriculum included a series of short lectures on contemporary French language and culture delivered by some of France's "great minds," including the philologist Ferdinand Brunot, novelists André Demaison and Maurice Martin du Gard, dramatist Tristan Bernard, philosopher Léon Brunschvicg, and of course, Paul Valéry. The Comédie Française actress and vocal coach Beatrix Dussane offered diction courses, while a cadre of Parisian *lycée* teachers provided instruction in foreign languages (German, English, Italian, and Spanish) and later that year, in drawing and art appreciation. Finally, a series of after-school broadcasts for adolescents focused on professional orientation aired during the early evening hours between 5:00 and 8:00 p.m. Talks entitled "Beautiful Woodworking Trades!" and "I Use Household Appliances ... What does that mean for my budget?" targeted urban youth, while lectures on "Fertilizers" and "Trades of Today: Working the Land and the Joys of the Peasantry," addressed rural students who might not ever leave their villages. If these topics suggest a somewhat

---

[90] Charles Rabette, "La radio scolaire: quand les élèves écoutent M. Paul Valéry sans le voir," *Le Figaro*, January 23, 1937, 5–6.

[91] "L'actualité pédagogique: radiophonie scolaire," *Journal des instituteurs et des institutrices*, January 30, 1937, 282. The three teachers were Mme Desmettre and Mlles B. and J. Auroy, authors of *Les beaux disques expliqués aux enfants*, 6, 11.

reductive conception of student audiences, they illustrate the government's commitment to reaching adolescents anxious about their future employment prospects.[92]

Yet despite the fears of far-right critics like Clément Vautel, the content of the school radio programs displayed few overt ideological biases. The first week of primary programs featured a discussion about winter sports and a profile of the recently deceased aviator Jean Mermoz, whose plane disappeared over the South Atlantic in December 1936. If the school radio commission judged Mermoz to be an appropriately modern hero to inspire children, the aviator had been a convinced man of the right, serving as the vice-president of the Parti Social Français (PSF), the legal successor to the banned Croix de Feu, which deployed Mermoz's image in life and after his death to represent the traditional values of work, family, and self-sacrifice that its members believed would save France from decadence.[93] Nor did the commission select its intellectual luminaries from a roster of left-wing ideologues. Bernard and Brunschvicg boasted a close friendship with Léon Blum, but the political views of Valéry and Demaison, among others, resisted easy classification along a left-right political axis.[94] Many of the public school teachers selected to participate, including a significant number of women, had already been active in pedagogical reform movements. While the proportion of the broadcasts devoted to modern foreign languages might have alarmed some conservatives, the programs displayed no expressly anti-militarist bent.[95]

By the winter of 1937, however, the fraying political consensus between radicals and communists and growing hostility toward the Blum government's economic policies created a far from receptive climate for *radio scolaire*. Despite widespread interest in educational broadcasting, the programs quickly garnered criticism from cultural critics, political pundits, and even teachers. Some questioned the very legitimacy of the pedagogy of the ear, claiming that listening – as opposed to visual observation – could never cultivate rational thinking and intelligence, particularly given the ephemeral qualities of broadcast sound. "True education must contain reiterated recreation, or even a more durable, written form. Only repetition permits [something] to be inscribed in the memory of the

---

[92] "Radiophonie scolaire," *L'Ecole libératrice*, January 31, 1937; Susan Whitney, *Mobilizing Youth*, 80–89.

[93] Sean Kennedy, *Reconciling France Against Democracy*, 217–19.

[94] Nord, *France's New Deal*, 299. Demaison would become the director of broadcasting under the Vichy regime.

[95] Siegel, *The Moral Disarmament of France*, 11–12, 160–61. Propositions from left-wing reformers to initiate a second foreign language (including Esperanto) were greeted with suspicion by many on the right. See Ory, *La belle illusion*, 646.

child until adulthood," complained the theater director Gabriel Boissy, a regular contributor to the PSF newspaper *Le Flambeau*. Classroom broadcasting could never be more than "radiophonic recreations" that "strike the imagination and the imagination only," for the "notions that remain [in the mind] are those slowly learned [and] slowly *written*."[96] "I have always been struck by the impression of artifice, of extreme abstraction when I listened to a lecture broadcast over the radio," M. Beauduc, a Limoges *lycée* philosophy teacher, concluded in an *enquête* about *radio scolaire* conducted by the *Revue universitaire*. "A string of ideas of a literary or philosophical nature needs to be constructed by gestures, rendered alive by the intensity of an expressive look," and it would "thus be dangerous for students, the majority of whom are visually oriented, for a lesson, already too abstract and cold for many of them, to come from afar and be dispensed by an anonymous being."[97]

Although physicians had just a few years earlier embraced radio's "prosthetic" capacities for replacing the damaged ears of veterans, complaints about the harmful effects of the disembodied radio voice on students exposed pervasive anxieties about the physical and psychological effects of broadcast sound on the body and mind, a shift in attitude that accompanied radio's transformation from the hobbyist's toy into a full-fledged mass media. Many teachers now feared an excessively mechanized future where machines would replace human capital and eliminate their jobs.[98] Even worse, this "mechanization" of teaching appeared at odds with the government's efforts to increase employment by expanding the size of the teaching corps, a reform backed by the Syndicat National des Instituteurs during the 1936 elections. "What a temptation for the State, in a period of financial difficulties and economic needs, to replace the teacher in a classroom with an overseer and a loudspeaker!" the *lycée* instructor M. Simon complained to the *Revue universitaire* in 1937.[99]

Even Yvette and Antonin Pagès, PCF members who had previously endorsed classroom phonograph use, worried that *radio scolaire* would undermine active learning. Radio broadcasts disrupted the careful equilibrium between activity and passivity demanded by the pedagogy of the ear, they argued, for the "listener of a radio broadcast senses himself diminished, even humiliated, in front of a loudspeaker whose vibrations

[96] Gabriel Boissy, cited in "En lisant nos confrères … contre la radio-scolaire," *Le Petit radio*, March 1, 1935, 28.

[97] "Notre enquête sur la radiophonie scolaire et l'enseignement secondaire," *Revue universitaire*, June 1936, 5.

[98] Panchasi, *Future Tense*, 37–39.

[99] "Notre enquête sur la radiophonie scolaire et l'enseignement secondaire," *Revue universitaire*, March 1937, 234.

he cannot stop to ask for explanations" or to "refute an argument that seems erroneous . . . Only the loudspeaker has rights: it speaks, it sings, it plays as it wants, when it wants." For teachers wishing to employ auditory and vocal training, the phonograph remained a "devoted servant . . . you stop the record at will; you can pose questions, comment on this or that portion, restart the record, repeat it . . . complete liberty is perfectly assured." In contrast, "Wireless at the School is the most complete passivity; it is not for the partisans of the active school."[100]

Other teachers interpreted the radio scolaire initiative as a deliberate assault on their freedom in the classroom, and by extension, on France's regional cultures and traditions. M. Taillebot, a foreign-language teacher in Lyon, complained to Langues modernes, the bulletin of the Association des Professeurs de Langues Vivantes, that school broadcasting would standardize classroom activities by over-regulating teachers' schedules. Instructors who wished to employ the broadcasts would be forced to restructure their teaching, generating disorder and confusion among students accustomed to a fixed routine. The "introduction of wireless could bring us unruly [behavior], disruption, and a loss of time," Taillebot argued, "and for what?"[101] Provincial teachers' hostility, the Journal des instituteurs et institutrices explained, resulted from a strong tradition of rural independence, where "up to now they were free to treat the chapters of the school program in the order that appeared best for their students, their region, and their own temper." Despite long-standing Parisian proscriptions against the use of regional dialects, teachers continued to employ them well into the 1930s to explain key concepts to their students. Now they feared a "return of the University of a century ago, when the Minister of Education could state: 'at this moment, all the children of the troisième are studying a Latin theme.'"[102]

On a more humorous note, the radio dramatist and journalist Georges-Armand Masson offered up a satirical vision of the future in Le Haut-parleur. The "dictator of National Education or the People's Commissar of International Education" would only be content when "every citizen, from the moment he reaches the age of understanding . . . is equipped with a headset," he quipped, permitting rural children to learn the "marvels of

---

[100] Yvette and Antonin Pagès, "Disques et radio," L'Educateur prolétarien, February 10, 1936, 175–76.

[101] Letter from M. Taillebot at the Lycée du Parc in Lyon, reprinted in "Chronique radiophonique," Langues modernes. Bulletin de l'Association des Professeurs de Langues Vivantes de l'Enseignement public, March 1937, 268–69.

[102] L. Lamorlette, "Radiophonie scolaire," Journal des instituteurs et institutrices, February 6, 1937, 291. Jean-François Chanet, "Maîtres d'école et régionalisme en France," Ethnologie Française, 18, 1988, 244–56. Chanet determined that rural schoolteachers continued to use regional dialects well into the 1930s.

the alphabet and the joys of arithmetic" while keeping their hands free for agricultural labor. Such standardized learning violated the key principles of the republican education tradition, Masson claimed, for the "individual school, the greatest progress of our modern times ... is founded upon the immortal principles of '89, the most sacred of which is the right of children to dispose of their little brains themselves."[103]

Right-wing critics of the Popular Front, regardless of their specific political views, typically interpreted *radio scolaire* as evidence that the government was attempting to force "totalitarian" educational methods on schoolchildren, a maneuver they condemned as antithetical to French values. Not unlike Jean Zay's own team of education reformers, far right parties saw adolescents as France's only salvation from its current decadence. Hubert Bourgin, the *lycée* teacher who directed the youth wing of the extra-parliamentary Faisceau in the 1920s, campaigned against the "false scientism" of the republican school, which undermined the strict moral discipline he believed could only be instilled through a Catholic and nationalist curriculum.[104] Colonel de La Rocque and members of the PSF accused the Popular Front of trying to produce a passive generation of youth incapable of physically or spiritually leading the nation through its current crisis, a view echoed by Catholic lay organizations.[105] For the non-conformist intellectuals who staffed the rabidly anti-Semitic dailies *Gringoire* and *Je suis partout*, the democratization of education, presented in a standardized form over the airwaves, threatened the survival of France's humanist tradition, which historically prepared the nation's elite through a grounding in classical languages, philosophy, and French literature.[106] *Radio scolaire* embodied the modern technological rationalization that, they feared, would overpower the human spirit, producing a future generation of automatons.

The criticisms of classroom radio listening that surfaced during the early months of *radio scolaire* both reflected and fueled the political confusion of the late 1930s, throwing into relief the rhetorical and ideological fluidity that existed between the parties of the left and right. Speaking from a position of political disempowerment, right-wing opponents of the Popular Front unilaterally condemned the government's policies. Yet if the PSF and Jacques Doriot's newer Parti Populaire Français viewed the Third Republic as weak and ineffectual, in the dispute over classroom

---

[103] Georges-Armand Masson, "La vie des ondes. L'école individuelle," *Le Haut-parleur*, May 15, 1937, 262.
[104] Kalman, *The Extreme Right in Interwar France*, 154–60, 165–67.
[105] Kennedy, *Reconciling France Against Democracy*, 101–3.
[106] David Carroll, *French Literary Fascism: Nationalism, Anti-Semitism, and the Ideology of Culture* (Princeton NJ, 1994), 110–16; Mazgaj, *Imagining Fascism*, 80–83.

listening they positioned themselves as defenders of individual "liberty" against a "tyrannical" centralized state – political claims historically advanced by republicans. Attacking the Popular Front for endangering the "freedom" of schoolchildren by forcing them to listen against their will, Pierre Laclau of *Je suis partout* condemned the purely auditory format of the broadcasts more than their content. "If students learned anything in class," he argued, it was only because the "teacher imposed it on them by his presence, by making them repeat his explanations until they have understood and retained it." The ephemerality of radio sound, combined with the physical distance separating the radio teacher and his students, rendered retention impossible. Moreover, when the principal "method of work in primary schools ... is to continually repeat," the results proved disastrous when teachers attempted such methods over the airwaves. In one recent broadcast, Laclau observed, a "conservatory professor teaching children *solfège* announced nine times out of ten that their teachers taught them to sing falsely" even though he couldn't hear the students in their classrooms.[107]

Yet even as right-wing critics insisted that listening rendered true learning impossible, they paradoxically accepted the premise that repeated exposure to school broadcasts would negatively affect students. Moreover, the requirement that students listen collectively created a situation in which listening ceased to serve the individual by making him a slave to the voices emerging from a receiver. "Mr. Zay was counting on this dissipation, on this sort of intellectual dazing to spread in his way, by shameful motives, dogmas that students will accept without any monitoring, leaving an indelible mark on them," Laclau charged. Consequently, *radio scolaire* would not elevate intelligence, as Popular Front spokesmen claimed, but would only "sink the minds of French youth – so alive, personal, original, [and] resistant to moral and intellectual constraints." Instead, school broadcasting would create "a dull-witted generation ... inept at all work [and] disarmed for life to the great profit of Israel, whose sons will occupy the best places [in society] and will no longer find the means to resist their nonsense and their hegemony."[108]

During the winter of 1937, criticisms of radio pedagogy thus blended with direct attacks on the Blum government to produce an image of schoolchildren chained to their desks and forced to listen to radio broadcasts produced by a cabal of socialist teachers and Jewish politicians. The

[107] Pierrep, "La radiophonie: Propos en l'air," *Je suis partout*, January 16, 1937, 4.
[108] Pierre Laclau, "La radiophonie ... persevarere diabolicum," *Je suis partout*, November 4, 1938, 2; Pierre Laclau, "La radiophonie. Une duperie: La radiophonie scolaire," *Je suis partout*, May 20, 1938, 9.

technical and financial problems plaguing *radio scolaire*, however, reveal a far more complex reality of reception. Despite the Eiffel Tower's iconic status as France's oldest station, by the late 1930s many listeners heard it as little more than a sputtering relic whose low transmitting power limited its reach outside Paris.[109] Equipping schools with radios posed another major challenge to the government, a fact that the radio press, as propagandist *par excellence* for broadcasting, was only too eager to point out.[110] Most of the students who heard the first broadcasts attended schools with wealthy donors. School cooperatives, through which students and families pooled resources to purchase radios, supplied only a minority of institutions.[111] The prefect of the Puy-de-Dôme reported that teachers in Riom brought their home radios to school for use during the primary school and early-evening career orientation broadcasts, but many of his schools had no access to the airwaves.[112] "Even though my company and I are part of these broadcasts," the children's radio performer René-Paul Groffe concluded in *Le Haut-parleur* later that spring, "I declare that the programs truly do not exist; there is not in France a single radio put *officially* into the hands of *radio scolaire*."[113]

Zay's staff had calculated that approximately eight hundred radios were already in the hands of secondary school teachers, but possessed no realistic picture of how they were used at the primary level, and called on regional school inspectors to investigate classroom wireless usage.[114] The responses to this survey have disappeared from the archives of the Ministry of Education, but teachers' periodicals complained into the summer about the shortage of radios and the government's failure to determine which models would be approved for the state subsidy. "This list is certainly not easy to establish," Charles Charlot, a teacher from Joigny (Yonne), admitted to the *Journal des instituteurs et institutrices*. Yet, classrooms did not require "luxurious" radios, but only hardy receivers with the most basic

[109] Antonin Pagès, "Radio-scolaire," *L'Educateur prolétarien*, February 15, 1937, 219.
[110] Danielle Semeur, "Dès janvier nos écoliers pourront prendre l'écoute de la Tour, mais les écoles auront-elles toutes des postes récepteurs?" *Comoedia*, December 19, 1936; "Radiodiffusion scolaire," *Radio-Magazine*, January 10, 1937, 12.
[111] "L'école en fête," October 14, 1933, and "Coopérative scolaire de Noailles (Corrèze)," *L'Ecole et la* vie, March 31, 1934.
[112] Rapport du Préfet, *Procès-verbaux des délibérations du Conseil Général du Puy-de-Dôme*, 1937 (Clermont-Ferrand, 1937), 33; "Rapport de l'Inspecteur d'Académie sur la situation de l'Enseignement primaire dans la département pendant l'année scolaire 1936–1937," *Rapports et procès-verbaux des séances du Conseil Général de la Haute-Marne*, October 1937 (Chaumont, 1937), 66–86.
[113] René-Paul Groffe, "La radio des gosses," *Le Haut-parleur*, April 18, 1937, 201.
[114] CARAN F60-573. Présidence du Conseil. Conseil Supérieur des Emissions, section de l'enseignement, des sports, des loisirs, et du tourisme. Procès-verbal de la séance de lundi, 31 janvier, 1937; F17-16007. A. Chatelet, le Ministère de l'Education Nationale à M. les Recteurs d'Académie, Paris, February 10, 1937.

features.[115] In the interim, many teachers and school directors, armed with an intimate knowledge of the state's bureaucratic machinery, were reluctant to purchase radios for fear of being denied an eventual reimbursement.[116] The Chambre Syndical des Industries Radioélectriques and the Syndicat Professionnel de l'Industrie Radioélectrique, who had campaigned since the 1920s against the intrusion of multinational corporations in the French radio market, successfully pressured officials to approve subsidies only for radios manufactured in France. Schools already using radios would have to prove that their receivers contained no more than 10 percent foreign-made parts in order to obtain the 400-franc subsidy, even though this sum would barely cover the purchase of a new radio.[117]

Nor did the right-wing critics who condemned the intellectual and ideological premises behind *radio scolaire* refrain from criticizing its organization. "Well-conceptualized, well-equipped, radio in the school *could* unify all the little schoolchildren of France in the same sentiment of fraternal camaraderie," Clément Vautel wrote in *Radio-Magazine*, fostering a suspension of class conflict like that of the early years of the war, but such a "*union sacrée* in the Republic of Children" could never exist without radios. Why could the state not simply install a receiver in each school?[118] Moreover, when many schools possessed only one radio, could the airwaves truly facilitate educational listening? "Do you think it is possible to make several hundred students listen silently to a loudspeaker, as in the case of the Parisian school presented to me," René-Paul Groffe wondered, when "the small listeners – the youngest – placed next to the loudspeaker – are overwhelmed by the machine that booms," with the same programs "poorly heard by those at the other extremity of the courtyard?"[119] Listening sessions like the one Groffe described were not uncommon, whether in urban or rural schools, raising perplexing questions about the potential success of the modern

---

[115] Yvette and Antonin Pagès, "Radio-scolaire. Critiques et suggestions," *Radio-Liberté*, June 11, 1937, 4; Charles Charlot, "Sons de cloches. Récepteurs scolaires," *Journal des instituteurs et institutrices*, June 12, 1937, 592.

[116] Major Watts, "On demande la liste des récepteurs agrées," *Le Haut-parleur*, April 11, 1937, 185. *Le Haut-parleur* reported that the competition for state-approved receivers was completed in April, although schools did not receive the list until July 13, 1937.

[117] "La radio scolaire," *Revue générale des industries radioélectriques*, July 1937, 18–19. Ministère de l'Education Nationale. Centre National de Documentation Pédagogique, *Appareils de radiophonie scolaire, phonographes, et tourne-disques. Bulletin du Musée Pédagogique*, 1938. Charles Charlot, "L'actualité pédagogique pour la radiophonie scolaire," *Journal des instituteurs et institutrices*, February 20, 1937, 323.

[118] Clément Vautel, "Radio chronique," *Radio-Magazine*, August 8, 1937, 2. Domène, "La politique des ondes. Dans les désert," *Radio-Magazine*, January 24, 1936. *Choisir* criticized the fact that the government made no provisions for private or religious schools to obtain radios. See J.M., "Comment va reprendre la radio scolaire," *Choisir*, October 3, 1937.

[119] René-Paul Groffe, "La radio des gosses," *Le Haut-parleur*, April 18, 1937, 201.

Figure 4.1 Students in Saint-Ouen listening to *radio scolaire* broadcasts, *Manuel général de l'instruction primaire* (1937). Image courtesy of the Bibliothèque Nationale de France.

pedagogy of the ear.[120] Sixty students gathered around a radio in a single village schoolroom might gain exposure to the wider world outside their commune by listening to a talk about aviation, philosophy, or art, and indeed, many rural children enjoyed their first prolonged encounter with a radio in their school. But using a single receiver to reform students' speaking habits or auditory capital would prove challenging. A promotional photo published on the cover of the *Manuel général de l'instruction primaire* in February 1937, which depicted schoolgirls clustered around a large radio receiver, illustrated perfectly this dilemma. Displaying none of the active engagement promised by reformers, they appeared to be passive listeners, disciplined into silence and immobility [Figure 4.1].[121]

Reforming *radio scolaire*

Jean Zay took seriously his contemporaries' complaints about the technical limitations of the *radio scolaire* broadcasts. In the spring of 1937, he ordered relays of the Eiffel Tower's school broadcasts to the regional state stations in Rennes, Strasbourg, Limoges, Grenoble, Toulouse, and Marseille so that even the most isolated schools could receive the programs. Radio-Paris, whose signal covered much of France, also began transmitting a few programs, increasing the volume of educational broadcasting on state stations to twenty-eight hours per week. *Radio scolaire* could "finally begin its real career," *Mon programme* announced in April 1937.[122] However, these relays of school broadcasting coincided with another important transformation to the state airwaves: the synchronization of public stations. For years, audiences complained that many of the state stations' most entertaining programs aired during competing time slots – a problem that particularly plagued listening in the Parisian region, with its three "national" stations Radio-Paris, Paris PTT, and the Eiffel Tower. Synchronizing the stations would, at least in principle, ensure that a maximum variety of programming aired at a given moment.[123]

---

[120] *L'Educateur prolétarien*, December 25, 1934. Two teachers from Noyarey (Isère), A. and R. Faure, described ninety students around a single radio in their school to hear the Alpes-Grenoble broadcasts.

[121] *Manuel général de l'instruction primaire*, February 20, 1937. This photo originally appeared in *L'Humanité* to coincide with the inauguration of the program.

[122] "Pour le corps enseignant," *Mon programme*, April 17, 1937.

[123] CAC 19870714-2. Archives de la Direction de la Radiodiffusion. Exposé de M. Jardillier, October 20, 1936. Robert Jardillier placed synchronization at the top of his agenda as PTT minister, given that his predecessor Mandel had proposed the reform years earlier. Stations were divided into five groups, each featuring a different daily program during a given time slot – whether symphonic music, variety shows, or radio plays – to allow listeners to hear five different programs at any given moment.

This scheme always looked better on paper than it sounded over radios, but when combined with the *radio scolaire* relays, synchronization reduced the diversity of programs available in certain areas, sparking renewed complaints about Blum's broadcasting reforms.[124] At a spring meeting of the Education, Sports, Leisure, and Tourism sub-committee of the Conseil Supérieur des Emissions de la Radiodiffusion, station directors and advisory board presidents complained that they had sacrificed as many as five weekly hours of their schedules to educational programming, "abruptly depriving listeners" of entertainment and filling the airwaves with excessive talk, rather than popular music or radio dramas. Listeners interpreted these decisions as a deliberate attempt to restrict their choice of programs, and thus to define the terms by which they participated in the "radio nation."[125]

This defense of audiences' right to listen to a variety of programs surfaced on the eve of a major challenge to the Popular Front's broadcasting policies: the radio elections of February 1937, in which listeners across France who had paid their annual radio license fee voted for representatives to their local state station's advisory board. The first radio elections, held in 1935, had attracted only a minority of listener-voters in urban areas, but the subsequent growth in radio ownership ensured that nearly 1.5 million people went to their post office in 1937 to cast ballots, including many women otherwise disenfranchised in politics. Two national pressure groups fielded slates of candidates: the Popular Front offshoot Radio-Liberté, and Radio-Familles, the latter backed by the Fédération Nationale Catholique, a lay Catholic organization formed in the 1920s to combat the "secular" policies of the first *cartel des gauches* coalition.[126] Appealing to conservative voters through its associational bulletin *Choisir* and in right-leaning newspapers ranging from *Le Figaro* to the PSF's *Le Flambeau* and *Le Petit journal*, Radio-Familles attracted numerous voters on the far right.

In the months leading up to the elections, Radio-Familles presented itself to voters an apolitical organization that represented the interests of

---

[124] Méadel, *Histoire de la radio*, 149–52. The Parisian stations seldom picked up relays of regional stations, while stations in the provinces felt obligated to relay live performances from national theaters and Parisian concert halls.

[125] AN F21-4699. Administration des Beaux-Arts. Ministère des PTT Direction de la Service de Radiodiffusion. Procès-verbal. Réunion des MM les membres de la section d'enseignement, des sports, des loisirs, et du tourisme du Conseil Supérieur des Emissions, et MM les Présidents des Conseils de Gérance, April 24, 1937. See also "Emissions scolaires," *Le Haut-parleur*, April 24, 1938. In late 1937, the state began to decentralize some of the secondary school broadcasts, permitting the regional advisory boards to coordinate the efforts of regional teachers for the programs. However, primary school programs remained centralized in Paris.

[126] Méadel, *Histoire de la radio*, 79–99.

devout, bourgeois families who desired nothing more than "clean, artistic, entertaining [and] family programing" in the place of political speeches and the Popular Front's educational programming. Radio-Familles composed its electoral lists from regional elites and the former members of regional radio advisory boards, while Radio-Liberté put forward a list of candidates known for their allegiance to the Popular Front. The Paris PTT list, for example, included the Radio-Liberté president Paul Langevin, as well as Victor Basch, the president of the Ligue des Droits de l'Homme (Human Rights League), while its regional lists featured a high proportion of public schoolteachers and members of left-leaning cultural organizations.[127] On the eve of the vote, *Gringoire* instructed its readers to reject the "revolutionaries directly inspired by Moscow" in favor of Radio-Familles' "properly national list," while the Popular Front urged its supporters to defeat the "fascist" and religious impulses of its opponents.[128] When the ballot counting ended, Radio-Familles won the election handily with 51 percent of the vote. These results, subjected to repeated analyses by media historians, have been interpreted as evidence of the strength of Catholic influence, or more recently, as radio listeners' rejection of the Popular Front's politicization of the airwaves.[129] But broadcast sound had long been political, as we have already seen. If voters rejected Radio-Liberté's candidates, it was less a reaction to the presence of politics on the airwaves than the absence of a right-wing perspective. More important, the election results signaled listeners' disapproval of being told *how* to listen by politicians and Parisian intellectuals.

* * *

By the summer of 1937, France's ongoing economic crisis and the unsuccessful devaluation of the franc provoked Blum to resign and the creation of a second Popular Front government under the radical Camille Chautemps. The socialist Jean-Baptiste Lebas replaced Robert Jardillier as postal minister – the latter judged ineffectual and overly intellectual by many of his colleagues, and by many radio voters as well.[130] But even as

---

[127] "Les élections radiphoniques: votez et faire voter," *L'Ecole libératrice*, February 20, 1937, 473–78.

[128] "Les élections radiophoniques," *Gringoire*, February 26, 1937; "Les élections radiophoniques. Nos adversaires utilisent tous les procédés pour s'assurer de bonnes élections," *Le Populaire*, February 26, 1937, 3.

[129] Neulander, *Programming National Identity*, 71–96.

[130] Méadel, *Histoire de la radio*, 177–83. Jardillier's departure from the PTT came after a full hearing in the Senate. The senator Paul Laffont produced a report accusing Jardiller of neglecting construction work on new transmitters and of tampering with the "democratic" structure of the advisory boards, claims made by the recently deposed Marcel Pellenc.

the Popular Front had lost its mandate to control the airwaves, Zay introduced an expansion of school broadcasting that autumn. A new series of broadcasts aired to correspond with the institution of *loisirs dirigés*: a program of "directed leisure activities" intended to complete the "culture and moral education" of children by requiring students to join field trips to museums, factories, and national monuments or to participate in art, singing, and drama lessons on weekdays and Saturday afternoons.[131] Designed to combat the overwork associated with secondary schools' traditional emphasis on memorization and written exercises, reformers thought school-based *loisirs* would foster individual cultural development.[132] "The reduction in hours of schoolwork creates the duty to fill free time with happy, disciplined, and fruitful occupations," Zay explained to students in a radio address. Juxtaposing the value of spontaneity with the importance of discipline, he noted that radio "addresses itself above all to the imagination," while simultaneously imposing an "effort of concentrated attention." This statement reiterated a recurring tenet in the modern pedagogy of the ear – that listening would enable students to cultivate their individuality, as well as develop traits that bound them to their fellow citizens.[133]

With many schools still lacking in radios, Zay again urged school inspectors to draw the attention of local charitable organizations and municipalities to the "importance and variety of services that school radio, seconded by the support of friends of education, can render to the entire country."[134] He also reassured teachers that machines would not replace them in their classroom since they had a duty to teach students how to listen. "Communal listening is the original and new element that school radio brings to pedagogy," read one ministerial missive to the teaching corps, and "when the subjects treated are known in advance by the master . . . nothing is easier than to apply a new genre of exercises to the recent listening session." Zay directed teachers to first "assess the manner in which the students listen, whether collectively or individually"

---

[131] CARAN F17-17501. Le Ministre de l'Education Nationale (Direction de l'enseignement du second degré) à MM les Recteurs de l'Académie, June 8, 1937. Zay institued the *loisirs dirigés* by decree on May 22, 1937. A. Chatelet, Ministre de l'Education Nationale (Direction de l'enseignement du second degré) à MM les Recteurs de l'Académie, Paris, June 8, 1938.

[132] Ory, *La belle illusion*, 176–78, 649, 667, 685–88. During the mid-1930s, the Union Ouvrière offered course for workers in languages, science, and history while the Ligue d'Enseignement Laïc demanded civic education programs for students past the school leaving age featuring the "critical study of means of information," including the content and form of radio broadcasts.

[133] CAC 19890313-53. Draft of Zay's speech inaugurating the second year of radio scolaire, reprinted as "La radio scolaire," *Documentation radiophonique*, December 1937.

[134] CARAN F17-16008. Jean Zay à MM les Inspecteurs d'Académie, October 5, 1937.

and then "lead them as he pleases to reflect upon what they have just heard" by posing questions, assigning written analyses of the broadcasts, or asking students to repeat what they heard in speech or in song – "all in a manner different from habitual assignments" – instructions echoed in pedagogical magazines.[135] To encourage schools to employ both sets of broadcasts, the Ministry of Education began publishing brochures with detailed program listings and workbooks containing maps, illustrations, texts of radio lectures, questionnaires, and other aids to guide listening sessions.[136]

Responding to complaints that the first broadcasts lacked "radiophonic" elements such as a sophisticated sound décor, the new school broadcasts featured historical "evocations" designed to transport children to a distant time and place, as well as on-the-ground reportages – programs not dissimilar to those enjoyed by adults during the evening.[137] Two series of the after-school broadcasts, which aired from February 1937 to December 1938, drew favorable reviews from radio critics, teachers, and parents: "Ancient and Modern Thought," which focused on the history and philosophy of science; and "The Voices of Distant France," a series of interviews with ethnographers and colonial bureaucrats working in France's overseas empire.[138] The *solfège* lessons provided a breath of fresh air to airwaves saturated with the voices of Mistinguette or Fernandel, *Ric et Rac*'s Pierre Varigny concluded, and the "youthful and slightly awkward voices" of schoolgirls heard via radio microphones "please us infinitely more than numerous so-called opera singers."[139] School administrators also dispatched positive feedback to the Ministry of Education. The regional inspector for the Bouches-du-Rhône described how "in the twenty schools in possession of a wireless receiver ... the children impatiently await the *radio scolaire* hour," even if their first listening sessions left them a little confused.[140] In a gesture toward democratization, the state tasked regional stations with the responsibility for organizing a portion of the *loisirs* radio curriculum, which put local school choirs, scout troops, and folklore societies on the

[135] CARAN F17-15701. Jean Zay, Ministre de l'Education Nationale à Messieurs les Recteurs de l'Académie, July 7, 1938; "Radio scolaire. Le rôle du professeur avant, pendant, et après l'émission," *Le Haut-parleur*, June 20, 1937.
[136] Paul Vernoy, "Il faut illustrer l'enseignement par les ondes," *Le Haut-parleur*, December 5, 1937; *Programme des émissions de la radiophonie scolaire du second degré. Publication trimestrielle* (Paris, 1937) and *Radiodiffusion scolaire. Enseignement du second degré. Bulletin trimestrielle. Initiation artistique* (Paris, 1937).
[137] René-Paul Groffe, "La radio des gosses," *Le Petit radio*, August 8, 1937.
[138] *Programme des émissions de la radiophonie scolaire du second degré*, January 1938.
[139] Pierre Varigny, "Radio," *Ric et Rac. Grand hebdomadaire pour tous*, February 23, 1938, 6.
[140] Rapport d'Inspecteur d'Académie Garçon, *Rapports et délibérations du Conseil Général du département du Bouches-du-Rhône* (Marseille, 1938), 244.

air, although Parisian teachers continued to conduct the bulk of the classroom lessons.[141]

Unfortunately, the new after-school *loisirs* broadcasts had the misfortune of sharing the same time slot on the Eiffel Tower station, albeit on different weekdays, with a series of worker education programs offered by the Centre Confédéral d'Education Ouvrière (CCEO), an offshoot of the Confédération Générale du Travail (CGT), France's largest federated trade union. Since 1932, the husband-and-wife team of Georges and Emilie LeFranc had taught CCEO courses in economics, philosophy, law, and labor history to industrial workers, but the airwaves allowed their instruction to reach a much larger audience. Their programs did not appear in the official *radio scolaire* program, but far right critics judged their scheduling to be far from coincidental, providing evidence of the deliberate blurring of "educational broadcasting" with political propaganda. Courses entitled the "Role and Mechanisms of the CGT" and the "Labor Movement and the Idea of the Nation" enraged right-wing pundits, who wondered why the CCEO was "disposed *at its will* to speak over the microphones of the State . . . permitting it to sow hate and dispense . . . hogwash to listeners?"[142] One CEEO broadcast juxtaposed the unwise tourist who, on a visit to the capital, chose to tour the Invalides and the Arc de Triomphe versus the well-organized worker who made time to drop in at the CGT headquarters. For *Je suis partout*, this episode provided clear evidence that "crackpots" were being allowed to "inculcate their benevolent listeners with false and inadequate ideas" informed by anti-militarism and Marxist economics.[143] *L'Epoque*'s Jean Dorbal complained about Georges LeFranc's "foreign"-sounding accent, regular lisp, and supposedly poor grasp of grammar, the latter a reminder of his working-class background, to contest his "Frenchness."[144]

[141] "L'actualité. Nos écoliers chantent," *Radio-Magazine*, October 17, 1937; *Programme des émissions de la radiophonie scolaire du second degré. 2e année,* January 1938. The *loisirs* broadcasts featured chorales from the elite Parisian *lycées* Molitor, Victor-Hugo, and Jules Ferry.

[142] Program listings for the week of Sunday, February 7, 1937, in *Mon programme*. Ory, *La belle illusion*, 59, 683. Georges LeFranc, *Emissions du Centre Confédéral d'Education Ouvrière. Poste de la Tour Eiffel, 1937–1939* (Paris, 1939); "Une centralisation abusive," *Choisir*, July 11, 1937, 4. In addition to the CCEO broadcasts, another series of "Social and Economic Broadcasts" debuted in the winter of 1937 on the Eiffel Tower station. Topics included "English Money in 1937" and "Economic Aspects of the Civil War in Spain." The "Economic and Social Committee" of the Conseil Supérieur des Emissions directed these programs, and included among its members Célestin Bouglé, Emile Courrière, Léon Jouhaux.

[143] Pierre Laclau, "La radiophonie: une école de démoralisation," *Je suis partout*, April 29, 1938, 2.

[144] Jean Dorbal, "Chose entendues: L'éducateur sans éducation," *L'Epoque*, September 8, 1937, 8; "Propagande internationale," *La Documentation radiophonique*, October 1937.

What now angered right-wing critics, and some listeners as well, was their perception that the government not only sought to transform education through the radio, but wished to make the entire "radio nation" more expressly pedagogical. During the winter of 1937, children "were asked to listen for several hours a day, which did not appear harmful," *Choisir* observed, but "little by little the hours increased" until they spilled outside of the school hours into the early evenings.[145] The entire concept of "organizing free time" was a contradiction, Pierre Domène sneered in *Radio-Magazine*. "Leisure, which contains an element of liberty and fantasy, must it suffer from being militarized? The presence in the home of a radio answers the question. It is at one's leisure that one turns on and off the condensers of one's radio," just as "following one's desire and taste one chooses from the immense quotidian repertory of the airwaves."[146] Parisian "educating educators" were violating their own republican principles by impinging upon the "rights" of individual listeners, *L'Epoque* agreed.[147] If controlling *what* people listened to was not bad enough, the government also tried to determine *how* the nation's citizens listened, as if radio owners did not know how to listen on their own. Indeed, what most offended Pierre Laclau was the presumption that the "education of the listener be undertaken, and he be taught to listen," or as his colleague Jean Dorbal rephrased it, that politicians wished to "haggle with the listeners over the right to *direct listening*."[148]

Protests against *radio scolaire* culminated in the spring of 1938, when the mayor of La Rochelle, Léonce Vieljeux, refused to purchase radios for his city's schools after being ordered to do so by the prefect of his *département*. Vieljeux argued that the broadcasts represented an unwarranted intrusion of the state into local politics. "One of the charms of the French spirit," Vieljeux reportedly stated, "resides in its diversity, in its independence, and it would be a serious attack upon it to try and standardize young minds in the manner of a Hitler, a Stalin, or a Mussolini." For Clément Vautel, the moral to be taken from this episode was that "young brains must not be crammed mechanically, in a long series, like the stomachs of geese called upon to produce *foie gras* …." Vieljeux had responded appropriately, Vautel believed, for "regimes that are too

---

[145] "Encore la radio scolaire …." *Choisir*, February 1939.
[146] Pierre Domène, "La politique des ondes: l'instrument des loisirs," *Radio-Magazine*, January 24, 1936.
[147] Jean Dorbal, "Choses entendues: ceux qui narguent les auditeurs," *L'Epoque*, September 14, 1937, 6.
[148] Pierre Laclau, "La radiophonie: autour d'un projet," *Je suis partout*, October 15, 1937, 2; Jean Dorbal, "Choses entendues: les voix couvertes," *L'Epoque*, September 5, 1937, 8.

centralized suffer from an extreme fragility."[149] Unfortunately for him, politicians and state bureaucrats would very shortly impose even greater restrictions on the airwaves under the auspices of national defense.

Training the nation's ears

Given the controversy surrounding *radio scolaire*, why did the school broadcasts stay on the air after the collapse of the Popular Front, and indeed, continue to flourish under greater state investment in 1938 and 1939? The condemnation of the school broadcasts by right-wing intellectuals and Catholic pressure groups provides abundant evidence of audiences' rejection of the Popular Front's political strategies for broadcasting, as well as its *pédagogique* programming. Radio listeners "do not wish to frequent evening classes," *Radio-Magazine* concluded in 1938, but only "want good humor . . . which explains the success of the private stations, who are less infatuated than the state stations with a pedantic radio where . . . M. Bellac, the 'dear master' of *The World of Irritation* holds forth."[150] Who would not prefer listening to Radio-37's *Bar of the Stars*, which featured intimate interviews with celebrities of the stadium and screen, or Radio-Cité's innumerable game shows in which fiancés and young married couples sparred for prizes of household goods?[151] Why would listeners turn their radio dials away from the fast-paced, upbeat, and humorous dialogue of commercial broadcasting for the dry lectures by university professors and various "experts" featured on state stations? The specialized radio press, claiming to speak in the interest of listeners, raised this question again and again.

The political battle over *radio scolaire*, however, coincided with a much broader series of public debates about the impact of France's burgeoning mass culture of sound on the cultural capital of the nation's citizenry. The educational reformers who developed the modern pedagogy of the ear first sounded the alarm about the deleterious effects of broadcast sound on the musical tastes and speech habits of youth, but their concerns resonated widely among elites anxious about the fate of French literature, language, and art in a globalized economy of mass cultural production. Although the left and right disagreed about what "true" French culture should be, elite critics concurred that mass culture, often the product of foreign or American influence, was overly standardized and derivative, and thus a danger to France both domestically and internationally. That

---

[149] Clément Vautel, "Chronique sans fil," *Radio-Magazine*, March 13, 1938; "Le maire de La Rochelle contre la radio-scolaire," *Le Haut-parleur*, March 13, 1938.
[150] Clément Vautel, "Chronique sans fil," *Radio-Magazine*, May 8, 1938.
[151] Neulander, *Programming National Identity*, 52–60.

the *classes populaires* empowered by the Popular Front at times preferred commercial broadcasting, with its advertising jingles, game shows, comedy sketches, or popular songs, to the more sophisticated cultural content of state radio only confirmed their conviction that "the people" required education.

Reading the weekly columns of listeners' complaints in the major radio magazines "is edifying because it informs us precisely of the state of mind of our countrymen," the composer Gustave Mouchet wrote in 1936. Yet he professed confusion over the frequency of "angry opinions directed at certain state stations accused of inciting boredom among listeners," for "it is difficult to understand how a page of Beethoven could be so contemptuously devalued when other works, so trivial to *our* ears, are elevated to a pinnacle." Despite the predominantly middle-class readership of the radio press, listeners' complaints to editors proved to Mouchet that the "current proletarian mass has no ears – radiophonic or otherwise – for anything but the triumphant and whiny accordion." The expansion of radio ownership among workers had ensured that "this instrumental parasite has become King, in a kind of paradoxical monarchy of the 'Popular Front.'"[152] In the magazine *Disques*, Germaine Weill argued that working-class audiences too often thrilled to superficial songs about romantic tribulations, the trials of factory labor, or household politics: "easy music of trivial intonations" with "skin-deep melodies of the Tino Rossi genre, enlivened by texts whose indigence makes one shudder." Listeners' requests to radio stations demonstrated all too clearly that the state should take a more active role in acquainting citizens with France's *true* musical patrimony, she believed, whether classical pieces or folk songs – "the most simple and charming form of our musical literature."[153]

For Mouchet and Weill, the quantity of sounds that infiltrated everyday life through the airwaves mattered as much as their quality, a view shared by many of their contemporaries. For the Russian-born composer Igor Stravinsky, *how* people listened mattered almost as much as what they listened to. "Today, the resident of any country only has to turn a button to play a record or hear a musical selection of his choice," he lamented in a 1936 *Mon programme* interview, and "it is precisely in that amazing facility, in that absence of an effort that lies the vice of so-called progress." Presaging Theodor Adorno's later critiques of popular music, Stravinsky claimed that constant listening supercharged listeners' ears, leaving them with a craving for the repetitive and superficial melodies that dominated

[152] Gustave Mouchet, "Notes piquées," *La Musique à l'école*, February 1937, 82.
[153] Interview with Germaine Weill, "Le disque dans l'éducation," *Disques*, September 1938, 8.

commercial radio. The only remedy to this mass distraction lay in cultivating active listening by giving audiences challenging and high-quality
classical selections in lieu of the *chanson populaire*.[154]

Radio also generated a heightened concern with the quality of broadcasting language. "Never before have we been made as aware of the
phonetic insufficiencies of the speakers of France as after radio's cruel
revelations which forgive nothing," José Germain wrote in *Mon programme* in 1936. "The ears of millions of listeners are scorched every
day by those who believe that to speak is to speak well."[155] Radio
announcers' vocal peculiarities had long been the subject of jokes in the
press, and for nearly a decade, *Radio-Magazine* ran a column titled "The
Complaints' Bureau" (*Le Bureau de réclamations*) in which the critic
Francis Dorset annotated listeners' commentaries on the poor diction,
faulty pronunciation, and grammatical mistakes they heard in the
airwaves.[156] Middle-class audiences regularly wrote in to the magazine
to denounce everything from the use of improper *liaisons* to the incorrect
pluralization of words. Describing the constant mispronunciation of the
word "peace," one listener insisted that the "*Radio-Journal de France*
(state broadcasting's nightly news program) must avoid these affronts to
correct language." Recalling his former teacher's efforts to "definitively
destroy these uses" among his students, he insisted that "there *are* correct
rules of pronunciation" that should be followed, particularly by those
reporting on events in an official capacity.[157]

Complaints from listeners about radio announcers' language and
speaking habits – not unlike teachers' commentaries on their students'
speech patterns – reflected regional, class, and political biases. While
some listeners adored the heavy southern accent of Jean Roy, the "unri-
valed station signal" of Radio-Toulouse, others insisted that "one single
accent must be dispersed by radio stations: that of the center of France, of
Tours, of Bourges, of Nevers, of Orléans" – and thus neither Parisian
slang nor the "vulgar, silly, and coarse Marseille jargon."[158] Right-wing
journalists whined about the "Yiddish" or foreign accents of state stations

[154] Igor Stravinsky, "Grandeurs et dangers de la musique radiodiffusée," *Mon programme*,
February 14, 1936; Pierre Descaves, "Initiation musicale," *Nouvelles littéraires*, October
19, 1935, 8.
[155] José Germain, "Le rudiment nécessaire. Pour la radiophonie, diction S.V.P.," *Mon
programme*, February 28, 1936.
[156] Francis Dorset, "Bureau de réclamations," *Radio-Magazine*, August 30, 1930, and
September 13, 1936.
[157] Francis Dorset, "Bureau de réclamations," *Radio-Magazine*, August 23, 1936.
[158] Georges Rivoire, "Jean Roy, speaker de Radio-Toulouse," *Mon programme*, March 11,
1932, 1; Santillane, "Points de vue," *Radio-Magazine*, July 10, 1938.

in a deliberate jibe at Léon Blum and Jean Zay.[159] The Popular Front, "which talks constantly of intelligence, technical subjects, and culture," François Robin wrote in *Gringoire*, "is not even capable of sending those in charge of publicly interpreting its thought to night school. The declaration that radio was going to become *scolaire* clearly did not succeed among our official announcers."[160]

The quality of broadcasting language mattered, these critics concluded, because radio listeners unconsciously absorbed the tone and speech patterns of announcers through daily listening.[161] "Of all the forces contributing to the destruction of the French language, radio has contributed to it with a great unconsciousness," Paul Crouzet, a Latinist and school inspector, wrote in the educational revue *L'Ecole et la vie*. Crouzet particularly condemned the advertising jingles that relied on popular melodies to tout the virtues of dishwashing soap or over-the-counter medicines. If adults suddenly found themselves humming along to a radio spot in the middle of the day, children loved to imitate these jingles, which truncated the ends of words and dropped *liaisons*, encouraging a "trend toward the least effort that transforms languages, for better or worse, and corrupts them."[162] At the same time, the journalist Paul Dermée proposed, radio offered politicians the "most efficacious means of imposing on an entire people, with gentleness, but with authority, the pronunciation of difficult or new words, and we must equally use it to standardize the pronunciation of the French."[163]

These repeated calls for the standardization of broadcast language corresponded with a rise in cultural chauvinism hastened by the perceived decline of French on the world stage, where it was increasingly subordinated to English.[164] This fear of foreign tongues supplanting French animated the oeuvre of André Thérive, a right-leaning literary critic for the Parisian daily *Le Temps* and the author of the long-running column, "Querelles de langage," published by *Nouvelle littéraires*.[165] In his 1933

[159] Kaplan, *Reproductions of Banality*, 134.
[160] François Robin, "La radio française sous la botte," *Gringoire*, January 1, 1937, 3; François Robin, "La radio française sous la botte," *Gringoire*, January 22, 1937, 3.
[161] Jacques Néjà, "La radio et les accents régionaux," *Alger-Radio*, December 26, 1937, 3.
[162] Paul Crouzet, "La défiguration du français à la radio," *La Grande revue*, October 1936, 564–71.
[163] Paul Dermée, "La radio, école de prononciation," *Mon programme*, December 20, 1935, 41.
[164] Panchasi, *Future Tense*, 110–59.
[165] Pierre-Marie Diouonnat, *Les 700 rédacteurs de Je suis partout, 1930–34. Dictionnaire des écrivains et journalistes qui ont collaboré au "grand hebdomadaire de la vie mondiale" devenu le principal organe du fascisme français* (Paris, 1993), 86. Thérive (pseud. Roger Puthoste) contributed regularly to the PSF newspaper *Le Flambeau* during the 1930s and to *Je suis partout* during the Second World War.

essay *Chantiers d'Europe*, Thérive described the French language as engaged in near-Darwinian struggle for survival in post-Versailles Europe. He blamed the intertwined evils of immigration and American mass culture for its demise, as well as the elevation of German and other "new" national languages in Central Europe. "A people who lets its idiom be invaded has already submitted to humility and passivity," Thérive concluded, before condemning the advertising and popular music imports that resulted in people peppering their speech with words such as "baby" or "speaker."[166]

More important, critics argued that the state should worry about the quality of French voices in the airwaves because audiences overseas were increasingly listening in to French radio. "The foreigner who speaks our language fluently ... must be edified to hear our state stations, as well as our commercial stations, accumulate so many incorrect [words] and mistakes, without talking of the effect produced abroad," the columnist Francis Dorset sneered in *Radio-Magazine*. "Is our language so insufficiently grated upon at home that official and national radio must contribute to its corruption?"[167] While the government could do little to control the sounds broadcast by commercial radio stations, whose content and programming remained outside its purview, the state radio administration could play a role in shaping the language used by its own announcers.[168] Anticipating eventual intervention in this domain, in 1937 the left-leaning linguist Ferdinand Brunot, author of the ten-volume *Histoire de la langue française*, and the poet Paul Valéry, announced the creation of the Office de Langue Française, an organization committed to "preserving the French language from corruption." Uniting longstanding republican preoccupations with recent right-wing impulses, the Office de Langue Française offered itself as a consulting service that could verify the accuracy of "French expressions ... to substitute for the barbarisms ... of other languages" that had invaded the

[166] André Thérive, *Chantiers d'Europe* (Paris, 1933). Thérive cited in Claude Désirat and Tristan Hordé, *La langue française au XXe siècle* (Paris, 1976), 82, 89; André Thérive, *Querelles du langage*, 3 vols. (Paris, 1929, 1933, 1940). In 1937–1938, Thérive hosted a ten-minute program on the Poste Parisien called "Let's Speak French" in which he offered listeners practical tips to improve their grammar and French-speaking skills.
[167] Francis Dorset, "Bureau de réclamations," *Radio-Magazine*, August 23, 1936; Paul Dermée, "La radio, école de prononciation," *Mon programme*, December 20, 1935, 41.
[168] Pierre Domène, "La politique des ondes. L'âge de la parole," *Radio-Magazine*, December 6, 1936, 3. Paul Dermée, "La radio, école de prononciation," *Mon programme*, December 20, 1935, 41. PTT minister Georges Mandel reportedly created a pronunciation course for radio announcers at the Institut de Phonétique. Dermée called for a "National Committee of Pronunciation" modeled on an equivalent British state institution to regulate announcers' speech habits.

French tongue.[169] The members of the Office de Langue Française, who straddled partisan divides, included the linguists Albert Dauzat, André Mary, Charles Bruneau, and Thérive; the literary critics André Billy and Mario Rocques; and Julian Cain, the director of the National Library of France.[170] Their presence illustrates a prevailing consensus among cultural elites from across the political spectrum that "radio today has the mission of unifying the pronunciation of all those who speak French."[171]

These increasing calls for language standardization and government intervention in regulating the state airwaves coincided with the collapse of the Popular Front and a rightward shift in politics. In the spring of 1938, just days before the *Anschluss*, the radical Edouard Daladier proposed a government of public safety to secure France in the face of Nazi Germany's eastward expansion. Daladier promised to maintain the Popular Front's social gains, but his government slid toward authoritarianism as he began to govern by decree, actions he justified in the interest of maintaining social peace.[172] To safeguard the nation's ears, Daladier further expanded the state's control over the airwaves. With an anxious public eager for up-to-the-minute news, the security services worried about the harmful effects of false news reports, prompting Daladier to create a special Service de Contrôle de la Radio in December 1938 to monitor their content.

Even more than his predecessors, Daladier privileged intellectuals' role in shaping the "radio nation." He reappointed to the Conseil Supérieur des Emissions de la Radiodiffusion Georges Duhamel, André Maurois, and Paul Valéry, all of whom shared his view that the state should promote what Philip Nord has termed a "culture of quality" to compete with Americanized mass culture.[173] Interviewed by *Radio-Magazine* about his role on the Conseil Supérieur, Maurois told the journalist A.H. Flassch "radio is a marvelous enough instrument that it can be used with success to 'remodel' an entire country." The state should exploit the airwaves for "this unique and determined goal: the prestige of the country, both internally and externally." For Maurois, this meant broadcasting classic works of literature and musical masterpieces to ensure that "the French language is heard overseas as much as possible."[174] Despite earlier condemnations of

[169] "Propos du samedi: Sur le trottoir de boulevard Saint-Michel, des passants faciles à reconnaître L'Office de Langue Française..." *Le Figaro*, May 8, 1937, 5.
[170] Georges Ravon, "Dans le No-Man's Land de la grammaire française. Visite au tranquille Office De Langue Française," *Le Figaro*, July 17, 1937, 5.
[171] Paul Dermée, "La radio au service de la langue française," *Mon programme*, May 28, 1937.
[172] Wardhaugh, *In Pursuit of the People*, 202–8.   [173] Nord, *France's New Deal*, 248–53.
[174] A.H. Flassch, "André Maurois et la radio," *Radio-Magazine*, June 26, 1938.

the Popular Front's educational broadcasting, state stations continued to transmit large quantities of "high" cultural content, from lectures about the Enlightenment to live broadcasts from the Comédie Française and the Théâtre de l'Odéon.[175]

The continuation of radio scolaire and "high" cultural content on the state airwaves after the Popular Front's defeat suggests that the battle over classroom radio listening owed much to the fierce polemics of mid-1930s politics, as well as to similar expectations for state radio shared by critics and social elites on the left and right. Although far right pundits condemned the Popular Front's progressive centralization of the airwaves and the pedagogical strategy behind in the school radio broadcasts, they did so primarily because the left controlled state radio microphones. While many people expressed anxieties that collective listening would undermine teachers' authority in the classroom and endanger students' development as rational, free-thinking individuals, in the end radio scolaire came to be seen as a viable method to combat the harmful effects of mass culture on the cultural capital of France's youth.

Under the Daladier government, the state radio administration continued to expand and professionalize radio scolaire, which remained on the air until the summer of 1940. By the spring of that year, thirty-nine schools possessed "central" radios: a single receiver wired through a public address system so that it could be heard in multiple classrooms. Eighty percent of lycées and collèges claimed to own at least one radio, although in many cases it was shared between multiple teachers and classrooms. The Ministry of Education also committed itself to equipping teachers with printed materials to help guide their students through listening sessions.[176] In 1938, a cabinet report summarized the lessons learned from the political battle over radio scolaire and proposed strategies for ensuring its future. Teachers' initial hostility toward the broadcasts owed much to their independence and reluctance to embrace modern technology, particularly in a depression-era economy in which many feared for their jobs. For radio scolaire to be successful, the state needed to remind teachers that they were vital to the broadcasts' success, for "in education, the essential is not that students listen, but that they listen for themselves. Here, as in other subjects, the progress of each lies in the personal effort put forth." The very best teachers would help their

[175] Jeanneney, ed., L'écho du siècle: dictionnaire historique de la radio et de la télévision en France (Paris, 1999), 33–34, and Hélène Eck, La guerre des ondes. Histoire des radios de langues françaises pendant la deuxième guerre mondiale (Paris, 1985), 26.
[176] E. Chamoux, "Enquête sur la radiophonie scolaire dans les établissements du second degré," La Classe à l'écoute, Avril–Juin, 1939, 6.

students learn to listen independently so they might reject "passive listening sessions" outside of class or turn off poor-quality radio programs when they came on the air. For even if it was against their will, citizens of France needed to learn how to listen so they might survive in a twentieth-century world that would assuredly be defined by broadcast sound.[177]

[177] CAC 19890313-53. No author. Note sur la radiodiffusion scolaire, 1938.

5 Dangerous airwaves
Propaganda, surveillance, and the politics of listening in French colonial Algeria

In September of 1934, Algerian Governor-General Jules Carde asked the Algiers police prefecture to investigate a rumor circulating through the colonial bureaucracy that "natives" in the *cafés maures* (Arab cafés) of Algiers were tuning into biweekly Arabic radio broadcasts transmitted by an unspecified Italian station that featured "commentaries unfavorable to France" and "openly attacked France's Muslim policy."[1] As the governor-general of three strategic overseas *départements*, Carde had already received warnings that the airwaves over North Africa were becoming dangerous. A few months earlier, Jean Berthoin, the director of national security for France's Interior Ministry, warned regional prefects "in numerous cities a large portion of the radio-electric industry – the sales and construction of devices – is in the hands of foreigners." Staff in the Sûreté (state security services) feared that the large number of multinational radio companies operating in France would permit enemy agents to mask radio transmitters beneath the cover of radio sales and report clandestinely on troop maneuvers and defense preparations. Berthoin instructed the police in each *département* to begin "discreet investigations" into the civil status, political affiliations, and nationality of local radio vendors and any affiliated personnel.[2] Although ostensibly directed at prefects in metropolitan France, the Sûreté directives generated considerable unease in Algeria – home to a large European population of German and Italian descent as well as to multiple garrisons of France's Armée d'Afrique (Army of Africa). By 1935, the governor-general had ordered the construction of a colony-wide surveillance web to monitor radio sales, investigate Algerians' listening habits, and assess the effects of

---

[1] ANOM 15H32. GGA Direction des Affaires Indigènes et Territoires du Sud. Le Gouverneur Général à M. le Préfet d'Alger (copiée à M. le Directeur des Affaires Indigènes), November 22, 1934.
[2] ANOM 15H32. J. Berthoin, le Directeur de la Sûreté Nationale pour M. le Ministre de l'Intérieur à M. les Préfets, September 27, 1934. The governor-general asked the prefects of the *départments* of Alger, Oran, and Constantine to begin their investigation on December 31, 1934.

broadcasting – or what one official termed a "new genre of oral propaganda" – on the "native mentality."[3]

In the mid-1930s, while Popular Front politicians and their opponents on the far right were fighting over *radio scolaire*, another battle over broadcast sound was unfolding in the Mediterranean, where transnational radio broadcasts fueled anxieties within Algeria's colonial administration, the security services, and in metropolitan political circles about the combined threats of foreign subversion and political instability in France's North African colonies. Nazi Germany and fascist Italy had already begun to challenge France's geopolitical status on the Continent with their streamlined propaganda machines. However, foreign radio propaganda did not become a serious problem meriting state intervention until the broadcasts reached North Africa, a region many policymakers regarded as vital to France's territorial security, but where the loyalty of its colonial subjects could not be assured. For proponents of the empire, the demographic devastation wrought by the First World War reaffirmed the value of *la plus grande France* (Greater France) as a source of manpower and material resources. In fact, the French empire reached its zenith during the interwar decades, absorbing the Middle Eastern protectorates of Syria and Lebanon as well as newly "pacified" territories along the internal borders of French West and Equatorial Africa. Still, legislators in Paris and colonial administrators overseas worried about managing a geographically vast and ethnically diverse empire amid the rise of indigenous nationalist movements whose leaders demanded not only reforms to discriminatory colonial policies but also complete independence from European rule.[4]

This chapter examines how radio broadcasting and an auditory culture of mass-reproduced sound transformed the politics of everyday life and imperial policymaking in colonial Algeria by turning listening into a new site of struggle between Algerians and the French colonial state. Although European nations from Britain and the Netherlands to Germany and Italy all developed imperial broadcasting schemes during the 1930s, the impact of radio on colonial societies has thus far sustained limited scholarly attention.[5] Scholars have instead regarded colonialism as a

[3] ANOM 15H32. Le Gouverneur Général à M. le Préfet d'Alger (copiée à M. le Directeur des Affaires Indigènes), November 22, 1934.
[4] Martin Thomas, *The French Empire Between the Wars: Imperialism, Politics, and Society* (Manchester, 2005), 1–53; Raoul Girardet, *L'idée coloniale en France de 1871 à 1962* (Paris, 1972).
[5] The bulk of the existing literature on imperial broadcasting focuses on the BBC's Empire Service, including Simon J. Potter, *Broadcasting Empire: The BBC and the British World, 1922–1970* (Oxford, 2012); Alasdair Pinkerton, "Radio and the Raj: Broadcasting in British India, 1920–1940," *Journal of the Royal Asiatic Society*, 18, 2, 2008, 167–91;

preeminently visual enterprise, emphasizing how the imperial epis-
temologies of anthropology and ethnography deployed painting, photography, and film to reinforce ideologies of Western superiority while
furnishing Europeans with discursive and material tools to "enframe"
and contain their African and Asian subject populations.[6] Yet broadcasting quickly became a centerpiece of colonial modernity, as imperial
lobbyists and colonial bureaucrats experimented with radio as a novel
form of distance communication, a source of entertainment, and a
weapon of propaganda.[7]

When a coalition of businessmen and settler elites persuaded the
Algerian colonial state to construct Radio-Alger (Radio-Algiers) in 1929
as the French empire's first public broadcasting station, they hoped to
advance their own economic and political interests within France's emerging "radio nation" while reinforcing the *mission civilisatrice* (civilizing
mission) among the indigenous population. But even before hostile foreign radio propaganda reached North Africa, broadcasting began to
challenge French authority as Algerian musicians used Radio-Alger's
microphones to question the racial and cultural boundaries undergirding
colonial society and to demand a greater role in colonial governance. The
concomitant emergence of a global market of Arabic-language records
threatened to further destabilize colonial politics by giving Algerians
access to Arab cultures outside the sphere of French control, in turn
suggesting troubling links between broadcast sound and the rise of pan-
Arabism and anti-colonial nationalism.

When Governor-General Carde ordered his staff to investigate
Algerian radio listening in the autumn of 1934, he hoped to uncover
direct links between broadcasting and the growing nationalist challenges

Joselyn Ziven, "Bent: A Colonial Subversive and Indian Broadcasting," *Past and Present*,
162, 1999, 195–220; Ziven, "The Imagined Reign of the Iron Lecturer," *Modern Asian
Studies*, 32, 3, 1998, 717–34; John MacKenzie, "'In Touch With the Infinite': The BBC
and The Empire, 1923–53," in McKenzie, ed., *Imperialism and Popular Culture*
(Manchester, 1986), 165–91. One notable exception is Rudolf Mrazek's *Engineers of
Happy Land: Technology and Nationalism in a Colony* (Princeton NJ, 2002), which examines broadcasting in the Dutch Indies.
[6] On the visual culture of imperialism, see Edward Said, *Orientalism* (New York, 1978);
Bernard S. Cohn, *Colonialism and Its Forms of Knowledge: The British in India* (Princeton
NJ, 1996); Timothy Mitchell, *Colonizing Egypt* (Cambridge, 1998); and Annie Coombes,
*Reinventing Africa: Museums, Material Culture, and Popular Imagination in Late Victorian
and Early Edwardian England* (New Haven CT, 1997).
[7] David R. Headrick, *The Invisible Weapon: Telecommunications and International Politics,
1851–1945* (Oxford, 1991), 136–40, 225–27. Headrick surveys the use of radio for
military and administrative communication in the colonies before the First World War
and during the interwar decades. In the French empire, long-wave wireless telegraphy
stations at Saigon, Bamako, and Tannarive connected colonial bureaus, but none of these
stations were used for public radio broadcasts.

to French rule. Yet the efforts of colonial police to monitor Algerians' radio listening habits were hampered by their reliance on visual surveillance techniques, the short duration of radio broadcasts, and the very subjective nature of listening itself. Where historians of colonial Algeria have portrayed the 1930s as a period of escalating violence and repression, revisiting this period through its contested auditory culture instead exposes the very limitations of colonial hegemony. As we shall see, the battle to control the airwaves over North Africa fueled contests of power between Algerians and colonial authorities, metropolitan politicians and colonial "old hands," and ultimately, between France and its diplomatic rivals. The Mediterranean, much to the dismay of policymakers in Algiers and Paris, became the first theater of an impending *guerre des ondes* (war of the airwaves), propelling metropolitan lawmakers to adopt more proactive counterpropaganda measures and reshape the French "radio nation" as the prospect of another world war loomed. But to understand how broadcasting first arrived in North Africa, we turn first to the politics surrounding the construction of Radio-Alger in 1930.

The politics of broadcasting in interwar Algeria

Radio broadcasting debuted in Algeria against the backdrop of what the Maghribi historian Jacques Berque once termed the "false apogee" of *Algérie française*: a decade when the triumphant imperial self-confidence of the year-long celebrations commemorating the Centenary of the French conquest in 1930 could barely mask the rising ethno-racial and class tensions that would shortly explode into violence.[8] Algeria had long occupied a symbolic stronghold in France's empire as its largest settler colony, but many colonial elites felt the need to reassert its strategic importance to the metropole. In the countryside, the wealthy *colons* (settlers) who had dominated the agricultural economy of wine and wheat production for much of the nineteenth century felt increasingly threatened by a discontented population of impoverished laborers. In Algeria's cities, the multi-ethnic European community of French, Italian, Maltese, and Spanish descent witnessed its dominance over urban politics challenged by the rise of working-class solidarities and the emergence of a vocal Muslim professional elite composed of civil servants, magistrates, public school teachers, physicians, and lawyers. These Algerian elites, who included both naturalized "citizens" and colonial "subjects," also began to demand political rights and reforms to

[8] Jacques Berque, *Le Maghreb entre deux guerres* (Paris, 1962).

discriminatory colonial legislation, calling into question the very legitimacy of the colonial enterprise.

When European businessmen persuaded the Algerian colonial government to construct Radio-Alger as the French empire's first profes-
sionally run radio station to coincide with the Centenary, they hoped the
"Voice of Algeria" would promote settlers' interests in France's "radio
nation" and combat European depopulation by advertising Algeria's
agricultural products and tourist destinations in the airwaves over
Europe.[9] To this end, the colonial state invested over two million francs
in Radio-Alger's 12-kW transmitter, making it one of the most powerful
stations of the era.[10] Emile Garcin, an early station promoter, hailed
Radio-Alger as an "incomparable instrument of propaganda and exterior
influence."[11] The Algerian Office of Economic and Tourist Action
(OFALAC), a public relations agency attached to the governor-general's
office, hired the English expatriate journalist R.C. Lee to regale radio
listeners with the thrills of the "Sahara Rally" and the beauties of an
"Algerian Spring in an Automobile," while the famous Parisian sports
reporter Edmond Dehorter (popularly known as *le parleur inconnu*) provided live reportage of the President Gaston Doumergue's visit to Algiers
and accompanying "Venetian Festival of Lights" staged in the city's
harbor.[12]

Radio-Alger's sponsors hoped the station would convey the pleasures
of everyday life in a modern colonial capital to listeners in Europe, but
they also understood the political imperative of situating their project
within contemporary Parisian debates about imperial broadcasting. In
the late 1920s, and nearly five years before the creation of the PTT
network of regional stations, Parisian colonial lobbyists had begun campaigning for the development of a state-run imperial broadcasting system
to complement the privately owned amateur stations operating in

---

[9] *La T.S.F. en Algérie: bulletin mensuel de la Radio-Club d'Algérie* (Algiers, 1925). In 1924 the
amateur-based Radio-Club d'Algérie began broadcasting recorded music, weather
reports, and stock reports from its small transmitter. The Amicale de Radio-Alger
absorbed the radio club after the inauguration of Radio-Alger.

[10] *Le livre d'or du Centenaire de l'Algérie Française. L'Algérie. Son histoire. Oeuvre française
d'un siècle. Les manifestations du Centenaire* (Algiers, 1930), 597; Jonathan K. Gosnell, *The
Politics of Frenchness in Colonial Algeria, 1930–1954* (Rochester NY, 2002), 29–30.

[11] ANOM 64S73. GGA Instruction Publique et Beaux-Arts. Transcription of a speech by
Garcin, president of the Amicale de Radio-Alger, November 1929. Press reports from
1930–1931 confirm that Radio-Alger could be heard in France and across the Continent.
See "Le président de la République devant le micro de Radio-Alger," *Le Petit radio*, May
31, 1930, 9; "Ondes par-ci, ondes par-là," *Paris-midi*, February 3, 1930; and "La portée
de Radio-Alger," *Radio-Magazine*, January 26, 1930, 6.

[12] ANOM 64S73. Commissariat Général du Centenaire. Memos dated March 5, 1930, and
June 5, 1930. Correspondence between Edmond Dehorter and the Commissariat
Général du Centenaire dated April 15 and 19, 1930.

Tunisia, Madagascar, and Indochina.[13] Members of the Paris-based Institut Colonial and prominent colonial administrators, including Julian Maigret, a former governor-general of French Indochina, argued that broadcasting would enable France to compete against its primary imperial rivals of Great Britain and the Netherlands. Radio coalesced neatly with colonial lobbyists' postwar efforts to recast imperial violence through the lenses of "colonial humanism" and economic *mise en valeur*.[14] Maurice Martelli, the president of the Association Colonies-Sciences, told an audience at the Congrès National de la Radiodiffusion (National Congress of Radio Broadcasting) in 1929 that France's colonial subjects, in the majority non-literate "auditory beings" accustomed to purely oral communication, would readily absorb messages transmitted to them via the airwaves.[15] These arguments eventually compelled lawmakers to endorse the construction of the short wave Poste Colonial, which debuted to great fanfare at the 1931 Colonial Exposition in Vincennes.[16]

The Constantine lawyer and Centenary Commissioner Gustave Mercier paid lip service to these larger imperial designs at Radio-Alger's inauguration, describing how the North African station would advance a spiritual conquest of Arab hearts and minds by reaching into Algerian domestic life, long the fixation of colonial elites, to advance France's

[13] Europeans in Saigon and Hanoi created private stations that broadcast for several hours a day. See the *Bulletin officiel du Radio-Club de l'Indochine du Nord*, 1935. Radio clubs in French West Africa and Madagascar transmitted short broadcasts and entrepreneurs constructed small transmitters in Tunis and Rabat in the mid-1930s. Neither of these stations possessed the cultural influence of Radio-Alger until after 1937.

[14] Albert Sarraut, *Grandeur et servitude coloniales* (Paris, 1931), 133–34; Alice L. Conklin, *A Mission to Civilize: The Republican Idea of Empire in France and West Africa, 1885–1930* (Stanford, 1997) 6–7, 46–53; Girardet, *L'idée coloniale en France*, 121–25; Michael Adas, *Machines as Measures of Men: Science, Technology, and Ideologies of Western Dominance* (Ithaca NY, 1989) 380–81.

[15] Maurice Martelli, "Rapport présenté au Congrès National de la Radiodiffusion," *Actes & comptes-rendus de l'Association Colonies-Sciences*, 5e année, N54, December 1929, 241–42.

[16] The lobbying groups Radio-Agricole Française, the Association Colonies-Sciences, and the Institut Colonial together petitioned parliament to construct the short-wave Poste Colonial. The station drew frequent criticism for broadcasting only in Western languages to settler audiences before 1935. No comprehensive study of French imperial short wave exists, although several studies illuminate the politics surrounding the construction of the Poste Colonial. The journalist Frédéric Brunnquell's *Fréquence monde: Du poste colonial à RFI* (Paris, 1992) is based heavily on André Moosmann, "Histoire des émissions internationales de la radiodiffusion française, 1931–1944," an unpublished manuscript in the Fonds Radio France archives written for the fiftieth anniversary of French overseas broadcasting. Additional accounts can be found in Jean Charron's "Les ondes courtes et la radiodiffusion française. Le service des émissions vers l'étranger, période 1931–1974. Problèmes physiques, législatives, et politiques" (PhD diss., Université de Bordeaux, 1984); Cécile Méadel, "Les postes coloniaux," in Jean-Noël Jeanneny, *L'écho du siècle: dictionnaire historique de la radio et de la télévision en France* (Paris, 1999), 678–80; Derek Vaillant's "At the Speed of Sound," 888–921, examines the Poste Colonial through the framework of global short-wave broadcasting.

mission civilisatrice. In a country where "space remains a large obstacle," Mercier proposed, Radio-Alger would "link together all the pioneers of the countryside, all the isolated towns and farms of the interior, and all the lost stations ... with the heart and mind of the Algerian capital." By filling the airwaves over North Africa with French voices, Radio-Alger could draw together a vast, multi-ethnic audience to "constitute the permanent affirmation of the union ... of *all* the diverse races of the country," rallying Europeans and Algerians behind *l'Algérie française*.

These competing mandates for the station – to reach North Africa and France, as well as European and Algerian audiences – in turn shaped Radio-Alger's unique administration. The Amicale de Radio-Alger a private, for-profit association of colonial businessmen and dues-paying subscribers, shared governance of the station with a steering committee appointed by the governor-general.[17] The colonial budget provided annual subsidies for the technical maintenance of the transmitter, but Radio-Alger derived its primary revenues from commercial advertising purchased by colonial firms and metropolitan companies including Royal Kébir (the "doyen of Algerian wines"), Ducretet, Pathé, Radiola, Philips, André shoes, Lustucru pasta, and Renault – an unusual arrangement that continued long after the state banned commercial advertising on public stations.[18]

With radio receivers still comparatively rare outside of Algeria's larger cities, Radio-Alger's staff collaborated with local merchants to convince potential European customers that their political and economic futures hinged on the future of the station itself. In 1931, the daily *La Dépêche algérienne* co-sponsored a "Radio-Tourist Circuit" that encouraged readers to tune into broadcasts nightly to trace the course of several fictional automobiles as they traversed the colony, tying the expansion of the radio audience to the symbolic unification of Algeria through French voices.[19] Glossy photo spreads in *L'Afrique du Nord illustrée* and *Annales africaines* juxtaposed Radio-Alger's recurring performers against advertisements depicting radios as indispensable commodities in a modern colonial

---

[17] ANOM 15H32. La Direction de la Sûreté Générale à M. le Directeur des Affaires Indigènes, March 16, 1933; Le Directeur des Affaires Indigènes à M. le Directeur des Beaux-Arts; Le Gouverneur Général à M. le Directeur des Affaires Indigènes, July 1, 1933; *L'Echo d'Alger*, January 28, 1931, 4.
[18] *Radio-Alger: bulletin official mensuel de l'Amicale de Radio-Alger. Supplement*, November 10, 1933. ANOM 15H-32. Amicale de Radio-Alger. Rapport de M. Foussat, président du Conseil d'Administration, et de M. Garros, trésorier de l'Amicale sur l'activité de la station en 1934, 16.
[19] Jules Cazenave, "Concours du radio-circuit touristique d'Algérie organisé par *La Dépêche algérienne et* Radio-Alger," *La Dépêche algérienne*, January 6, 1931, 4. See also the Délégations Financières, session ordinaire, délégation des non-colons, 3e séance, Saturday, June 1, 1935.

household.[20] The appearance of a "talking machine" or radio in the countryside, the settler Pierre Mannoni later recalled, constituted a veritable local "event," propelling friends to the homes of those with wireless to listen to music or news.[21] For the journalist Fred Bédeil of *L'Echo d'Alger*, it was precisely these rural European listeners, far more than the cosmopolitan urbanites of Algiers, for whom broadcast sound offered the greatest benefit, reducing the potential threat of "going native" by establishing permanent contact with Algiers, Paris, or other French cities.[22] Radio-Alger's publicity campaigns appear to have succeeded, for the number of registered radios in Algeria rose from a few hundred in the late 1920s to 60,000 by 1936, though most remained in European hands.[23]

Before 1935, Radio-Alger transmitted daily from noon to midnight, serving up a repertory of classical music performed by the station orchestra, radio plays (including heavy doses of Molière and Racine), readings of modern literature and colonial fiction, and viticulture advice programs.[24] The announcer André Hughes provided live reportage from important events in the European community: the Christmas Eve midnight mass at the Eglise St. Augustin, opening galas at the Algiers opera, and Bastille Day concerts performed by the French Foreign Legion orchestra.[25] The remaining professional staff, including Henri Defosse, the former conductor of the Stravinsky orchestra, and Alec Barthus, the director of Radio-Alger's theater troupe, came directly from Paris.[26] Their connections enabled the station to capture interviews with celebrities wintering in North Africa or touring on Algiers's stages.

[20] Lucien Goetz, "Le salon algérien de la T.S.F. en 1935," *Annales africaines: la revue de l'Afrique du Nord*, October 20, 1935, 354; "Le Xe salon algérien de la T.S.F.," *L'Afrique du Nord illustrée*, November 1, 1935; Mrazek makes a similar claim about colonial radio in the Dutch East Indies in *Engineers of Happy Land*, 166–73.

[21] Pierre Mannoni, *Les français d'Algérie: vie, moeurs, mentalité de la conquête des Territoires du Sud à l'indépendance* (Paris, 1993), 46. Radio newspapers and colonial periodicals debated the best receivers for the colonies given the challenges facing settlers: lack of electricity, the constant need for new batteries, and the corrosion caused by excessive heat and humidity to fragile wiring. See Fred Bédeil, "T.S.F. Parmi les nouveautés de la saison 1934–1935," *L'Afrique du Nord illustrée*, September 15, 1934, 8.

[22] Fred Bédeil, "T.S.F.," *L'Echo d'Alger*, August 31, 1930, 2; Fred Bédeil, "Le développement de la T.S.F. dans le département de Constantine," *L'Echo d'Alger*, June 16, 1930, 5; Bédeil, "La T.S.F. et les vins," *L'Echo d'Alger*, July 13, 1930.

[23] ANOM 15H32. "La radiodiffusion et les populations indigènes d'Algérie," June 1937. Report prepared for the Haut Comité Méditerranéen.

[24] Georges Martin, "Prosper au micro," *Alger-Radio: le premier magazine de T.S.F. de l'Afrique du Nord*, January 1, 1936, and July–August, 1936. Program listings for the week of March 18, 1935, in *Radio-Alger*.

[25] Program listings for the week of December 24, 1934, in *Radio-Alger*.

[26] Jean Gustave, "Les prochaines transformations à Radio-Alger," *Mon programme*, September 22, 1933.

The comic duo Pills and Tabet, Josephine Baker, and the film director Julien Duvivier, who used the Casbah as a set for his 1937 heist drama *Pépé Le Moko*, all spoke over the station's microphones, bestowing the sheen of glamour on what the Parisian *chansonnier* and short-lived Radio-Alger cabaret performer René Devilliers regarded as the station's otherwise "conformist and bourgeois mentality."[27]

Radio-Alger did attract metropolitan listeners, to be sure, but the Amicale's administrative council, a veritable roster of the colony's professional and political elite, expected the station's sound to align with their largely conservative worldview.[28] News broadcasts deliberately avoided references to unsettling events such as the anti-Semitic pogroms that erupted in 1934 or the divisive elections that ushered the Popular Front into political power in 1936.[29] If the station promoted no single cultural agenda, the *algérieniste* intellectuals Robert Randau, Jean Pomier, and Lucienne Favre exercised considerable influence over its programming. Headlining the 1936 season of radio plays was a dramatization of Favre's novel *Prosper*, which celebrated the robust Latin race of European "Algerians" forged in the ethnically diverse *creuset algérien* ("melting pot") of the southern Mediterranean who would rise up to rejuvenate a decadent metropolitan France.[30]

These efforts to cultivate European audiences for the station in both North Africa and metropolitan France stood in sharp relief to the station's comparable disregard for potential Algerian listeners. Even as Parisian colonial lobbyists devised elaborate schemes to promote indigenous radio listening through the installation of central village radios or loudspeakers in markets and public squares, Radio-Alger took no deliberate measures to cultivate radio ownership among Arab-Algerians. In fact, colonial civil servants judged metropolitan fantasies of creating a mass of docile Algerian listeners to be woefully impractical and politically naïve.[31] Jean

<hr>

[27] René Devilliers, *Butte Boul'Mich' et Cie: souvenirs d'un chansonnier* (Paris, 1946), 171–75. The Algerian-born Devilliers was an early radio celebrity on Paris PTT before joining Radio-Alger's staff.
[28] "Ondes par-ci, ondes par-là," *Paris-midi*, February 3, 1930; "La portée de Radio-Alger," *Radio-Magazine*, January 26, 1930, 6. See also "L'assemblée générale de l'Amicale de Radio-Alger," *Le Petit radio*, March 22, 1930, 10. When the journalist A. Tony Zannett of the daily *La Dépêche algérienne* tackled the topic of European-Muslim relations in his weekly "Algerian Column," he emphasized the need for Algerians to assimilate to Western norms. Rabah Zenati, "Zannett au micro," *La Voix indigène*, January 19, 1935.
[29] Délégations Financières, délégation des colons. 8ᵉ séance, October 10, 1932, 335.
[30] "Les émissions parlées à Radio-Alger," January 1, 1936. Peter Dunwoodie, *Writing French Algeria* (Oxford, 1998), esp. Chapter 4. Randau, Pomier, and Favre all served on Radio-Alger's programming board.
[31] Maurice Martelli, "Rapport présentée au Congrès National de la Radiodiffusion," 250. The governor-general's office occasionally authorized the use of loudspeakers for retransmissions of state funerals or other "official" celebrations. Fred Bédeil, "La musique de

Mirante, the director of the Algerian Bureau of Native Affairs, feared that broadcasting would only open up another space for dissent against French rule in an already heavily censored colonial public sphere. In the aftermath of the First World War, the colonial administration attempted to quell the rising tide of Algerian discontent by peacefully co-opting Muslim elites into the political process. However, the 1919 Jonnart Law, which opened up civil service positions to Muslims and expanded the Muslim electorate to allow limited Algerian participation in local government, only galvanized colonial politics.[32] By the mid-1930s, a range of Algerian political organizations, including the reformist Association des Oulémas Musulmans Algériens (Muslim Ulama), the liberal Fédération des Elus de Constantine (Federation of Elected Muslims of Constantine), and the openly nationalist Etoile Nord-Africaine (North African Star), aired their grievances against the colonial state in municipal assemblies, at political demonstrations, and in the pages of numerous French- and Arabic-language indigenous newspapers.

Elected spokesmen for the Francophone, pro-assimilation Muslim elite declared their loyalty to France while appropriating the language of republican universalism to demand an expansion of the suffrage, expose the hypocrisies of colonialism, and condemn the repressive native legal code, the *code indigénat*. Algerian political figures even allied themselves with European opposition parties, such as the French Communist Party (PCF) or the far right, extra-parliamentary Croix de Feu, in ways that the colonial government and conservative settler population found worrisome and confusing. To govern Algeria, the colonial administration had historically relied upon a tenuous balance of violence, repression, and manipulation of indigenous elites, even subsidizing Algerian-run newspapers that promoted assimilation and acquiescence to French policy. By the early 1930s, colonial authorities no longer knew which sectors of Algerian society represented their best allies.[33] In such a contentious political climate, Mirante feared that radio broadcasting would only exacerbate challenges to French authority, and he warned Governor-

Bourgeuil," *L'Echo d'Alger*, May 28, 1930, 4. See Jean-Jacques Jordi and Jean-Louis Planche, eds., *Alger 1860–1939: le modèle ambigu du triomphe colonial* (Paris, 1999), 174.

[32] Claude Collot, *Les institutions d'Algérie durant la période coloniale, 1830–1962* (Algiers, 1972), 56–105. For a discussion of Muslims' evolving citizenship status, see Todd Shepard, *The Invention of Decolonization: The Algerian War and the Remaking of France* (Ithaca NY, 2006), 19–54.

[33] Important studies of Algerian politics include Charles-Robert Ageron, *Les algériens musulmans et la France, 1871–1919* (Paris, 1968); Mahfoud Kaddache, *Histoire du nationalisme algérien. Question nationale et politique algérienne, 1919–1951* (Algiers, 1981); Pascal Le Pautremat, *La politique musulmane de la France au XXᵉ siècle. De l'héxagone aux terres d'Islam. Espoirs, réussites, échecs* (Paris, 2003); Jacques Bouveresse, *Un parlement colonial? Les Délégations financières algériennes, 1898–1945* (Rouen, 2008).

General Carde that "broadcasting is far too effective a means of propaganda for the administration not to minutely oversee all communications addressed to the natives."[34]
In a concession to dialogue with the expanded Muslim electorate, the governor-general's office approved intermittent talks in Arabic and French by a list of politically "safe" Algerian personalities whom Mirante determined would "receive without difficulty the counsels and direction of the Bureau of Native Affairs": Ahmed Ben Lakahal, the muezzin at an Algiers mosque; several French-educated lawyers and physicians; and teachers from French-controlled madrasas. Even with these precautions in place, Mirante recommended that a French civil servant stand by in the studio to "discreetly observe" all talks given by Algerians to ensure that no criticism of the colonial administration escaped speakers' lips.[35] That the colonial state intended these "native" broadcasts (a mere tenth of the weekly broadcast schedule) to reach a limited audience of literate Muslim elites is further evidenced by its selection of an Arabic-language radio announcer: Omar Guendouz, an Arabic teacher at Algiers's Ecole Sarrouy and a contributor to the state-funded "assimilationist" newspaper *La Voix des humbles*.[36] Between 1933 and 1935, Guendouz acted as an intermediary between the administration and Muslim elites of Algiers, proposing an array of Algerian lecturers that he introduced in literary Arabic and occasionally even in French.[37] However, the majority of the Algerian population spoke Algerian Arabic or Berber dialects, as colonial education policies had for decades rendered classical Arabic the preserve of a small population of Algerian men: civil servants, professors, merchants, native chiefs, and others who had received a private Qur'anic education – a group that included many French speakers for whom Radio-Alger's French broadcasts would have been readily accessible.[38]

---

[34] ANOM 15H32. Jean Mirante, le Secrétaire des Affaires Indigènes à M. le Secrétaire Général du Gouvernement, February 21, 1933.

[35] ANOM 15H32. Note à M. le Directeur des Affaires Indigènes, January 23, 1933. Published program listings, while sometimes inaccurate, document only a few talks by Algerians before 1936: a lecture by the miniaturist Mohamed Racim (winner of the colonial state's Grand Prix d'Algérie) and a 1935 talk by Chérif Benhabyles, a French-trained lawyer from Constantine, both of which were delivered in French. See Benhabyles, "Ménages mixtes," *Radio-Alger*, January 11, 1935, and *Radio-Alger*, May 9, 1935. Benhabyles self-identified in his talk as both a "European" and a "Muslim" by his use of the pronoun "nous." He discouraged unions between Muslim men and French women without precluding their eventual possibility once Algerians had "evolved."

[36] Mahfoud Kaddache, *Histoire du nationalisme algérien*, 208.

[37] Mahieddine Bachetarzi, *Mémoires, suivi d'une étude sur le théâtre dans les pays islamiques* (Algiers, 1968), 367. Allalou, *L'aurore du théâtre algérien, 1926–1932* (Oran, 1982), 11.

[38] Alain Messaoudi, "The Teaching of Arabic in French Algeria and Contemporary France," *French History*, 20, 3, 2006, 297–317. An analysis of how French authorities

"Oriental concerts" composed of live performances by Algerian musicians or selections from commercial Arabic-language records instead comprised the bulk of Radio-Alger's "native" broadcasts. These programs aired intermittently and during the late evening hours, although the station extended them during Ramadan, when its staff assumed that Algerians would seek out music for their fast-breaking celebrations.[39] Mahieddine Bachetarzi, the first Algerian musician to perform on Radio-Alger, viewed this relegation of Algerian performers to the station's "off hours" as a veritable denial of Algerian voices in colonial affairs. "Radio-Alger gave us no place at the beginning," Bachetarzi recalled in his memoirs, a policy that translated into paying Algerian musicians nothing or significantly less than their European counterparts.[40]

This deliberate segregation of performers and potential listeners into the bifurcated categories of "European" and "native" reflected interwar political imperatives and the colonial state's historic taxonomic impulses, which since the late nineteenth century had sought to fix Algeria's population into easily governable racial and legal categories.[41] However, the station's efforts to delimit radio publics ultimately failed, instead revealing the difficulty of controlling broadcast sound and its varied meanings in a diverse, multi-ethnic colonial society. Broadcasting, as we shall see, created opportunities for Algerians to challenge the authority of the colonial state, first by demanding that the "Voice of Algeria" represent their concerns, and later by tuning into foreign stations outside the sphere of French control. Two of the station's recurring programs, which blended "Western" and "Arab" cultures to create hybrid comedy acts

viewed Algeria's linguistic breakdown can be found in ANOM 10 APOM 830 (CHEAM) M. Delahaye, "Les émissions de langue arabe du poste Radio PTT-Alger." Exposé fait par M. Delahaye au cours de perfectionnement des Affaires Indigènes, February 1937.
[39] Amicale de Radio PTT-Alger. Rapports de M. Foussat, président du Conseil d'administration et de M. Garros, sur l'activité de la station en 1934, 10; Program listings can be found in *Radio-Alger*, November 10, 1933. "Oriental" concerts for the week of November 19, 1933, aired on Monday from 6:00 to 7:00 p.m., Tuesday from 9:00 to 9:30 p.m., and Thursday from 10:00 p.m. to 11:00. For 1934 listings, see the supplement of November 23, 1934. "Oriental" concerts for the week of December 2, 1934, included a Sunday and Wednesday concerts from 6:00 to 6:45 p.m. as well as evening concerts at 9:00 p.m. on Thursday and 10:00 p.m. on Tuesday and Friday.
[40] Bachetarzi, *Mémoires*, 355–56, 366–68. Bachetarzi claims he participated in the trials of the Radio-Club d'Algérie's transmitter several years before its inauguration as Radio-Alger. He suggests the station's Arabic-language broadcasts began as early as 1928, although no archival records confirm this. Bachetarzi's El-Moutribia Orchestra received a mere 100 francs per performance to be shared between twenty and twenty-five musicians.
[41] Ann Laura Stoler, *Carnal Knowledge and Imperial Power: Race and the Intimate in Colonial Rule* (Berkeley, 2002), 206–7; Patricia M. Lorcin, *Imperial Identities: Stereotyping, Race, and Prejudice in Colonial Algeria* (New York, 1995).

and musical genres, illuminate why contemporaries quickly came to hear broadcast sound as subversive and politically dangerous. More importantly, a close examination of these on-air performances offers insights into the perspectives of Algerian listeners, whose voices are frequently obscured in the archives of the colonial state.

Subversive sound? cultural *métissage* on the airwaves

Shortly after Radio-Alger's inaugural broadcasts, metropolitan radio magazines and colonial newspapers began urging their readers to sample the station's most distinctive programs: its "savory *sabir* chronicle" and its "oriental concerts," which together showcased the "unique and local physiognomy" of colonial Algeria and promised sonic novelties for ears fatigued by the jazz bands and café-concerts that saturated the European airwaves.[42] In the first of these programs, a European comedian bantered in *sabir*, a dialect that *Radio-Magazine* hailed as one of the "originalities of Algeria." In the second, Algerian musicians and comedians blended multiple languages and "Western" and "Eastern" aesthetic styles to create new, modern genres of Algerian popular songs.[43] Both programs defied the station's efforts to cultivate separate "European" and "native" radio audiences by attracting a seemingly multi-ethnic audience. Yet the broadcasts' linguistic and cultural *métissage* disconcerted other listeners, both European and Algerian, who feared that metropolitan audiences would be unable to identify the ethnic and racial origins of the performers. The ensuing debate over the artistic quality of these programs highlights how broadcasting and recorded sound politicized language and music in novel ways, threatening to disrupt the racial and class boundaries undergirding colonial society. As a result, colonial policymakers began to view broadcasting as a dangerous medium that merited strict surveillance by the colonial state.

Radio-Alger's comedy sketch *La Chronique du cireur* (*The Shoe-Shiner's Column*), which aired weekly for nearly a decade, featured a European comic christened "Jeannot" who played a host of Arab stock characters – a rug merchant, shoe shiner, or army conscript – while offering up humorous assessments of colonial politics and Arab-Algerian customs in *sabir*, a mixture of French, Arabic, Italian, Maltese, and Spanish spoken in Algeria's coastal cities.[44] Before taking his act to the

[42] *Radio-Magazine*, August 23, 1930, 2.
[43] *Radio-Magazine*, June 1, 1930, 7; Jean Gustave, "Nouvelles de l'Afrique du Nord," *Mon programme*, February 3, 1933.
[44] "La Chronique des disques," *La Presse libre*, June 29, 1930. Jeannot's records for Parlophone included 46.551 *Carnaval d'un tirailleur*, 46.549 *La guerre au Maroc*,

microphone, Jeannot honed his comedic skills in cinema entr'actes, on the stages of Algiers's theaters, and in smaller comedy clubs (*salons du rire*).[45] *Sabir* sketches borrowed heavily from the *comique troupier* genre that flourished in turn-of-the-century café-concerts and in the interwar films of the comedian Fernandel, who donned an army uniform and sang humorous ditties about military life in a heavy Marseilles accent that played up racial, class, and gender stereotypes for laughs.[46] Colonial critics, however, celebrated Jeannot as an undisupted *local* star. On evenings when Jeannot performed, *L'Echo d'Alger* reported in 1930, "numerous *colons* gathered in the homes of those with wireless to spend several minutes in laughter," while in the Mitidja, "café owners ... have even installed radios in their establishments to permit their clientele, who deserted them every Thursday, to listen to the stories told by the priceless shoe-shiner of 'Radio-Batata.'"[47]

The transcripts of Jeannot's sketches have disappeared alongside his recordings for the Parlophone label, but he often employed dialogues written by the Algerian-born cabaret and radio star Dominus, whose own *sabir* act animated Parisian stages during the 1930s.[48] These dialogues illuminate the structure and themes of the *sabir* performances, which employed verbal slapstick – comprised of puns, comic wordplay, vocal manipulation, and linguistic *métissage* – for humorous ends.[49] In the following scene from Dominus's *Le marchand de tapis* (*The Rug Merchant*), a French woman chats with the Arab rug merchant Ali, who pressures her to purchase items from his stall.

ALI: Alli, madame, achite moi ! ... J'en it tot ça qui ti vox. Je vends di tot!
FEMALE CLIENT: Tu n'as rien d'alimentaire?

46. 562 *Mustapha vient de Paris*. *La Presse libre* suggested that Jeannot was an actor named Jean Chiariani, but other accounts claim he was a comic named Soler. For the latter, see Eveline Caduc, "Une capitale culturelle," in *Alger 1860–1939*, 91.
[45] "Aux Folies-Bergères," *Annales africaines*, December 26, 1924, 33; Fred Bédeil, "T.S.F. La comique Jeannot à Radio-Alger," *L'Echo d'Alger*, July 6, 1930; Fernand Arnaudiès, *Histoire de l'Opéra d'Alger: épisodes dans la vie théâtrale algérienne* (Algiers, 1941), 206; Alain Ruscio, *Le crédo de l'homme blanc. Regards coloniaux français, XIX–XXᵉ siècles* (Brussels, 1996), 165.
[46] Susan Hayward, *French National Cinema*, 2nd ed. (New York, 2005), 154–58.
[47] Fred Bédeil, "Le développement de la T.S.F. dans le département," *L'Echo d'Alger*, July 20, 1930, 2. Lucien Goetz, "Le salon algérien de la T.S.F. 1935," *Annales africaines*, October 20, 1935, 361. See also "Jeannot: Le kébir des sabirs," *Alger-Radio*, March 1, 1936, 9.
[48] Dominus. *Sabir avec le marchand de tapis. Scènes, fables, récits* (Paris, 1934), 9–11. The Algerian-born Dominus performed his *sabir* act *Le marchand de tapis* (*The Rug Merchant*) in a Montmartre cabaret before becoming a regular player in Paris PTT's *T.S.F. à l'hôpital* broadcasts.
[49] Douglas, *Listening In*, 101–8.

ALI: Ali-mentaire, non, madame. Ji souis pas Ali-mentaire. Ji suis Ali Makmal ben Zlabiya, commarçant.

FEMALE CLIENT: Tu as ta license?

ALI: De l'issence, oui, j'en i ... Ouala c'it di l'issence di roses di Tourquie ... di vrai ... C'it fabriqui à Pantin ...[50]

Here a *bourgeoise* asking for food (*alimentaire*) in clipped French diction received the reply "*Ali-mentaire*? No I'm Ali Makmal ben Zlabiya, merchant." The scene relied upon Ali's malapropisms to generate a laugh – mistaking a woman's query about his license (*license*) as a request for perfume (*l'essence*) and the juxtaposition of two very different accents. The sketch concluded with a monologue by the "Sidi" Ali, who described leaving his native Kayblia for military service on the Western Front, where he fought savage *boches* at Verdun, an experience that cemented his loyalty to "Madame la République." Radio-Alger's *Chronique du cireur* employed a similar structure, with the announcer André Hughes playing straight man to Jeannot's Arab-Algerian, or on occasion, European stock characters.[51]

The widespread popularity of *La Chronique du cireur* raises an interesting question: how did Jeannot's unique linguistic humor resonate in a multicultural and multilingual colonial society? Contemporary scholars consider *sabir* to be a centuries-old manifestation of the Maghrib's cultural cosmopolitanism, tracing its deep historical roots to the *lingua franca* spoken by merchants, traders, and Ottoman clerks as early as the thirteenth century.[52] Colonial-era writers, in contrast, located *sabir*'s origins in France's conquest of Algeria, which had produced a vocabulary necessary for exchanges between French soldiers and Arabs, including words such as *toubib* (doctor), *cadi* (chief), and *bléd* (countryside). Over time, they suggested, *sabir* degenerated from a medium of exchange into evidence of Arabs' inability to speak French properly. "Today in North Africa," Dominus claimed, "the Frenchman speaks to the Native in his language or in common Arabic, when he knows it. The Arab or Kabyle

---

[50] Dominus, *Sabir avec le marchand de tapis*, 15–16. Bibliothèque Nationale de France. Dominus, Parlophone 80.990 *Le renseignement d'Ali/Le sidi parigot* and Parlophone 80.761 *La visite à la mosquée/Le Mariage d'Ahmed*.

[51] Bédeil, "T.S.F. La comique Jeannot." Jeannot's sketches typically featured an "Arab" in conversation with a Frenchman.

[52] Jocélyne Dahklia, "No Man's *langue*: une rétraction coloniale," in Dahklia ed., *Trames de langues: usages et métissages dans l'histoire du Maghreb* (Paris, 2004), 260–62; Kmar Kchir-Bendana, "Kaddour Ben Nitram: chansonnier et humoriste tunisien," in *Revue des mondes musulmanes et de la Méditerranée*, 77, 77–78, 1995, 165. Kchir-Bendana argues that the *sabir* sketches of artist Edmond Martin (who performed under the sobriquet Kaddour Ben Nitram) exploited the linguistic diversity of colonial Tunis to humorous ends, thus diffusing interpretations of *sabir* as exclusively racist humor.

who struggles to express himself in French is obliged to speak *sabir* or in a pidgin manner."[53]

For Europeans who felt their political dominance in the colony threatened by the rise of indigenous nationalism, *sabir* sketches reinforced their sense of cultural hegemony by emphasizing Algerians' inability to assimilate to European linguistic or cultural norms. Hence Jeannot's frequent use of racialized minstrel tropes, or what one critic termed the "childlike" and "good-natured" qualities of Arabs, as evidenced in Ali's cheerful sales pitches.[54] The humor of *sabir* resided in the knowledge that Jeannot was not a "real" Arab but a Westerner. By imitating Arabs "perfectly," Jeannot doubled the comedic value of his performances while emphasizing his own racial difference. "One asks oneself whether one is in the presence of an old *turc* or an authentic shoe-shiner," *L'Echo d'Alger* declared, while another critic praised Jeannot's authentic "guttural" dialect when playing a jasmine merchant of the Casbah.[55] *Alger-Radio* magazine reinforced this interpretation of Jeannot's performances by printing a photo spread depicting him in the uniform of an Algerian *tirailleur* and the *burnous* typically worn by Algerian men [Figure 5.1].

To suggest that all of Radio-Alger's listeners would have heard Jeannot's sketches as aural blackface is far too simplistic, however, for colonial authors consistently struggled to distinguish *sabir* from *patatouète*, the urban slang spoken by Algeria's multi-ethnic working-class population and popularized in Musette's early nineteenth-century stories about the street-wise adventurer Cagayous, who became the preeminent symbol of a wily new Latin race emerging in North Africa.[56] *Patatouète*, one colonial dictionary proposed, constituted a hybrid of European Mediterranean languages (Spanish, Italian,

---

[53] Dominus, *Sabir avec le marchand de tapis*, 14–15.

[54] Emmanuel Sivan, "Colonialism and Popular Culture in Algeria," *Journal of Contemporary History*, 14, 1, 1979, 21–53. Colonial minstrelsy flourished during the nineteenth century and produced *petit nègre* tropes that persisted for decades. Michael Pickering, "Mock Blacks and Racial Mockery: the 'Nigger' Minstrel and British Imperialism," in J.S. Bratton, et al., eds., *Acts of Supremacy: The British Empire and the Stage, 1790–1930* (Manchester, 1991), 179–236.

[55] Fred Bédeil, "T.S.F. La comique Jeannot à Radio-Alger," *L'Echo d'Alger*, July 6, 1930. See also Georges Martin *Alger-Radio*, "Les secrets du studio," May 1, 1936, 4. Martin describes Jeannot's performance in the play *Prosper*. Another account described Jeannot as a "Parisian" who had mastered Algiers dialects. "Aux Folies-Bergères," *Annales africaines*, December 25, 1924, 333. I am indebted to Joshua Cole's analysis for this point. See Joshua Cole, "'*A chacun son public*': Performing Publics and Culture in Interwar French Algeria" (unpublished paper cited by permission of the author).

[56] Noah Arcenaux, "Blackface Broadcasting in the Early Days of Radio," *Journal of Radio Studies*, 12, 1, 2005, 61–73; David Prochaska, "History as Literature, Literature as History: Cagayous of Algiers," *American Historical Review*, 101, 3, 1996, 671–711. Dunwoodie, *Writing French Algeria*, 141–43.

Figure 5.1 "Jeannot," *Magazine* (1936). Image courtesy of the Archives Nationales d'Outre-Mer.

and French) with only a few Arabic additions, making it "less common [and] richer, denser, and more colored than *sabir*," the latter being merely a pidgin spoken by "Algerian *tirailleurs* and Muslim artisans."[57] Because Jeannot played "all the special Algerian types, whether they are natives or come from the lands bathed by the Mediterranean," in alternating accents that were "sometimes Arab, then Neapolitan, and then Spanish," only slight linguistic and aural cues separated Jeannot's portrayals of Arab-Algerians from his caricatures of Europeans. By playing a Cagayous type who targeted the pretensions of colonial elites, civil servants, and the "different characters of the Government Square," Jeannot indirectly celebrated the language and manners of Algiers's working classes, whose lifestyles and modes of speech shared more with *sabir* speakers (whether European or Arab-Algerian) than with wealthy *colons*.

Yet given the fact that journalists frequently hailed Jeannot as the "*kabir* of *sabirs*" and the "only man who can make the Moors laugh," it merits asking whether Arab-Algerians found Jeannot's sketches funny.[58] While there is no clear answer to this question, by emphasizing the cultural and

[57] No author, "Algérie, Petit dictionnaire," in "Les pieds noirs: la question du jour," *Documents de la Revue des Deux Mondes*, 18, 1961, 46–57.
[58] Bédeil, "T.S.F. Le comique Jeannot." Bédeil suggested that "Jeannot expressly imitated the *bon enfant et bourru*" Cagayous type; see the unauthored description of Jeannot in *L'Antenne*, November 8, 1931, 691, and *La Presse libre*, June 13, 1930.

linguistic *métissage* that flourished among Algiers's "little people," Jeannot appears to have attracted a cross-cultural audience for his comedy sketches.[59] When mimicry of French language and manners lay at the heart of France's civilizing mission, the multiple levels of parody in *sabir* sketches may have permitted Europeans and Algerians to laugh at Jeannot – albeit for different reasons – for exposing the arbitrary nature of colonial hierarchies and fluidity of racial and cultural identities.

This potential cross-cultural appeal of *La Chronique du cireur* is evidenced by the cultural mixture that defined Algerian theatrical productions between 1925 and 1935, where Jeannot performed onstage alongside the first generation of Algerian recording artists, including many of the musicians who animated Radio-Alger's "oriental concerts."[60] Radio and the emerging Arabic-language recording industry offered performers such as Mahieddine Bachetarzi – a musician, singer, and pioneer of dialectical Arabic theater – new spaces for artistic and personal expressions, provided they could navigate the strictures of colonial censorship.[61] Already a celebrity before his radio debut, Bachetarzi first achieved notoriety as a teenage *hazzab* (reader of the Qur'an) in an Algiers mosque. He later became the star performer and director of El-Moutribia, an Arab-Andalusian orchestra dedicated to preserving and democratizing Algeria's centuries-old "classical" music repertory, making the group a pivotal player in the emerging Muslim civil society of the 1930s.[62]

---

[59] Lucien Goetz, "Le salon algérien de la T.S.F. 1935," *Annales africaines*, October 20, 1935, 361. Nancy Rose Hunt, "Tintin and the Interruptions of Congolese Comics," in Paul S. Landau and Deborah D. Kaspin, eds., *Images and Empires: Visuality in Colonial and Postcolonial Africa* (Berkeley, 2002), 90–123. Hunt argues that Congolese sometimes found the blackface images of Belgian Tintin cartoons highly amusing, but for very different reasons than settlers.

[60] "Fêtes et concerts. Gala franco-oriental organisé par El-Andalousia," *La Presse libre*, June 11, 1930, 5. In May 1930, Jeannot performed his *sabir* sketches alongside the "famous Oranais tenor and Hispano-Moorish singer" M. Dahon, the El-Andalousia Orchestra, and a dancer named Zoubida, and a jazz band.

[61] Bouziane Daoudi and Hadj Miliani, *L'aventure du raï: musique et société* (Paris, 1996), 37–84; Hadj Miliani, *Sociétaires de l'émotion: études sur les musiques et les chants d'Algérie d'hier et d'aujourd'hui* (Oran, 2005); Rabah Saadallah, *El-Hadj M'hamed El-Anka: maître et rénovateur de la musique 'chaabi'* (Algiers, 1981), 36–73. The roots of contemporary North African music, from the Algiers-based *chaabi* to Oranais *raï*, date to this first generation of Maghribi recording artists. The station's lineup included the Arab-Andalusian orchestras El-Andalousia, El-Mossilia, El-Djaizairia, and El-Ghernatia as well as solo performers Ali Soufi and Lili L'Abassi.

[62] Miliani, *Sociétaires de l'émotion*, 31–32, 62. The Jewish musician Edmond Nathan Yafil founded El-Moutribia in 1912. Nathan and the amateur French musicologist Jules Rouanet began transcribing Algeria's Arab-Andalusian repertory, seeking out scores from the ninth to fifteenth centuries and modern variations of secular and religious pieces. Omar Carlier, "Médina et modernité: l'emergence d'une société civile

By the time El-Moutribia began performing on Radio-Alger, Bachetarzi had already recorded numerous religious and secular pieces for the Gramophone and Pathé labels, whose directors were eager to capitalize on Europeans' taste for colonial exoticism and "authentic" ethnographic music. The Lebanese-Egyptian Baidaphone Company, which wielded star-making power across the Arabic-speaking world, thanks to its global network of subsidiary recording labels, film studios, and distributors, also attracted Bachetarzi and other North African performers, many of whom hoped to become household names like the Egyptian singer Oum Kalthoum.[63] "The natives are already very fond of the phonograph," the critic Gabriel Audisio commented in *La Revue musicale* in 1930. "The tiniest *café maure* and the rich residences of the bourgeoisie, as well as the dens ... of the Casbah are decorated with one, most frequently set up with a gleaming horn," demonstrating that the "native clientele ... constitutes an important market for the phonograph industry."[64] Radio-Alger's "oriental concerts" offered Algerian musicians the opportunity for even greater exposure across North Africa and Europe.[65]

However, Bachetarzi's performances, like Jeannot's *sabir* sketches, rapidly acquired multiple and conflicting meanings. Classical Arab-Andalusian music comprised the majority of El-Moutribia's repertory, but Bachetarzi and several of the orchestra's solo performers – including the comic impresario Rachid Ksentini, the *châabi* singer Lili L'Abassi, and the teenage Mohammed El-Kamal, together pioneered new genres of culturally hybrid and humorous songs. The singers penned lyrics in multiple languages to sounds of fox-trots, rumbas, and big-band numbers, often borrowing their vocal styling from the French singers Tino Rossi and Maurice Chevalier or the Egyptian Mohammed Abdul Wahab, who became popular after his musical films played in Algerian cinemas. The linguistic fluidity of these songs, in which the performers moved from dialectical Arabic to *sabir* and then to French, reveals the singers' efforts to reach a working-class, rather than exclusively elite North African audience, while their occasional use of the Orientalist musical motifs

«musulmane» à Alger à l'entre-deux-guerres," in Pierre-Robert Baduel, ed., *Chantiers et défis de la recherche sur le Maghreb contemporain* (Paris, 2008), 199–228.
[63] Pekka Gronow, "The Record Industry Comes to the Orient," *Ethnomusicology*, 25, 2, 1981, 262–74.
[64] Gabriel Audisio, "Un aperçu de la musique algérienne," *La Revue musicale*, August–September 1930, 153–54.
[65] Bachetarzi, *Mémoires*, 366–68. The Tunisian singer Fadila Khetemi agreed to perform unpaid on the radio after refusing to sing in a concert for free. Bachetarzi used his radio exposure to sign lucrative advertising deals with metropolitan firms.

common to the French-language *chanson coloniale* also suggests their songs' potential appeal to French listeners.[66]

Algerian performers used these hybrid musical numbers to satirize the effects of Western modernity (represented by automobiles, telephones, and high fashion) on Algerian family life or to parody the Muslim bourgeoisie in the form of stock characters such as the stupid *cadi* or greedy *muphti*. Ksentini's song "The Councilor" mocked a recently elected Muslim municipal official who appealed to his "dear brothers" on the eve of an election only to become a pretentious pawn of the French who sported sunglasses, drove a Citroën, and demanded that fellow Algerians address him as "Monsieur." Ksentini and his fellow Algerian comedian Allalou also performed *comique troupier*-style sketches that while similar in style to Jeannot's, featured titles such as "Kouider at the Dentist" and "Kaci Returns from Mecca."[67] During live performances, these songs and sketches relied heavily on double entendre or the accentuation of particular words and syllables to seal a joke, enabling the artists to subtly criticize colonial society while escaping the attention of state censors.[68] If these performers' hybrid musical performances proved difficult to interpret, El-Moutribia's membership, which included both Jews and Muslims, or naturalized citizens and colonial subjects, likewise resisted easy classification within colonial ethnic and legal categories.[69] Photos of El-Moutribia, its members posed in Western evening attire while holding Arab musical instruments, further complicated interpretations of their performances [Figure 5.2].[70]

In the absence of detailed program guides, determining precisely *how* political Algerian musicians' radio performances may have been

---

[66] Miliani, "Variations linguistiques et formulations thématiques dans la chanson algérienne au cours de XXe siècle. Un parcours," in Dakhlia, ed., *Trames de langues*, 427. See Rachid Ksentini's "Un coup de téléphone au cadi," Mohammed El-Kamal's "Tik-tak," and Aissa's "Qui veut des tapis?" and "Arrouah, je t'y cire," on the CD *Algérie: Fantaisistes des années 1930*, Buda Musique, 2009. Miliani notes that many of these French-Arabic songs featured orientalist motifs common to the popular *chansons coloniales* of the era (such as Maurice Chevalier's "Ali Ben Baba"). Gabriel Audisio reviewed the latter in "Enregistrements algériens," *La Revue musicale*, July 1930, 57–58.

[67] The lyrics to "Le conseiller" can be found in Saaddine Bencheneb, "Chansons satiriques d'Alger (1er moitié du XIVe siècle de l'Hégire)," *La Revue africaine*, 74, 1933, 75–117. See also *L'Echo musicale de l'Afrique du Nord*, March 1934, 9–10. One "Gala Franco-Oriental" starring Mahieddine, Louis Chaprot, and Ksentini, featured a Franco-Arab military vaudeville titled "The Peasant in the Regiment" whose "*dialogue narquais*" was understood by the multi-ethnic audience.

[68] Ahmed Cheniki, *Le théâtre en Algérie: histoire et enjeux* (Aix-en-Provence, 2002), 23–29.

[69] Bachetarzi, *Mémoires*, 60–61, 99–100, 133–34. The socio-economic and ethno-religious diversity of El-Moutribia's members produced internecine tensions.

[70] On El-Moutribia's style of performance as a form of political expression, see Joshua Cole, "*A chacun son public*"; See the photo of El-Moutribia in *Alger-Radio*, February 1, 1937.

Figure 5.2 "El-Moutribia Orchestra," *Alger-Radio Magazine* (1936).
Image courtesy of the Archives Nationales d'Outre-Mer.

remains difficult. The governor-general's office deemed Bachetarzi to
be a politically safe performer, and many European critics heard him as
the embodiment of France's *mission civilisatrice*, christening him as the
"Caruso of the Desert."[71] In fact, French critics tended to interpret
this linguistic and musical *métissage* broadcast by Radio-Alger either as
evidence of Algerians' successful assimilation or the lamentable corruption of "pure" Arab music by Western mass culture.[72] Bachetarzi
later recalled that Jean Mirante, the director of the Bureau of Native
Affairs, warned him not to sing "little songs which risked being misinterpreted" on the radio, but there is no evidence that the singer
listened, and Ksentini performed his comedy sketches on the radio

[71] Nadja Bouzar-Kasbaji, *L'émergence artistique algérienne aux XXᵉ siècle: contribution de la
musique et du théâtre algerois à renaissance culturelle et à la prise de conscience nationaliste*
(Algiers, 1988), 28–32.
[72] "La musique indigène," *La Dépêche de Constantine*, July 7, 1937. In the 1960s, sociologist
Jacques Berque interpreted this musical and linguistic *métissage* as evidence of the
psychological *déracinement* of Algerians who were "trapped between 'Western' and
'Eastern' versions of themselves." See Berque, *Le Maghreb entre deux guerres*, 391–92.

for years.[73] In fact, colonial authorities displayed little interest in censoring Arab orchestras before 1935. When the Bureau of Native Affairs pulled the predominantly Muslim Arab-Andalusian El-Djazairia Orchestra off the air in 1933, the decision came only after the multi-confessional Jewish-Muslim orchestra El-Andalousia denounced the former for engaging in nationalist politics in order to obtain their radio spot.[74] Algerian musicians, as these examples suggest, found opportunities to manipulate the colonial state's censorship regime and exploit the new auditory culture to their advantage.

However, if some listeners laughed at Jeannot's *sabir* sketches or danced to the sounds of "oriental concerts," the liminality of these performances clearly disconcerted others, whether European or Algerian. Precisely because Jeannot, Mahieddine, and Ksentini challenged prevailing notions of authenticity (who was the real "Arab" and who was the real "European"?), their performances disrupted racial categories, producing complaints that unsophisticated radio audiences, particularly in metropolitan France, would be unable to decipher the subtle linguistic cues required to identify the performers. Criticisms of the *sabir* sketches and the "oriental concerts" first surfaced in the Délégations Financières, the closest equivalent to a colonial parliament, where Europeans condemned the "concerts of alleged oriental music in which one hears three or four tired primitive themes rubbed, banged, and bellowed" on Arab instruments, featuring singers "turned into sopranos (*sopraniser*) in Mans, with listeners told that they are Arabs!" Radio-Alger should not give voice to "the most barbarous products of the Age of Dancing," the settler Marcel Gatuing argued, and while such programs "might have been pleasing at one time, in favor of the Centenary and Colonial Exposition," Algeria's sole radio station needed "not only to hold its own among the great European stations but at the very least give us good musical performances, with programs chosen in view of the artistic education of the different races of this new country."[75]

---

[73] Bachetarzi, *Mémoires*, 109–10. For Ksentini's radio performances during Ramadan in 1936, see *La Libre parole*, November 27, 1936, and December 12, 1936. See also ANOM 15H-32. Jean Mirante, le Directeur des Affaires Indigènes à M. le Directeur de la Sécurité Générale, March 16, 1933. No evidence suggests that regular censorship took place before 1935.

[74] ANOM 15H32. La Société El-Andalousia à M. le Directeur des Affaires Indigènes, August 10, 1933, Le Directeur des Affaires Indigènes à M. le Directeur des Beaux-Arts, August 17, 1933. See also Bachetarzi, *Mémoires*, 156, 215. Bachetarzi's memoirs suggest that ethnic-religious tensions contributed to this dispute. In 1932, Muslim members of the mixed Jewish/Muslim El-Andalousia Orchestra abandoned the group to join the Muslim El-Djazairia. Tensions within these confessionally mixed orchestras grew after the 1934 pogroms.

[75] Assemblées Financières Algériennes, délégation des colons, 8e séance, October 10, 1932, 335.

René Foudil, an Algerian businessman from Blida, likewise called upon the station to "suppress the *sabir* comedies," conflating their "vulgar" content with certain songs performed by Algerian musicians. "I don't know if people in the metropole have a taste for these trivialities," Foudil argued, "but much would be gained in replacing them with *true* Arab concerts ... we are already viewed poorly enough and we don't need to put forward the image of a disastrous culture that we don't have." The physician Abdelkader Smati concurred, declaring that he "wished to see disappear from the program of Radio-Alger these comedies in *sabir* that are not at all pleasant and are totally deprived of an artistic sense, and which have a burlesque character." While disapproving of Jeannot's stereotypical portrayal of Arab-Algerians, the deputies also demanded music that sounded "Arab," rather than Western, and which represented Algerians' "true" patrimony.[76]

More important, Algerian delegates' complaints about the "oriental broadcasts" provided them with an opportunity to demand inclusion on Radio-Alger's governing board, in a direct parallel to nationalists' growing demands for political representation in the colony. "When a native buys a radio that is already expensive, generally a sacrifice for entertaining his family, and for which he is required to pay a tax," Abedlkader Smati argued in the Délégations Financières in 1936, "does he not have the right to expect something from Radio-Alger on this point?"[77] When European delegates responded that not enough Algerians listened to the radio to merit a voice in the station's management, Mohammed Bendjelloul, a leading spokesman for the Fédération des Elus de Constantine, insisted that "the use of radio is widespread among Muslims; they exist in *cafés maures*, among individuals, in towns and in the countryside," and demanded that "an effort be made to increase the [Arabic] broadcasts."[78] During Radio-Alger's first five years of broadcasting, the station failed to produce the passive "native" audience colonial ideologues once

---

[76] Assemblées Financières Algériennes, session ordinaire de 1935, délégation indigène, section kabyle, June 6, 1935, 399. Biographical information on Foudil and Smati comes from Bouveresse, *Un parlement colonial*, 954, 974.

[77] CARAN F60-739. Délégations Financières, section arabe, November 23, 1936, 175–77; Procès-verbal de l'Assemblée Algérienne, session ordinaire, 1933, section arabe. May 1933 (?). See also Délégations Financières, session ordinaire de 1935, délégation indigène, section arabe, 37. Radio-Alger's director Raymond Brossard responded by asking the governor to nominate one "native representative" to the council. ANOM 15H32. Note du Comité directeur de Radio-Alger à M. le Directeur des Affaires Indigènes, June 24, 1933. Several Algerians joined the Amicale as dues-paying members, but the European members tended to ignore their requests. See the minutes of the meeting of the general assembly of the Amicale de Radio PTT-Alger in *Alger-Radio*, March 21, 1937.

[78] CARAN F60-739. Délégations Financières, 7e séance, November 23, 1936, 175–76.

imagined, instead fueling Algerians' demands for a greater "voice" in colonial politics and the "radio nation" in the airwaves. Moreover, the station failed to create separate and distinct "European" and "native" listening publics, instead generating fierce disputes over the meaning of broadcast sound. This potential for radio listeners to develop competing interpretations of radio broadcasts posed new challenges to the colonial state, fueling European anxieties that the airwaves over North Africa would undermine French authority in the region.

Capturing sound: radio, records, and French surveillance

During the winter of 1934–1935, the squabbles between Arab and French representatives to the Délégations Financières over Radio-Alger's programming suddenly paled in the face of more serious political challenges posed by the airwaves in North Africa. After Mussolini's 1933 visit to Egypt signaled his sympathy for Muslims living under foreign domination, Italy's expansionist aims in Tunisia and France's Levant protectorates began to alarm diplomats and colonial civil servants alike. Shortly thereafter, the Italian short-wave station Radio-Bari began broadcasting in Arabic and Italian from the boot of the Italian peninsula, proclaiming daily Italy's support for emerging nationalist movements in Egypt, Syria, and Lebanon and their promotion of a pan-Arab and pan-Islamic identity.[79] When Franco's coup against the republican government of Spain ignited the Spanish Civil War in July of 1936, Arabic-language transmissions from Spanish nationalist stations in Seville (retransmitted through Tétouan in Spanish Morocco) and Ceuta (on the strait of Gibraltar) reached Algeria, as did broadcasts from Cairo, Alexandria, Zagreb, Istanbul, and occasionally even Moscow. The mere existence of the Moscow broadcasts provoked alarm in colonial circles because the Comintern and the anti-imperialist PCF openly declared their support for the Etoile Nord-Africaine, the sole nationalist movement to demand Algeria's complete independence from France. The Algerian airwaves, once dominated by French radio signals, now swelled with voices chattering in Arabic and other European languages.[80] Broadcasting in turn fueled fears within the colonial administration and the metropolitan security

---

[79] Basheer M. Narif, "The Arabs and the Axis, 1933–1940," *Arab Studies Quarterly*, 19, 2, 1997, 1–24; Manuela Williams, *Mussolini's Propaganda Abroad: Subversion in the Mediterranean and the Middle East* (London, 1996), 63–87.

[80] ANOM 15H32. Ministère de la Défense Nationale et de la Guerre, Etat-Major de l'Armée, section d'outre-mer, Bulletin des renseignements des questions musulmanes, July 1, 1937. Labeled "Secret."

services about the conjoined threats of foreign subversion, political instability, and rising nationalism in North Africa.

When Governor-General Carde first ordered the police to construct a surveillance web to monitor Algerian radio listeners in late 1934, his response to the threat of foreign radio propaganda in North Africa proved strikingly different from that of Parisian politicians and security services in the metropole. Since the early 1920s, audiences in metropolitan France had regularly exercised their "right" to tune into radio programs from across Europe without a great deal of interference from the state. Rising diplomatic tensions prompted the creation of a radio listening service in 1935 to record and evaluate the content of foreign broadcasts (primarily the speeches of European statesmen) and the Interior Ministry's radio police (Police de l'Air) patrolled the airwaves in search of clandestine and unlicensed amateur transmitters, but the security services rarely conducted surveillance of listeners. Such a task would have proven logistically challenging given the density of radio receivers in France, but likely provoked the ire of voters as well.[81] For Carde, however, evaluating the content of Radio-Bari's early propaganda broadcasts proved less important than locating Algerian listeners in order to uncover their programming preferences and listening habits.

This fixation with watching people reflected the rising political tensions in the colony as well as longstanding preoccupations within the security services and the troubled dynamics of the interwar colony–metropole relationship. Since the mid-nineteenth century, the colonial civil services had developed a wide range of visual surveillance techniques to identify, categorize, and control their colonial subject populations. From the 1880s onward, police tracked Muslim pilgrims en route to Middle Eastern holy sites. Colonial authorities worried about Algerian Muslims' exposure to nationalist currents in the French protectorates of Syria and Lebanon, particularly after the spectacular rise of the Lebanese pan-Arab propagandist Shakib Arslan in the mid-1920s, whose Geneva-based newspaper La Nation arabe attacked French interventions in North Africa and the Levant.[82] Police-state measures adopted during the war further fueled metropolitan and colonial bureaucrats' fantasies of maintaining internal political stability and securing France's external borders through the control of subject and foreign populations. Faced with an

---

[81] CAC 19950218–2. Rapport sur le fonctionnement du Centre d'écoute, Direction générale de radiodiffusion, n.d. On the Police de l'Air, see Vaillant, "La Police de l'Air," 1–24.

[82] Martin Thomas, Empires of Intelligence: Security Services and Colonial Disorder after 1914 (Berkeley, 2008), 204; William L. Cleveland, Islam against the West: Shakib Arslan and the Campaign for Islamic Nationalism (Austin, 1985), 90–114.

onslaught of postwar immigration from Eastern Europe and the colonies, the security services modernized older methods of visual surveillance, turning to photographs, passports, and work permits to track immigrants at border crossings, political demonstrations, and ports – strategies that acquired increasing importance after the Etoile Nord-Africaine began seeking financial support from Algerian laborers living in France.[83]

These visual modes of surveillance employed by indigenous and French civil servants in the post office and the Bureau of Native Affairs, policemen, and eventually, the army's security services, all informed the colonial state's investigation of Algerian radio listening. However, if state power historically relied upon strategies designed to render populations "legible," colonial authorities employed no single or coherent logic in their surveillance of listeners, but rather deployed a shifting series of tactics driven by fear, racial prejudice, and above all, a profound uncertainty about how broadcast sound operated in a diverse, multi-ethnic society. Despite the eventual scope of the colonial state's surveillance web – which stretched from the cities of Oran and Algiers to tiny communes such as Bou-Sâada – the invisibility of the airwaves and the short duration of radio programs resisted the attempts of colonial civil servants to render broadcast sound legible to the state. Radio listening turned out to be highly individualized and subjective, and thus difficult to manipulate, monitor, and control.[84]

The governor-general's office had no idea how many Algerians even owned radios in 1934. Carde consequently asked the post office to begin compiling registers of radio owners who had paid their license fee. As in metropolitan France, colonial PTT registers included the owners' name and the receiver's classification as "public" or "private." However, colonial postal agents also documented Algerians' état civil: their marital status, profession, and classification as French "subjects" or naturalized French "citizens" – this latter category presumably less suspect from a political point of view. These early lists of radio ownership produced several surprises. First, the price of personal radio receivers (ranging from 500 to 1,500 francs in 1933–34) prohibited many Algerians outside the educated Muslim elite from making purchases. In Algeria's three départements, postal agents counted only 225 total radios in "native" hands, with forty three in Oran, versus sixty six in Constantine and 116 in Algiers. Algerian radio ownership appeared concentrated in middle-class urban neighborhoos (for example, eighteen in the cities of Constantine and Bône, versus seven in Bougie), with the majority of radio owners living in Algiers.[85] Although the number of

[83] Rosenberg, *Policing Paris*, 17–43.   [84] Scott, *Seeing Like a State*, 5–8.
[85] ANOM 15H32. PTT, Direction de Constantine. Liste des indigènes ayant déclaré un poste de radiodiffusion. November 30, 1934. See also the lists of radios owned by individuals in the départements of Algiers (1934) and Oran (December, 1934).

registered radios in Algerian hands rose to an estimated 2,000 by 1937, the Bureau of Native Affairs believed this figure to be far below the reality.[86] Many Algerian radio owners, like their counterparts in France, resisted declaring their radios to escape paying the license fee. Moreover, colonial civil servants consistently doubted the validity of statistics based on self-reporting, believing that Algerians frequently lied or misreported information to escape the scrutiny of the colonial state.[87]

Personal radio ownership statistics also proved indecisive because of the large numbers of public radios in use. Early reports detailing Algerian radio usage stressed the growing numbers of *cafés maures, cremeries françaises* (greasy spoon restaurants), brothels, and *cercles* (Muslim associations) where Algerian men gathered to listen to the radio and where foreign propaganda might reach a potentially unlimited number of listeners. For colonial civil servants, public radio listening threatened to be a far more dangerous phenomenon than domestic listening, for groups could discuss and debate the broadcasts, in turn lending them a greater authority. In fact, the police had long targeted the *café maure*, a traditional site of Muslim male sociability and a gathering place for transient laborers, as a special target for surveillance, and after the First World War, as a breeding ground for nationalist and communist politics.[88] Although memoirs testify that North African women (especially in wealthier families who enjoyed the luxury of a home receiver) became avid radio enthusiasts, that policemen focused their surveillance almost exclusively on public and collective listening betrayed their assumption that Algerian men alone represented a significant political threat.[89]

Moreover, colonial civil servants had for decades privileged the information that could be gathered from cafés and public spaces – based on rumors, whispers, and hearsay – as the most reliable indicators of the "native" mentality, often bribing café proprietors to serve as informants and report on political dissidence in their businesses.[90] Radio threatened

[86] ANOM 15H32. Ministère de la Défense Nationale et de la Guerre, Etat-Major de l'Armée, section d'outre-mer, Bulletin des renseignements des questions musulmanes, July 1, 1937. This report from the Ministry of Defense noted that the Bureau of Native Affairs questioned the veracity of the PTT's radio ownership statistics, believing the numbers to be much higher.

[87] Kamel Kateb, *Européens, "indigènes" et juifs en Algérie (1830–1962): représentations et réalités des populations* (Paris, 2001), 109–10, 197.

[88] Omar Carlier, "Le café maure, sociabilité masculine et effervescence citoyenne (Algérie XVIIᵉ–XXᵉ siècles)," *Annales ESC*, July–August, 4, 1990, 975–1003.

[89] Fatima Mernissi, *Dreams of Trespass: Tales of a Harem Girlhood* (New York, 1995), esp. Chapters 1, 10, and 12. Mernissi describes the pivotal role that radio played in her early childhood by inspiring the women in her extended family to imagine alternative lifestyles outside the family harem.

[90] Thomas, *Empires of Intelligence*, 27, 78.

to disrupt this time-honored method of information collection. Café owners who used radios to attract a clientele for their businesses were less likely to volunteer details about customers' listening habits or the stations their radios received. Moreover, Radio-Bari's initial broadcasts were short and irregular (ranging from five to fifteen minutes in length), making it difficult for colonial policemen to catch Algerians in the act of listening.[91] For the European policemen and agents in the Bureau of Native Affairs accustomed to recording applause or cheers during theatrical performances and film screenings or monitoring the shouts of political demonstrators, deciding precisely when radio listening became a political act proved enormously challenging, in part because it relied upon a visual register on a listeners' face. Foreign radio broadcasts soon appeared to colonial civil servants as a technological manifestation of the *téléphone arabe* – or what some Algerians referred to as "Radio-Burnous" – the elusive indigenous information network that Europeans always sought to tap into, but consistently feared.[92]

Yet in their initial forays into *cafés maures* and radio shops across the colony, colonial policemen and civil servants made a surprising discovery: record listening, perhaps even more than radio listening, had become a widespread phenomenon among Algerians. Edouard Estaudié, director of the Algerian PTT, reported that "no [foreign] station broadcasting in Arabic could be heard" in the Algiers cafés that he visited, but that proprietors frequently used their radios as "pick-up" devices for playing records.[93] Policemen deployed to investigate foreigners working in radio-electric sales turned up several suspect merchants in Algiers: the German Herbert Kofahl, the Italian Ferruccio Menini (reputedly a member of the "Young Fascists"), and the Hungarian communist Nicholas Koves. They also learned that those same radio merchants frequently made more profits by selling Arabic-language records than wireless receivers.

---

[91] Daniel Grange, "Structure et techniques d'une propagande: les émissions arabes de Radio-Bari," *Relations internationales*, 2, 1974, 165–85. In 1934, Radio-Bari transmitted short bulletins three times a week ranging from five to fifteen minutes in length.

[92] Thomas, *Empires of Intelligence*, 27. European colonial powers displayed an inordinate interest in indigenous communication networks. In his *Empire and Information: Intelligence Gathering and Social Communication in India, 1780–1870* (Cambridge, 1996), C.A. Bayly argues that British colonial civil servants constantly feared the political threat posed by gossip in Indian communities, particularly after the 1857 rebellion, when rumors circulated that runners had secreted messages between rebel groups via "chapatis." During the Algerian War, Europeans feared the role of the "téléphone arabe" in facilitating communication between members of the nationalist National Liberation Front. See Fanon, *A Dying Colonialism* (New York, 1967), 78. Mahieddine Bachetarzi employed the term "Radio-Burnous" to refer to this same phenomenon in his *Mémoires*, 324.

[93] ANOM 15H32. Edouard Estaudié, Chef de services centraux des PTT. Note pour Louis Millot, le Directeur Général des Affaires Indigènes. December 18, 1934.

Because phonographs required no electricity or batteries to work, they proved to be a more practical entertainment choice than radios for those without electricity or those living in rural areas, making them accessible not only to the Muslim middle classes but also to the Algerian laborers who flocked to Algiers and other port cities in search of work.[94] Record listening turned out to be a more widespread and popular pastime than the authorities previously supposed, revealing the existence of a semi-autonomous Algerian auditory culture and a global market of recorded sound that had thus far escaped French control.

Staff in the Bureau of Native Affairs had long harbored suspicions of Algerian oral culture, for the satirical (and sometimes openly polemical) songs and poems performed by itinerant musicians in souks and Muslim orchestras in private homes too often escaped the colonial state's surveillance web. The new media of 78-rpm records, which could be easily transported, sold and resold, and played in a variety of environments, defied the temporality of live performances by offering listeners the possibility of recreating a sonic experience again and again.[95] Thanks to Radio-Alger's "oriental concerts" and the research of a few savvy staff members in the Sûreté, the colonial state already possessed some knowledge of the vogue for recorded sound in the Maghrib. However, before 1934 many civil servants dismissed phonographs and records as the playthings of the educated Muslim elite, such as the men who performed in El-Moutribia.[96]

---

[94] ANOM 15H32. Le Ministre de l'Intérieur à M. les Préfets, September 27, 1934. Prefects in France responded in limited numbers to this memo, suggesting that colonial authorities took the request more seriously given Algeria's cosmopolitan and multiethnic population.

[95] Miliani, *Sociétaires de l'émotion*, 58–60. French policemen typically learned of these performances only after they ended. See ANOM 2I48. Préfecture d'Alger. Le Gouverneur Général, Direction de la Securité Générale à M. le Préfet du département d'Alger, December 20, 1935. The governor-general asked the Bureau of Native Affairs to analyze a text by the singer Cheihk Mohammed El-Anka performed at a religious ceremony in August 1934.

[96] ANOM 15H32. Département de Constantine, Sûreté Départementale, Commissariat spéciale de Bône. Report dated October 26, 1936, and Le Directeur de la Sécurité Générale à M. le Directeur des Affaires Indigènes au Gouvernement Général, January 26, 1931. During the 1920s, the Bureau of Native Affairs monitored the recording activities of a few Algerian artists who traveled to Europe to record for Continental labels and their North African subsidiaries. Policemen in Bône noted the departure of Mohammed El Kourd and several other musicians for Paris, where they planned to record albums "on the account of Resaici Anouar [sic]." See also ANOM 9H37 GGA Affaires Indigènes. "Note sur la censure artistique," July 1, 1936. In December 1935, another agent proposed the creation of an "artistic censorship committee." Although the Bureau of Native Affairs drafted a proposed law requiring an entry visa for records that remained in a file, the governor's office only developed more concrete proposals for record censorship once sales became linked to foreign subversion.

Although French record companies initially dominated record sales in North Africa, colonial police soon fixed their attention on the Lebanese-Egyptian Baidaphone Company, run by the self-proclaimed "Doctor" Michel Baida and his brothers Pierre and Gabriel from their joint headquarters in Beirut, Cairo, and Berlin. Between 1930 and 1935, Baida attracted the attention of the police as a visible "foreigner" traveling through France's three North African possessions with his German sound engineer Max Printz, where he secured recording contracts with local performers and established a network of distributors to sell Baidaphone records.[97] Citing Baida's relations with a host of unsavory characters, the Algiers Police Prefecture warned regional bureaus in 1935 that he was a likely German spy and that Printz had participated in "contraband sales of weapons" in neighboring Morocco during the First World War.[98]

Even arms trafficking did not compare to the Baidas brothers' supposed subversive trade in Arabic records. In June of 1935, Tunisian authorities overheard gossip that Pierre Baida was planning to smuggle records "clandestinely by car" across the Moroccan-Algerian border to avoid customs duties and inspections at Algerian ports.[99] Although no evidence tied the Baida brothers directly to political agitation, Constantine police reported in January of 1936 that Dr. Bendjelloul, one of the leaders of the Fédération des Elus de Constantine, had recently shared a drink with Michel Baida.[100] If this insistence on the Baidas' subversive intentions appears extreme, the Sûreté possessed one prior example of dangerous trafficking in recorded sound. In 1917, the Interior Ministry discovered that German spies were using phonograph cylinders and records to smuggle communications concerning troop maneuvers and munitions from France into Germany.[101] This precedent, combined with Germany's wartime history of distributing pan-Islamic propaganda to France's colonial armies, convinced many within the security services that the expanding global trade in Arabic records – and particularly Baidaphone records – comprised a covert and sophisticated strategy

---

[97] ANOM 15H32. Renseignement Tunisie. Source: très bonne. A/S du nommé Michel Baida, suspect.

[98] ANOM 15H32. Undated note, "Agents allemands Berlin" and Chef du département de Sûreté d'Alger à M. les Préfets (Cabinet, Police Générale, Sécurité Générale), December 28, 1937. Operating on suspicions of espionage, French authorities in Tunisia "invited" Michel Baida to leave the Regency in January of 1936.

[99] ANOM 15H32. Renseignement A/S du Dr. Pierre Baida, June 17, 1935.

[100] ANOM 15H32. Préfecture de Constantine, section des Affaires Indigènes et de la Police Générale, transmis à M. le Gouverneur Général d'Algérie, Direction Générale des Affaires Indigènes et des Territoires du Sud, January 1936. Labeled "Secret."

[101] CAC 19940500–64. M. le Ministre des Finances à M. le Ministre de l'Intérieur, March 25, 1917, and December 24, 1918.

deployed by France's diplomatic enemies to inflame Algerian nationalism and in turn to undermine French authority in North Africa.

Fears of imported Arabic records inciting political subversion in North Africa became entrenched within the colonial bureaucracy after 1936, when an Algerian agent working for the Bureau of Native Affairs, the Bachaga Smati, produced a detailed study of Arabic-language records and Algerian listening habits and disseminated his findings through a training course for officers. Echoing French tropes about Arabs' natural proclivities for sound, Smati argued that the "traditional taste of Mediterranean peoples for music" and the inexpensive price of phonographs had made records into a popular commodity that transcended the predominantly masculine spaces of cafés to reach into the "cloistered life" of Muslim women, with the result that "there is hardly a *café maure* or family – however modest their condition – that does not have a phonograph and a collection of popular songs."[102] While this vogue for records began harmlessly enough, the popularity of local Maghribi artists soon dwindled in the face of a foreign invasion of Middle Eastern "oriental records" facilitated by the Baida brothers.

According to Smati, Baidaphone records contained elaborate codes of hidden meaning masked beneath "declamations on the beauty and charm of the oriental countries." Polemical phrases such as "my country" (*biladi*) or "homeland" (*al watan*) recurred in song lyrics while Arabic spoken-word recordings featured *hadith* from the Qur'an and phrases such as "you were the best people to appear on the surface of the earth."[103] Algerian musicologists confirm that the transnational Arabic-language record trade transformed North African music and Arabic dialects by introducing novel musical styles and providing Maghribi performers with a new political vocabulary lifted from the Middle Eastern nationalist press, in turn fostering hybrid Algerian musical genres and contributing to the emergence of modern standard Arabic.[104] Yet Smati viewed the resulting transformations to Maghribi music less as the product of benign cross-cultural mixing than as evidence of Algerians' suggestive mentality and ingrained superstitions,

---

[102] ANOM 9H37. Surveillance politique des indigènes. Smati began his investigations into the recording industry in 1936. Earlier versions of the 1937 talk can be found in "Note sur la censure artistique" from July 1, 1936. According to this document, Smati's first report on records dated to December 1935.

[103] ANOM 15H32. Bachagha Smati, Causerie faîte par M. Bachagha Smati au cours de perfectionnement des Affaires Indigènes, "Le disque en langue arabe," February 1937. Civil servants drafted these translations, but little is known about their identity or linguistic skills.

[104] Miliani, "Variations linguistiques," in Dakhlia, ed., *Trames de langues*, 427.

recapitulating a view of native psychology advanced by European physicians since the turn of the century.[105]

To an audience "whose dominant trait remains a profound if unreasonable attachment to Islam," Smati argued, Baidaphone served up "official or unofficial songs of the different Muslim countries: Cherifien hymns, Tunisian, Egyptian, Lebanese, Syrian, Iraqi, etc ... [and] while this might appear anodyne, in fact they inculcate in the native the idea that there exist in the world peoples having his faith ... who have kept more or less the façade of Arab states and who proclaim their desire for liberty in their maternal language and not in that of a foreign *Marseillaise*."[106] The Baidas had tested "the reaction of the public powers" to their propaganda records by slowly introducing into Algeria songs with subtle nationalist or religious themes. Once a performer acquired a following, they sold records with more overtly political lyrics. As an example, Smati cited a recent recording by Elie Baida (a cousin of the Baida brothers) that featured the refrain "Awaken Oriental!" and sought to "captivate and awaken the spirit of the listeners" by nourishing "xenophobia" toward the French.[107]

The Bachaga Smati's analysis of the Arabic-language recording industry encapsulated the mixture of paranoia and pragmatism displayed by colonial bureaucrats and the security services in the face of widespread Algerian record listening and its perceived challenges to French authority. Citing Michel Baida's relations with German politicians from the liberal Gustav Stresseman to the Nazi propaganda minister Joseph Goebbels, Smati portrayed the global distribution of Arabic records as nothing less than an expansive German strategy for geopolitical dominance. Yet even as his report displayed a competent knowledge of the Arabic recording industry, his depiction of ostensibly Christian Lebanese businessmen serving as the vehicles for Nazi-sponsored pan-Islamist and pan-Arab propaganda left logic wanting. Were the Baidas really German pawns, or just ambitious and clever businessmen eager to make a profit?[108]

If the metropolitan security services found the distinction between foreign espionage and internal social disorder relatively clean-cut,

[105] Richard C. Keller, *Colonial Madness: Psychiatry in French North Africa* (Chicago, 2007).
[106] ANOM 15H32. Bachagha Smati, "Le disque en langue arabe," February 1937.
[107] *Ibid.*
[108] *Ibid.* Smati claimed that Jewish merchants were responsible for the vogue for records because of their competitive sales techniques, "easy methods of payment" (layaway), and "large knowledge of native languages." Jewish merchants displayed a complete indifference to the "good or bad influence that a popular record could have on the clientele," Smati believed, making them complicit in this pernicious anti-French propaganda.

Martin Thomas suggests that colonial policymakers struggled to "distinguish between foreign subversion and indigenous resistance to European rule" because the loyalty of their subject population could never be assured. Even after Ben Badis and his Muslim reformist Ulama movement sought out exchanges with influential Middle Eastern clerics during the mid-1930s in order to reclaim a purer, pre-colonial Islamic past, the Algerian governor-general's office possessed little evidence of a direct connection between foreign pan-Islamic propaganda and manifestations of anti-French dissent.[109] When Smati worried about Arabic records inciting nationalist agitation, he disavowed Algerians' political agency by portraying Arabs as passive, superstitious listeners who lacked the intellectual sophistication to resist the entreaties of foreign agents. The Baidas' powers of seduction even extended to Radio-Alger performers Mahieddine Bachetarzi and El-Hadj Mohammed El-Anka, who both traveled to Berlin to record for Baidaphone on the promise of lavish dinners, automobiles, and untold financial rewards.

For these reasons, the Bachaga Smati believed the auditory polemics of Arabic records to be far more dangerous than propaganda disseminated through films or print media, particularly when records passed through Algerian ports without examination by colonial censors. In one notorious example of administrative failure, censors removed the nationalist song "Hymn to the Green Flag" from the popular Egyptian musical film *Tears of Love* before its premiere in Algiers, while a Baidaphone record of the song passed through customs to sell hundreds of copies across the colony.[110] Moreover, records could be played repeatedly for effect, in conjunction with political meetings or simply to permit listeners to memorize their lyrics.

On Smati's urging, policemen and agents in the Bureau of Native Affairs began combing Algerian shops and cafés for subversive, anti-French recordings, compiling deep files on Baidaphone and its local subsidiaries and following cartons of records as they traveled from Constantine to Tlemcen or Algiers to Bône.[111] In 1937, when an Algerian named

---

[109] Thomas, *Empires of Intelligence*, 282. Michael Miller agrees that surveillance reports reveal as much about the fears, prejudices, and incapacities of policemen than they do about the objects of their surveillance. Michael B. Miller, *Shanghai on the Metro: Spies, Intrigue, and the French Between the Wars* (Berkeley, 1994), 76–77, 83.

[110] ANOM 9H37. Note sur la censure artistique, July 1, 1936. Film imports required a visa, permitting those "containing spoken or sung passages that attacked French sovereignty" to be suppressed or edited, but the same was not true for records. The Bureau of Native Affairs had drafted a proposed law requiring a visa for records several years earlier, but the project lapsed.

[111] ANOM 15H32. Centre d'information et d'études, December 14, 1936. The Bureau of Native Affairs compiled a file on Baida's nephew Theodore Khayat, who ran the family business in Constantine and neighboring Tunisia.

Boulbina tried to sell a collection of records produced by the little-known Diamophone label to Radio-Alger, the police interrogated him and learned that Diamophone's owner, the Constantine-based merchant Taieb ben Amor, was "in relations with Dr. Baida," and placed him under surveillance.[112] The staff of the Bureau of Native Affairs then began to transcribe and translate the lyrics of hundreds of Diamophone records (and those of other labels), underlining particularly subversive passages in red. Unlike radio broadcasts that escaped the eyes of colonial censors, records appeared to contain a precise script that could be lifted off the vinyl, transcribed, and analyzed.[113]

However, producing definitive interpretations of song lyrics remained challenging amid the social and political turmoil of the mid-1930s, when Muslim and "nationalist" organizations remained highly fragmented and Algerian political figures competed for political influence. Colonial bureaucrats sought to identify nationalist activity by linking anti-French behavior to specific political organizations (typically the "militant" Muslim Ulama or the Etoile Nord-Africaine), although Algerians confounded their efforts by modifying their political rhetoric or shifting their political allegiances. In this volatile political climate, the very definitions of the terms "nation," "religion," and "community" used in political songs relied upon the identity of the singer and the precise context in which they were uttered, factors that only a few savvy colonial agents understood.[114] This situation complicated the work of record translators, particularly when they possessed little knowledge of Arabic dialects spoken outside the Maghrib or lacked the cultural capital to understand slang.[115] A un-authored report analyzing Baidaphone record translations in the files of the Bureau of Native Affairs highlighted numerous errors in the transcriptions, noting

---

[112] ANOM 5I54. Centre d'information et d'études. Renseignement A/S des Etablissements Taieb ben Amor de Constantine, December 29, 1937; ANOM 15H32, Lettre de Louis Millot, Directeur Général des Affaires Indigènes, January 14, 1938.

[113] Miliani, *Sociétaires de l'émotion*, 58–60. French policemen typically learned of these performances only after they ended. See ANOM 2I48. Le Gouverneur Général, Direction de la Securité Générale à M. le Préfet du département d'Alger, December 20, 1935.

[114] James McDougall, *History and the Culture of Nationalism in Algeria* (Cambridge, 2006).

[115] ANOM 15H32. Affaires Indigènes, unauthored note from April 1, 1938. This evaluation of the Diamophone record translations in the files of the Bureau of Native Affairs suggested the translator(s) had made plentiful errors in their "purely phonetic" transliterations. Not only did the translator incorrectly attach syllables to words, but he also ignored the songs' informal structure, which employed simple rhyming phrases, and in turn misinterpreted their intent. Bachtarzi used the argument of mistranslation as his defense in when the governor's office accused him of singing "tendentious" songs in the late 1930s. See Bachetarzi, *Mémoires*, 173. Le Pautremat argues colonial civil servants' language skills could not adequately meet the needs of the administration. Le Pautremat, *La politique musulmane de la France au XXᵉ siècle*, 312.

that the songs' "esoteric language" and use of parables to convey a message made it "difficult to understand word-for-word Arabic songs and often impossible to get a hold of their true, *hidden* meaning."[116]

Amid the wave of strikes, political demonstrations, and street violence that accompanied the Popular Front's arrival into political power in the summer of 1936, colonial officials continued to rely on time-honored methods of visual surveillance to contain Algeria's burgeoning auditory culture, with civil servants attempting to link "dangerous" records to politically suspect individuals. Such was the case with an infamous record produced by the local North African label Rsaissi. In December of 1937, the head of the Sûreté in Algiers warned police prefects across the colony that the Algeriaphone shop had sold an estimated forty Rsaissi records bearing the false label "Piano solo 65075A/65075B." The record did not contain a piano selection but instead featured a song by an unknown vocalist singing the lyrics "Muslims, listen to me, join the Association; get rid of this mentality with which you are afflicted [and] unite together so that we might chase away our enemies and make religion live again." The song also enjoined Algerians to purchase *El Ouma*, the newspaper of the Parti du Peuple Algérien (Algerian People's Party), confirming policemen's fears that record listening encouraged political dissidence.[117] Coming just a few months after Messali Hadj had reconstituted the banned Etoile Nord-Africaine as the Parti du Peuple Algérien, this discovery confirmed the ties between record listening and the rise of political dissidence in Algeria. In an attempt to slow the diffusion of the *Piano Solo* record across the colony, police interrogated its primary distributor, a Swiss-German national named Jean Zupiger, who reportedly employed an Algerian named Bechir with ties to the leading Ulama Tawfiq al-Madani.[118] That Anouar Rsaissi, the owner of the local Rsaissi label and a Baidaphone distributor, was a reputed "Lothario" with an avowed Neo-Destourian (Tunisian nationalist) brother only further substantiated the seditious intent of the *Piano Solo* record.[119]

[116] CARAN F60-707. Note pour M. le Secrétaire Général de la Présidence du Conseil, July 25, 1939.
[117] ANOM 4I66. Préfecture d'Alger. Service des liaisons nord-africaines. Le Chef du Département de Sûreté d'Alger à MM le Préfets (Cabinet, Police Générale, Direction de la Sûreté Général), December 28, 1937.
[118] ANOM 15H32. Centre d'information et d'études, November 16, 1939. Police detained Zupiger repeatedly but never arrested him, even after placing him on the notorious Carnet B (a list of foreigners to be deported in case of war) in 1937 for distributing Nazi propaganda.
[119] ANOM 15H32. Centre d'information et d'études. November 11, 1940. In the 1920s, Rsaissi built up a two million-franc business for Baidaphone in Tunis, Constantine, and Bône, earning the gift of a Mercedes as a reward, before breaking from the company in 1930. See also Hadj Miliani, "Le cheik et le phonographe: Notes de recherche pour un

Over the next few years, policemen fanned out across the colony in search of the *Piano Solo* record, attempting to track its distribution to record merchants in regional cities and then on to individual *cafés maures*, restaurants, market stalls, and brothels in the tiniest villages.[120] The fact that a "clientele in the countryside" now listened to records alarmed the colonial state, which had thus far targeted urban areas for surveillance.[121] As if to confirm the authorities' worst fears, the *Piano Solo* record turned up across Algeria, and police searches found additional Rsaissi records bearing false labels, including one song misattributed to the popular *malouf* singer Mohammed El Kourd and titled "I Weep Alone for My Country" (tr. *Abki biladia*). The song demanded the suppression of the repressive *code indigénat* and included "seditious" phrases such as "If God grants us our wishes ... we will be delivered from our enemies and all of our sorrows" and "Oh Muslims, awaken yourselves from your slumber."[122] The "care with which these labels were forged proves the criminal intent of the editors," the police chief in Constantine wrote to the Algiers Police Prefecture in 1938.[123] Backed by the 1935 Régnier decree, which criminalized "anti-French" activity and "civil disorder" incited by Algerians and "foreigners," colonial police invaded cafés across the colony, seizing records and demanding that proprietors inform on their clientele. In 1938, police in Constantine, Phillipeville, and Bône closed three cafes for a month after uncovering *Piano Solo* and other seditious records inside.[124] Record listening, which Algerian café habitués and their families once enjoyed as a benign evening pleasure, now placed Algerians under the greater scrutiny of the state, further fueling authorities' fears about the dangers of radio broadcasting.

corpus de phonogrammes et des vidéogrammes des musiques et chansons algériennes," *Les Cahiers du CRASC*, 8, 4, 43–67.

[120] ANOM 2I48. Le Sous-Préfet, Commissaire de Police de Médéa à M. le Sous-Préfet des Affaires Indigènes d'Alger, October 29, 1938; the Rapport de Commissaire de Police, ville de Tizi-Ouzou, October 29, 1938; ANOM 15H32, Le Préfet de Constantine à M. le Gouverneur Général d'Algérie, Direction de la Sécurité Générale, September 1, 1938.

[121] ANOM 5I54. Préfecture d'Oran. Service des liaisons nord-africaines. Response to questionnaire, July 1937.

[122] ANOM 15H32. Rapport du Police d'Etat d'Alger. December 30, 1937.

[123] ANOM 15H32. Rapport du Chef de la Police Spéciale de Constantine, Surveillance politique des indigènes, September 8, 1938.

[124] John Ruedy, *Modern Algeria: The Origins and Development of a Nation* (Bloomington, 1992), 140. ANOM 2I48. Préfecture d'Alger. Administration des indigenes. M. le Sous-Préfet de Médéa à M. le Préfet d'Alger, March 22, 1938; 15H32. Préfecture de Constantine à M. le Gouverneur Général d'Algérie, Direction de la Sécurité Générale, Alger, September 1, 1938.

Fugitive sound: tracking "native" radio listeners

The colonial administration's obsession with tracking and confiscating politically "subversive" Arabic records betrayed civil servants' persistent fears about the nefarious influence of broadcast sound – and particularly "oriental music" – on Algerian minds. Although colonial authorities consistently failed to observe Algerians in the act of listening to radio broadcasts, records provided a means to capture and render legible the intangible qualities of broadcast sound. During a training course for staff in the Bureau of Native Affairs in February of 1937, the agent Delahaye reminded agents of its "essentially fugitive" character: "the radio broadcast has liberated itself from the ties that bind the written word, crossing the most protected borders, the most firmly closed doors, and the thickest walls" to the point that "nothing can stop it except jamming."[125]

Thanks to summaries of radio programs provided by the state's Paris-based listening service and reports from the security services, by 1937 colonial authorities had amassed considerably more data about the structure and content of propaganda broadcasts and the technical capacities of foreign transmitters. Radio-Bari redoubled its attacks on France's North African possessions after a brief hiatus following the 1935 Laval-Mussolini Accords, while Radio-Seville and Radio Tétouan urged North Africans to rally behind Franco.[126] Bureaucrats now knew that Radio-Bari, Radio-Seville, and even Radio-Cairo all introduced their news reports with concerts of "oriental music" to attract listeners, suggesting a direct correlation between Algerian record consumption and increased radio listening.[127] In September of 1937, after the *Gazette de la Maritime* reported that Italian spies had begun distributing fixed-frequency receivers in Algeria and Morocco tuned to Radio-Bari's frequency, colonial police began recording the manufacturer, model number, and provenance of the radio receivers

[125] ANOM 10 APOM 830. Delahaye, "Les émissions de langue arabe du poste Radio PTT-Alger."
[126] SHD 7N4093. Etat-Major de l'Armée. "La radiodiffusion en Afrique du Nord," Bulletin des renseignements de questions musulmanes, October 14, 1937; Thomas, *The French Empire Between the Wars*, 316–19. The Iberian Anarchist Federation, which seized control of a Barcelona station in September of 1936, called upon Muslim troops to rise up against their colonial oppressors in a jihad. Army reports claimed that these broadcasts had provoked small rebellions within the Armée d'Afrique.
[127] SHD 7N4095. Etat-Major de l'Armée. The army's *Revue analytique* published summaries of Radio-Bari's broadcasts, which typically lasted thirty minutes. One December 1937 broadcast began with ten minutes of music followed by a lecture on Muslim law in Sicily and a twenty-minute "news" report on the Neo-Destour nationalist movement in Tunisia and nationalist advances in Spain.

they found in Algerian hands.[128] Simply owning an Italian- or German-made radio became enough to implicate an Algerian in nationalist politics. As a policeman in Aumale wrote to his superior, "during our operations we found in the café of Mohammed El Imam ... a radio of a German label, purchased from an agent of the merchant Meyzoret and Zupiger in Algiers ... [and] it is well know that this establishment is one of the preferred meeting places for sympathizers of the Algerian People's Party."[129] The Maison Zupiger, of course, had previously fallen under suspicion for selling the seditious *Piano Solo* record.

The files complied by the colonial state between 1935 and 1938 over-flowed with contradictory reports about Algerian radio listening as police-men, civil servants, and municipal authorities disagreed about the degree to which foreign propaganda influenced local populations. Policemen who visited a café at the appointed hour of a Radio-Bari broadcast might hear no Arabic emerging from radio loudspeakers, but later uncover rumors of people tuning into the news bulletins. As one anon-ymous report directed to the Bureau of Native Affairs concluded in 1937, "in the different sales outlets for radios in Oran nearly all the natives coming in to purchase a radio ask for one capable of picking up the Cairo station. Some even demand BOMBAY." These requests signaled Algerians' growing desire to participate in the wider world outside the sphere of French control. Yet the very same report concluded that foreign broadcasts had not as yet exerted a "*profoundly* harmful influence" on the native mentality, for "it is undeniable that the local broadcasts of Radio-Alger are followed with interest."[130]

Disagreements between staff in the various branches of the colonial administration about radio listening pivoted around two key problems. First, colonial civil servants could not settle on the number and type of radios in Algerian hands, and consequently, the social class of the Algerian radio audience. Algerian radio ownership rose dramatically from 2,000 receivers in July of 1937 to 2,966 in March of 1938 – a startling increase matched by a growth in the number of "public" radios in use.[131] In Bône, forty-seven radios could be heard in cafés, whereas

[128] ANOM 15H31. GGA Affaires Indigènes. "Note dans la partie du sans-filisme," Blida, July 31, 1938.
[129] ANOM 2I48. Commissariat de Police d'Aumale. Number 1461, July 2, 1938. The Maison Zupiger, somewhat ironically, still operated in Algiers in the early 1950s, even advertising its products in *Ici Alger: revue des émissions arabe et kabyle de Radio-Algérie*.
[130] ANOM 5I54. Département d'Oran. Services des liaisons nord-africaines. Memo on "Emissions radiophoniques," July 10, 1937.
[131] ANOM 15H31. Report on "Emissions radiophoniques," July 1, 1937, and the Déclarations d'appareils récepteurs de radiodiffusion. Relevé, par bureau de poste, des auditeurs indigènes et européens. March 31, 1938.

only thirty-six individual Algerians owned home receivers.[132] In Constantine, thirty-five public radios broadcast to listeners in *café maures* and restaurants.[133] Radio sales would be even higher in Oran, one agent noted, if "merchants did not demand the full price of a radio upon its delivery." However, the all-wave radios required to receive the short-wave broadcasts of Radio-Bari were found only among "native notables and several well-off functionaries," thus diffusing the enormous danger posed by the Italian station's broadcasts.[134]

Policemen and staff in the Bureau of Native Affairs also disagreed about whether Algerians could understand the "literary" (i.e. classical) Arabic employed by the announcers of foreign stations, since most of the working-class Algerian population spoke Arabic or Berber dialects and the foreign stations (whether Radio-Bari or Radio-Seville) typically hired announcers of Middle Eastern descent. According to the subprefect of Tizi-Ouzou, very few people in his region could understand the polemics of Radio-Seville, for a "broadcast in Arabic, is generally speaking, for the Kabyle listeners, less interesting than listening in French."[135] Historians disagree about whether the nineteenth-century colonial state deliberately fostered illiteracy in Arabic in order to promote Algerian assimilation to French values, but the fact that multiple interwar "nationalist" movements promoted the Arabization of Algeria's populations in their political platforms aroused suspicions among French authorities. In 1933, Messali Hadj had reclaimed Arabic as the "official" language of Algeria in the Etoile Nord-Africaine's manifesto, while the Ulama made reviving the Qur'anic language a centerpiece of their desired religious renewal by offering private Arabic courses to Algerians.[136] However, as a report from the army's General Staff concluded in 1937, illiteracy did not necessarily prohibit reception when so many Algerians gathered to listen in *cafés maures*, where a single individual could translate a foreign program to a crowd gathered around a loudspeaker. Moreover, even the most educated, assimilated middle-class Algerians might prove susceptible to

---

[132] ANOM 15H31. Relevé numérique des postes récepteurs de radiodiffusion existant dans le département de Constantine. October 5, 1938.

[133] ANOM 15H31. Rapport de Guilhermet, Police Spéciale Départementale de Constantine à M. le Directeur des Affaires Indigènes, April 14, 1938.

[134] ANOM 15H31. Report on "Emissions radiophoniques," July 1, 1937.

[135] ANOM 2I48. Le Sous-Préfet de Tizi-Ouzou à M. le Préfet d'Alger, November 18, 1938. Policemen reported similar incidents involving records. ANOM 15H-32. Romatet, le Commissaire Général de Police à Tlemcen à M. le Préfet. January 13, 1938. A Tlemcen policeman reported listeners' enthusiasm for a record of the "Egyptian National Anthem," but given that the "the majority of the natives in the region, who only know imperfectly the language in which it is performed, mistake it for the 'Algerian National Anthem,'" this explained the song's popularity.

[136] Messaoudi, "The Teaching of Arabic," 297–317.

the entreaties of foreign announcers. "The current listeners who belong to the most evolved classes are very sensitive," the author claimed, and "lacking a critical mind, they are often considerably taken with adverse propaganda and in turn reproduce these harmful ideas among the popular classes, who are very easily influenced."[137]

Taken together, these documents reveal more about the fears and suspicions of colonial civil servants, their varied linguistic and cultural competencies, and the incomplete and ever-shifting nature of colonial hegemony than they do about Algerian listening habits or the effects of foreign radio propaganda on Algerian politics. Both Claude Collot and Charles-Robert Ageron point to the general disorganization of the colonial civil services (police, Native Affairs, municipal governance) and the poor education of lower-level French administrators and their Algerian reinforcements.[138] Although the colonial state offered annual salary subsidies for Arabic proficiency, in 1938 only seventy individuals (excluding interpreters and Arabic teachers) received the bonus for their ability to write in Arabic, alongside another 300 for conversational skills in dialectical Arabic or Kabyle.[139]

These statistics illuminate why the modern, oral medium of radio challenged the observational capacities of civil servants as well as the colonial state's reliance on visual observation and rumor to generate knowledge, or alternatively, on direct surveillance and mediated queries through Algerian informants, none of which proved entirely effective. Thus the police commissioner of Cherchell, fully accepting the veracity of his informants' data, wrote to the prefect of Algiers that "in the conversations I have had with several natives who own a radio receiver, I had the very clear impression that none of them paid much attention to the talks and news broadcast by wireless, preferring oriental music," while the subprefect of Médéa claimed that native informants were unlikely to be truthful about their listening habits and that even direct surveillance failed to catch Algerians listening to subversive broadcasts in public.[140] However, if the Bureau of Native Affairs consistently sought out direct physical evidence of radio's impact on

---

[137] CARAN F60-710. Etat-Major de l'Armée, section d'outre-mer. Note sur la radiodiffusion en pays musulmanes, 1937.
[138] Ageron, Les algériens musulmans et la France, esp. 612–43; and Collot, Les institutions d'Algérie durant la période coloniale, 50–129.
[139] CARAN F60-702. Gouverneur Général d'Algérie, Direction des Affaires Indigènes et des Territoires du Sud, Deuxième bureau, Administration générale. Note sur l'extension de la connaissance des langues indigènes parmi les fonctionnaires et même parmi les divers éléments de la population européenne. March 1, 1938.
[140] ANOM 2I41. Préfecture d'Alger. Le Commissaire de Police de Cherchell à M. le Préfet (Affaires Indigènes-Police générale), Alger, July 6, 1938; Le Sous-Préfet de Médéa à M. le Préfet d'Alger (Affaires Indigènes-Police générale), January 10, 1939.

Algerian politics, members of the army's radio-goniometry services who listened to foreign propaganda broadcasts required no such proof.

By the autumn of 1937, staff in the army's information and intelligence services began to worry about the effects of foreign propaganda on the morale of North African troops in the Armée d'Afrique, and called upon Parisian politicians to adopt more proactive counterpropaganda measures. Invoking the cliché of the *téléphone arabe*, a reservist captain in Algiers mailed a quasi-hysterical letter to the headquarters of the state radio administration in Paris, describing how "rumors spread within Islam that France is afraid of Mussolini."[141] The indigenous French- and Arabic-language press further fueled European fears about Algerian listeners by printing summaries of foreign propaganda broadcasts. "In periods of political tension or in case of a European war, a campaign of false news unleashed by enemy powers could have grave consequences if we have no means of protection," one army report cautioned, making it "necessary to put into place an organization permitting us not only to protect the natives under our guardianship, but even more to exert a positive action over them."[142] Despite the vast scope of the colonial state's surveillance web – which stretched from the cities of Algiers, Constantine, and Oran to tiny communes such as Bou-Sâada – radio listening remained highly individualized, and therefore difficult to measure and control. Even worse, by challenging the loyalties of indigenous troops, broadcast sound not only threatened domestic political stability in Algeria but also the territorial security of France, demonstrating the need to shore up the borders of the "radio nation" in the airwaves over North Africa.

Remaking the voice of France in the Mediterranean

The summer of 1936 – bracketed by the May elections that ushered the left-leaning Popular Front coalition into political power and the start of the Spanish Civil War – transformed metropolitan policymakers' attitudes toward foreign radio propaganda in the Maghrib. The long-term psychological effects of foreign propaganda on the "native" mentality notwithstanding, the Ministry of Defense worried that the conflict in Spain, as the first major European war in which radio propaganda played

---

[141] CARAN F60-710. Le Directeur du Service de la radiodiffusion à M. le Président du Conseil, November 27, 1937.
[142] CARAN F60-710. Note sur la radiodiffusion en pays musulmanes from the Etat-Major de l'Armée, section d'outre-mer, 1937. Similar extracts in ANOM 15H32. Ministère de la Défense Nationale et de la Guerre. Bulletin des renseignements des questions musulmanes, October 14, 1937.

a central role, might spread into Morocco and then engulf the entire region.[143] Right-wing politicians now joined colonial lobbying groups, who had for years campaigned to expand imperial broadcasting, in demanding that the state rebut the entreaties of Radio-Bari and Radio-Seville.[144] In October 1936, the newly elected premier Léon Blum responded to the flurry of correspondence that landed on his desk from the Ministries of Colonies, Foreign Affairs, and War by calling for the creation of a centralized committee to develop an Arabic-language broadcasting policy, a task, he believed, that could not be left to individual colonial administrators since it concerned all of North Africa.[145]

During the First World War, the Colonial and War ministries had demanded a coordinated "Muslim policy" to respond to German-sponsored propaganda in North Africa and the Middle East, but only after foreign radio propaganda exposed the potential links between indigenous nationalism, pan-Arabism, and fascism did legislators take definitive steps to coordinate counterpropaganda, political surveillance, and defense for the region.[146] In January of 1937, Blum recalled to life the dormant Haut Comité Méditerranéen (Mediterranean High Committee, or HCM) – an advisory body whose members included the reform-minded Maghribi sociologist Charles-André Julien, former colonial governors-general Maurice Violette and Albert Sarraut, and representatives from relevant cabinet ministries – by granting it a permanent secretariat. Charged with formulating strategies to shore up security in the Maghrib by "seeking out the most efficacious means of defense against the Muslim peril that exalts communism, espionage … pan-Islamic propaganda, [and] nationalist dreams," the HCM became a clearinghouse for security analysis and policy formation in North Africa.[147] Radio featured prominently on the HCM's agenda, given that Arabic-language broadcasting

---

[143] Davies, "The First Radio War," 473–513.

[144] F. Soulier-Valbert, "Il faut un budget de radio coloniale," *La France outre-mer*, November 11, 1937.

[145] CAC 1987071425. Copie d'une lettre de Marius Moutet, le Ministre des Colonies à M. le Ministre des Affaires Etrangères, August 13, 1936. Moutet worried about Radio-Bari's "very tendentious" reporting on the Constantine pogroms of 1934 and Zeezen's broadcasts that commented on partisan political violence in Paris in 1935. German and Soviet broadcasts could both be heard in West Africa. CARAN F60-710. Propagande par radio en Afrique du Nord, October 20, 1936. Blum signaled his agreement to a proposal by the general secretary of the Haut Comité Méditerranéen.

[146] Le Pautremat, *La politique musulmane de la France*, 354; Thomas, *The French Empire Between the Wars*, 316–19.

[147] William A. Hoisington, Jr., "France and Islam: The Haut Comité Méditerranéen and French North Africa," in George Joffé, ed., *North Africa: Nation, State, and Region* (London, 1993), 80–82. ANOM 3CAB-35. Haut Comité Méditerranéen et de l'Afrique du Nord. Session de mars 1937. Pierre Laval appointed the first HCM in 1935 in response to parliamentary pressure for more coordinated North African policy.

had exposed the linguistic incompetency of colonial civil servants and the failures of the colonial state's surveillance mechanisms – both factors that would contribute to the restructuring of the Algerian Bureau of Native Affairs in May 1937.[148]

Discussions between the members of the Haut Comité Méditerranéen and a host of cabinet subcommittees over North African broadcasting policies continued from the fall of 1936 into the spring of 1938, and provoked a series of fierce turf battles between Parisian politicians and colonial authorities over who had the right to direct Arabic-language counterpropaganda. Although the Popular Front would prove to be no less imperialist than previous governments, colonial reforms designed to quell nationalist unrest took center stage on the government's agenda, albeit subordinated to the larger goal of fighting fascism.[149] In December 1936, the socialist Marceau Pivert, the Popular Front's media adviser, cautioned Blum about Radio-Alger's "fascist" politics and the "excessive privilege" enjoyed by European elites in the Amicale, as well as the station's tendency to extract news reports from the right-wing newspapers *La Dépêche algérienne* and *La Presse libre*, which "have reproduced the communiqués of Radio-Seville and General Franco since the beginning of the Spanish Civil War."[150] Nor were Pivert's concerns about the political sympathies of colonial elites unfounded. Military intelligence reports suggested that Radio-Bari and Radio-Seville already exerted an influence over the Italian population living in Tunisia and Morocco. In September of 1937, the Sûreté noted that Oran's right-leaning mayor, the Abbé Lambert, had given a talk on Radio-Seville in which he "compared General Franco to Joan of Arc" and enjoined citizens to embrace the cause of Nationalist Spain.[151] Was it any wonder, Pivert asked, that Radio-Alger had failed in its "role as the educator of the Muslim population?"[152]

---

[148] CARAN F60-710. Réunion du Sous-commission des affaires musulmanes, December 16, 1937. This committee predated the HCM but was subsumed into it in 1937. Charles-Andre Julien complained that the linguistic incapacities of French colonial civil servants in North Africa exacerbated the security challenges posed by transnational broadcasting.

[149] Thomas, *Empires of Intelligence*, 273–81; Benjamin Stora, *Nationalistes algériens et révolutionnaires français au temps de Front Populaire* (Paris, 1987), 52–53.

[150] CARAN F60-739. "La radiodiffusion en Algérie," un-authored and undated report written by Marceau Pivert (ca. December 1936).

[151] CARAN F60-710. Fava Verde, le Commissariat divisionnaire de Fes. Note de renseignement confidentiel, September 12, 1937. In the same file, see A.P., "Une propagande dangereuse: Le maire d'Oran au micro de Radio-Séville," *La Dépêche marocaine*, September 15–16, 1937. For right-wing politics in Algeria, see Samuel Kalman, "Le combat par tous les moyens: Colonial Violence and the Extreme Right in 1930s Oran," *French Historical Studies*, 34, 1, 2011, 125–53.

[152] CARAN F60-739. "La radiodiffusion en Algérie," un-authored and undated report, likely written by Marceau Pivert (ca. December 1936).

Pivert's arguments received further ammunition after PTT minister Robert Jardillier dispatched the radio administrator Marcel Pellenc to North Africa to investigate the "reach" of Radio-Alger and metropolitan stations across the region.[153] Although Pellenc lacked specialist knowledge of North African cultures, his final report painted a dismal picture of the airwaves over North Africa, where French stations, received intermittently during the day if more clearly in the evenings, were drowned out by Arabic propaganda broadcasts. "It is sufficient to have seen at the hour of the Arabic broadcasts, in any Arab town, the natives gather round ... the shop door of a merchant with a radio ... and remain there," Pellenc wrote, to understand the potential impact of propaganda on an economically distraught and superstitious population "always ready to be guided by its instincts, its religious passions, [and] its beliefs ... so cleverly exploited by foreign agents." Although Radio-Maroc and the privately run Radio-Tunis each broadcast programs for several hours a day, Pellenc judged Radio-Alger to be the most important North African station, even though it lacked the cultural resources and technical capacity to serve the entire region. France "has with radio perhaps the sole means to peacefully win over the Arab mind and maintain its influence, already unfortunately compromised ... in its North African empire," he concluded, but the solution lay in coordinating counterpropaganda initiatives in Paris and putting radios "in the hands of the masses."[154]

Before the ink had dried on the report, the newly appointed governor-general Albert LeBeau dispatched a series of missives to Paris denouncing Pellenc's findings. Condemning Parisian radio announcers for reporting on North African politics with little regard for the impact of their words on colonial populations, LeBeau insisted that metropolitan radio programmers lacked sufficient knowledge of Maghribi affairs to produce politically safe propaganda broadcasts. Moreover, any North Africans recruited as Arabic-language announcers from Paris would "already be won over by the ideals of nationalism and xenophobic sentiments" against the French, a position supported by the security services.[155] LeBeau

[153] Méadel, *Histoire de la radio*, 116–17. Shortly after arriving in power, Robert Jardillier orchestrated an investigation of Marcel Pellenc's activities during his tenure as the director of radio broadcasting, which ended with Pellenc's demotion to Inspector General, a position he held until the war.

[154] CARAN F60-710. Marcel Pellenc, "Etude sur la radiodiffusion nord-africaine," December 7, 1936. Pellenc called for the construction of a North African radio network (with new stations in Oran and Tunis) linked by telephone lines to metropolitan transmitters.

[155] F60-710. Albert LeBeau, Gouverneur Général d'Algérie à M. le Ministre des PTT, December 8, 1936; Le Ministère de l'Intérieur, le Directeur du Contrôle et Comptabilité des Affaires Algériennes à Robert Jardiller, le Ministre des PTT, January 4, 1937.

eventually capitulated to Parisian demands for the creation of an advisory board to govern Radio-Alger, but he fixed its membership by decree to ensure that he could appoint two-thirds of its members.[156] Many Europeans interpreted this bureaucratic dispute over the "voice" of Algeria as a microcosm of a larger battle unfolding over control of the colony itself. In the months leading up to the sole election for Radio-Alger's advisory board, Europeans listened to Maurice Violette defend the Popular Front's proposal to extend citizenship to 25,000 Muslim men over the microphones of Radio-Paris, while the right-wing colonial press denounced Radio-Liberté for filling its list with unapologetic *indigénophiles* who would allow Algerian "nationalists" on the airwaves.[157] In Paris, the far right newspapers *Gringoire* and *La Libre parole* backed the settlers' position while condemning the Popular Front's failure to organize sufficient counterpropaganda.[158] Radio-Liberté, for its part, promised to use Radio-Alger to combat "the propaganda directed ... at our Muslim brothers by Radio-Bari."[159] Unsurprisingly, the former Amicale's conservative list handily won the radio elections of 1937.

However, policymakers on both sides of the Mediterranean did agree on one matter: that the entreaties of Radio-Seville, which promised Muslim listeners that the "government of Burgos would improve their lot" in exchange for supporting the nationalists, posed the most immediate danger to security in Algeria, while Radio-Bari threatened the status quo in Tunisia. In February of 1937, Le Beau ordered the installation of a temporary jamming station in Oran to block Seville's wavelength. The Ministry of Foreign Affairs debuted a trial of news broadcasts in Arabic (lifted directly from the state's official *Radio-Journal de France*) on the coastal station Marseille-Provence PTT and on the short wave Poste Colonial designed to counteract the foreign

---

[156] Jean Foussat, President of the Amicale de Radio PTT-Alger, "Rapport Moral de 1936," *Alger-Radio*, March 7, 1937. In September 1937, LeBeau created a Conseil Supérieur de Radiodiffusion, appointed directly by his office, to oversee Radio-Alger's programs. See ANOM 15H32. Gouverneur Général d'Algérie, Arrêté du 15 septembre 1937 modifié par arrêté du 11 mars 1938.

[157] "Dans une allocution radiodiffusée, M. Violette défend son projet de représentation parlementaire des indigènes," *La Dépêche de Constantine*, January 28, 1937. See also "Les élections à Radio-Alger," *La Libre parole*, May 4, 1937, 6.

[158] François Robin, "La radio française sur la botte," *Gringoire*, November 5, 1937. ANOM 4I66. Radio-Liberté's list included two Algerians – the lawyer Robert Amrouche and Mahieddine Bachetarzi. The anti-Semitic Algiers daily *La Défense* offered a scathing critique of Radio-Liberté on December 3, 1937, describing a recent meeting where the president Leon Weinmann spoke in Arabic before introducing Cheikh El-Okbi and Cheikh BenBadis, the leader of the reformist *Ulama* and Amar Ouzegane, the regional secretary of the PCF.

[159] "Notre association," *Radio-Liberté*, March 3, 1938.

transmitters.[160] Yet over the course of the next year, two radically divergent perspectives about North African broadcasting and indigenous listeners emerged.

In October 1937, the HCM advised Camille Chautemps, who headed the Popular Front's second government, that Arabic-language counter-propaganda should be coordinated and directed from Paris, with the goal of attracting a mass audience of Muslim listeners, a decision supported by the PTT and Ministry of Foreign Affairs.[161] To this end, lawmakers voted credits for the construction of a powerful new radio transmitter in Tunis to cover much of the Maghrib, and ordered the construction of a more powerful transmitter for the short-wave Poste Colonial, to be rechristened Paris-Mondial. The short-wave station's broadcasts, which debuted in April of 1938, were intended to transmit a distinctly "French perspective" on global affairs through broadcasts in multiple European languages, while providing a synthetic daily news report in Arabic that clarified French diplomatic policies across the Muslim world.[162]

Despite the inherent paternalism of these counterpropaganda measures designed to "protect France's subjects," the war of the airwaves in the Mediterranean forced colonial propagandists to rethink their earlier preconceptions about radio sound as a malleable weapon of social control, and even more significantly, to acknowledge North African listeners as political subjects whose sensibilities might not be so easily manipulated. When the under-secretary of state, François de Tessan, pressed his colleagues to "re-baptize" the Poste Colonial in 1938, he argued that its former name – too reminiscent of colonial oppression – would never

[160] ANOM 15H32. Ministère de la Défense et de la Guerre. Etat-Major de l'Armée, section outre-mer, Bulletin des renseignements des questions musulmanes, July 1, 1937.
[161] AN F60-710. J.B. Lebas, Le Ministre des PTT à M. le Président du Conseil, Secrétariat Général, August 18, 1937. Lebas argued that Algerian elites who owned personal radio receivers could understand "most of the news included in the programs of metropolitan stations." It was therefore imperative to "organize public listening or to facilitate the natives' acquisition of receivers." A summary of the HCM's work on the subject appears in F60-704. Haut Comité Méditerranéen et de l'Afrique du Nord, session de mars 1938. Rapport n. 2: La radiodiffusion en Afrique du Nord et dans les pays d'Islam. See also Frédéric Brunnquell, Fréquence monde, 34–42. In November 1936, Jardillier authorized ten million francs from the PTT budget to construct Radio-Tunis, but later abandoned the project. Legislators later accused him of subordinating France's overseas interests to his metropolitan radio projects.
[162] CARAN F60-710. Note sur la propagande par radio en Afrique du Nord, October 20, 1936. Paris-Mondial's broadcasts were produced by a team consisting of Jean Fraisse, the former cabinet secretary to Albert Sarraut; the left-leaning reporters Georges Pioch and Henri Jeanson; and several mainstream journalists such as Frédéric Pottecher. See André Moosmann, Histoire des émissions internationales, 35–38.

attract Muslim audiences, whereas Paris-Mondial would communicate France's distinctly republican and "universal values."[163]

Rejecting the metropolitan viewpoint, staff in the Bureau of Native Affairs continued to resist any broadcasting initiatives they believed would further "Arabize the indigenous population of North Africa" or generate political unity among Algeria's ethnically diverse population. Despite the fact that colonial bureaucrats' early vision of creating bifurcated "European" and "native" listening publics had failed, they now applied even more finite categories to Algerian radio audiences: those literate in Arabic (including civil servants, chiefs, and former *madrasa* students); those speaking dialectical Arabic but literate only in French (civil servants who attended French schools and soldiers in the Armée d'Afrique); women and children; Algerian Jews; and the mixed Arab public of *cafés maures*, where literate and illiterate populations intermingled. Moreover, the Bureau of Native Affairs maintained that it had already fulfilled its duties vis-à-vis the Algerian population, and claimed to have transmitted nearly 200 Arabic-language broadcasts by North African speakers between 1935 and early 1937.[164]

Above all, the new "native" broadcasts that debuted on Radio-Alger in the late 1930s demonstrated the colonial government's persistent anxieties about exploiting broadcasting for counterpropaganda purposes and its general reluctance to engage in overtly "political discussions" with an Arab and Berber population whose political loyalties to France remained questionable. To host the programs, Radio-Alger hired Salah Arzour, a young French *diplomé* hailing from Constantine, whose family had worked for the colonial state for several generations, and whose political loyalties appeared unquestionable.[165] Arzour read news broadcasts lifted from the state radio network's nightly *Radio-Journal de France* and introduced a number of Algerian lecturers who spoke on such illuminating subjects as "The Wheat Office" or "The History of the Microscope" as well as arts, antiquities,

---

[163] CARAN F60-702. Haut Comité Méditerranéen, compte-rendu de la séance du samedi matin le 12 mars 1938. Tessan also proposed the name "Radio-universel." See also F60-710. Procès-verbal de la Commission du travail de la radiodiffusion en langue arabe, February 22, 1938. Tessan argued that "we should profit from the construction of the new station to change the name of the Poste Colonial. The name alone suffices to awaken the suspicions of Arabic-language speakers and renders a great part of our efforts sterile before they have begun."

[164] ANOM 10 APOM 830. Delahaye, "Les émissions de langue arabe du poste Radio PTT-Alger."

[165] ANOM G/1B/14/Arzour. Gouvernement Général de l'Algérie, Direction du Personnel. Feuille signalétique. n.d.; Service des liaisons nord-africaines 93/4239 Arzour; and 4I/111/Arzour. Arzour taught in several *lycées* before becoming a civil servant. He worked as Radio-Alger's announcer under the Vichy regime.

literature, and cuisine. A young Algerian woman named Leila Abed offered talks on childcare, hygiene, and Western medicine – a clear attempt to reinforce the *mission cilivilisatrice* among Muslim women. The station provided live reportage from events presumed to be of interest to the Algerian population: sports matches, the departure of ships transporting pilgrims to Mecca, and Ramadan concerts.[166] The languages used for these programs varied from dialectical to literary Arabic, and occasionally included Berber, demonstrating the state's effort to appeal to diverse local constituencies as well as Middle Eastern listeners.[167] The use of literary Arabic, according to one report from the Bureau of Native Affairs, struck a "blow to the prestige of the Ulama" and knocked a "hole in the quasi-superstitious respect the public attached to these savants" by demonstrating that Algerian nationalist or Muslim religious organizations did not hold a "monopoly on the privilege and use of the Arabic language."[168]

However, musical concerts still constituted the bulk of Radio-Alger's "native" programs. The Bureau of Native Affairs forbade the use of Baidaphone recordings on air, but artists whose records previously appeared on censorship lists continued to perform live over the station's microphones. The colonial state banned sales of Mahieddine Bachetarzi's song lyrics in 1937 on the grounds that they contained nationalist propaganda, yet he remained a station regular until 1940.[169] This appeal to popular cultural figures such as Mahieddine, regardless of their ambiguous political sympathies, high-lights colonial bureaucrats' desperation to cultivate listeners for Radio-Alger as the prospect of another European war loomed on the horizon.

Few of Radio-Alger's European audiences heard the new Arabic-language broadcasts as an improvement to the airwaves. They complained in the press about the increased air time given over to potential Muslim audiences, and some even questioned the utility of counterpropaganda. Multiplying the "Arabic language broadcasts without consideration

[166] See Radio-Alger's program listings in *La Presse libre*, February 25, 1937, 6, and March 11, 1937.
[167] ANOM 15H32. Département d'Alger. L'Administrateur principal de la commune mixte de Fort-National à M. le Gouverneur Général d'Algérie, Direction des Affaires Indigènes. Objet: T.S.F. Emission en langue kabyle, November 4, 1936.
[168] ANOM 10 APOM 830. Delahaye, "Les émissions de langue arabe du poste Radio PTT-Alger."
[169] Bachetarzi, *Mémoires*, 332–34. ANOM 5I54. Notes du Centre d'information et d'études, October 11, 1938, and November 24, 1938. Paris-Mondial hired musicians previously suspected of nationalist activity, including Mohammed El-Kamal. On this point, see also SHD 7N4093. Bulletin des renseignements des questions musulmanes, November 16, 1938, 438.

would promote the resurrection of Arabic in opposition to French,"
Edmond Esquirol wrote in *Alger-Radio*, in turn "reinforcing the actions
of certain groups that the governor-general finds worrisome, and by all
means slowing the predominance of French culture, and by consequence,
the much-desired assimilation" of the native population.[170] Nor did the
Algerians whose voices surfaced in the French- and Arabic-language press
appreciate the broadcasts. In the Délégations Financières, Abbenour
Tamzali criticized the broadcasts' repetitive content and the fact that
Radio-Alger possessed no Arabic-language discotheque, forcing it to rely
on loans from local merchants.[171] *El Bassair*, the newspaper of the reformist Ulama movement, proclaimed Radio-Alger to be a "calamity and
danger for good values" and a symbol of the "artificial, licentious, and
amoral Western civilization" forced upon Algerians by the French.[172] The
assimilationist newspapers *La Voix indigène* and *La Défense* similarly complained that the news programs had been sanitized to the point that they
contained no relevant information, but only reported on subjects such as
the "Tricentenary of the Académie Française," topics that were of no
interest to Algerians.[173]

Closing down the airwaves

In 1938 and 1939, colonial police continued their forays into *cafés maures*
to assess Algerians' reception of Radio-Alger's latest programs and the
Arabic news broadcasts of Paris-Mondial. Policemen found that
Algerians could indeed hear Paris-Mondial and tuned in regularly to
Radio-Alger, but they could not determine whether the French broadcasts swayed Algerians from tuning into foreign stations. However, the
chief of police in Blida observed worrying behavior, writing to Algiers that
"yesterday evening . . . one of my native inspectors surprised the owner of
a *café maure* in the process of playing several records of nationalist propaganda." The agent immediately seized the records, but the police chief
remained troubled by the fact that the "customers picked up the refrains
of the chorus," confirming that broadcast sound – whether surfacing from
phonograph or radio speakers – had become the soundtrack to anti-
colonial resistance. By singing along to the refrain on the record,

[170] Edmond Esquirol, "Opinions et propos sur la radio en Afrique du Nord," *Alger-Radio*, September 12, 1937.
[171] F60-710. *Supplément spécial du Journal officiel de l'Algérie*, June 9, 1937.
[172] ANOM 15H31. "La radiodiffusion et les populations indigènes d'Algérie," *El Bassair*, cited in a report prepared for the HCM.
[173] CARAN F60-739. Un-authored note from May 1937; "Radio d'Alger," *La Voix indigène*, July 18, 1935.

Algerian café customers had become political activists rather than passive listeners.

Despite contradictory surveillance reports about the impact of foreign propaganda on Algerians and the turf battle that pitted colonial bureaucrats against metropolitan authorities, both popular perceptions of foreign propaganda and the most sophisticated security analyses continued to rely upon deeply rooted prejudices about Algerians' psychology. "All that is bad in North Africa comes from outside," the journalist Jules Cazenave asserted in January of 1938, but what made foreign broadcasts particularly dangerous were propagandists' attempts to exploit the emotional weaknesses of the "natives." Citing Antoine Porot, the founder of the Algiers School of Psychiatry, Cazenave argued that the "three aspects of the native mind were a lack of emotionalism and anxiety; credulity and suggestibility; and finally the legendary passivity." These should all be taken into account, he argued, when developing strategies to "protect Muslim workers" from anti-French propaganda.[174] A similar claim appeared later that year in the army's internal "Bulletin de renseignements des questions musulmanes," which commented that despite North African nationalists' use of newspapers and records to reach a wider audience, Algerians remained victims of their "traditional psychology, so often different from our own," which in turn made them "prone to listen to the most violent speakers and follow them blindly."[175] This racialized view of native psychology ultimately propelled the colonial state to shut down Algeria's burgeoning auditory culture and restrict Algerian listening.

By a decree of February 14, 1938, the governor-general banned the import of any *"foreign* language records" (defined as "records in any language other than the French language") without specific authorization. The same decree forbade the recording of any live performances in languages other than French, shutting down many of the local recording labels that flourished during the interwar decades.[176] The army General Staff banned the playing of Baidaphone records in barracks and camps housing North African troops, provided officers with a list of permissible Arabic records, and ordered them to confiscate "subversive" records circulating among their men, including the elusive Rsaissi *Piano Solo* record, which the security services feared was avail-

[174] Jules Cazenave, "En Afrique du Nord, la propagande contre la France a repris de plus belle," *De la Kabylie française,* January 22, 1938.
[175] SHD 7N4093. Bulletin des renseignements des questions musulmanes, February 16, 1938, annexe 1, 76–77.
[176] ANOM 2I48. Arrêté du Gouvernement Général de l'Algérie, Direction de Sûreté Général, February 14, 1938.

able in both metropolitan France and the colonies.[177] Colonial police in the town of Arba restricted radio use in public cafés after 8:00 p.m. to prevent Algerians from receiving broadcasts from "Nationalist Spain."[178] By the end of the year, the security services had installed jamming stations in Algiers and Tunis to block access to Radio-Bari, and in 1939, to Nazi propaganda broadcasts in Arabic transmitted by the German stations Zeezen and Radio-Berlin. Whereas authorities once feared Algerians listening in public, by 1939 the new restrictions placed on the colonial public sphere ensured that clandestine listening – undetected by the colonial surveillance web – provoked the greatest anxiety.[179] Similar attempts to restrict radio listening through controls on public listening or the jamming of foreign stations would only be adopted in metropolitan France after the start of the Second World War, revealing how the colonial periphery became the first battle-ground in the impending *guerre des ondes*.

[177] CARAN F60-707. Note pour Monsieur le Secrétaire Général du Présidence du Conseil. July 25, 1938, and SHD 7N4133. Etat-Major de l'Armée. Ministère de la Defense Nationale et de la Guerre, section d'outre-mer. Le Président du Conseil à MM le Gouverneurs Militaires de Paris, Metz, et Lyon; le Commandant Général de la région de Paris; les Généraux commandants; le Général commandant en chef des troupes du Maroc; le Général commandant le corps 19e d'armée; Généraux commandants des troupes de Tunisie et le Levant. Paris, March 31, 1939.

[178] ANOM 2I41. Le Commissaire de Police de la ville d'Arba à M. le Chef du Bureau du service des Affaires Indigènes et de Police générale de Préfecture d'Alger, January 17, 1939.

[179] SHD 2N243. Conseil Supérieur de la Défense Nationale. Le Général d'Armée Noguès, Commandant en Chef de théâtre d'opérations de l'Afrique du Nord to M. le Général Commandant en Chef des forces terrestres, October 26, 1939.

Conclusion
Paris-Mondial: globalizing the voice of France

In April of 1938, a new short-wave station named Paris-Mondial began transmitting from the outskirts of Paris. With broadcasts that could be heard around the world, Paris-Mondial became the "voice" of France on the eve of the Second World War. Few listeners outside of France, however, knew anything about the complicated history behind its creation. Several years earlier, lawmakers had approved funding for a new short-wave transmitting center to replace the outdated Poste Colonial, the latter station built to coincide with the 1931 Exposition Coloniale at Vincennes. As France's first short-wave transmitter, the Poste Colonial had attracted worldwide attention upon its debut, but the imperial propagandists and settlers' associations who lobbied for its construction envisioned the station serving primarily as a liaison between France and its colonial possessions in Africa, Asia, and the Caribbean.[1] During the Poste Colonial's first years in operation, letters poured in to the PTT's headquarters in Paris from across the empire testifying to the station's reach, but by 1934, France had lost its position as a leader in long-distance radio broadcasting as Britain, Germany, Italy, and the Soviet Union each began building more powerful short-wave transmitters with directional antennas that could reach distant regions of the globe.[2] French settlers overseas began to complain that they could no longer hear the Poste Colonial's 15-kW transmitter, while imperial lobbyists and journalists of varied political convictions demanded that the state increase the station's broadcasting power and improve the quality of its programs.

By the mid-1930s, staff within the state radio administration also became convinced that France needed to increase the space occupied by its "radio nation" in the airwaves in order to compete with rival nations in the wider concert of Europe. The PTT minister Georges Mandel and

---

[1] ANOM 100 APOM 134. Le Comité Central Français pour l'Outre-Mer. In 1930–1931, the Union Coloniale Française dispatched a survey to chambers of commerce in France's colonial cities to investigate how well the station could be heard and who was listening. Approximately forty responses came from Africa and Asia. The archives also include transcripts of talks given by members of the Union Coloniale.

[2] For a look at France's short-wave broadcasting through a transnational perspective, see Derek Vaillant, "At the Speed of Sound," 888–921.

the engineer Marcel Pellenc, the director of the radio broadcasting administration for nearly a decade, were particularly insistent that France expand its short-wave capacities in order to showcase "French culture and the expansion of our national genius" around the world.[3] When Mandel appealed to parliament in July of 1935 to fund the powerful new short-wave transmitters that would later serve Paris-Mondial, he reminded deputies that the hostile foreign radio propaganda of Nazi Germany and fascist Italy had rendered imperative a French station with a truly global reach. Yet cognizant of his contemporaries' distaste for fascist broadcasting strategies, Mandel reassured deputies that no nefarious motivations lay behind the proposed short-wave station. "Some might suspect us of employing [a new] station for indiscreet national propaganda," he asserted, but "that is not our intention. To serve our country well, it suffices to present an impartial display of our national effort every day." The strength of France's universal republican values ensured that "we should only have to inform people overseas ... about all forms of our material and intellectual activity for them to recognize that France has nothing to be jealous of ... compared to the nations that surround it."[4] Mandel's appeal won over legislators, who quickly endorsed the project, but the construction of the new transmitter foundered amid the political turmoil of the Popular Front years. Not until late 1936, when colonial authorities became anxious that the Arabic-language propaganda broadcast by fascist transmitters was stirring up anti-colonial nationalism in North Africa, did radio counterpropaganda become a serious political problem meriting significant government attention.[5]

When Paris-Mondial finally debuted in the spring of 1938, it boasted a new 25-kW transmitter, and in 1939, began transmitting at 100 kW from an even newer broadcasting facility at Allouis, which also housed a 900-kW transmitter for France's national long-wave station Radio-Paris. "France can finally speak to its North African populations in the language of reason, justice, and humanity," the socialist postal minister Jean-Baptiste Lebas proclaimed triumphantly at the station's inauguration. "The French Republic today possesses a marvelous instrument that will permit it to inform peoples, however distant they may be, about its international politics, or that's to say, about its firm desire for peace."[6] Mainstream

---

[3] CAC 19870714–1. Marcel Pellenc, Le Bilan des réalisations effectuées en 1935 par le Ministère des PTT. Speech made at the Salon de la T.S.F., June 21, 1935.

[4] Georges Mandel, "Rapport au Président de la République. Station de radiodiffusion coloniale," *Journal officiel de la République française*, July 15, 1935, 7581.

[5] CAC 19870714–2. Marcel Pellenc, Rapport de l'Inspecteur Général de la Radiodiffusion à M. le Ministre des PTT sur le centre émetteur colonial, September 18, 1937.

[6] CAC 19870714–2. Discours de Jean Lebas à l'inauguration du poste Paris-Mondial. August 16, 1938.

dailies and the radio press greeted with enthusiasm a station that took as its mission the defense of French values in the Mediterranean and around the world. Yet despite the careful planning that surrounded Paris-Mondial's new name, which had undergone vetting by the Ministry of Foreign Affairs and the North African experts of the Haut-Comité Méditerranéen, considerably less attention went into designing the station's broadcasts, outside of those destined for North Africa.[7]

Paris-Mondial's programs, which aired in Arabic, French, English, German, and Italian, and by 1940, in twenty different European and non-Western languages, were initially prepared by a hodgepodge of journalists recruited by the station's new administrator. Signaling a break from the Poste Colonial's history as a station catering exclusively to French settlers, the state dismissed its longtime director Julien Maigret, a former governor-general of Indochina and the author of the popular "exotic" African novel *Tam-Tam*. Into his place stepped the young Jean Fraisse, an inexperienced but politically well-connected secretary to the radical politician Albert Sarraut. Fraisse brought on board the left-leaning journalists Henri Jeanson and Georges Pioch, as well as the screenwriter Frédéric Pottecher. Pascal Copeau, a correspondent covering German culture for *Nouvelles littéraires*, took over editing the station's news bulletins.[8] A corps of international announcers, selected from a population of émigrés and political refugees who had made Paris their home in the 1930s, read Paris-Mondial's programs over the air. Because many Europeans, including many French people, were only beginning to purchase short-wave receivers, the Quai d'Orsay supplemented Paris-Mondial's programs with foreign-language broadcasts on medium wavelengths transmitted by stations along France's periphery: Italian from Nice-Côte d'Azur PTT; English from Lille PTT and Rennes PTT; Spanish from Toulouse-Pyrénées PTT; and German from Strasbourg PTT. Yet it was Paris-Mondial, the station promising to expand France's "radio nation" around the globe, that became the preeminent symbol of French broadcasting on the eve of the Second World War.[9]

What did Paris-Mondial have to tell the world about France and its values as another global conflict loomed on the horizon? No transcripts of Paris-Mondial's broadcasts remain in the archives, but a brochure for the station provides some insights into the logic undergirding its propaganda strategy. The programs destined for North Africa and the Mediterranean

---

[7] CARAN F60-702. Haut-Comité Méditerranéen. Session de mars 1938; Compte-rendu de la séance du samedi matin le 12 mars 1938.

[8] Moosmann, "Histoire des émissions internationales de la radiodiffusion française."

[9] Brochand, *Histoire générale de la radio*, 1: 341.

featured news bulletins, agricultural market reports, and concerts of live and recorded music by Maghribi performers. Recurring programs included "Letters from France: Life in Paris" or "The French Man and Woman of Today." Broadcasts directed to the Middle East included a translated lecture by André Maurois about "Chateaubriand in Old Age," a concert of classical music, and a retransmission of Molière from a Parisian theater.[10] All of the station's news broadcasts consisted of excerpts from the *Radio-Journal de France* that had been edited to reflect "regional interests." Perhaps most striking, Paris-Mondial's announcers deliberately refrained from direct rebuttals to German and Italian propaganda unless the fascist stations aired false information demanding "correction."[11] The composition of these programs reflected the trend toward elite cultural programming begun during the Popular Front's final years in power and solidified by Daladier's centralization of the state broadcasting administration in 1938. France was a nation of universal humanist values with a rich literary and musical heritage and a beautiful language, according to Paris-Mondial, serving as a beacon of civilization in a world already decimated by fascist aggression.

Concerned about Paris-Mondial's reception overseas, in the summer of 1938 the Daladier government solicited feedback from French consulates and embassies around the world, as well as from colonial bureaucrats and army officers. The reports that made their way to Paris over the course of the next year focused primarily on the technical quality of the broadcasts rather than the content the programs, reflecting the longstanding preoccupation of French radio audiences and bureaucrats alike with interference-free reception. Paris-Mondial could be heard clearly in North America, with listeners in Boston reporting that the station's intensity compared favorably to that of Rome and Berlin, although Caribbean audiences experienced fading during the day. The Turkish ambassador claimed that an Italian station sometimes blocked his reception of the short-wave signal.[12] Reports from France's overseas colonies in Africa once again revealed the difficulties of gauging audience reception in a multicultural environment. In Algeria, agents in the Bureau of Native Affairs reported that many North Africans did not possess the short-wave receivers necessary to pick up Paris-Mondial, while those who

[10] CAC 19870714–1. Paris-Mondial brochure, 1939.
[11] CARAN F60-710. Ministère des Affaires Etrangères, Direction des Affaires politiques et commerciales. Le Ministre des Affaires Etrangères à Monsieur le Président du Conseil, November 23, 1938.
[12] CARAN F60-739. Reports on Paris-Mondial, n.d. (late 1938?); F60-710. Le Ministre des Affaires Etrangères a Monsieur le Président du Conseil. Services des oeuvres françaises a l'étranger. January 28, 1939.

did appreciated the Arabic records and live concerts played on air, even if they found the news bulletins to be lacking in "up-to-the-minute" information vis-à-vis its foreign competitors.[13]

Responses to Paris-Mondial's broadcasts from radio critics and journalists in France were also mixed. Le Monde colonial illustré, claiming to speak for French settlers around the world, praised the station's broadcasts in rapturous tones, although Le Temps offered a searing indictment of the station's influence in Latin America, where its "insipid" programs garnered reproaches in the local Spanish-language press.[14] Writing for the left-leaning internationalist revue L'Europe nouvelle, André Labrousse described Paris-Mondial's broadcasts as "retrograde, bureaucratic, and academic" in tone, providing evidence of the "ravages of appeasement" in certain political and intellectual circles.[15] Similar critiques were echoed by a number of foreign observers, including the American Harwood Childs, a researcher at Princeton University, who studied the content and quality of European short-wave propaganda during the 1930s. He found Paris-Mondial's programs to be woefully lacking when compared to those if its competitors. France's refusal to directly attack its enemies, its "highly intelligent" if overly detailed analyses of diplomatic questions, and its tendency to only "answer contentions" by German and Italian stations, rather than introduce political ideas, rendered the station highly ineffective, in his opinion. "By the time the French woke up" to the dangers posed by radio propaganda, he concluded, the "Germans already had the decisive advantage."[16]

Historians have been no kinder to Paris-Mondial, citing the station's broadcasts as evidence of France's inexperience in the domain of propaganda and its overall lack of preparedness for the Second World War. France had already lost the guerre des ondes before it fully began, Christophe Charle suggests, thanks to its "elitist" propaganda style and its refusal to engage in the conversational and informal mode of broadcast talk employed by fascist propagandists. Following the 1938 agreement that solidified Germany's annexation of the Sudetenland, Nazi propagandists for the first time began bombarding radios with hostile propaganda in French. The Daladier government responded by creating

[13] ANOM 2I48. Gouverneur Général d'Algérie à M. le Préfet d'Alger, August 16, 1938. Responses from Miliana, Tizi-Ouzou, and Médéa.
[14] No author, "Allô! Paris Mondial," Le Monde colonial illustré, May 1938, 9. Georges Dumas, "Lettre au Directeur du Temps. La radiodiffusion de la pensée française dans l'Amérique Latine," Le Temps, November 38, 1938, 1–2.
[15] André Labrousse, "La propagande à l'ordre du jour," Europe nouvelle, July 1939.
[16] Harwood L. Childs and John B. Whitton, Propaganda by Short Wave (New York, 1942, 1972), 8, 183. On Paris-Mondial's reception in the United States, see also Thomas Dickenson Kernan, France on Berlin Time (New York, 1941), 40–41.

a new Commissariat Général d'Information (General Commission for Information) to coordinate French counterpropaganda. All media outlets, including commercial and public radio stations, were placed under the direct control of the cabinet and tasked with defending the government's perspective on the diplomatic crisis. Yet the Commissariat's entire budget, as Charle points out, was approximately one-third of the German budget for radio propaganda in 1933, when radio was still a relatively young media.[17] Daladier also appointed Jean Girardoux, a respected member of the diplomatic corps and well-spoken man of letters, to head the new agency. But Girardoux lacked the administrative skills necessary for the job, in Philip Nord's estimation, and more importantly, "spoke in a polished, poetic diction that made him well-nigh incomprehensible to many listeners." When he went on air to speak about the "peaceful nature of the average Frenchman," he was no match for a master propagandist such as Joseph Goebbels.[18]

Although most scholars have interpreted Paris-Mondial's programs as evidence of France's failure to prepare for a future war, both the logic undergirding the station's propaganda and the state's broadcasting policies in 1938–1939 might better be seen as a product of the tensions undergirding France's interwar auditory culture. As I have argued in this book, radio broadcasting transformed the dynamics of politics in France and its empire as people began to imagine the airwaves as a "radio nation": a new kind of collective space in which they could come together to debate the definition of the body politic and the terms by which citizens could participate in national life. In the late 1920s, and long before a radio receiver had entered every French home, a series of political debates about how to reintegrate disabled veterans of the First World War into civil society encouraged people to conceive of listening as a form of political participation and a quotidian practice of citizenship. The "radio nation" that subsequently emerged in the airwaves occupied a space at once physical and discursive, and was created through the radio signals that carried sounds as well as the social and political tasks that contemporaries assigned to the new media. Nor did the "radio nation" emerge solely through the efforts of politicians and state bureaucrats, but in constant dialogue with radio audiences. When pedagogical reformers and Popular Front politicians set out to discipline the ears of the nation's schoolchildren through *radio scolaire*, or when colonial policymakers in Algiers tried to mold the worldview of colonial subjects, they

---

[17] Christophe Charle, *La crise des sociétés impériales. Allemagne, France, Grande-Bretagne, 1900–1940*. Essai d'histoire sociale comparée (Paris, 2001), 532.

[18] Nord, *France's New Deal*, 251–52.

encountered resistance from listeners. Not only did audiences contest elite constructions of listening, but they also found ways to participate in separate and overlapping publics both within and outside the boundaries of the "radio nation," challenging elites' attempts to use the airwaves to promote social or political cohesion.

More importantly, the boundaries of France's "radio nation" remained in constant flux throughout the interwar decades, subject to the ever-shifting ratio of signals and sounds that audiences received through their radios, as well as their desire to tune into French stations, particularly when foreign stations sometimes offered higher-quality artistic programming and more up-to-the-minute news. A recurring tension emerged between listeners' demands that politicians create a strong and stable French radio network in the airwaves over Europe and their insistence that the state protect individuals' "right to listen" in any way they chose. Even after the Blum and Daladier governments began to exert greater control over broadcasting in the late 1930s, guaranteeing audiences' ability to tune into foreign stations remained central to policy-makers' conception of France's democratic "radio nation" as compared to those of neighboring fascist regimes. These tensions between promoting France's national interests in the airwaves and securing the individual rights of listeners recapitulated in the domain of broadcasting the Third Republic's struggle for political legitimacy. They also illuminate Paris-Mondial's unique strategy of presenting French "strengths" to the world while refraining from aggressive and combative radio propaganda to defend France's interests on the global stage. The fascist regimes, many policymakers believed, had violated their own citizens' "right to listen" by assaulting their ears with propaganda and restricting their access to foreign voices, practices deemed unacceptable in republican France.

The start of the Second World War brought an abrupt end to the "radio nation" of the Third Republic. In early September of 1939, radios once again appeared on the sidewalks of Paris and in the windows of homes in rural villages, as people gathered to listen for news of a formal declaration of war against Germany. Although the ensuing *drôle de guerre* witnessed no military action in Western Europe, it intensified the battle for political loyalties already unfolding in the airwaves, as Germany unleashed a new wave of hostile and sophisticated radio propaganda in French, targeting soldiers stationed along the Franco-German border, industrial workers laboring in factories, and housewives fretting about their children's future. Critical to the Nazi offensive on French ears were the broadcasts of Radio-Stuttgart, featuring a right-wing French journalist named Paul Ferdonnet who had defected to Germany before the start of the war.

Although the Daladier government publicly identified Ferdonnet in October, the announcer hailed by the press as the "traitor of Stuttgart" provoked panic by convincing some listeners that a network of spies in France was feeding him information about domestic politics.[19] The Germans also used the airwaves for "black propaganda": deliberately misleading information transmitted by secret radio stations whose broadcasts supposedly originated in France. The German station Radio-Humanité, whose name resembled the recently banned newspaper of the French Communist Party, claimed to represent the voices of communist laborers, while a station calling itself La Voix de la Paix (The Voice of Peace) served up vitriolic attacks portraying the Daladier government as bellicose warmongers, and a third, Réveil de la France (The Awakening of France), appealed to French nationalists. For the first time since the *guerre des ondes* erupted in the Mediterranean, the state began jamming foreign radio signals to prevent French radios from receiving Nazi propaganda, albeit with limited success.[20]

When France fell to Nazi Germany during the summer of 1940, Nazi forces in the occupied northern zone quickly seized all the radio stations, whether public or commercial, that had survived the bombing raids of the invasion. The powerful transmitters at Allouis formerly used by Radio-Paris and Paris-Mondial would henceforth be used to broadcast pro-German propaganda in French, Arabic, and Kabyle to audiences across France and North Africa.[21] After the signing of the Armistice on June 22, Radio-Paris became the voice of the occupier, even as its announcers continued to speak in French. The station's German administrator, Alfred Bofinger, hired a staff of journalists from prewar right-wing newspapers including the anti-Semitic *Je suis partout* and the Catholic, family-oriented *Choisir* to produce racist and openly collaborationist talk programs, and he found recording stars ranging from Charles Trenet to Maurice Chevalier and Tino Rossi only too willing to perform with the station's swing orchestra for extra income.[22]

[19] Julian Jackson, *France: The Dark Years, 1940–1944* (Oxford, 2001), 117. Hélène Eck, *La guerre des ondes: histoire des radios de langue française pendant la deuxième guerre mondiale* (Paris, 1985), 32–36.
[20] Derek Vaillant, "Occupied Listeners: The Legacies of Interwar Radio for France During World War II," in David Suisman and Susan Strasser, eds., *Sound in the Age of Mechanical Reproduction* (Philadelphia, 2009), 141–58.
[21] Raffael Scheck, *French Colonial Soldiers in German Captivity during World War II* (Cambridge, 2014), 134–36; Brochand, *Histoire générale de la radio*, 1: 569–74.
[22] Eck, *La guerre des ondes*; Cécile Méadel, "La propagande par le divertissement, un masque de normalité. Cinéma et radio en France pendant la deuxième guerre mondiale," *Convegno del Istituto Luce e dell'Università La Sapienza, 80 anni di storia, Un confronto tra le cinematografie europee* (Rome: 2004), 1–10.

In the southern zone, the Vichy regime quickly seized control of the public stations below the demarcation line, but brokered a deal with the remaining six commercial stations that allowed them to continue operating, provided that they broadcast up to sixty hours per week of state-supervised programming, while the remainder of their content would be evaluated by Vichy-appointed censors with veto powers.[23] The government hired several well-known producers from prewar commercial broadcasting to produce youth and family programs for its Radiodiffusion Nationale, and continued to expand the educational broadcasting of the Popular Front era through its own *radio scolaire* program, albeit with a curriculum dedicated to promoting the use of regional languages and the government's conservative agenda of *travail, famille*, and *patrie* ("work, family, and homeland").[24]

Yet if radio permeates the historical memory of the Second World War in France, this is due less to the broadcasting policies of the German occupiers or the Vichy government than to radio's role in the origin myth of the French Resistance. On June 18, 1940, a few days before the Armistice, a little-known French general named Charles de Gaulle broadcast an appeal to the French population from the London studios of the BBC, calling on them to resist surrender to the invading German army. Most historians agree that in the chaos of the *exode*, few people in France even heard this broadcast, though many would later claim that they had as a demonstration of their loyalty to de Gaulle's Free French resistance movement.[25] By September, Radio London was broadcasting a daily thirty-minute news and current affairs program titled *Les Français parlent aux français* ("The French Speaking to the French"), written by a team of French journalists who had fled into exile in London. Over the course of the next few months, the BBC became the voice of the French Resistance.

Fearful of the BBC's influence and the growing power of Resistance movements in France, in 1941 both the German occupiers and the Vichy regime banned listening to foreign stations (or any "non-national" stations from outside France's borders) and actively worked to jam their signals.[26] For the remainder of the war, audiences who wished to tune into the BBC's broadcasts had to do so in secret, relying on the tuning and listening skills they had acquired in the interwar years to navigate an "ocean" of static and deliberate *brouillage*. For these reasons, the historian

---

[23] Nord, *France's New Deal*, 297–301.
[24] See also Lebovics, *True France*, 175–76, and Faure, *Le project culturel de Vichy*, 245–46.
[25] Aurélie Luneau, *Radio Londres: Les ondes de la liberté, 1940–1944* (Paris, 2010), 32–36; Vaillant, "Occupied Listeners," 141–44.
[26] CAC 19070714–1. Extrait du *Journal Officiel* du 28 octobre 1941.

Aurélie Luneau views the listening practices of the Second World War as a rupture from prewar habits, as clandestine listening became more explicitly politicized and audiences had to learn to reject the sometimes familiar voices of Radio-Paris and the Vichy-run stations in favor of the "legitimate" French voices broadcast by a foreign station overseas.[27] However, as this book has shown, international listening was already quite commonplace in the 1930s and radio listening itself was a highly contested act. In many ways, the clandestine listening practices of the Second World War built upon prewar listening patterns. Moreover, the large numbers of tech-savvy radio amateurs that existed in France ensured that many people possessed skills in wireless construction that would become vital to the Resistance once it began preparing for the D-Day invasion of 1944.[28]

However, the complex politicization of the airwaves during the Second World War did have a significant impact on post-1945 broadcasting policy. Politicians of the nascent Fourth Republic, armed with an intimate knowledge of the oppositional listening practices of the 1930s and the war years, but cognizant of the difficulties of controlling audience reception to broadcasts, sought to eliminate the diversity of voices in the airwaves by nationalizing broadcasting through the creation of a new Office de Radiodiffusion-Télévision Française (French Radio Broadcasting and Television Office, or ORTF) in 1946.[29] This restructuring of the airwaves marked an end to commercial broadcasting in France for the next three decades. The imperative to nationalize the airwaves reflected left-wing politicians' desire to punish commercial broadcasters for their collaboration with the Vichy regime, but it also signaled the desire of the Liberation government to break permanently with the "prewar mercantile era" by solidifying state control over the media and eliminating any commercial competition to the state airwaves.[30]

The postwar decades did not represent a complete break from the broadcasting policies of the Third Republic, however. The interwar years had cemented the notion among political and social elites, state bureaucrats, and radio audiences that listening constituted a critical means of participation in civil society and political life, and that access to the airwaves was a social right of citizenship that should be guaranteed by the state. Even after the advent of the transistor radio reduced the cost of receivers, audiences were still required to pay an annual radio license fee to support the cost of state radio programming. To ensure full access to the airwaves, a 1953 law offered exemptions from the license fee to any

[27] Luneau, *Radio Londres*, 66–89.   [28] Vaillant, "Occupied Listeners," 141–58.
[29] Jeanneney, *L'écho du siècle*, 46–47.   [30] Nord, *France's New Deal*, 311–59.

disabled veterans, retired salaried workers, any individuals receiving state welfare, and several categories of civilian invalids. Any elderly person living on a state pension could obtain a 50 percent reduction in the license fee.[31] At the same time, the debates over mass culture in the 1930s cemented the notion that the state had an obligation to shape the cultural tastes and political values of France's citizenry through the mass media. Many radio programs of the 1950s reasserted the Popular Front's emphasis on the pedagogical uses of radio for cultural formation. After the Second World War, culture and language would become the primary arbiters of France's national identity in an era that saw its military and economic power progressively eclipsed by the United States.[32] As the first mass broadcast media, radio would remain a pivotal technology for projecting the French language and French culture around the globe, in turn shaping the political goals of state-run media in the emerging era of television.

---

[31] Christian Brochand, *Histoire de la radio et de la télévision en France. Vol. 2: 1944–1974*, 483–484. A subsequent law of 1974 extended these exemptions to televisions.
[32] Chaplin, *Turning on the Mind*, 1–16.

Bibliography

Archives

Archives Municipales de Paris

Archives du Crédit Municipal de Paris
Délibérations du Conseil Municipal de Paris
Inventaires de la Lycée Molière

Archives de la Préfecture de Police de Paris

BA 1862-1863	Manifestations
DA 460	Fêtes nationales
DB 143	Bruit

Archives Nationales d'Outre-Mer (ANOM), Aix-en-Provence

Archives Privées d'Outre-Mer
10 APOM	Le Centre des Hautes Etudes sur l'Afrique et l'Asie Moderne
100 APOM	Le Comité Central Français pour l'Outre-Mer

Gouvernement Général d'Algérie (GGA)
Sous-série CAB	Cabinets Civils des Gouverneurs Généraux
Sous-série H	Affaires Indigènes
Sous-série S	Instruction Publique et Beaux-Arts

Algérie. Préfecture d'Alger
Sous-série I	Administration des Indigènes

Algérie. Préfecture de Constantine
Sous-série B	Cabinet du Préfet

Algérie. Préfecture d'Oran
Sous-série I	Administration des Indigènes

Bibliothèque Fourney

Bibliothèque Historique de la Ville de Paris

Collection Rondel

Bibliothèque Nationale de France

Archives de l'Audiovisuel
Fonds Germinet-Vinot
Institut National de l'Audiovisuel, sound recordings

Centre des Archives Contememporaines (CAC), Fontainbleau

Série 199850023	Salon des Arts Ménagers
Série 199870714	Histoire de la Radiodiffusion en France et à l'Etranger
Série 19950218	Archives de la Direction Générale de la Radiodiffusion Française

Centre des Archives Nationales (CARAN), Paris

Série F^{12}	Commerce et Industrie
Série F^{17}	Education Nationale
Série F^{21}	Administration des Beaux-Arts
Série F^{60}	Présidence du Conseil
Série 94AP	Fonds Albert Thomas

Service Historique de la Défense (SHD), Vincennes

Série 2N	Conseil Supérieur de la Défense Nationale
Série 7N	Etat-Major de l'Armée
13ydd444	Dossier personnel, Général Mariaux

Maison de Radio France, Service des Archives Ecrites et Musée (Fonds Radio France)

Published primary sources

Newspapers and periodicals

L'Afrique du Nord illustrée
Alger-Radio. Le premier magazine de T.S.F. de l'Afrique du Nord
Alger-Républicain
Annales Africaines. La revue de l'Afrique du Nord

Annales des PTT. Revue mensuelle publiée par les soins d'une commission nommée par le
  Ministre des Postes, Télégraphes, et Téléphones
Annales de prothèse auriculaire. Revue d'acoustique physique appliquée à l'étude de
  l'ouïe
L'Année psychologique
L'Antenne. Journal français de vulgarisation de T.S.F.
L'Avenir médical
Bulletin de l'Académie de Médecine
Bulletin du Musée Pédagogique
Bulletin de la Société Française de Pédagogie
Bulletin de l'Union des Aveugles de Guerre
Les Cahiers de Radio-Paris
Catalogue du Salon des Arts Ménagers
Choisir . . . la radio, le cinéma
La Classe à l'écoute. Bulletin trimestriel des émissions radiophoniques pour les enseigne-
  ments du second degré
Comoedia
La Dépêche algérienne
La Dépêche de Constantine
La Dépêche coloniale
La Documentation radiophonique (éditée par la Radio Française)
L'Echo d'Alger
L'Echo des débitants-hôteliers, restaurateurs. Organe du Syndicat des Marchands de
  Vins en Détail de Bordeaux et de la Sud-ouest
L'Echo musical de l'Afrique du Nord
L'Eclair. Journal du Midi
L'Ecole et la vie
L'Ecole libératrice. Organe hebdomadaire du Syndicat National des Institutrices et
  Instituteurs de France et des Colonies
L'Echo de Paris
L'Echo du studio: Revue de T.S.F. artistique-littéraire-technique
L'Edition musicale vivante. Revue critique mensuelle de la musique enregistrée
L'Educateur prolétarien. L'imprimerie à l'école. Le cinéma. La radio. Les techniques
  modernes d'éducation populaire
Entendre. Organe de l'Association Amicale des Durs d'Oreille de la Région Parisienne
Europe nouvelle
Gringoire
Guérir. Revue mensuelle de vulgarisation médicale et scientifique
Le Haut-parleur: journal pratique, artistique, amusant des amis de la radio
L'Humanité
L'Illustration
L'Intransigeant
Je sais tout: la revue de la découverte
Je suis partout
Journal des débats politiques
Le Journal des instituteurs et institutrices
Journal des mutilés et combattants

Journal officiel de la République Française

Les Langues modernes. Bulletin de l'Association des Professeurs des Langues Vivantes de l'Enseignement public

La Libre parole (Algiers)

Lumière et radio. Sciences. Lettres. Arts. Magazine synthétique de la vie moderne

Machines parlantes et radio. Publication officielle de l'Office Général de la Musique

Le Matin

Mercure de France

Le Miroir du monde: hebdomadaire illustré

Le Monde hôtelier: revue périodique de documentation et d'informations hôtelières

Mon programme T.S.F.

La Musique à l'école. Organe corporatif et pédagogique des professeurs de musique

Le Mutilé des yeux. Organe de la Fédération des Mutilés des Yeux de France et des colonies

La Nature. Revue des sciences et de leurs applications aux arts et à l'industrie

L'Oeuvre

L'Ouest-Eclair

Ondes coloniales. Bulletin d'information coloniales d'éclairage et de la radio

Les Ondes scolaires. Bulletin des émissions radiophoniques pour les écoles primaires et l'education postscolaires

Oran républicain

Le Petit parisien

Le Petit radio: journal hebdomadaire des sans-filistes

Le Phonographe à l'école. Revue critique des enregistrements convenant aux discothèques scolaires

Le Populaire

La Libre parole T.S.F.

Programme des émissions de la radiophonie scolaire du second degré. Publication trimestrielle.

Radio LL Revue. Organe mensuel de documentation technique et commerciale

Radio-Agricole française: revue illustrée de la vie moderne à la campagne. Organe mensuel de la Fédération Nationale de Radiophonie dans les Campagnes

Radio-Alger. Bulletin officiel de l'Amicale de Radio-PTT-Alger

Radio-Espéranto. Organe trimestriel du Radio-Club Espérantiste de France

Radiola. La grande marque française. Bulletin mensuel

Radio-Liberté. Bulletin de l'Association des Auditeurs de T.S.F.

Radio-Magazine. Hebdomadaire illustré de T.S.F.

Radio-Phil. Bulletin d'information et de liaison entre Philips-Radio et ses bons clients

Revue de France

Revue générale des industries radioélectriques. Organe mensuel de la Chambre Syndicale des Industries Radioélectriques

La Revue municipale. Recueil hebdomadaire d'études édilitaires pour la France et l'étranger

La Revue de l'ouïe

La Revue universitaire

La Semaine radiophonique

Sonora. Gazette de la Foire. Journal distribué par Sonora-Radio et Sonora-Distribution

Le Temps
La T.S.F. en Algérie: bulletin mensuel du Radio-Club d'Algérie
T.S.F.-Phono-Ciné
T.S.F. Programme
T.S.F. Tribune
Le Tympan
L'Urbanisme
Le Valentin Haüy: revue française des questions relatives aux aveugles
La Voix indigène (Algiers)
Vendre. Tout ce qui concerne la vente et la publicité. Revue mensuelle

Books, manuals, and pamphlets

Actes et comptes-rendus de l'Association Colonies-Sciences, 5, 54, December 1929.
Annuaire de la radiodiffusion française 1933. Paris: Administration des Postes, Télégraphes, et Téléphones, 1933.
Annuaire de la radiodiffusion française 1934. Paris: Administration des Postes, Télégraphes, et Téléphones, 1934.
Annuaire de Radio-Télévision 1947. Ouvrage patronné par la Radiodiffusion Française. Paris: Chambre Syndicale des Editeurs d'Annuaires, 1947.
Annuaire statistique de la ville de Paris. Paris: Imprimerie municipale, 1943.
Arnaudiès, Fernand. *Histoire de l'Opéra d'Alger: épisodes dans la vie théâtrale algérienne*. Algiers: Ancienne imprimerie V. Heintz, 1941.
Arnheim, Rudolph. *Radio*. Translated Margaret Ludwig and Hebert Read. London: Faber and Faber, 1936.
Association des Professeurs de Langues Vivantes. *Emissions anglaises organisées par l'Association des Professeurs de Langues Vivantes de l'Enseignement public*. Paris: Henri Didier, 1938.
Bachetarzi, Mahieddine. *Mémoires: suivi d'une étude sur le théâtre dans les pays islamiques*. Algiers: Editions nationales algériennes, 1968.
Bernardin, Charles. *Le bruit: danger social. Le bruit à Toulouse. Thèse pour le doctorat en médecine*. Toulouse: Ateliers "Apta-France," 1938.
Bloch, Jean-Richard. *Naissance d'une culture. Quatre essais sur mon temps*. Paris: Imprimerie des presses universitaires de France, 1936.
Bonain, A. *L'oreille et ses maladies. L'audition et ses troubles. Les organes de l'équilibre*. Paris: G. Doin et Cie, 1933.
Chevais, Maurice. *L'éducation musicale de l'enfance*. 2 vols. Paris: Alphonse Leduc, 1937.
Coeuroy, André. *Le phonographe*. Paris: Editions Kra, 1929.
   Panorama de la radio. Paris: Editions Kra, 1930.
Courtin, Mlle and Louis Zivy, "La radiophonie scolaire," *L'Enseignement scientifique. Organe général de l'enseignement des sciences*, 25 October 1936, 86–89.
Deharme, Paul. *Pour un art radiophonique*. Paris: Le rouge et le noir, 1930.
   "Proposition d'un art radiophonique," *La Nouvelle revue française*, n. 174, 1 March 1928.
Defert, André. *Le bruit au point de vue juridique*. Paris: Imprimerie Lang, Blanchet, et Cie., 1930.

De Parrel, Gérard. *La rééducation de la voix parlée. Collection des manuels de la rééducation.* Paris: G. Doin et Cie, 1932.
La rééducation de l'ouïe. Collection des manuels de la rééducation. Paris: G. Doin et Cie, 1932.
La surdité et son traitement: manuel de rééducation auditive à l'usage du sourd et de son entourage. Paris: Albin Michel, 1927.
Les centres de rééducation, ateliers de récupération humaine. Paris: L'œuvre de la réadaptation de l'enfant, 1938.
and B. de Gorse. *Sous la menace de la surdité.* Paris: Editions Albin Michel, 1934.
De Parrel, Gérard and E. Junca. *L'éducation vocale. Manuel à l'usage des membres de l'enseignement.* Paris: Fernand Nathan, 1933.
Descaves, Pierre. *Quand la radio s'appelait Tour Eiffel.* Paris: La table ronde, 1962.
Desmettre, Mme, Mlles B. Auroy and J. Auroy, *Les beaux disques expliqués aux enfants.* Paris: Librarie Fernand Martin, 1935.
Devilliers, René. *Butte Boul'mich' et Cie: souvenirs d'un chansonnier.* Paris: Aux portes du large, 1946.
Dominus. *Sabir avec le marchand de tapis. Scènes, fables, récits.* Paris: Dominus, 14 rue Girardon, 1934.
Duhamel, Georges. *Querelles de famille.* Paris: Mercure de France, 1932.
Radiophonie et culture intellectuelle. Séance publique annuelle des cinq Académies, présidée par M. Petit-Dutaillis, président de l'Académie des Inscriptions et Belles-Lettres. Paris: Typographie de Firmin-Didot, 1938.
Fargue, Léon-Paul. *Le piéton de Paris.* Paris: Gallimard (1932), 2001.
Fouret, Louis André. *IIIe Congres International des Professeurs de Langues Vivantesr.* Extrait de la revue *Les Langues modernes*, January–February 1936. Cahors: Imprimerie Couselant, 1936.
Germinet, Gabriel. *Théâtre radiophonique: mode nouveau d'expression artistique.* Paris: Chiron, 1926.
Guiraud, Georges-Jean. *Pour un statut démocratique et rationnel de la radiodiffusion.* Rennes: Imprimerie Ouest-Eclair, 1930.
Hemardinquer, Pierre. *La surdité et l'acoustique moderne.* Paris: Chiron, n.d.
Huth, Arno. *La radiodiffusion: puissance mondiale.* Paris: Librarie Gallimard, 1938.
Institut International de Coopération Intellectuelle. *La radiodiffusion et la paix. Etudes et projets d'accords internationaux.* Paris: Institut International de Coopération Intellectuelle, 1933.
Jouet, Robert. *Etudes sur les sourds-muets.* Paris: Jouve et Cie, 1917.
Kaddour. *Fables et contes en sabir.* Calvisson: Editions Jacques Gandini (1920), 1994.
Lacour-Gayet, Jacques. *La grande pitié de la radiodiffusion française. Extrait du Correspondent du 25 janvier 1930.* Paris: Imprimerie Louis de Soye, 1930.
Lallement, Jules, "Le Comité français du phonographe dans l'Enseignement," *Bulletin du Musée Pédagogique*, 10, October 1933, 285–290.
Larronde, Carlos. *Théâtre invisible. Le douzième coup de minuit. Le chant des sphères.* Paris: Imprimerie Lang, Blanchong, et Cie, 1936.
LeFranc, Georges. *Emissions du Centre Confédéral d'Education Ouvrière. Poste de la Tour Eiffel, 1937–1939.* Paris, 1939.
Legrand, Max-Albert. *L'oreille et la surdité. Hygiène, maladies, traitement.* Paris: Bibliothèque Larrousse, 1921.

Le livre d'or du Centenaire de l'Algérie Française. L'Algérie. Son histoire. Œuvre française d'un siècle. Les manifestations du Centenaire. Algiers: Imprimerie Fontana frères, 1930.

L'Hôpital, Charles. *Disques de divertissement sélectionnés spécialement par le Comité Français du Phonographe dans l'Enseignement à l'usage des écoles, établissements d'enseignements, et œuvres postscolaires.* Paris: Editions Phonomatiques, 1934.

Machet, Jean and Léo Joubert. *Aide-mémoire du mutilé des yeux.* Rennes: Imp. H. Riou-Renzé, 1933.

Malard, Suzanne. *Radiophonies.* Paris: Editions de la revue des poètes, 1931.

Marage, Georges René Marie. *Contribution à l'étude du sens de l'ouïe, surdités vraies et simulées consécutives à des blessures de guerre.* Paris: Au bureau du "Journal de Physique," 1917.

Masson, Georges-Armand. *Radio, quand tu nous tiens.* Paris: Editions Armand Fleury, 1932.

Maurice, Albert. *Surdité et rééducation auditive: traitement de surdité chronique par les exercices acoustiques.* Paris: Chez Malone, 1924.

Ministère de l'Education Nationale. "Appareils de radiophonie scolaire," *Bulletin du Musée Pédagogique*, n. 28, 1939, 2–8.

    "Appareils de radiophonie scolaire, phonographes, et tourne-disques," *Bulletin du Musée Pédagogique*, n. 25, 1938, 2–12.

Morche, Robert. *Guide du mutilé de l'oreille et des personnes sourdes, demi-sourdes, et dures d'oreille.* Paris-Asnières: Editions de la Revue des Mutilés d'Oreille, 1927.

    La lutte contre la surdité. Encyclopédie des mutilés d'oreille. Sanary: Revue des Mutilés d'Oreille, 1930.

Petit, Pierre. *Le bruit et ses effets dans la vie moderne.* Thèse pour le doctorat en médecine, diplôme d'état, Faculté de Médecine de Paris. Paris: E. Le François, Ed. 1936.

Piéron, Henri. "Revue générale d'acoustique psycho-physiologique," *L'Année psychophysiologique*, n. 35, 1934, 167–197.

Procès-verbaux des délibérations du Conseil Général du Puy-de-Dôme. Clermont-Ferrand: Imprimerie Mont-Louis, 1937.

Rapports et délibérations du Conseil Général du Département du Bouches-du-Rhône. Marseille: Imprimerie nouvelle, 1938.

Rapports et procès-verbaux des séances du Conseil-Général de la Haute-Marne. Chaumont: Les Imprimeries champenoises, 1937.

Ravizé, A. *Répertoire des disques de langue étrangère enregistrées et éditées sous les auspices du Comité Français du Phonographe dans l'Enseignement et l'Association des Professeurs de Langues Vivantes.* Paris: Editions Phonomatiques, n.d.

Rocher, Marguerite L. "La radiodiffusion scolaire," *IIIe Congrès des Professeurs de Langues Vivantes 1937.* Paris: Maison du livre français, 1937.

Sarraut, Albert. *Grandeur et servitude coloniales.* Paris: Editions du Sagittaire, 1931.

Soulier-Valbert, F. "Le Problème de la radiodiffusion coloniale," *Extrait du Bulletin de l'Agence Economique des Colonies Autonomes des Territoires Africains sous Mandat*, n. 303, June 1934.

Souquet, Jean. *Code des anciens combattants et des victimes de la guerre*. Paris: Editeurs Charles Lavauzelle et Cie, 1932.

Sudre, René. *La psychologie de la radio. Conférence donné à l'Institut général de psychologie*. Paris: Au siège de la société, 1929.

Thérive, André. *Querelles du langage*. 3 vols. Paris: Stock, Delmain, et Boutreau, 1929, 1933, 1940.

Tillot, Emile. *Le réveil de l'ouïe par les excitations fonctionnelles coup sur coup. Manuel de l'auxiliaire ou rééducateur de l'ouïe*. Rouen: Imprimerie commerciale du Journal de Rouen, 1930.

Touring Club de France. *La lutte contre le bruit. Etudes entreprises sur les matériaux dits insonores, sous les auspices du Touring Club de France, avec la collaboration du Laboratoire d'essais au Conservatoire National des Arts et Métiers*. Rouen: Touring Club de France, 1934.

T.S.F.-Phono-Ciné de Lyon et du Sud-est. Lyon, 1937.

Union des Aveugles de Guerre. Compte-rendus sténographiques des réunions du Conseil d'Administration, 1932–1935.

Union Internationale de Radiodiffusion. *Les problèmes de la radiodiffusion: exposé en français et anglais des études entreprises depuis cinq ans par l'Union Internationale de Radiodiffusion*. Chambéry: Imprimeries Réunis, 1930.

Vachet, Pierre. *Remèdes à la vie moderne*. Paris: B. Grasset, 1928.

Valentino, Charles Louis. *Militaires blessés et infimes. Réformes, gratifications, et pensions*. Paris: Berger-Lavrault, 1918.

Villey, Pierre. *Maurice de la Sizeranne: aveugle, bienfaiteur des aveugles*. Paris: Les Petit-fils de Plon et Nourrit, 1932.

Wicart, Alexis. *Les puissances vocales: Le chanteur*. 2 vols. Paris: Phillipe Ortiz, 1931.

Les puissances vocales: L'orateur. 2 vols. Paris: Editions Vox, 1935.

Zay, Jean. *Souvenirs et solitudes*. Le Roeulx, Belgium: Talus d'approche, 1987.

Secondary sources

Adorno, Theodor. "On the Fetish Character in Music and the Regression of Listening," *The Culture Industry: Selected Essays on Mass Culture*. London: Routledge, 1991, 29–60.

Allalou. *L'aurore du théâtre algérien, 1926–1932*. Oran: Dar el Gharb, 1982.

Alten, Michèle. "L'introuvable identité disciplinaire de la musique scolaire en France sous la IIIe République," *Paedagogica Historica*, 40, 3, 2004, 279–291.

"Un siècle d'enseignement musique à l'école primaire," *Vingtième Siècle*, 55, July–September 1997, 3–15.

Altman, Rick. *Silent Film Sound*. New York: Columbia University Press, 2004.

Adas, Michael. *Machines as Measures of Men: Science, Technology, and Ideologies of Western Dominance*. Ithaca, NY: Cornell University Press, 1989.

Ageron, Charles-Robert. *Les algériens musulmans et la France, 1871–1919*. Paris: Presses universitaires de France, 1968.

Amoundry, Michel. *Le Général Ferrié: naissance des transmissions et de la radio-diffusion*. Grenoble: Presses universitaires de Grenoble, 1993.

Anderson, Benedict. *Imagined Communities: Reflections on the Origins and Spread of Nationalism.* London: Verso, 1996.

Anderson, Malcolm. *In Thrall to Political Change: Police and Gendarmerie in France.* Oxford: Oxford University Press, 2011.

Arcenaux, Noah. "Blackface Broadcasting in the Early Days of Radio," *Journal of Radio Studies*, 12, 1, 2005, 61–73.

Auslander, Leora. *Taste and Power: Furnishing Modern France.* Berkeley: University of California Press, 1995.

Back, Les and Michael Bull, eds. *The Auditory Culture Reader.* London: Bloomsbury Academic, 2004.

Bailey, Peter. "Breaking the Sound Barrier: A Historian Listens to Noise," *Body and Society*, 2, 49, 1996, 49–66.

Baranowski, Shelley. *Strength Through Joy: Consumerism and Mass Tourism in the Third Reich.* Cambridge: Cambridge University Press, 2007.

Barral, Catherine, Florence Paterson, Henri-Jacques Stiker, and Michel Chauvière, eds. *L'institution du handicap. Le rôle des associations. XIXe–XXe siècles.* Rennes: Presses universitaires de Rennes, 2000.

Bayly, Christopher A. *Empire and Information: Intelligence Gathering and Social Communication in India, 1780–1870.* Cambridge: Cambridge University Press, 1996.

Beale, Marjorie. *The Modernist Enterprise: French Elites and the Threat of Modernity, 1900–1940.* Stanford: Stanford University Press, 1999.

Becker, Jean-Jacques. *The Great War and the French People.* Translated by Arnold Pomerans. New York: Bloomsbury Academic, 1986.

Ben-Amos, Avner. *Funerals, Politics, and Memory in Modern France, 1798–1996.* Oxford: Oxford University Press, 2000.

Bergeron, Katherine. *Voice Lessons: French Mélodie in the Belle Epoque.* Oxford: Oxford University Press, 2010.

Bergerson, Andrew Stuart. "Listening to the Radio in Hildesheim, 1925–1953," *German Studies Review*, 24, 1, 2001, 83–113.

Bergmeier, H. J. P. *Hitler's Airwaves: The Inside Story of Nazi Radio Broadcasting and Propaganda Swing.* New Haven, CT: Yale University Press, 1997.

Berque, Jacques. *Le Maghreb entre deux guerres.* Paris: La Table ronde, 1962.

Beyer, Robert T. *Sounds of Our Times: Two Hundred Years of Acoustics.* New York: AIP Press, 1999.

Bijker, Weibe E. *Of Bicycles, Bakelites, and Bulbs: Towards a Theory of Sociotechnical Change.* Cambridge, MA: MIT Press, 1995.

Bijker, Weibe E., Thomas D. Hughes, and Trevor Pinch, eds. *The Social Construction of Technological Systems: New Directions in the Sociology and History of Technology.* Cambridge, MA: MIT Press, 1987.

Bijsterveld, Karin. *Mechanical Sound: Technology, Culture, and Public Problems of Noise in the Twentieth Century.* Cambridge, MA: MIT Press, 2008.

   ed. *Soundscapes of the Urban Past: Staged Sound as Mediated Cultural Heritage.* Bielefeld: Verlag, 2013.

Birdsall, Carolyn. *Nazi Soundscapes: Sound, Technology, and Urban Space in Germany 1933–1945.* Amsterdam: Amsterdam University Press, 2012.

Blatt, Joel, ed. *The French Defeat of 1940: Reassessments.* New York: Berghahn, 1998.

Blower, Brooke L. *Becoming Americans in Paris: Transatlantic Politics and Culture Between the World Wars*. Oxford: Oxford University Press, 2011.

Bourke, Joanna. *Dismembering the Male: Men's Bodies, Britain, and the Great War*. Chicago: University of Chicago Press, 1996.

Bouveresse, Jacques. *Un parlement colonial? Les délégations financières algériennes, 1898–1945*. Rouen: Publication des Universités de Rouen et du Havre, 2008.

Bouzar-Kasbadji, Nadya. *L'émergence artistique algérienne au XXe siècle*. Algiers: Office des publications universitaires, 1988.

Branson, Jan and Don Miller. *Damned for their Difference: The Cultural Construction of Deaf People as Disabled*. Washington, DC: Gaullaudet University Press, 2002.

Bratton, J. S., Richard Allen Cave, Breandan Gregory, Heidi J. Holder, and Michael Pickering, eds. *Acts of Supremacy: The British Empire and the Stage, 1790–1930*. Manchester: Manchester University Press, 1991.

Briggs, Asa. *The History of Broadcasting in the United Kingdom*. 5 vols. Oxford: Oxford University Press, 1961–1995.

Brochand, Christian. *Histoire générale de la radio et de la télévision en France*. 2 vols. Paris: Documentation française, 1994.

Brodiez-Dolino, Axelle. *Combattre la pauvreté: vulnérabilités sociales et sanitaires de 1880 à nos jours*. Paris: Editions CRNS, 2013.

Bruilart, Luc et Gerald Schlemminger. *Le mouvement Freinet: des origines aux années quatre-vingts*. Paris: L'Harmattan, 1996.

Brunnquell, Frédéric. *Fréquence monde: du poste colonial à RFI*. Paris: Hachette, 1991.

Cabanes, Bruno. *The Great War and the Origins of Humanitarianism, 1918–1924*. Cambridge: Cambridge University Press, 2014.

Cardiff, David and Paddy Scannell. *A Social History of British Broadcasting. Vol 1: Serving the Nation, 1922–1939*. Oxford: Basil-Blackwell, 1991.

Carlier, Omar. "Le café maure, sociabilité masculine et effervescence citoyenne (Algérie XVIIe-XXe siècles)," *Annales ESC*, 4, July–August 1990, 975–1003.
"Médina et modernité: l'émergence d'une société civile 'musulmane' à Alger à l'entre-deux-guerres," *Chantiers et défis de la recherche sur le Maghreb contemporain*, ed. Pierre-Robert Baduel. Paris: Karthala, 2008.

Carroll, David. *French Literary Fascism: Nationalism, Anti-Semitism, and the Ideology of Culture*. Princeton, NJ: Princeton University Press, 1994.

Chanet, Jean-François, "Maîtres d'école et régionalisme en France," *Ethnologie Française*, 18, 1988, 244–256.

Chapfer, Tony and Amanda Sackur. *French Colonial Empire and the Popular Front: Hope and Disillusion*. New York: St. Martin's, 1999.

Chaplin, Tamara. *Turning on the Mind: French Philosophers on Television*. Chicago: University of Chicago Press, 2007.

Charle, Christophe. *La crise des sociétés impériales. Allemagne, France, Grande-Bretagne, 1900–1940. Essai d'histoire sociale comparée*. Paris: Editions du Seuil, 2001.

Charron, Jean. "Les ondes courtes et la radiodiffusion française. Les services des émissions à l'étranger, période 1931–1974." PhD diss., Université de Bordeaux, 1984.

Chatriot, Alain. *Philatélie et histoire. L'étude en cas: les émissions philatéliques surtaxées en France 1935–1940.* Paris: Mémoire de l'Institut des Etudes Politiques, 1995.

Cheniki, Ahmed. *Le théâtre en Algérie: histoire et enjeux.* Aix-en-Provence: Edisud, 2002.

Cheval, Jean-Jacques. *Les radios en France: histoire, état, et enjeux.* Rennes: Editions Apogée, 1997.

Chevandier, Christian. *L'hôpital dans la France du XXᵉ siècle.* Paris: Perrin, 2009.

Childers, Kristen Stromberg. *Fathers, Families, and the State in France, 1914–1945.* Ithaca, NY: Cornell University Press, 2003.

Childs, Harwood L. and John B. Whitton. *Propaganda by Short Wave.* New York: John Wiley and Sons, 1972 (1942).

Clark, T. J. *The Painting of Modern Life: Paris in the Art of Manet and His Followers.* Princeton, NJ: Princeton University Press, 1999.

Classen, Constance. *Worlds of Sense: Exploring the Senses in History and Across Cultures.* New York: Routledge, 1997.

Cleveland, William L. *Islam against the West: Shakib Arslan and the Campaign for Islamic Nationalism.* Austin: University of Texas Press, 1985.

Cohen, Deborah. *The War Come Home: Disabled Veterans in Britain and Germany, 1914–1939.* Berkeley: University of California Press, 2001.

Cohen, Evelyne. *Paris dans l'imaginaire national de l'entre-deux-guerres.* Paris: Publications de la Sorbonne, 1999.

Cohn, Bernard S. *Colonialism and its Forms of Knowledge: The British in India.* Princeton, NJ: Princeton University Press, 1996.

Collot, Claude. *Les institutions d'Algérie durant la période coloniale, 1830–1962.* Algiers: Editions du CRNS, 1972.

Conklin, Alice. *A Mission to Civilize: The Republican Idea of Empire in France and West Africa, 1885–1930.* Stanford: Stanford University Press, 1997.

Coombes, Annie. *Reinventing Africa: Museums, Material Culture, and Popular Imagination in Late Victorian and Early Edwardian England.* New Haven, CT: Yale University Press, 1994.

Corbin, Alain. *Time, Desire, and Horror: Towards a History of the Senses.* Translated by Jean Birell. Cambridge: Cambridge University Press, 1995.

Village Bells: Sound and Meaning in the Nineteenth-Century French Countryside. Translated by Martin Thom. New York: Columbia University Press, 1998.

Crary, Jonathan. *Techniques of the Observer: On Vision and Modernity in the Nineteenth Century.* Cambridge, MA: MIT Press, 1990.

Crisell, Andrew. *Understanding Radio.* London: Routledge, 1994.

Dakhlia, Jocélyne. *Trames de langues: usages et métissages linguistiques dans l'histoire du Maghreb.* Paris: Maisonneuve et Larose, 2004.

Daoudi, Bouziane and Hadj Miliani. *L'aventure du raï: musique et société.* Paris: Editions du Seuil, 1996.

Davies, Alan. "The First Radio War: Broadcasting in the Spanish Civil War, 1936–1939," *Historical Journal of Film, Radio, and Television,* 19, 4, 1999, 473–513.

Dean, Carolyn J. *The Frail Social Body: Pornography, Homosexuality, and Other Fantasies in Interwar France.* Berkeley: University of California Press, 2000.

de Certeau, Michel. *The Practice of Everyday Life*. Translated by Steven Rendall. Berkeley: University of California Press, 1984.

de Grazia, Victoria. *The Culture of Consent: The Organization of Mass Leisure in Fascist Italy*. Cambridge: Cambridge University Press, 1981.

Irresistible Empire: America's Advance Through Twentieth-Century Europe. Cambridge, MA: Harvard University Press, 2005.

Delaporte, Sophie. *Les gueules cassées. Les blessées de la face de la grande guerre*. Paris: Le grand livre du mois, 2001.

Dell, Simon. *The Image of the Popular Front: The Masses and the Media in Interwar France*. London: Palgrave-MacMillan, 2007.

Désirat, Claude and Tristan Hordé. *La langue française au XXe siècle*. Paris: Bordas, 1976.

Diouonnat, Pierre-Marie. *Les 700 rédacteurs de Je suis partout, 1930–34. Dictionnaire des écrivains et journalistes qui ont collaboré au "grand hebdomadaire de la vie mondiale" devenu le principal organe du fascisme français*. Paris: SEDOPOLS, 1993.

Douglas, Susan J. *Inventing American Broadcasting, 1899–1922*. Baltimore: Johns Hopkins University Press, 1989.

Listening In: Radio and the American Imagination from Amos 'n' Andy and Edward R. Murrow to Wolfman Jack and Howard Stern. New York: Time Books, 1999.

Doctor, Jennifer. *The BBC and Ultra-Modern Music, 1922–1936*. Cambridge: Cambridge University Press, 2002.

Downs, Laura Lee. *Childhood in the Promised Land: Working-Class Movements and the Colonies de vacances in France, 1880–1960*. Durham, NC: Duke University Press, 2002.

D'Souza, Aruna and Tom McDonough, eds. *The Invisible Flâneuse? Gender, Public Space, and Visual Culture in Nineteenth-Century Paris*. Manchester: Manchester University Press, 2008.

Dudley, Andrew and Steven Ungar. *Popular Front Paris and the Poetics of Culture*. Cambridge, MA: Harvard University Press, 2005.

Dunwoodie, Peter. *Writing French Algeria*. Oxford: Clarendon Press, 1998.

Duroselle, J. B. "The Spirit of Locarno: Illusions of Pactomania," *Foreign Affairs*, 50, 4, 1972, 752–764.

Duval, René. *Histoire de la radio en France*. Paris: Alain Moreau, 1980.

Eck, Hélène. *La guerre des ondes: histoire des radios de langue française pendant la deuxième guerre mondiale*. Paris: Armand Colin, 1985.

Eksteins, Modris. *Rites of Spring: The Great War and the Birth of the Modern Age*. New York: Anchor Books, 1989.

Eley, Geoff and Jan Palmoski, eds. *Citizenship and Nationality in Twentieth Century Germany*. Stanford: Stanford University Press, 2007.

Erlmann, Veit. *Sound Cultures: Essays on Sound, Listening, and Modernity*. Oxford: Berg, 2004.

Fanon, Frantz. *A Dying Colonialism*. New York: Grove Press, 1967. First published 1959 by François Maspero.

Faure, Christian. *Le project culturel de Vichy: folklore et revolution nationale*. Lyon: Presses universitaires de Lyon, 1989.

Faure, Olivier et Dominique Dessertine. *Combattre la tuberculose, 1900–1940*. Lyon: Presses universitaires de Lyon, 1988.

Fauser, Annegret. *Musical Encounters at the 1889 Paris World's Fair*. Rochester, NY: University of Rochester Press, 2004.

Favre, Muriel, "Quand le 'Führer parle': Le public des cérémonies radiophoniques du Nazisme," *Le Temps des médias*, 2, 3, 2004, 108–117.

Febvre, Lucien. *The Problem of Unbelief in the Sixteenth Century: The Religion of Rabelais*. Translated by Beatrice Gottlieb. Cambridge, MA: Harvard University Press, 1982. First published 1942 by Albin Michel.

Fijalkow, Claire. *Deux siècles de musique à l'école: chroniques de l'exception parisienne, 1819–2002*. Paris: L'Harmattan, 2003.

Foster, Hal, ed. *Vision and Visuality*. Seattle: Bay Press, 1988.

Frader, Laura Levine. *Breadwinners and Citizens: Gender in the Making of the French Social Model*. Durham, NC: Duke University Press, 2008.

Frost, Robert. "Machine Liberation: Inventing Housewives and Home Appliances in Interwar France," *French Historical Studies*, 18, 1, 1993, 109–130.

Führer, Karl Christian. "A Medium of Modernity? Broadcasting in Weimar Germany, 1923–1932," *The Journal of Modern History*, 69, 4, 1997, 722–753.

Führer, Karl Christian and Corey Ross, eds. *Mass Media, Culture, and Society in Twentieth-Century Germany*. London: Palgrave-MacMillan, 2006.

Fulcher, Jane. *The Composer as Intellectual: Music and Ideology in France, 1914–1940*. Oxford: Oxford University Press, 2005.

French Cultural Politics and Music: From the Dreyfus Affair to the First World War. Oxford: Oxford University Press, 1999.

Furlough, Ellen. *Consumer Cooperation in France: The Politics of Consumption, 1834–1930*. Ithaca, NY: Cornell University Press, 1991.

Galazi, Enrica. *Le son à l'école: phonétique et enseignement des langues*. Brescia, Italy: Editrice La Scuola, 2002.

Garrioch, David. "Sounds of the City: The Soundscape of Early Modern European Towns," *Urban History* 30, 1, 2003, 5–25.

Gerber, David, ed. *Disabled Veterans in History*. Ann Arbor: University of Michigan Press, 2000.

Germond, Carine and Henning Turk, eds. *A History of Franco-German Relations in Europe: From "Hereditary Enemies" to Partners*. New York: Palgrave-Macmillan, 2008.

Girardet, Raoul. *L'idée coloniale en France de 1871 à 1962*. Paris: La table ronde, 1972.

Gitelman, Lisa. *Always Already New: Media, History, and the Data of Culture*. Cambridge, MA: MIT Press, 2005.

Gitelman, Lisa and Geoffrey Pingree, eds. *New Media, 1740–1915*. Cambridge, MA: MIT Press, 2003.

Gosnell, Jonathan. *The Politics of Frenchness in Colonial Algeria, 1930–1954*. Rochester, NY: Rochester University Press, 2002.

Grange, Daniel. "Structure et techniques d'une propagande: les émissions arabes de Radio-Bari," *Relations internationales*, 2, 1974, 165–185.

Griset, Pascal, "Innovation and Radio Industry in Europe during the Interwar Period," in François Caron and Wolfram Fischer, eds. *Innovation in the European Economies Between the Wars*. Berlin: De Gruyter, 1995, 37–57.

Gronow, Pekka. "The Record Industry Comes to the Orient," *Ethnomusicology*, 25, 2, 1981, 262–274.

Guillaume, Pierre. *Du désespoir au salut: les tuberculeux aux XIXe et XXe siècles.* Paris: Aubier, 1986.

Gutton, Jean-Pierre. *Bruits et sons dans notre histoire: essai sur la reconstitution du paysage sonore.* Paris: Presses universitaires de France, 2000.

Hahn, Hazel. *Scenes of Parisian Modernity: Culture and Consumption in the Nineteenth Century.* London: Palgrave-MacMillan, 2009.

Hanley, David L., A. P. Kerr, and Neville H. Waites. *Contemporary France: Politics and Society Since 1945.* London: Routledge, 2005.

Hargrove, June and Neil McWilliam. *Nationalism and French Visual Culture, 1870–1914.* New Haven, CT: Yale University Press, 2005.

Haring, Kristin. *Ham Radio's Technical Culture.* Cambridge, MA: MIT Press, 2006.

Harp, Steven. *Marketing Michelin: Advertising and Cultural Identity in Twentieth-Century France.* Baltimore: Johns Hopkins University Press, 2001.

Hayward, Susan. *French National Cinema.* 2nd ed. London: Routledge, 2005.

Hendy, David. *Radio in the Global Age.* Oxford: Polity Press, 2000.

Hilmes, Michelle and Jason Loviglio, eds. *Radio Reader: Essays in the Cultural History of Radio.* New York: Routledge, 2002.

Howes, David. *Sensual Relations: Engaging the Senses in Culture and Social Theory.* Ann Arbor: University of Michigan Press, 2003.

Hull, Raymond, ed. *Rehabilitative Audiology.* New York: Grune and Stratton, 1982.

Ingram, Norman. *The Politics of Dissent: Pacifism in France, 1919–1939.* Oxford: Oxford University Press, 1991.

Iriye, Akira. *Cultural Internationalism and World Order.* Baltimore: Johns Hopkins University Press, 2000.

   Global and Transnational History: The Past, Present, and Future. Basingstoke, UK: Palgrave-MacMillan, 2013.

Isolo, Giana. "Italian Radio: History and Historiography," *Historical Journal of Film, Television, and Radio*, 15, 3, 1995, 393–399.

Jackson, Jeffrey H. *Making Jazz French: Music and Modern Life in Interwar Paris.* Durham, NC: Duke University Press, 2003.

   "Solidarism in the City Streets: La Société protectrice contre les excès de l'automobilisme and the Problem of Traffic in Early Twentieth-Century Paris," *French Cultural Studies*, 20, 3, 2009, 237–256.

Jackson, Julian. *France: The Dark Years, 1940–1944.* Oxford: Oxford University Press, 2001.

   The Popular Front: Defending Democracy, 1934–1938. Cambridge: Cambridge University Press, 1988.

Jay, Martin. *Downcast Eyes: The Denigration of Vision in Twentieth-Century French Thought.* Berkeley: University of California Press, 1993.

Jeanneney, Jean-Noël. *L'écho du siècle: dictionnaire historique de la radio et de la télévision en France.* Paris: Hachette, 1999.

Joffé, George, ed. *North Africa: Nation, State, and Region.* London: Routledge, 1993.

Johnson, James H. *Listening in Paris: A Cultural History*. Berkeley: University of California Press, 1995.

Jolly, Jean. *Dictionnaire des parlementaires français. Notices biographiques sur les ministres, députés, et sénateurs français de 1889 à 1940*. 8 vols. Paris: Presses universitaires de France, 1960.

Jones, Andrew. *Yellow Music: Media Culture and Colonial Modernity in the Chinese Jazz Age*. Durham, NC: Duke University Press, 2001.

Jordan, Matthew F. "Discophile ou Discomanie? The Cultural Politics of Living-Room Listening," *French Cultural Studies*, 16, 2, 2005, 151–168.

Jordi, Jean-Jacques and Jean-Louis Planche, eds. *Alger 1860–1939: le modèle ambigu du triomphe colonial*. Paris: Le grand livre du mois, 1999.

Julien, Charles-André. *Les algériens musulmans et la France, 1871–1919*. Paris: Presses universitaires de France, 1968.

Jütte, Robert. *A History of the Senses: From Antiquity to Cyberspace*. Cambridge: Polity Press, 2005.

Kaddache, Mafoud. *Histoire du nationalisme algérien. Question nationale et politique algérienne, 1919–1951*. Algiers: Société nationale d'édition et de diffusion, 1981.

Kahn, Douglas. *Noise, Water, Meat: A History of Sound in the Arts*. Cambridge, MA: MIT Press, 1999.

Kahn, Douglas and Gregory Whitehead. *Wireless Imagination: Sound, Radio, and the Avant-Garde*. Cambridge, MA: MIT Press, 1992.

Kalman, Samuel. *The Faisceau and the Croix de Feu: The Extreme Right in Interwar France*. Aldershot: Ashgate, 2008.

"Le combat par tous les moyens: Colonial Violence and the Extreme Right in 1930s Oran," *French Historical Studies*, 34, 1, 2011, 125–153.

Kaplan, Alice. *Reproductions of Banality: Fascism, Literature, and French Intellectual Life*. Minneapolis: University of Minnesota Press, 1996.

Kateb, Kamel. *Européens, "indigènes" et juifs en Algérie (1830–1962): représentations et réalités des populations*. Paris: Institut national des études démographiques, 2001.

Kchir-Bendana, Kmar. "Kaddour Ben Nitram: chansonnier et humoriste tunisien," *Revue des mondes musulmanes et de la Méditerranée*, 77, 1995, 77–78.

Keller, Richard. *Colonial Madness: Psychiatry in French North Africa*. Chicago: University of Chicago Press, 2007.

Kelly, Barbara L., ed. *French Music, Culture, and National Identity, 1870–1939*. Rochester, NY: University of Rochester Press, 2008.

Kennedy, Dane, ed. *Reinterpreting Exploration: The West in the World*. Oxford: Oxford University Press, 2014.

Kennedy, Sean. *Reconciling France Against Democracy: The Croix de Feu and the Parti Social Français*. Montreal: McGill-Queens University Press, 2007.

Kergoat, Jacques. *La France du Front Populaire*. Paris: La Découverte, 1986.

Kern, Stephen. *The Culture of Time and Space, 1880–1918*. Cambridge, MA: Harvard University Press, 1983.

Kittler, Friedrich A. *Gramophone, Film, Typewriter*. Translated by Geoffrey Winthrop-Young and Michael Wutz. Stanford: Stanford University Press, 1999.

Koshar, Rudy, ed. *Histories of Leisure*. Oxford: Oxford University Press, 2002.

Koven, Seth. "Remembering and Dismemberment: Crippled Children, Wounded Soldiers, and the Great War in Great Britain," *American Historical Review*, 99, 4, 1999, 1167–1202.

Kudlick, Catherine J. "Disability History: Why We Need Another 'Other'," *American Historical Review* 108, 3, 2003, 763–793.

Kudlick, Catherine J. and Zina Weygand. *Reflections: The Life and Writings of a Young Blind Woman in Post-Revolutionary France*. New York: New York University Press, 2001.

Laborie, Léonard. *L'Europe mise en réseau: la coopération internationale dans les postes et télécommunications, années 1850–1950*. Brussels: Peter Lang, 2010.

Lacey, Kate. *Feminine Frequencies: Gender, German Radio, and the Public Sphere, 1923–1945*. Ann Arbor: University of Michigan Press, 1996.

Listening Publics: The Politics and Experience of Listening in the Media Age. Oxford: Wiley-Blackwell, 2013.

Lacqua, Daniel. *Internationalism Reconfigured: Transnational Ideas and Movements Between the Wars*. London: IB Tauris, 2011.

Landau, Paul S. and Deborah D. Kaspin, eds. *Images and Empires: Visuality in Colonial and Postcolonial Africa*. Berkeley: University of California Press, 2002.

Lebovics, Herman. *True France: The Wars Over Cultural Identity, 1900–1945*. Ithaca, NY: Cornell University Press, 1992.

Leed, Eric. *No-Man's Land: Combat and Identity in World War One*. Cambridge: Cambridge University Press, 1979.

Le Mahieu, D. L. *A Culture for Democracy: Mass Communication and the Cultivated Mind in Britain Between the Wars*. Oxford: Oxford University Press, 1988.

Le Naour, Jean-Yves. *The Living Unknown Soldier: A Story of Grief and the Great War*. Translated by Penny Allen. New York: Henry Holt, 2005.

Le Pautremat, Pascal. *La politique musulmane de la France aux XXᵉ siècle. De l'héxagone aux terres d'Islam. Espoirs, réussites, échecs*. Paris: Maisonneuve et Larose, 2003.

Lerner, Paul and Mark S. Micale. *Traumatic Pasts: History, Psychiatry, and Trauma in the Modern Age, 1870–1930*. Cambridge: Cambridge University Press, 2001.

Levin, David Michael. *Modernity and the Hegemony of Vision*. Berkeley: University of California Press, 1993.

Lévy, Rosa Claude. *La T.S.F. ou comment danser avec le Kayser*. Paris: Editions Le Manuscrit, 2009.

Lewis, Robert W. "'A Civic Tool of Modern Times': Politics, Mass Society, and the Stadium in Twentieth Century France," *French Historical Studies*, 34, 1, 2011, 155–184.

Limoges, André, "La troupe de Radio-Alger," *Cahiers d'histoire de la radiodiffusion*, 26, 1990, 63–68.

Lommers, Suzanne. *Europe on Air: Interwar Projects for Radio Broadcasting*. Amsterdam: Amsterdam University Press, 2013.

Longmore, Paul K. and Laurie Umansky, eds. *The New Disability History: American Perspectives*. New York: New York University Press, 2001.

Lorcin, Patricia. *Imperial Identities: Stereotyping, Race, and Prejudice in Colonial Algeria*. New York: I.B. Tauris, 1995.

Loubes, Olivier. *L'école et la patrie: histoire d'un désenchantement, 1914–1940*. Paris: Belin, 2001.

"L'école et les deux corps de la nation en France, 1900–1940," *Histoire de l'éducation*, 126, 2010, 55–76.

Lowe, Donald M. *A History of Bourgeois Perception*. Chicago: University of Chicago Press, 1983.

Loviglio, Jason. *Radio's Intimate Public: Network Broadcasting and Mass Mediated Democracy*. Minneapolis: University of Minnesota Press, 2005.

Luneau, Aurélie. *Radio Londres: les ondes de la liberté, 1940–1944*. Paris: Perrin, 2005.

Lusseyran, Jacques. *Et la lumière fut*. Paris: Le Félin, 2005.

Maisonneuve, Sophie. *L'invention du disque: genèse de l'usage des médias musicaux, 1877–1949*. Paris: Edition des Archives Contemporaines, 2009.

Mannoni, Pierre. *Les français d'Algérie: vie, moeurs, mentalité de la conquête des Territoires du Sud à l'indépendance*. Paris: L'Harmattan, 1993.

Marcus, Sharon. *Apartment Stories: City and Home in Nineteenth Century Paris and London*. Berkeley: University of California Press, 1999.

Marks, Sally. *The Illusion of Peace: International Relations in Europe, 1918–1933*. 2nd ed. Basingstoke, UK: Palgrave-MacMillan, 2003.

Martin, Benjamin. *France and the Après-Guerre*. Baton Rouge: Louisiana State University Press, 1999.

Marvin, Carolyn. *When Old Technologies Were New: Thinking about Electric Communication in the Late Nineteenth Century*. Oxford: Oxford University Press, 1988.

Mazgaj, Paul. *Imagining Fascism: The Cultural Politics of the French Young Right*. Newark, DE: University of Delaware Press, 2007.

McDougall, James. *History and the Culture of Nationalism in Algeria*. Cambridge: Cambridge University Press, 2006.

McKenzie, John, ed. *Imperialism and Popular Culture*. Manchester: Manchester University Press, 1986.

McLuhan, Marshall. *The Gutenberg Galaxy: The Making of Typographic Man*. Toronto, 1962.

Understanding Media: The Extensions of Man. New York: Routledge, 2001 (1964).

Méadel, Cécile. *Histoire de la radio des années trente: du sans-filiste à l'auditeur*. Paris: Anthropos/INA, 1994.

Menduni, Enrico, "An Unheard Story? The Challenges for Radio Studies in Italy," *The Radio Journal: International Studies in Broadcast and Audio Media*, 2, 1, 2004, 15–26.

Mernissi, Fatima. *Dreams of Trespass: Tales of a Harem Girlhood*. New York: Addison-Wesley, 1995.

Messaoudi, Alain. "The Teaching of Arabic in French Algeria and Contemporary France," *French History*, 20, 3, 2006, 297–317.

Miliani, Hadj. *Sociétaires de l'émotion: études sur les musiques et les chants d'Algérie d'hier et d'aujourd'hui*. Oran: Dar El Gharb, 2005.

Miller, Michael B. *Shanghai on the Metro: Spies, Intrigue, and the French Between the Wars*. Berkeley: University of California Press, 1994.

Millington, Chris. *From Victory to Vichy: Veterans in Interwar France*. Manchester: Manchester University Press, 2012.

Mills, Mara. "Hearing Aids and the History of Electronics Miniaturization," *IEEE Annals of the History of Computing*, 33, 2, April–June 2011, 24–45.

Mirzoeff, Nicholas. *Silent Poetry: Deafness, Sign, and Visual Culture in Modern France*. Princeton, NJ: Princeton University Press, 1995.

Mitchell, Timothy. *Colonizing Egypt*. Cambridge: Cambridge University Press, 1998.

Morat, Daniel, ed. *Sounds of Modern History: Auditory Cultures in 19th and 20th Century Europe*. New York: Berghahn Books, 2014.

Mrazek, Rudolf. *Engineers of Happy Land: Technology and Nationalism in a Colony*. Princeton, NJ: Princeton University Press, 2002.

Narif, Basheer M. "The Arabs and the Axis, 1933–1940," *Arab Studies Quarterly*, 19, 2, 1997, 1–24.

Nelson, Michael. *War of the Black Heavens: The Battles of Western Broadcasting in the Cold War*. Syracuse: Syracuse University Press, 1997.

Neulander, Joelle. *Programming National Identity: The Culture of Radio in 1930s France*. Baton Rouge: Louisiana State University Press, 2009.

Nord, Philip. *France's New Deal: From the Thirties to the Postwar Era*. Princeton, NJ: Princeton University Press, 2010.

Nott, James. *Music for the People: Popular Music and Dance in Interwar Britain*. Oxford: Oxford University Press, 2002.

Ong, Walter J. *Orality and Literacy. The Technologizing of the Word*. New York: Routledge, 2012. First published 1982 by Meuthen and Co.

Ory, Pascal. *La belle illusion: culture et politique sous le signe du Front Populaire*. Paris: Plon, 1994.

Ott, Katherine, David Serlin, and Stephen Mihm, eds. *Artificial Parts, Practical Lives: Modern Histories of Prosthetics*. New York: New York University Press, 2002.

Otter, Chris. *The Victorian Eye: A Political History of Light and Vision in Britain, 1800–1910*. Chicago: University of Chicago Press, 2008.

Oudshoorn, Nelly and Trevor Pinch, eds. *How Users Matter: The Co-Construction of Users and Technologies*. Cambridge, MA: MIT Press, 2003.

Ozouf, Jacques and Mona. *La république des instituteurs*. Paris: Gallimard, 1992.

Panchasi, Roxanne. *Future Tense: The Culture of Anticipation in France Between the Wars*. Ithaca, NY: Cornell University Press, 2009.

Pedersen, Susan. *Family, Dependence, and the Origins of the Welfare State: Britain and France 1914–1945*. Cambridge: Cambridge University Press, 1993.

Peer, Shanny. *France on Display: Peasants, Provincials, and Folklore in the 1937 Paris World's Fair*. Albany, NY: SUNY Press, 1998.

Petricioli, Maria and Donatella Cherubini, eds. *Pour la paix en Europe: institutions et sociétés dans l'entre-deux-guerres*. Brussels: Peter Lang, 2007.

Picker, John M. *Victorian Soundscapes*. Oxford: Oxford University Press, 2003.

Pinch, Trevor and Karin Bijsterveld, eds. *The Oxford Handbook of Sound Studies*. New York: Oxford University Press, 2013.

Pinkerton, Alasdair. "Radio and the Raj: Broadcasting in British India, 1920–1940," *Journal of the Royal Asiatic Society*, 18, 2, 2008, 167–191.

Potter, Simon J. *Broadcasting Empire: The BBC and the British World, 1922–1970.* Oxford: Oxford University Press, 2012.

Price, Matthew. "Bodies and Souls: The Rehabilitation of Maimed Soldiers in France and Germany during the First World War." PhD diss., Stanford University, 1998.

Prochaska, David, "History as Literature, Literature as History: Cagayous of Algiers," *American Historical Review*, 101, 3, 1996, 671–711.

Prost, Antoine. *L'histoire de l'enseignement en France: 1800–1967.* Paris: A. Colin, 1968.

Jean Zay et le gauche du radicalisme. Paris: Presses de Sciences Po, 2003.

In the Wake of War: Les anciens combattants and French Society, 1914–1939. Translated by Helen McPhail. Oxford: Berg, 1992.

Prot, Robert. *Dictionnaire de la radio.* Grenoble: Presses universitaires de Grenoble, 1997.

Puren, Christian. *Histoire des méthodologies de l'enseignement des langues.* Paris: Cle International, 1988.

Quartararo, Anne T. *Deaf Identity and Social Images in Nineteenth-Century France.* Washington, DC: Gallaudet University Press, 2008.

Rabinbach, Anson. *The Human Motor: Energy, Fatigue, and the Origins of Modernity.* Berkeley: University of California Press, 1990.

Rearick, Charles. *The French in Love and War.* New Haven, CT: Yale University Press, 1997.

Paris Dreams, Paris Memories: The City and Its Mystique. Stanford: Stanford University Press, 2011.

Rifkin, Adrian. *Street Noises: Parisian Pleasure 1900–40.* Manchester: Manchester University Press, 1993.

Rioux, Jean-Pierre and Jean-François Sirinelli. *Histoire culturelle de la France. Vol. 4: Le temps des masses.* Paris: Editions du Seuil, 1998.

La culture de masse en France de la Belle Epoque à aujourd'hui. Paris: Fayard, 2002.

Riskin, Jessica. *Science in the Age of Sensibility: The Sentimental Empiricists of the French Enlightenment.* Chicago: University of Chicago Press, 2002.

Roberts, Mary Louise. *Civilization without Sexes: Reconstructing Gender in Postwar France, 1917–1927.* Chicago: University of Chicago Press, 1994.

Rosenberg, Clifford. *Policing Paris: The Origins of Modern Immigration Control Between the Wars.* Ithaca, NY: Cornell University Press, 2006.

Ross, Corey. *Media and the Making of Modern Germany: From the Empire to the Third Reich.* Oxford: Oxford University Press, 2008.

Roux, Alain. "L'évolution du radiorécepteur domestique en France entre 1931 et 1940." PhD diss., Ecole des Hautes Etudes en Sciences Sociales, 1987.

Ruedy, John. *Modern Algeria: The Origins and Development of a Nation.* Bloomington: Indiana University Press, 1992.

Ruscio, Alain. *Le crédo de l'homme blanc. Regards coloniaux français, XIXe-XXe siècles.* Brussels: Editions Complexe, 1996.

Saadallah, Rabah. *El-Hadj M'hamed El-Anka: maître et rénovateur de la musique 'chaabi'*. Algiers: La Maison du livre, 1981.

Scannell, Paddy. "Public Service Broadcasting and Modern Public Life," *Media, Culture, and Society*, 11, 1989, 135–166.

Schmidt, Eric Leigh. *Hearing Things: Religion, Illusion, and the American Enlightenment*. Cambridge, MA: Harvard University Press, 2000.

Schwartz, Hillel. *Making Noise: From Babel to the Big Bang and Beyond*. New York: Zone Books, 2011.

Schwartz, Vanessa. *Spectacular Realities: Early Mass Culture in Fin-de-Siècle Paris*. Berkeley: University of California Press, 1998.

Schneider, William. *Quality and Quantity: The Quest for Biological Regeneration in Twentieth-Century France*. Cambridge: Cambridge University Press, 1990.

Sconce, Jeffrey. *Haunted Media: Electronic Presence from Telegraphy to Television*. Durham, NC: Duke University Press, 2000.

Scott, James. *Seeing Like a State: How Certain Schemes to Improve the Human Condition Have Failed*. New Haven, CT: Yale University Press, 1998.

Scott, Joan. *Only Paradoxes to Offer: French Feminists and the Rights of Man*. Cambridge, MA: Harvard University Press, 1997.

Serlin, David. "Disabling the Flâneur," *Journal of Visual Culture*, 5, 2, 2006, 193–208.

Shepard, Todd. *The Invention of Decolonization: The Algerian War and the Remaking of France*. Ithaca, NY: Cornell University Press, 2006.

Siegel, Mona. *The Moral Disarmament of France: Education, Pacifism, and Patriotism, 1914–1940*. Cambridge: Cambridge University Press, 2004.

Sivan, Emmanuel. "Colonialism and Popular Culture in Algeria," *Journal of Contemporary History*, 14, 1, 1979, 21–53.

Smith, Mark Michael. *Hearing Histories: A Reader*. Athens, GA: University of Georgia Press, 2004.

    Sensing the Past: Seeing, Hearing, Smelling, Tasting, and Touching in History. Berkeley: University of California Press, 2007.

Smith, Timothy B. *Creating the Welfare State in France, 1880–1940*. Quebec City: McGill University Press, 2003.

Spohrer, Jennifer. "Ruling the Airwaves: Radio-Luxembourg and the Origins of European National Broadcasting, 1929–1950." PhD diss., Columbia University, 2008.

Squier, Susan Merrill. *Communities of the Air. Radio Century, Radio Culture*. Durham, NC: Duke University Press, 2003.

Sterne, Jonathan. *The Audible Past: The Cultural Origins of Sound Reproduction*. Durham, NC: Duke University Press, 2003.

    ed. *The Sound Studies Reader*. Abingdon: Routledge, 2012.

Stiker, Henri-Jacques. *Corps infirmes et sociétés*. Paris: Aubier Montaigne, 1982.

Stoler, Ann Laura. *Carnal Knowledge and Imperial Power: Race and the Intimate in Colonial Rule*. Berkeley: University of California Press, 2002.

Stora, Benjamin. *Histoire de l'Algérie coloniale, 1830–1954*. Paris: Editions La Découverte, 2004.

    Nationalistes algériens et révolutionnaires français au temps de Front Populaire. Paris: L'Harmattan, 1987.

Stovall, Tyler. *Paris and the Spirit of 1919: Consumer Struggles, Transnationalism, and Revolution*. Cambridge: Cambridge University Press, 2013.

Street, Sean. *Crossing the Ether: Pre-War Public Service Radio and Commercial Competition in the U.K.* Eastleigh, UK: John Libbey Publishing, 2006.

Suisman, David and Susan Strasser, eds. *Sound in the Age of Mechanical Reproduction*. Philadelphia: University of Pennsylvania Press, 2010.

Surkis, Judith. *Sexing the Citizen: Morality and Masculinity in France, 1870–1920*. Ithaca, NY: Cornell University Press, 2006.

Sweeney, Regina. *Singing Our Way to Victory: French Cultural Politics and Music During the Great War*. Middletown, CT: Wesleyan University Press, 2001.

Taithe, Bertrand. *Defeated Flesh: Welfare, Warfare, and the Making of Modern France*. Manchester: Manchester University Press, 1999.

Tartakowsky, Danielle, "Stratégies de la rue, 1934–1938," *Le Mouvement social*, 135, April–June 1986, 31–62.

Tenot, Frank. *Radios privées, radios pirates*. Paris: Denoël, 1977.

Thomas, Gregory N. *Treating the Trauma of the Great War: Soldiers, Civilians, and Psychiatry in France, 1914–1940*. Baton Rouge: Louisiana State University Press, 2009.

Thomas, Martin. *Empires of Intelligence: Security Services and Colonial Disorder after 1914*. Berkeley: University of California Press, 2008.

The French Empire Between the Wars: Imperialism, Politics, and Society. Manchester: Manchester University Press, 2005.

Thomas de la Peña, Carolyn. *The Body Electric: How Strange Machines Built the Modern American*. New York: New York University Press, 2005.

Thompson, C. W. *French Romantic Travel Writing: Chateaubriand to Nerval*. Oxford: Oxford University Press, 2002.

Thompson, Emily Ann. *The Soundscape of Modernity: Architectural Acoustics and the Culture of Listening in America, 1900–1933*. Cambridge, MA: MIT Press, 2002.

Thomson, Richard. *The Troubled Republic: Visual Culture and Social Debate in France, 1889–1900*. New Haven, CT: Yale University Press, 2004.

Tiersten, Lisa. *Marianne in the Market: Envisioning Consumer Society in Fin-de-Siècle France*. Berkeley: University of California Press, 2009.

Todd, Christopher. "Georges Duhamel: Enemy-cum-friend of the Radio," *Modern Language Review*, 92, 1, 1997, 48–59.

Tumbelty, Joan. *Remaking the Male Body: Masculinity and the Uses of Physical Culture in Interwar France and Vichy*. Oxford: Oxford University Press, 2012.

Ulmann-Mauriat, Caroline. *Naissance d'un média: histoire politique de la radio en France, 1921–1931*. Paris: L'Harmattan, 1999.

Vaillant, Derek, "La Police de l'Air: Amateur Radio and the Politics of Aural Surveillance in France, 1921–1940," *French Politics, Culture, and Society*, 28, 1, 2010, 48–59.

"At the Speed of Sound: Techno-Aesthetic Paradigms in U.S.-French International Broadcasting, 1925–1942," *Technology and Culture*, 54, 4, 2013, 888–921.

Vessel, Joel. *Drawing France: French Comics and the Republic*. Oxford, MS: University of Mississippi Press, 2010.

von Salhern, Adelheid, "Volk and Heimat Culture in Radio Broadcasting during the Period of Transition from Weimar to Nazi Germany," *The Journal of Modern History*, 76, 2, 2004, 312–346.

Wakeman, Rosemary. *The Heroic City: Paris, 1945–1948*. Chicago: University of Chicago Press, 2009.

Watson, Leland A. *Hearing Aids and Hearing Instruments*. Baltimore: Wilkins & Wilkins, 1949.

Wardhaugh, Jessica. *In Pursuit of the People: Political Culture in France, 1934–1939*. London: Palgrave-MacMillan, 2009.

Weber, Eugen. *Peasants into Frenchmen: The Modernization of Rural France, 1870–1914*. Stanford: Stanford University Press, 1976.

The Hollow Years: France in the 1930s. New York: W.W. Norton, 1994.

Weygand, Zina. *The Blind in French Society: From the Middle Ages to the Century of Louis Braille*. Stanford: Stanford University Press, 2010.

Whitney, Susan. *Mobilizing Youth: Communists and Catholics in Interwar France*. Durham, NC: Duke University Press, 2009.

Williams, Manuela. *Mussolini's Propaganda Abroad: Subversion in the Mediterranean and the Middle East, 1935–1940*. London: Routledge, 1995.

Williams, Rosalind. *Dream Worlds: Mass Consumption in Late Nineteenth-Century France*. Berkeley: University of California Press, 1982.

Woloch, Isser. *The French Veteran from Revolution to Restoration*. Chapel Hill: University of North Carolina Press, 1979.

Ziven, Joselyn. "Bent: A Colonial Subversive and Indian Broadcasting," *Past and Present*, 162, 1, 1999, 195–220.

"The Imagined Reign of the Iron Lecturer," *Modern Asian Studies*, 32, 3, 1998, 717–734.

Yvert, Benoît. *Dictionnaire des ministres de 1789 à 1989*. Paris: Perrin, 1990.

Index

Abed, Leila, 254
Abraham, Henri, 131
Abraham, Marcel, 173
Académie de Médicine, 54
Académie Française, 158–59, 255
Adam, Michel, 117
advertising cars, 35, 60
Adorno, Theodor, 10, 76, 161n9, 200
Ageron, Charles-Robert, 246
Algeria, 6, 154, 207–57; broadcasting
  politics in, 210–19; cosmopolitanism of,
  214, 221; cultural *métissage* in, 219–30;
  Jews of, 238n108, 253; radio owners in,
  231; surveillance in, 207–8, 230–47
Algerian Office of Economic and Tourist
  Action (OFALAC), 211
Altman, Rick, 15
Amitié des Aveugles, 71
amputees, 65, 91–92; pension for, 90n88;
  rehabilitation of, 108
Amrouche, Robert, 251n158
Annales School, 16–17
anti-Semitism, 151, 166, 187, 200–2, 265;
  in Algeria, 215; of Vichy regime, 94
Armand-Masson, Georges, 117,
  120–21, 125
Arnheim, Rudolph, 69n19
Arthaud, Yvane, 65–66
Arzour, Salah, 253
Ashbridge, Noel, 142–43
Association Colonies-Sciences, 212,
  212n16
Association des Durs d'Oreille de la Région
  Parisienne, 99–100
Association des Mutilés des Yeux, 73
Association des Oulémas Musulmans
  Algériens, 216, 238, 240, 245, 255
Association des Professeurs de Langues
  Vivantes, 186
Association Valentin Haüy (AVH), 73–75,
  83, 89
Auclair, F., 110

audiometer, 52, 97–98
Audisio, Gabriel, 225
Austria, Nazi *Anschluss* of, 204
Avron, Charles, 75–76

Bachetarzi, Mahieddine, 217, 224–28, 239,
  251n158, 254
Baida brothers, 236–40
Baidaphone Company, 225, 236–41, 254;
  restrictions on, 256
Barraud, Martial, 121
Basch, Victor, 169, 194
Bayly, C.A., 234n92
Bédeil, Fred, 214
Bell, Alexander Graham, 97
Bellonte, Maurice, 32–33
Ben Amor, Taieb, 240
Ben Badis, Abd al-Hamid, 239
Bendjelloul, Mohammed, 229, 236
Ben Lakahal, Ahmed, 217
Berché, Paul, 55, 129
Bergson, Henri, 121
Berlitz language courses, 123, 126, 172
Bernard, Tristan, 183
Berque, Jacques, 210
Berthoin, Jean, 207
Billy, André, 204
Bion, Paul, 141
Bleustein-Blanchet, Marcel, 13–14, 162
blindness, as a metaphor for radio
  listening, 69
blind veterans, 93; pensions for, 66, 90n88;
  postage stamp honoring, 73, 76, 77; radio
  charities for, 64–65, 70–90, 108–10;
  radio license fee exemption for, 65,
  86–95, 267–68; rehabilitation of, 86–91.
  See also disabled veterans
Bloch, Jean-Richard, 171, 182n88
Blum, Léon, 149, 169, 248; broadcast
  policies of, 193, 248, 249, 264; criticisms
  of, 201–2; educational policies of, 159,
  173; election of, 162; resignation of, 194

Social and Cultural Histories (CSC)

Printed in the USA
CPSIA information can be obtained
at www.ICGtesting.com
CBHW060602111124
17209CB00008BA/331

9 781107 519619